Lincolnshire's Great Exhibition

Treasures, Saints and Heroes

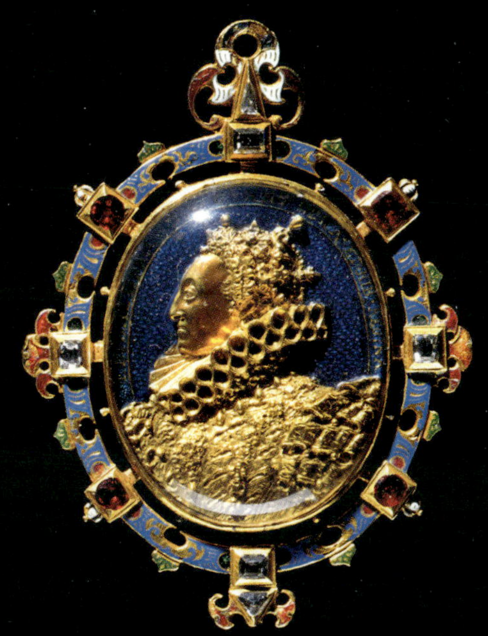

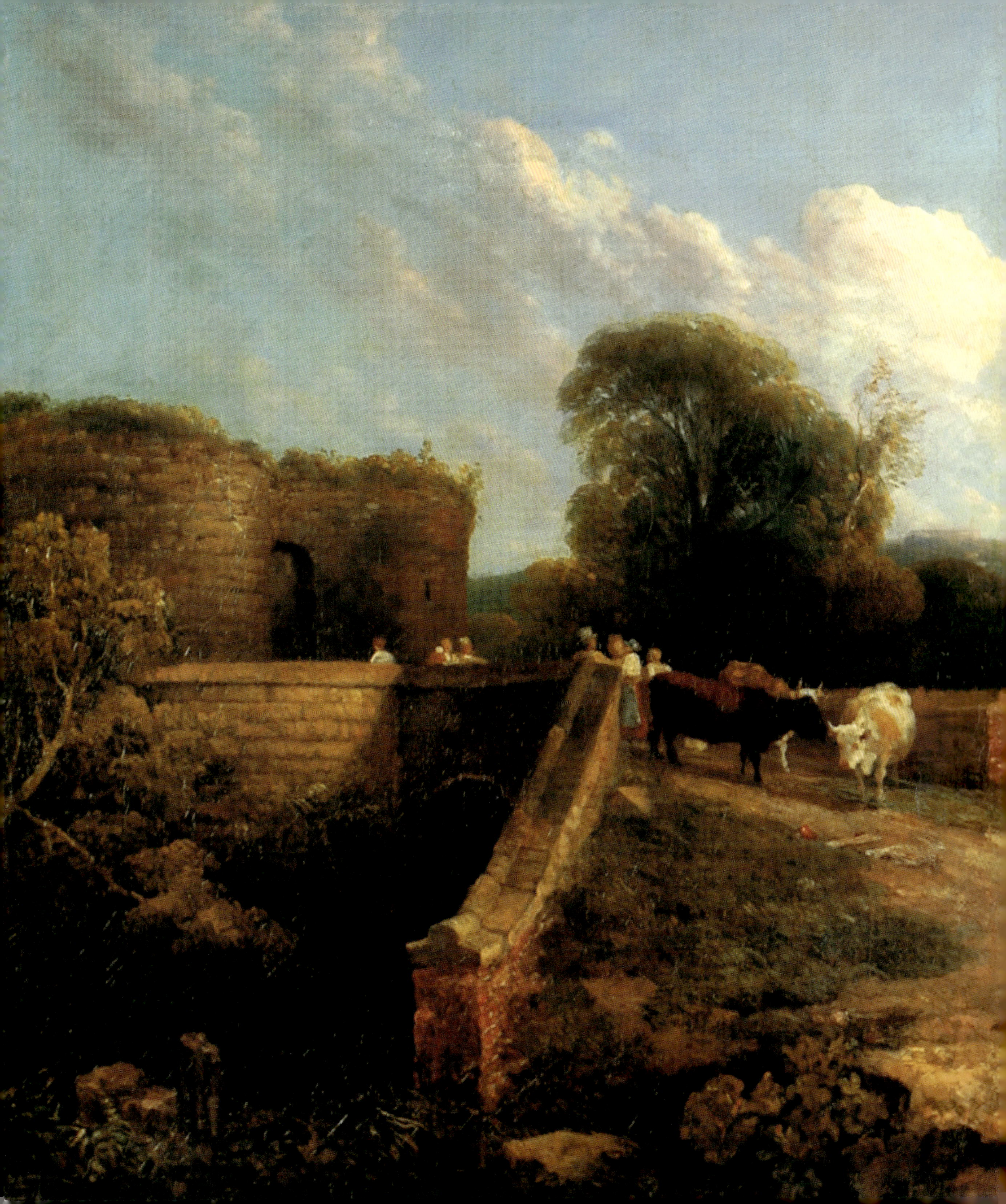

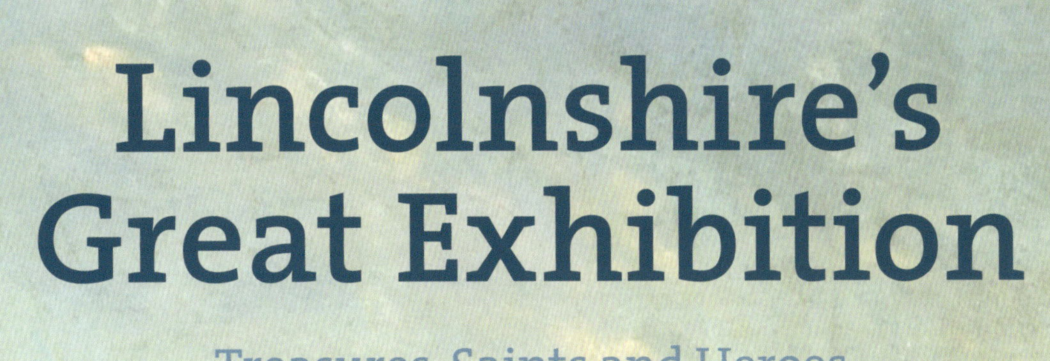

Lincolnshire's Great Exhibition

Treasures, Saints and Heroes

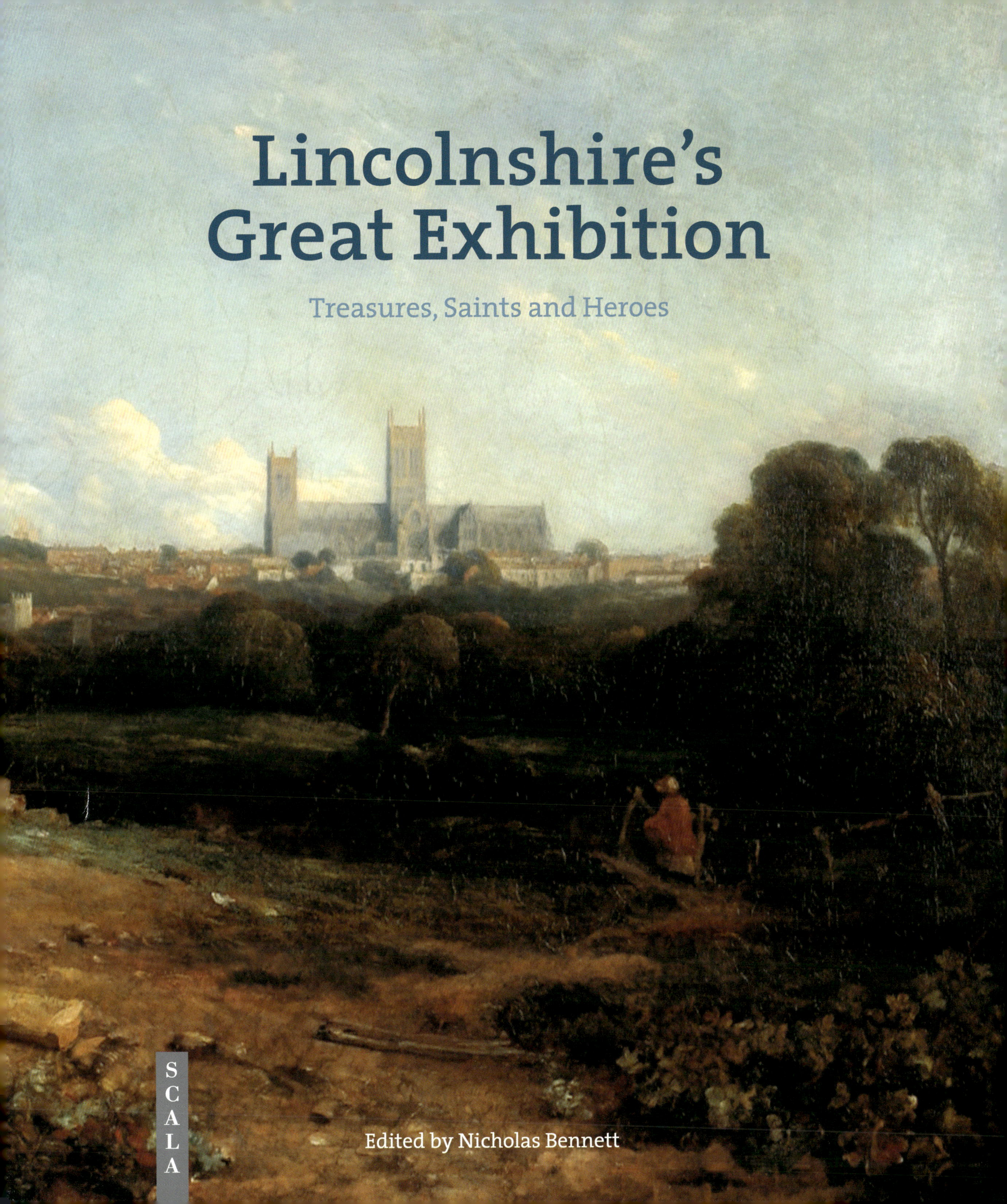

Edited by Nicholas Bennett

SCALA

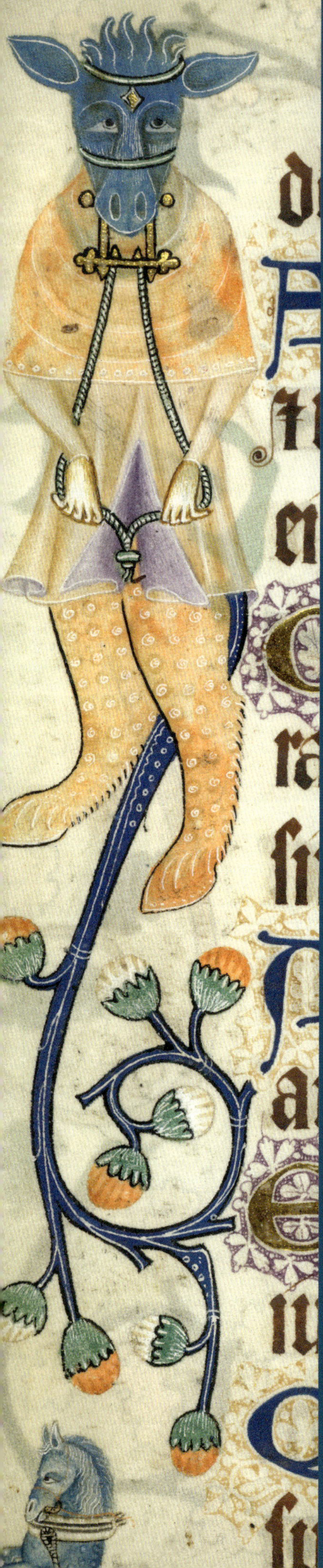

First published in 2015 by
Scala Arts & Heritage Publishers Ltd
10 Lion Yard
Tremadoc Road
London SW4 7NQ, UK
www.scalapublishers.com

In association with Lincolnshire County Council
and the Historic Lincoln Trust
The Castle
Lincoln LN1 3AA

ISBN 978-1-85759-932-9

Edited by Johanna Stephenson
Designed by Raymonde Watkins
Printed in Turkey
10 9 8 7 6 5 4 3 2 1

Page 1: The Heneage Jewel, about 1595 (Victoria and Albert Museum, London)

Pages 2–3: Peter De Wint (1784–1849) *Lincoln from the South with Bargate*, exhibited at the Royal Academy 1824 (Usher Gallery, Lincoln)

Front cover: David playing his harp: illuminated initial from the Luttrell Psalter, about 1325–40 (British Library, London)

Back cover: Samuel Laurence (1812–84) and Sir Edward Coley Burne-Jones (1833–98), *Alfred Tennyson, 1st Baron Tennyson (1809–92)*, about 1840 (National Portrait Gallery, London)

Back flap: George Stubbs (1724–1806), *Faddle, a black and white spaniel belonging to Sir John Nelthorpe*, 1792 (Courtesy of Scawby Hall)

Principal sponsor

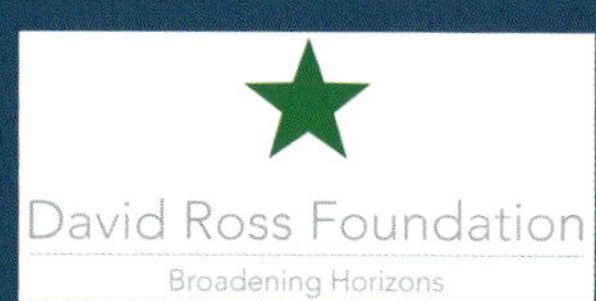

In partnership with

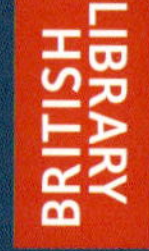

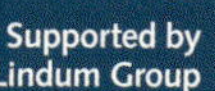

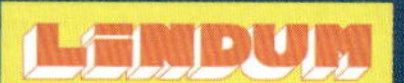

Contents

Preface

PATRICK, LORD CORMACK

Chairman of the Historic Lincoln Trust

After George Jones (1786–1869)
***Coronation Banquet of George IV*, about 1821–2**
Oil on panel
Palace of Westminster Collection

I CONCEIVED the idea for *Lincolnshire's Great Exhibition* during a dinner that I hosted for the Historic Lincoln Trust in September 2012. One of our guests was the Earl of Yarborough and as I talked to him I thought what a splendid idea it would be to have an exhibition of some of the treasures of Lincolnshire country houses during 2015. I asked him if he would be willing to lend some of Brocklesby's treasures to such an exhibition. His immediate and very positive reply encouraged me. I talked to others about the idea and especially to those who have charge of the Collection and the Usher Gallery. They responded enthusiastically but stressed that it would be necessary to have an Honorary Curator whose name would be well known in the world of museums and galleries and who would be able to help approach owners of suitable exhibits and advise on their display. By then the idea had somewhat snowballed and we were already thinking in terms of borrowing from major national collections as well as from local private ones. So I turned to a friend of many years standing, Dr Alan Borg, who had been Director of the Imperial War Museum and later of the Victoria and Albert Museum. He readily agreed to act as Honorary Curator for works of art and artefacts and Oliver Morley, then Chief Executive and Keeper of the National Archives, also agreed to be Honorary Curator for manuscripts and maps. Together they formed an admirable small team and when Oliver Morley left the National Archives to take charge of the DVLA in Swansea, his successor, Jeff James, took over the role from him. To indicate his continuing support for Lincoln and the exhibition Oliver Morley became one of our Patrons.

And so we now have what is the greatest exhibition ever staged in Lincoln, or Lincolnshire. We are enormously grateful to Her Majesty The Queen and the Director of the Royal Collection, and to the Trustees and Directors of all those great national institutions that have lent us wonderful things. Almost every request we have made has been met with supportive enthusiasm, as have our approaches to the owners of many fine, and often little-known, collections in and around the county. In that context I am particularly grateful not only to the lenders but to Robin Battle, one of our Trustees, who has a vast and professional knowledge of many of Lincolnshire's great houses and who came with me to visit a number of their owners, and introduced me to those I did not know.

As a result of all this, and in particular of the dedication and support, here in Lincoln, of Jonathan Platt and Andrea Martin (who has masterminded the detailed

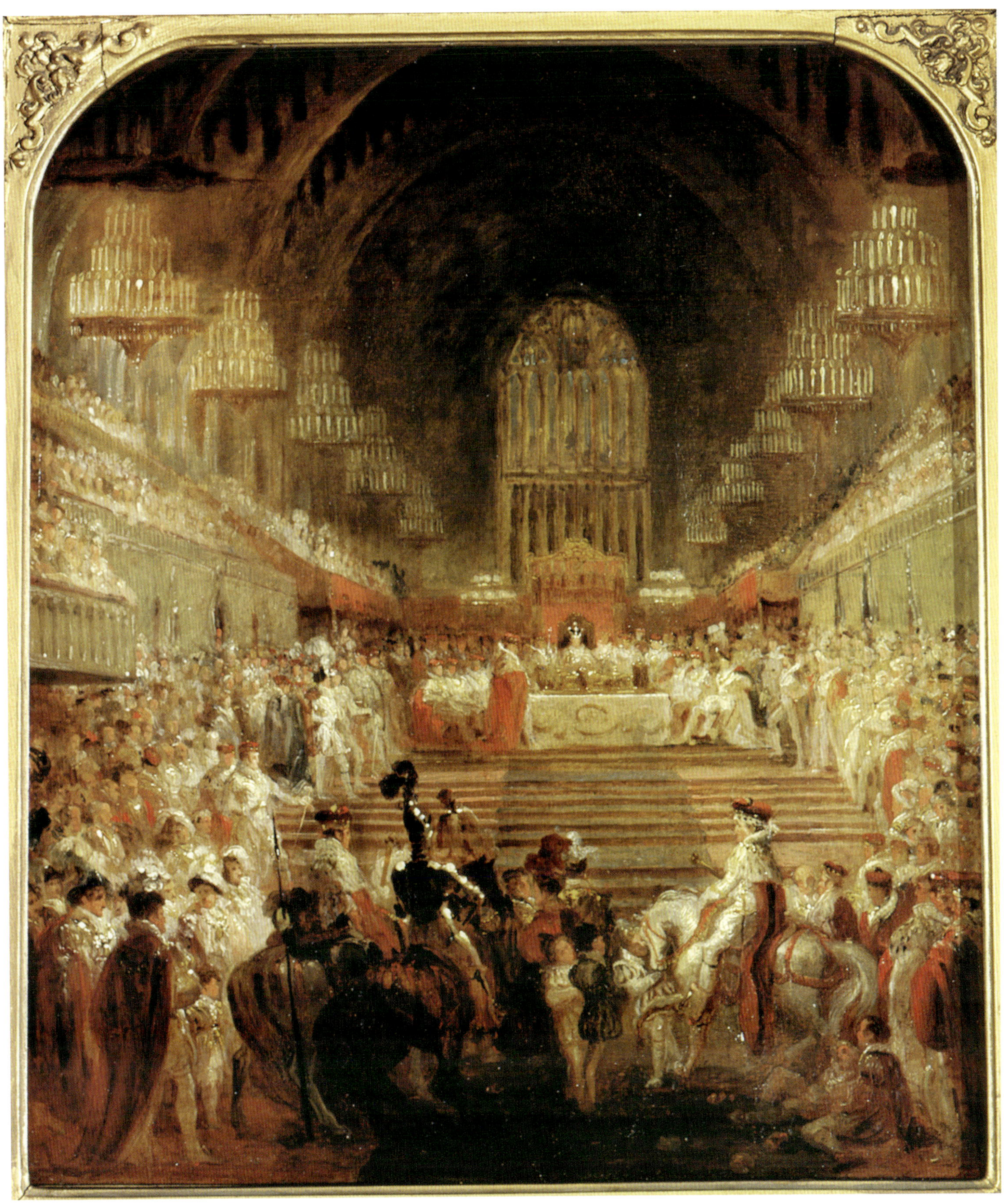

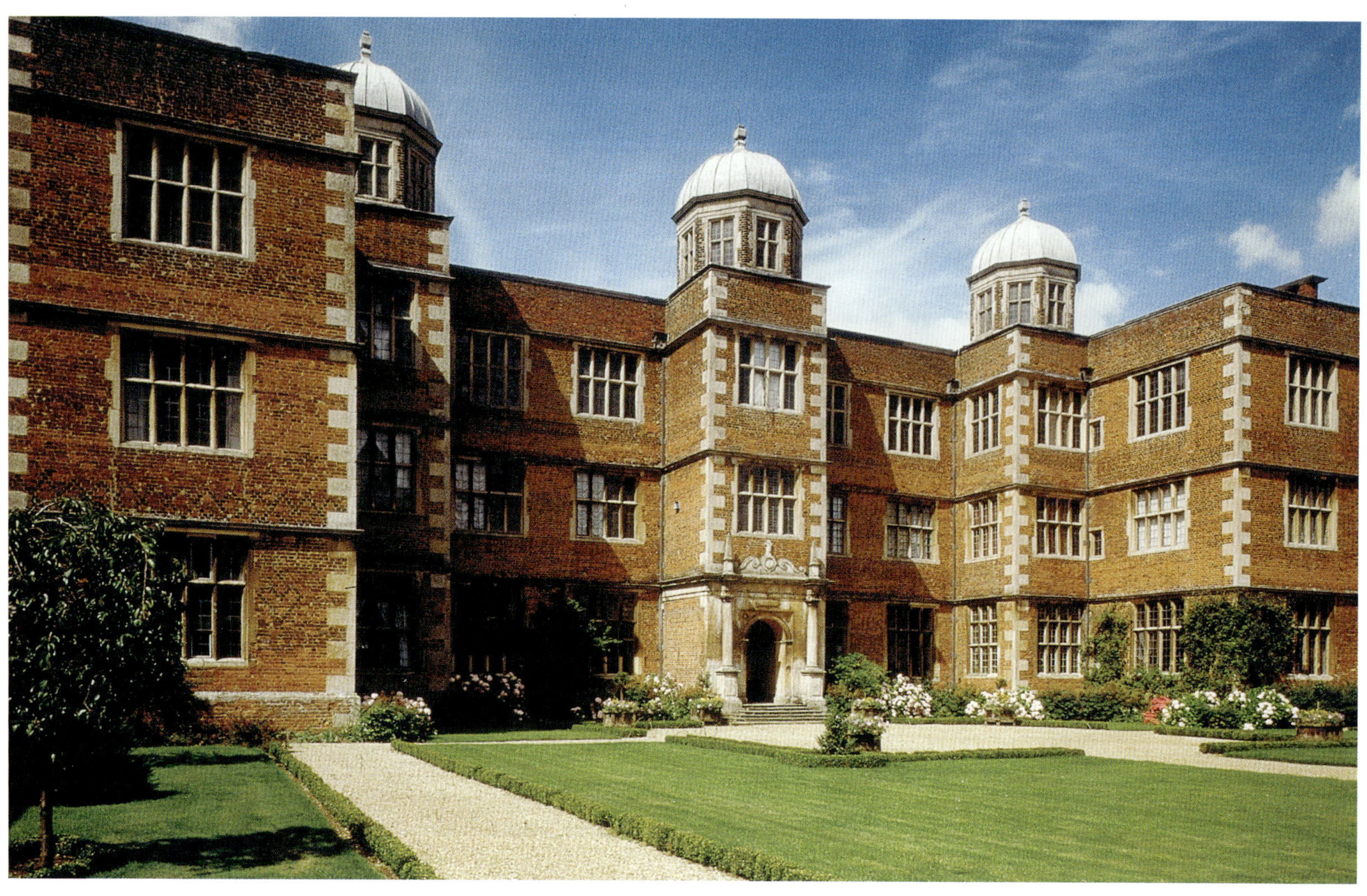

Doddington Hall
Photo: Andrew Tryner, copyright Lincolnshire County Council

arrangements for all our loans), we have an amazing artistic feast to lay before the people of Lincolnshire and to all of those who visit Lincoln between the end of June and the end of September 2015. Most of the exhibition is housed in the Collection and in the Usher Gallery but there are a number of very important manuscripts and printed books in the Medieval and Wren Libraries of the Cathedral. In the Ross Magna Carta Vault itself, within the Castle grounds, we have on display the Cathedral's Magna Carta of 1215 and the Charter of the Forest of 1217 (one of only two to survive), together with one of the rare 1225 copies of Magna Carta from the National Archives.

Although the exhibition lasts for just three months, we felt it important to have a book that would be a permanent and treasured reminder of *Lincolnshire's Great Exhibition* and I am most grateful to Dr Nicholas Bennett, Cathedral Archivist and, before that, for a quarter of a century Cathedral Librarian, for agreeing to edit the book, and to Dr Marianne Wilson who has assisted him in this task. Together they have produced a volume which I am sure will be cherished by all who acquire it. Thanks are also due to all our distinguished contributors who have produced some fascinating chapters on some of Lincolnshire's great figures of the past and on some of the treasures on display. I am grateful to Johanna Stephenson, the

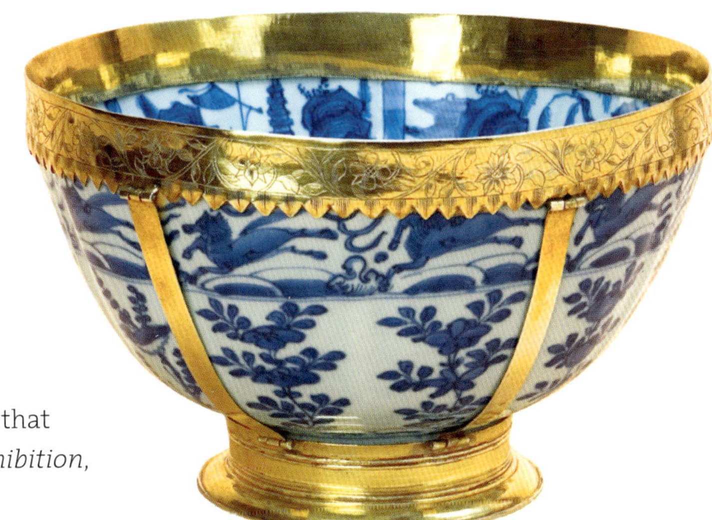

The Walsingham Bowl, about 1580–1600
Ceramic, mounted in silver gilt
The Burghley House Collection

Project Editor of the book, and Ray Watkins, the Designer, for all the work that they have put in to producing a volume worthy of *Lincolnshire's Great Exhibition*, and to Rosemarie McCabe, Laura Lappin and Sophie Neve of Scala.

The exhibition falls into various categories. We have a section devoted to great Lincolnshire figures, from Gilbert of Sempringham, the only Englishman to found a monastic order, to Margaret Thatcher, our first, and to date only, woman Prime Minister, and the longest-serving of modern times. Other great Lincolnshire figures such as Sir Isaac Newton, George Boole, John Wesley and Alfred, Lord Tennyson are represented, as are Lincolnshire's great explorers, Sir Joseph Banks, George Bass, Matthew Flinders and Sir John Franklin. We are particularly excited to be able to display Matthew Flinders's map of Australia, lent to us by the National Archives. Also in the exhibition are notable topographical views of Lincoln and Lincolnshire, including the only surviving panorama of an English town, the *Louth Panorama*. Elsewhere we have a group of pictures by George Stubbs, who did all his research and dissections for his great work, *The Anatomy of the Horse*, near the banks of the Humber at Horkstow. Many of the Lincolnshire gentry and aristocracy of the day were among his patrons and we are delighted to be able to display a number of the pictures commissioned by them.

In expressing the hope that you will enjoy your visit, and treasure this volume as a reminder of it, I would reiterate my thanks to all those who have made *Lincolnshire's Great Exhibition* possible. I would also like to thank the Dean of Lincoln, the Very Reverend Philip Buckler, who, within weeks of my returning to my native county, invited me to be the first Chairman of the Historic Lincoln Trust. To all my fellow Trustees, and to our Patrons, I am also grateful. Special thanks go to those who have worked so hard behind the scenes, particularly Mary Powell, without whom we would not have had the magnificent grant from the Heritage Lottery Fund, which has made it possible to restore and reveal Lincoln Castle as never before. To the Leader of the County Council Martin Hill, and to Councillor Nick Worth and their fellow members and officers, whose determination in difficult financial times never wavered, we owe a special debt of gratitude. Finally, thanks are due to Justin Brown, the County Council's Commissioner for Economic Growth, and to Will Wright, who has been the only person employed solely on working for the Historic Lincoln Trust over the last two years, and who has acted as a very assiduous PA.

Forewords

ALAN BORG

Honorary Curator (Works of Art and Artefacts)

THE IDEA for *Lincolnshire's Great Exhibition* in 2015 originated with Lord Cormack. He realised that, as one of the four surviving copies of Magna Carta is preserved in Lincoln, the 800th anniversary of the Great Charter provided an ideal opportunity to celebrate Lincoln and Lincolnshire more widely. Without his drive and enthusiasm for the project it would never have happened and I was delighted when he approached me to be one of the Honorary Curators of the proposed exhibition.

All curators of exhibitions embark on a journey that is both intellectual and actual. The intellectual journey involves establishing the theme of the exhibition and creating a framework into which the proposed exhibits will fit. In the case of *Lincolnshire's Great Exhibition*, it was immediately apparent that there were several themes that needed to be addressed. These range in time from the medieval period, when the county had a significant role in both the ecclesiastical and political history of Britain, to the modern era, in which Lincolnshire figures have played a part on the national and international stage. The obvious link was with individuals and the number of significant and historically important people who were born in the county proved to be larger than I had first thought. Many of these, from Isaac Newton to Margaret Thatcher, are immediately recognisable, while others, such as Bennet Langton, are not necessarily household names but are nonetheless distinguished national figures. We therefore decided to include as many Lincolnshire worthies as possible in the exhibition, although it was inevitable that some had to be omitted because of a lack of potential exhibits.

An extension of this category comprised people who were not actually born in Lincolnshire but who became closely associated with the county. Chief among these was George Stubbs, the great animal painter, much of whose work was commissioned by members of the landed gentry who devoted their time to hunting and horse racing. Several Lincolnshire houses contain a range of his work and he made the drawings for his famous publication of *The Anatomy of the Horse* while living at Horkstow. For this reason we decided to devote a whole room to the work of Stubbs.

Despite the predominance of these individual stories, it was also clear that we needed to include a range of other items in the exhibition. One category could simply be described as 'Treasures' and consisted of some of the rich and spectacular objects which were associated with the county. Two of the key examples were the

John Michael Rysbrack (1694–1770)
Tomb monument of Sir Isaac Newton (1642–1727), 1731
Marble
Westminster Abbey

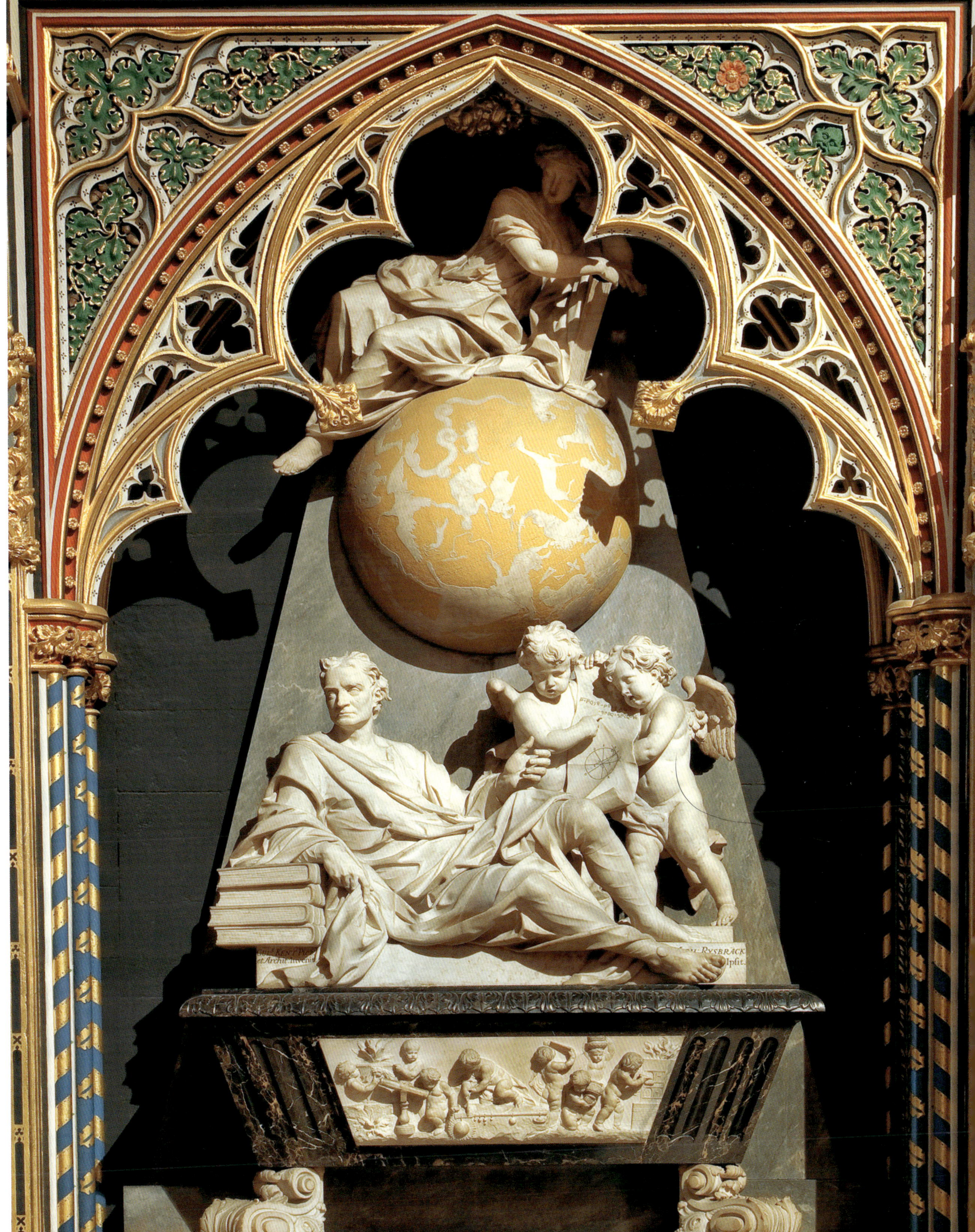
et Archit.
RYSBRACK

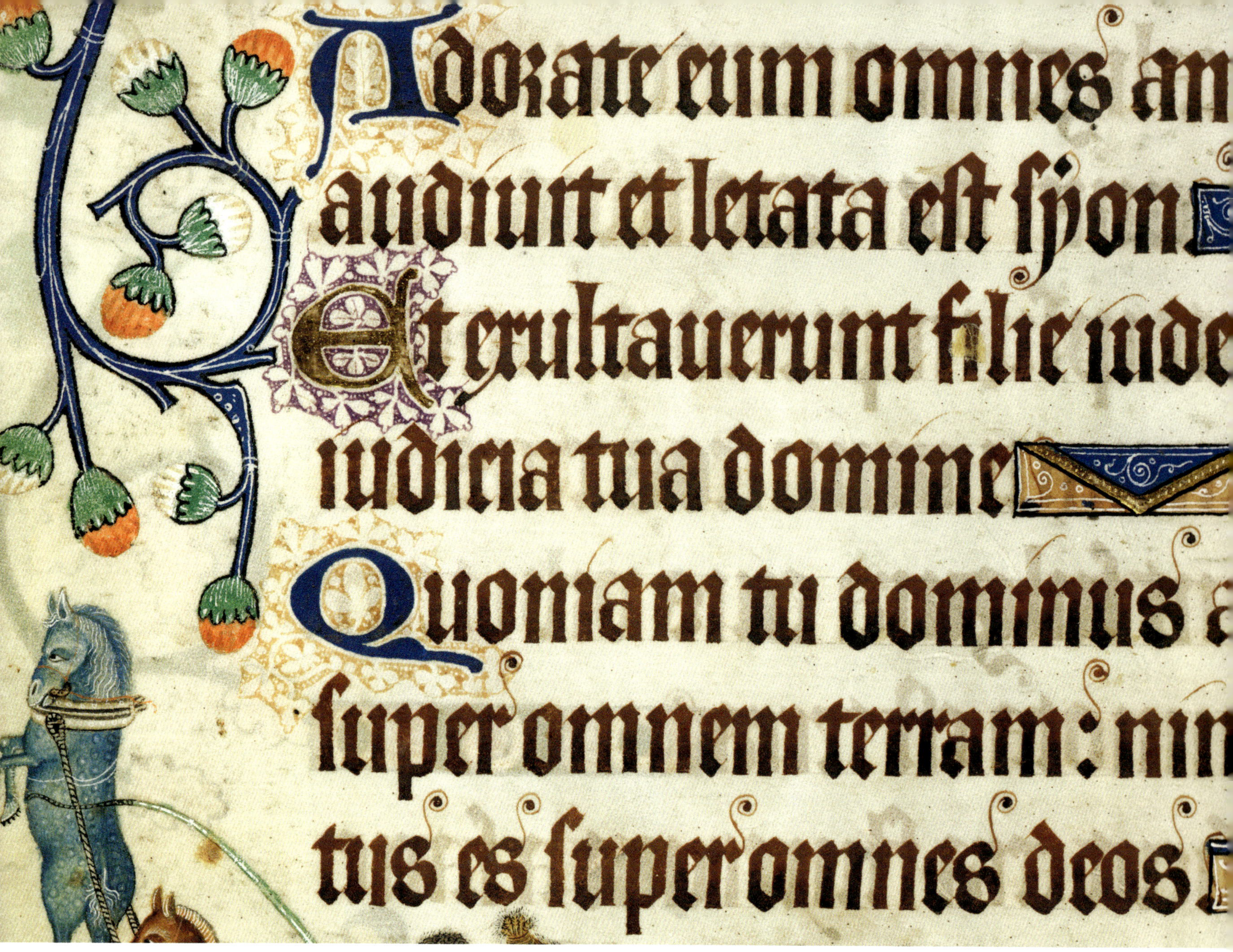

Luttrell Psalter and the Heneage Jewel, but all the objects in this section demonstrate that Lincolnshire has contributed to some of the most magnificent collections in the country.

A further category was 'Views of Lincolnshire', including the City of Lincoln itself. Here the magnificent cathedral and castle have led artists to portray them over the years and we were able to include a range of such views. But it was not just Lincoln itself and it was not solely about well-known artists. One of the most intriguing objects in the exhibition, the *Louth Panorama*, is a view of the entire town painted from the spire of St James's church in the mid nineteenth century by an amateur artist, William Brown. This gives us a social history of the area that is unique and endlessly fascinating.

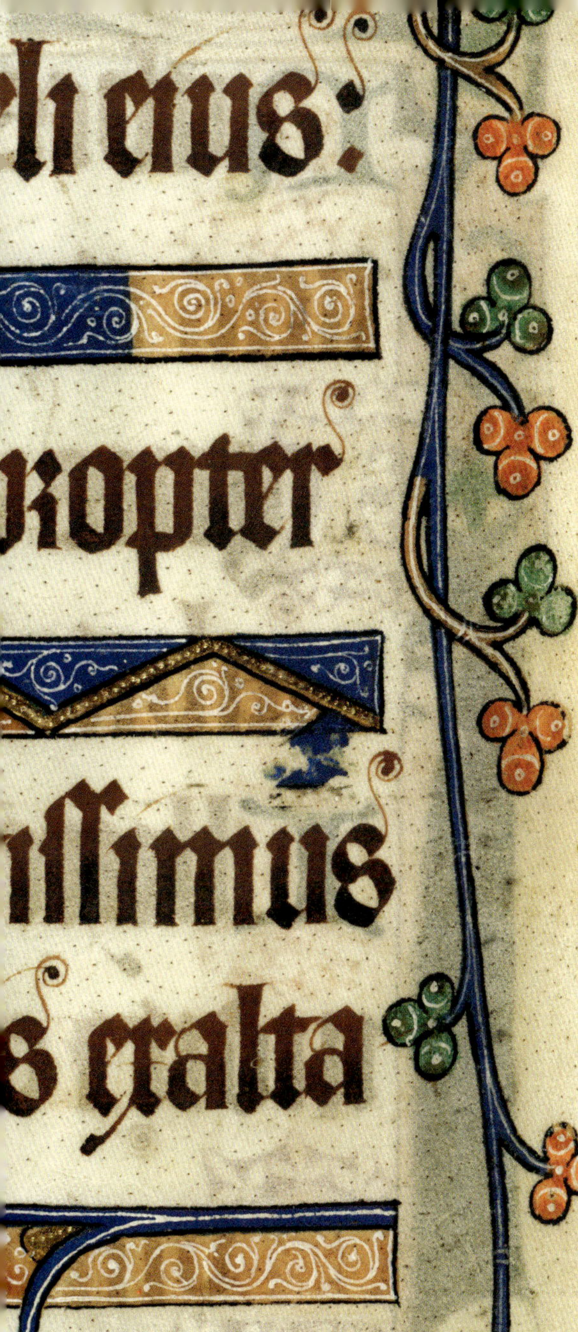

The Luttrell Psalter, about 1325–40
Verses from Psalm 96, 'Sion heard of it and rejoiced: and the daughters of Judah were glad'
British Library, Add MS 42130, f.173v

OVERLEAF
William Brown (1788–1859)
***Louth Panorama*, 1844–7**
View south-west from the top of Louth spire
Oil on linen
Louth Town Council

The intellectual journey of refining the concept of the exhibition developed in parallel with the actual journeys required to locate and select the exhibits. These involved visits to museums, galleries, archives, learned societies and local councils. The objects held by such institutions are usually (but not always) well recorded and so travel to the collection was normally to see one or two works of art or other objects which seemed to fit in with the theme of the exhibition. Along this road we were welcomed by directors, curators and other officials, who responded most generously to our requests for loans and we were able to borrow works of art and artefacts from several of our great national collections, as well as from some lesser-known ones. As a result we were able to include some of the greatest treasures associated with Lincolnshire in the exhibition and we are indebted to the staff and governing bodies of the institutions involved.

There was one other important source open to us, namely the numerous country houses within the county and more widely in Britain as a whole. On these visits we were invariably welcomed by the owners, who offered to lend generously to the exhibition and gave us free run of their property. In consequence, when we had gone to a particular house with a particular loan in mind, we often ended up with a list of several requests, including things that were entirely new and unexpected. It made for several highly enjoyable and memorable visits, and once again our sincere thanks go to all those who made this possible.

In practical terms, the exhibition was only made possible by the hard work of several people who dedicated many months to the creation of the finished display. In the first place, the Historic Lincoln Trust and the Exhibition Committee, both chaired by Lord Cormack, were at the centre of the entire enterprise. Everyone involved played a key role, but I must single out William Wright, who acted as Secretary to the Committee and kept track of the loan requests and responses. Above all, it was Andrea Martin of The Collection, serving as exhibition co-ordinator, whose tireless efforts made sure that the exhibition actually happened. She ensured that my role as Honorary Curator was entirely straightforward and I am most grateful to her. The end result, recorded in this volume which was edited by Nicholas Bennett, was an outstanding assemblage of works of art and artefacts that continues to celebrate the glories of this great county.

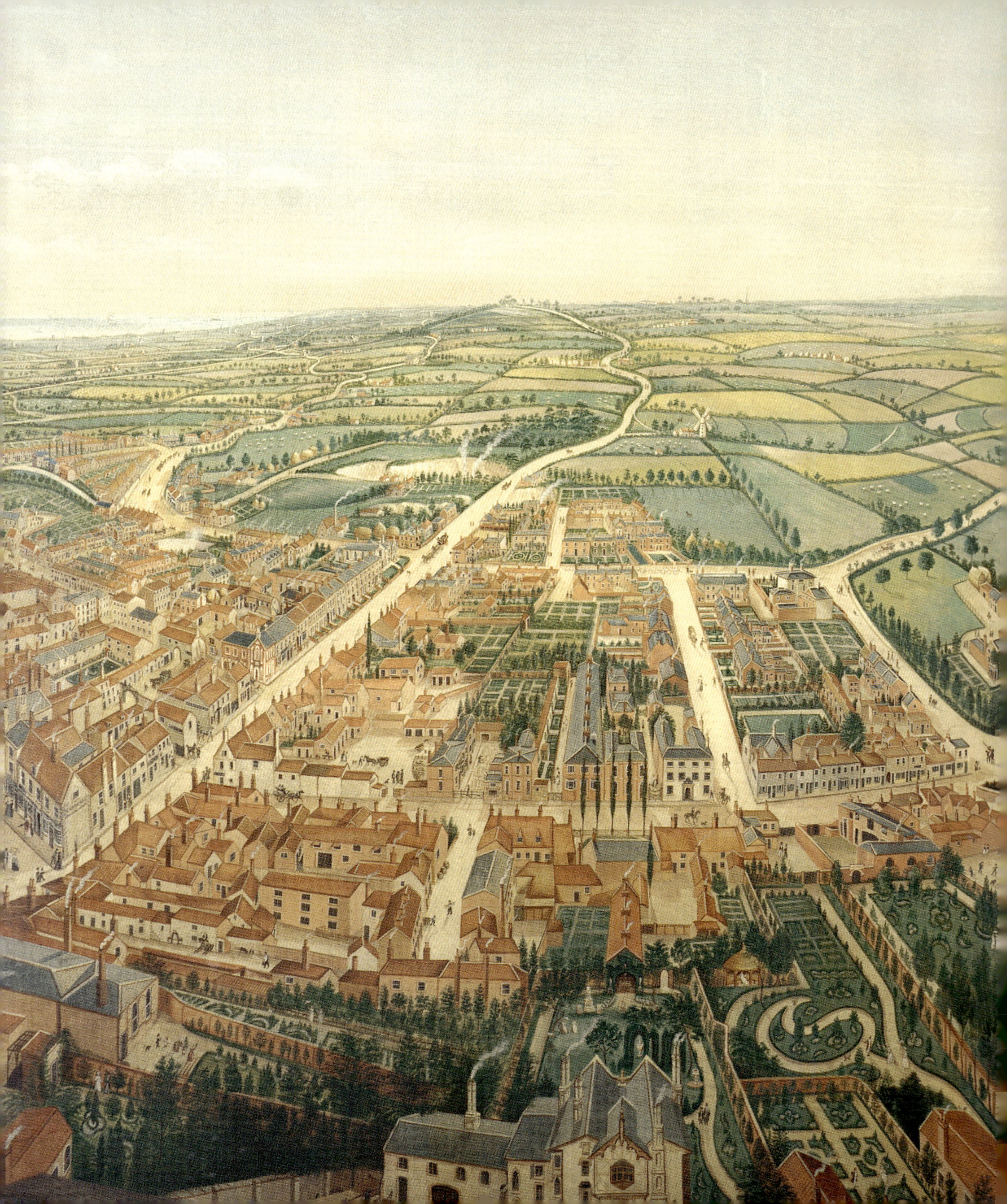

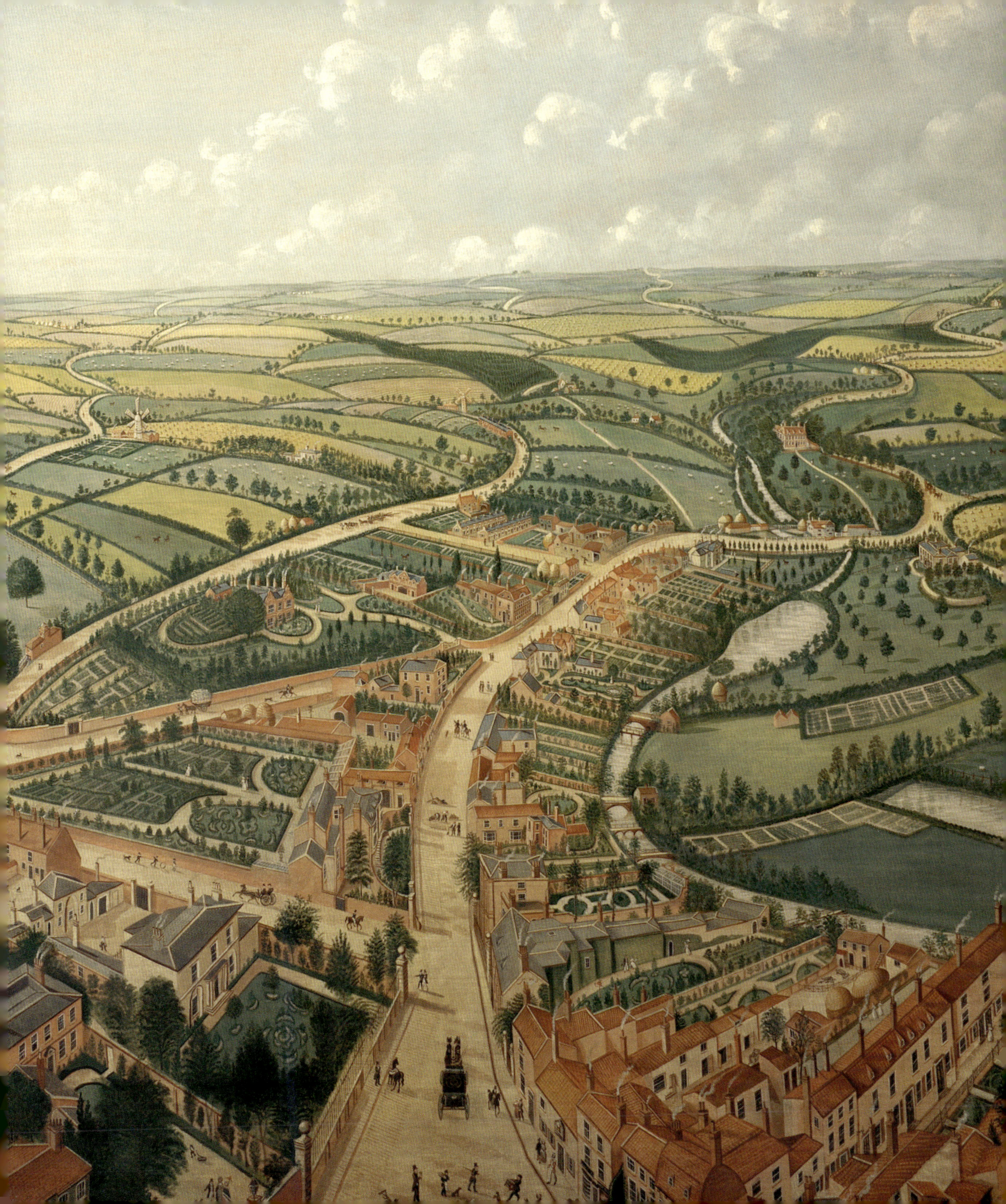

JEFF JAMES

Honorary Curator (Manuscripts and Maps)

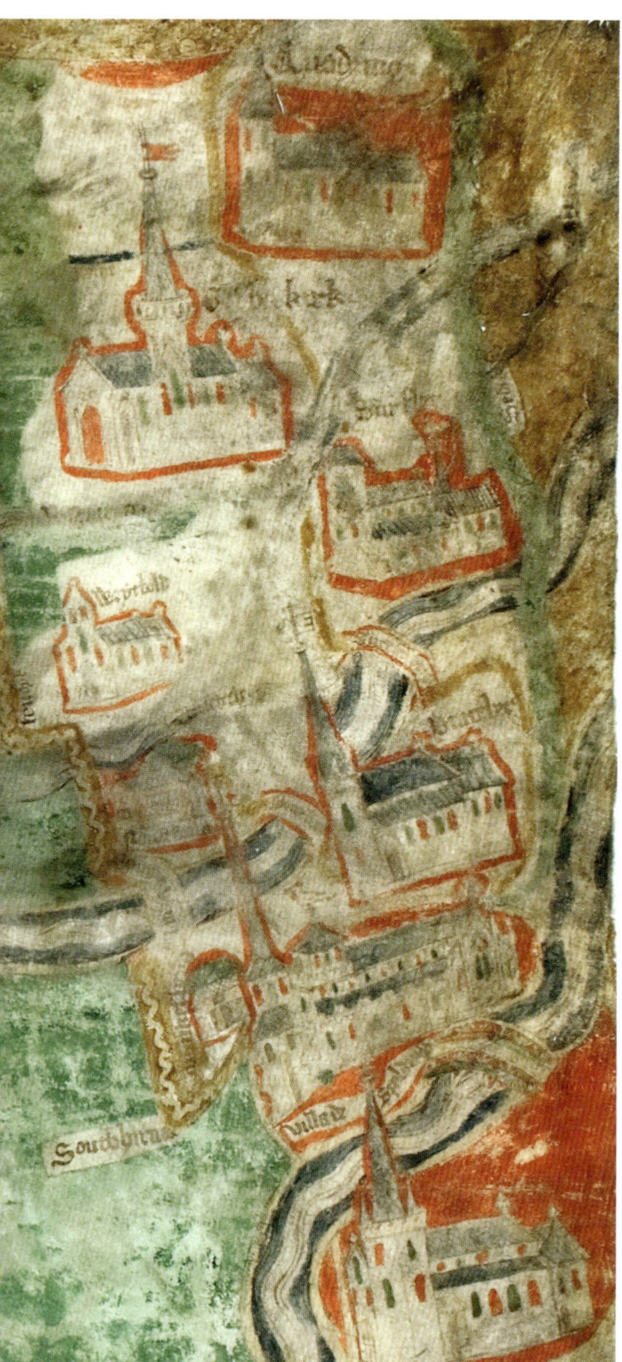

I AM delighted to be an Honorary Curator for *Lincolnshire's Great Exhibition* and to have been asked to provide this foreword. I took on this role from Oliver Morley, my predecessor as Chief Executive and Keeper at The National Archives and now a Patron of the Historic Lincoln Trust. Over several visits to Lincolnshire it has been a genuine pleasure to see the Exhibition – and the infrastructure supporting it – taking shape.

The National Archives is the official archive for the UK government and for England and Wales. We perform the functions of the Public Record Office, established by Act of Parliament in 1838 and the Historical Manuscripts Commission, first appointed by Royal Warrant in 1869. These historic responsibilities mean that we have obligations both to records in public hands and those held privately.

As the leader of the archive sector in England, we also play a leading role in promoting the value of archives as a vital component of the nation's heritage. These are challenging times and when we are making the case for archive services, often with colleagues in national or local government, it is always helpful to be able to refer to exemplars. Having seen the enormous dedication and work that has gone into its preparation, I cannot imagine a better example than *Lincolnshire's Great Exhibition*.

Our nation's documentary heritage is made up of thousands of archives, each with its own unique history. The richness of our archives is the result of generations of careful stewardship by countless individuals and institutions, including local authorities, families, businesses, religious groups and charities.

Lincolnshire's Great Exhibition amply demonstrates this richness and care, with its inclusion of so many rare and valuable documents and artefacts. And of course it shows the extraordinary contributions the people of Lincolnshire have made to the wider world. Archival and heritage collections contain remarkable stories. They help us understand better who we are, providing a window into the past so that we can make sense of the present and plan for our future.

Pinchbeck Fen Map, fifteenth century
Detail showing the lost church of Spalding Priory, with neighbouring churches
The National Archives, MPCC1/7

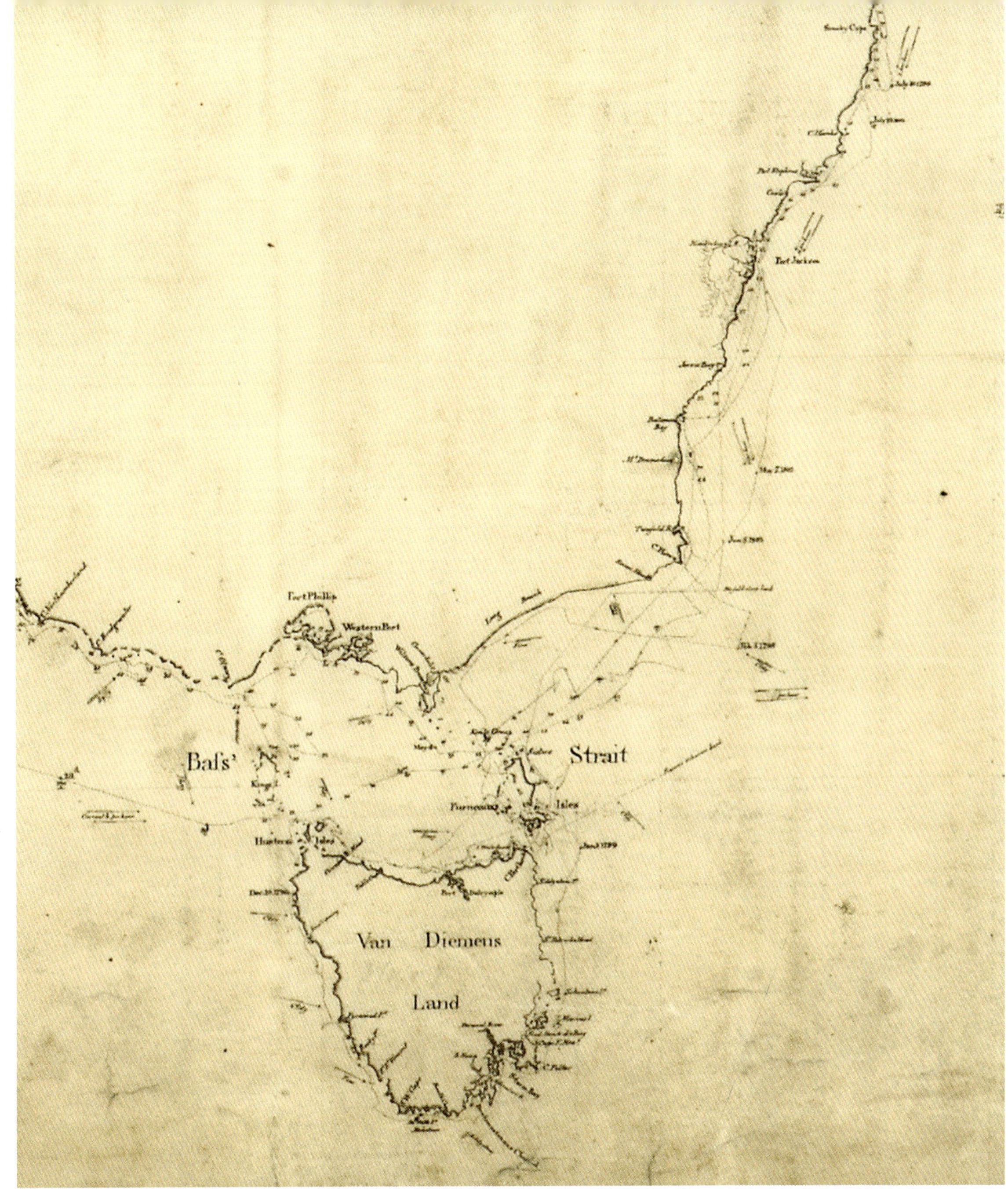

Matthew Flinders (1774–1814)
The Flinders Map, 1804: ***Chart showing such parts of Terra Australis and its vicinity, as were discovered or examined by the following vessels: Schooner Francis in 1798, Sloop Norfolk in 1798 and 9, Schooner Cumberland in 1803 and HMS Investigator in 1801, 2 and 3 by M Flinders, Commander***
Detail showing Port Jackson (Sydney) and the Bass Strait
The National Archives, ADM 352/477

The National Archives is the guardian of some of our most iconic national documents, dating back more than a thousand years. These include the 1225 Magna Carta and we are delighted to loan it to the exhibition. We are also very happy to be loaning three other documents of particular significance for Lincolnshire: the 1804 map of Australia by Matthew Flinders, the seal of Archbishop Langton and the fifteenth-century Pinchbeck Fen Map. These four records are among the most powerful and intriguing in our collection and it is good that they will be seen by so many people in the context of this impressive exhibition.

The National Archives is therefore very pleased to support *Lincolnshire's Great Exhibition.* We hope it will inspire people throughout the county and beyond and we wish it every success.

OVERLEAF
Lincoln Cathedral: the western towers
Photo: James Newton

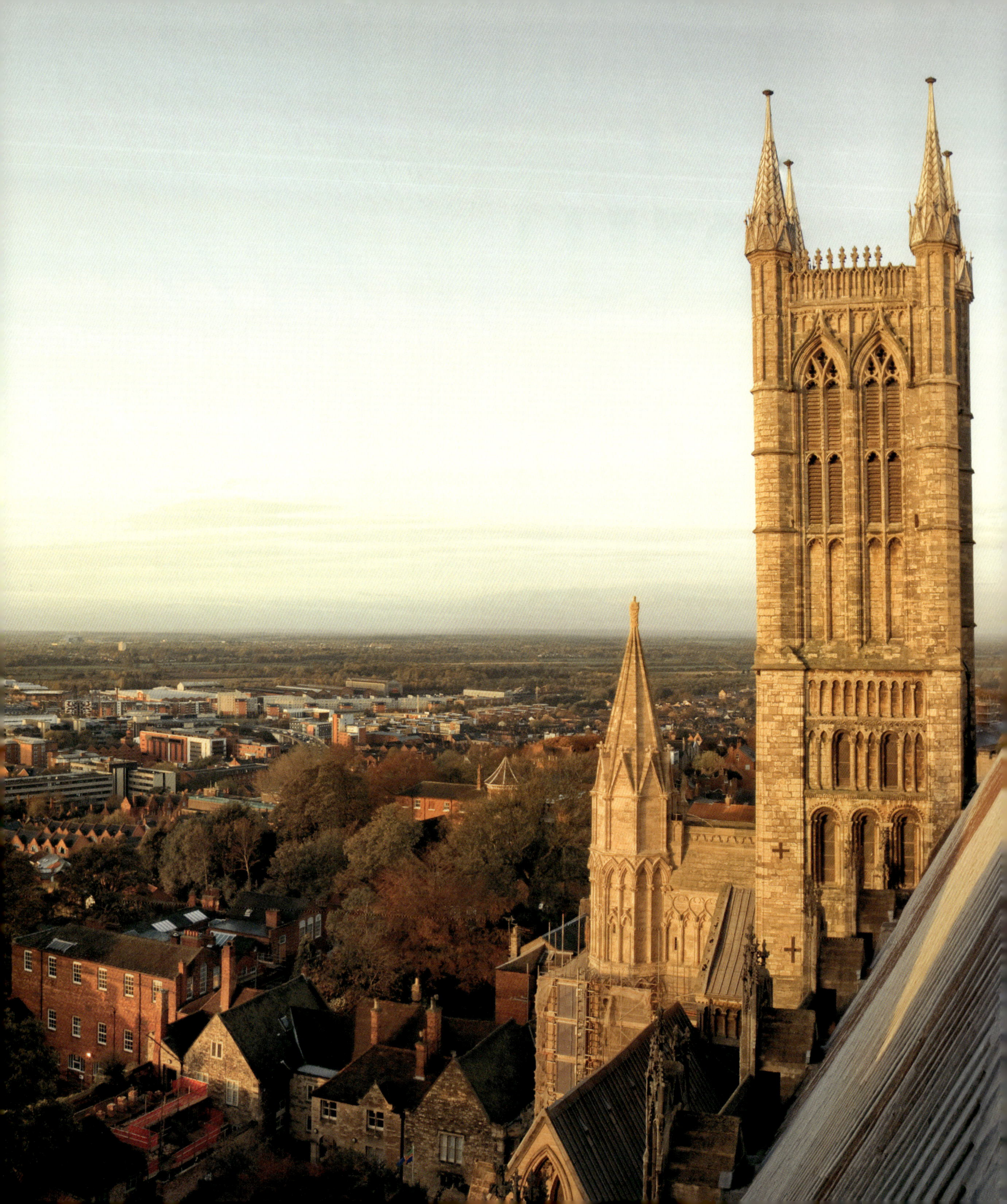

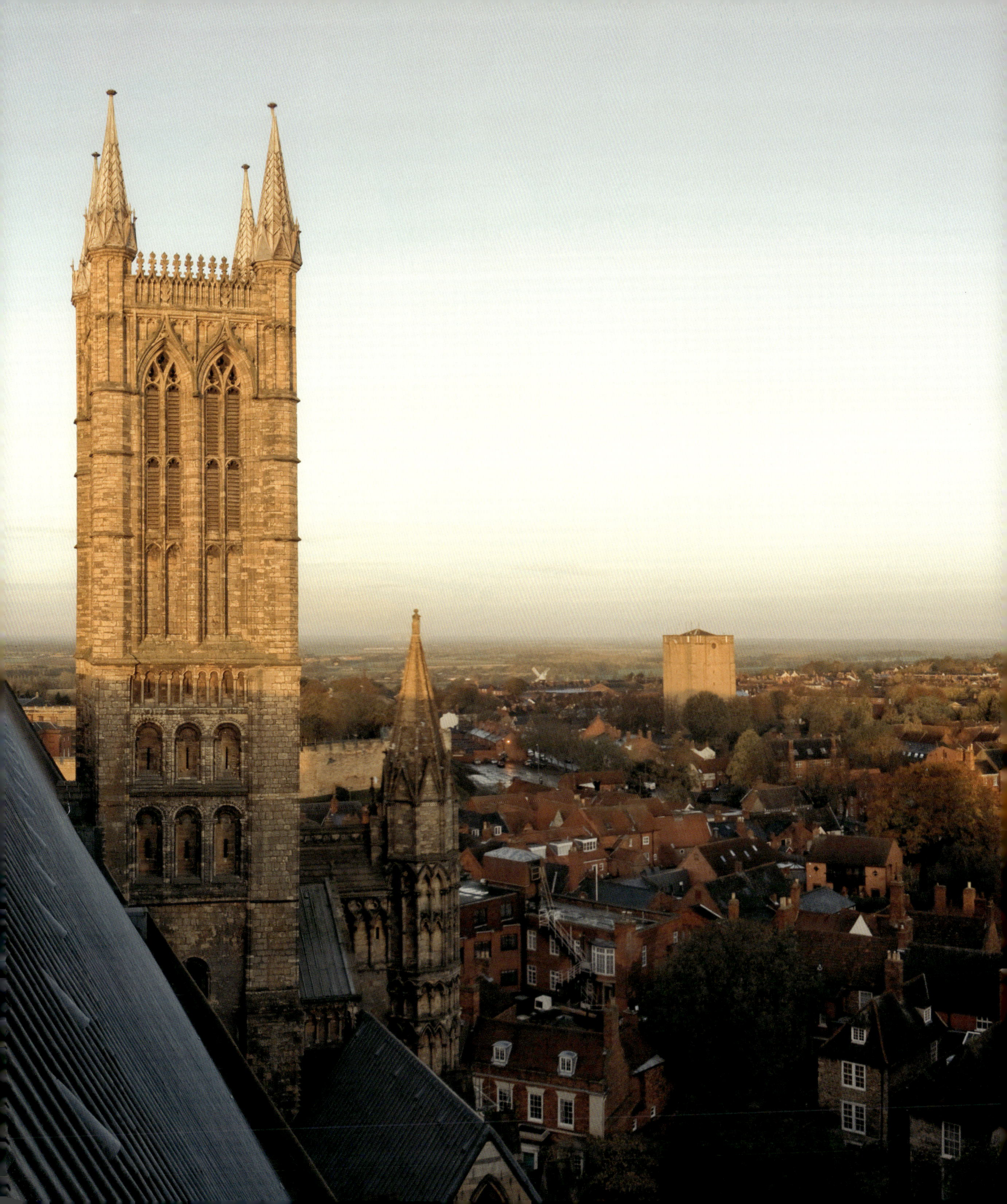

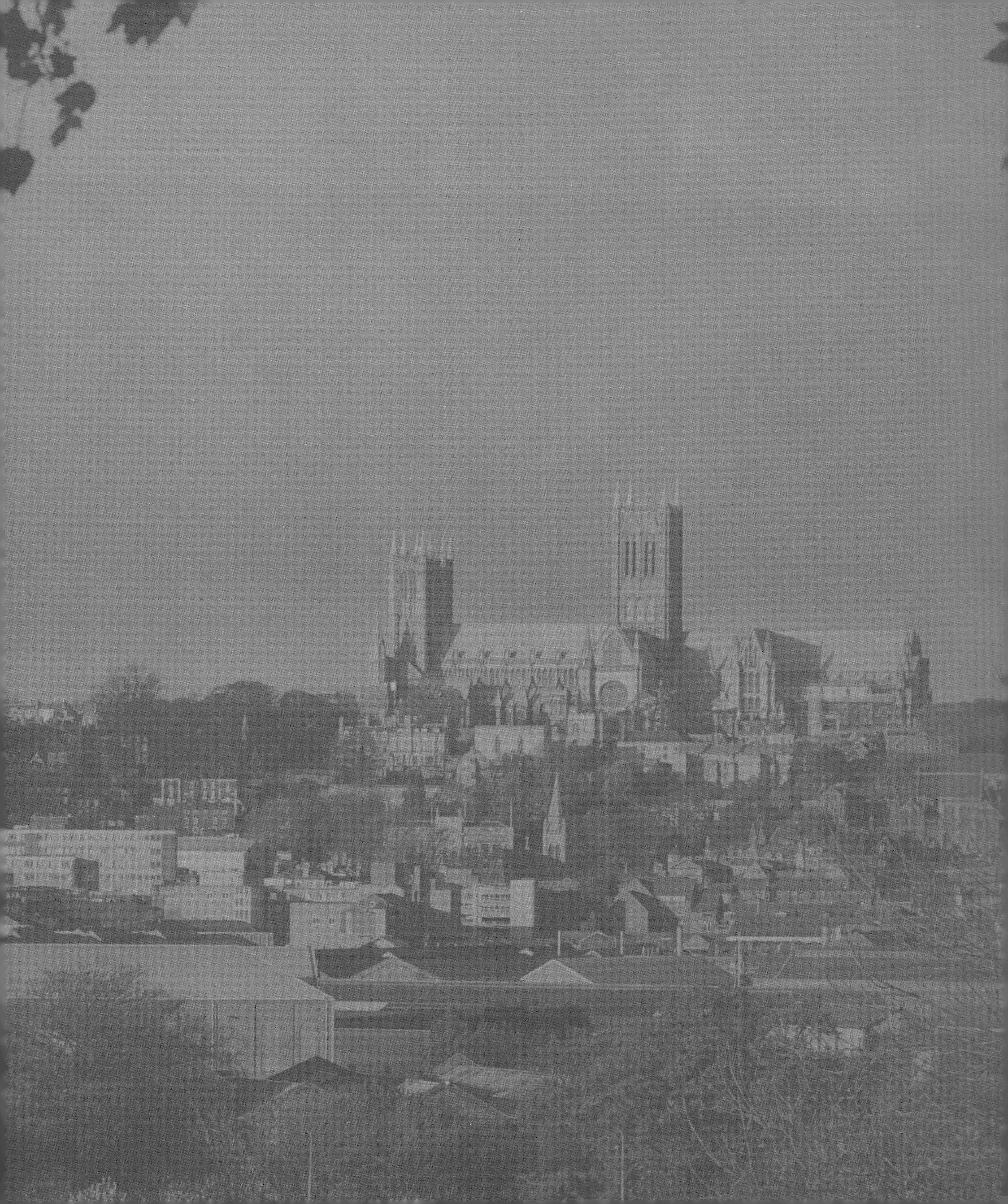

A sense of Lincolnshire

MARY POWELL

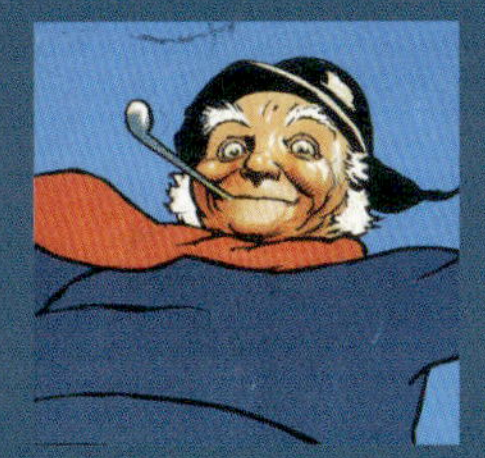

TOURISM is the fifth largest industry in the UK, bringing many billions of pounds into national, regional and local economies. With over 50 miles of coastline, it is not surprising that Lincolnshire had an early history of involvement in tourism and that it is of vital importance to Lincolnshire's economy. It began when the railway reached the village of Skegness in 1873 and the local landowner, the Earl of Scarbrough, believed that the popularity of the seaside could only grow. He engaged an architect to plan 'a model watering place' with wide, tree-lined streets on a grid system, promenades, gardens and a pier. The Earl turned out to be right, and when the Great Northern Railway Company commissioned John Hassall in 1908 to draw the 'Skegness is So Bracing' poster, its success as a destination was secured. This most famous of holiday advertisements was to promote a special three-shilling excursion from King's Cross. Skegness continued to make tourism history when in 1921 a poor travelling showman, Billy Butlin, set up his hoop-la stalls here. By 1929 he had opened a large amusement park and by 1935 had built the Butlin's Holiday Camp. However, we should not see the holiday coast as the only place vying for people's increasing leisure time. From 29 February 1884 the grounds of Lincoln Castle were opened to paying visitors. Frederick Quipp, the gate keeper, was made responsible for collecting the fees of tuppence per head and ensuring that the visitors' book was signed. Organisations such as the Lincolnshire Automobile Association started to apply to hold events in the Castle grounds.

OPPOSITE
John Hassall (1868–1948)
***The Jolly Fisherman*, 1908**
LNER poster, 1926
Skegness Town Council/National Railway Museum/Science & Society Picture Library

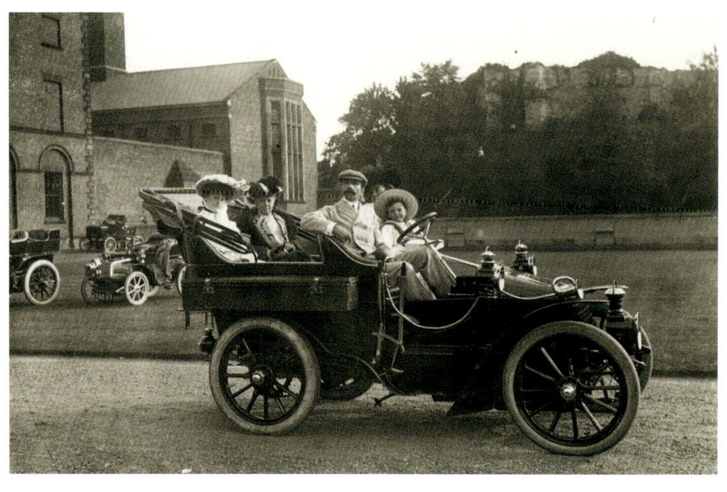

Automobile Association rally in Lincoln Castle, September 1902
Lincolnshire Libraries

Fast forwarding to the present, as Tourism Manager for Lincolnshire it is my great pleasure to promote the joys of this huge rural county. I would be the first to admit that the world over, tourism promotion is notorious for its clichés – the 'undiscovereds' and 'off the beaten tracks', and copy so bland that frankly it could apply to anywhere. Capturing that elusive sense of place, however, is easier said than done. James Beresford, Chief Executive of Visit England, once said to me, 'Above all, preserve and celebrate all that is unique in Lincolnshire. In a world where there is so much choice it is important to celebrate an area's distinctiveness.' He is right, of course, and as you travel across this country over relatively short distances the feel and look changes, and the differences

SKEGNESS

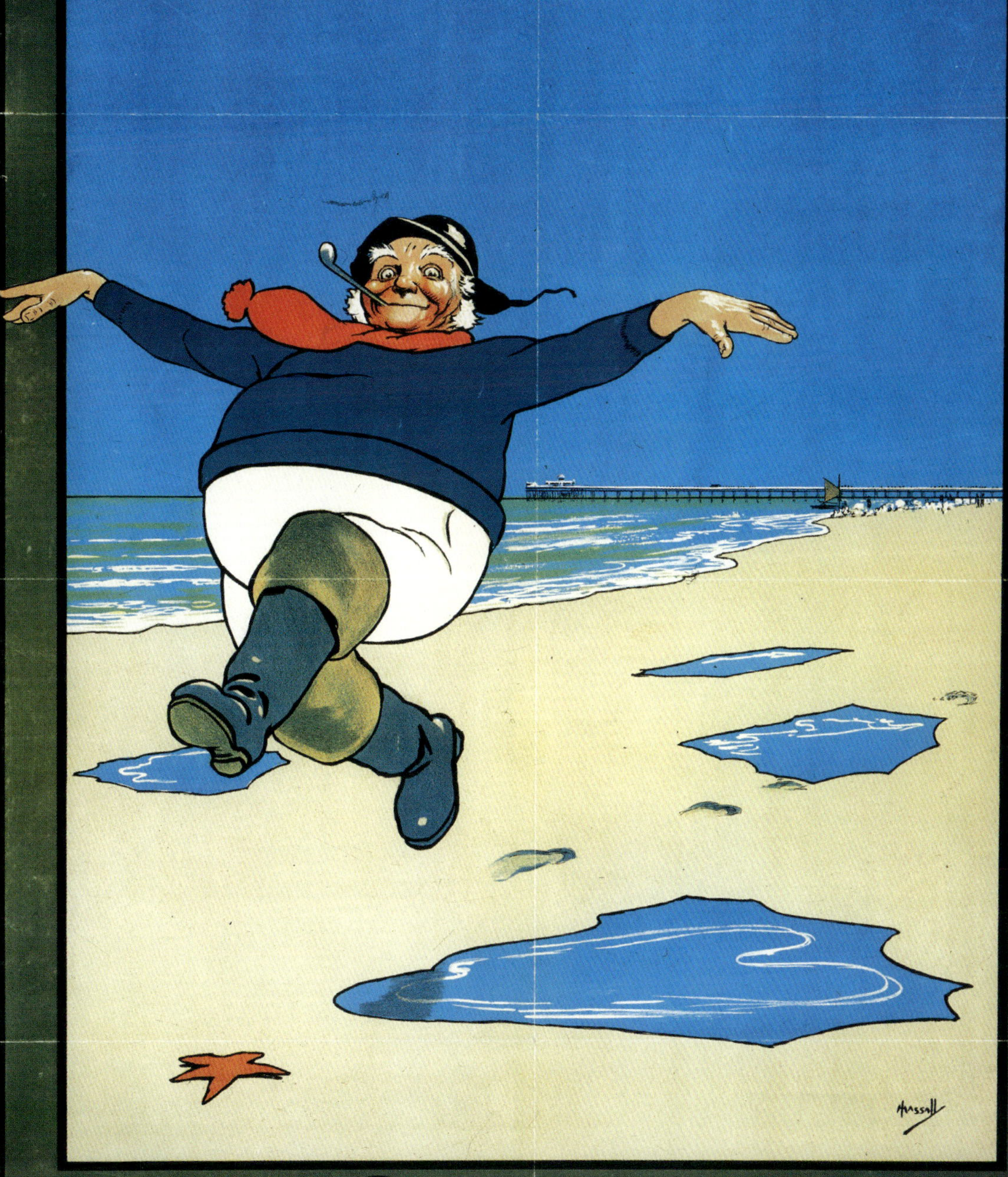

IS SO BRACING

Illustrated Guide from Secretary, Advancement Association, Skegness, or any L·N·E·R Enquiry Office.

Published by the London & North Eastern Railway. Printed in England. Vincent Brooks, Day & Son, Ltd. London. W.C.2

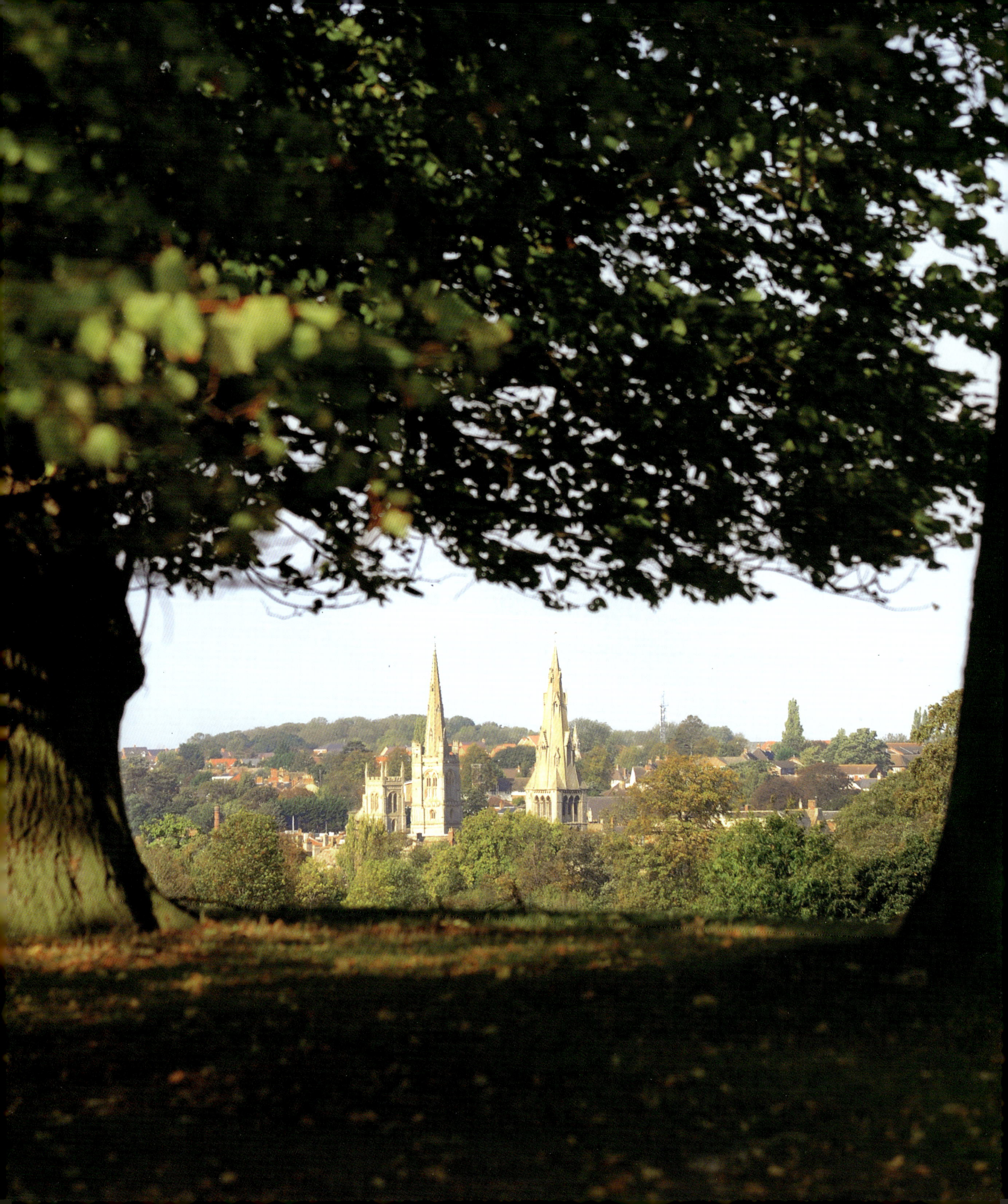

between the English counties in what can seem an increasingly homogenised world are surely something to be appreciated. We should celebrate that uniqueness, in terms of landscape, building materials, food specialities and of course, people – their voices, faces and achievements.

Taking care of Lincolnshire's assets comes first, in my book. Promotion is all very well but how you look after your heritage and countryside will always say more about your county. After spending several years encouraging local food sourcing and working on the regeneration of the county's waterways, in 2005 I was given the wonderful job of improving the uphill area of Lincoln, and so began ten years of some of the most challenging but satisfying work I have ever done.

It is not just Lincolnshire people who believe Lincoln Cathedral to be one of the finest buildings in the region, this country, Europe and beyond! So there you have it, I nail my colours to the mast as hopelessly prejudiced, but wherever your loyalties lie, I am sure you will agree that this is a wondrous building, whether viewed up close or seen on the skyline from afar. This is a building that tells stories of rich variety. William the Conqueror picked this strategic site of a former Roman fortress to build his castle (1068) and cathedral (1072) as very clear messages proclaiming his power and dominance to his new population; one the stick, the other the carrot. Now seen as something of a backwater, Lincolnshire in the early Middle Ages was, through the wool trade, wealthy and powerful. The diocese of Lincoln stretched from the Humber to the Thames and its extent is reflected in the

OPPOSITE
Stamford, viewed from the Burghley estate
Photo: Andrew Tryner, copyright Lincolnshire County Council

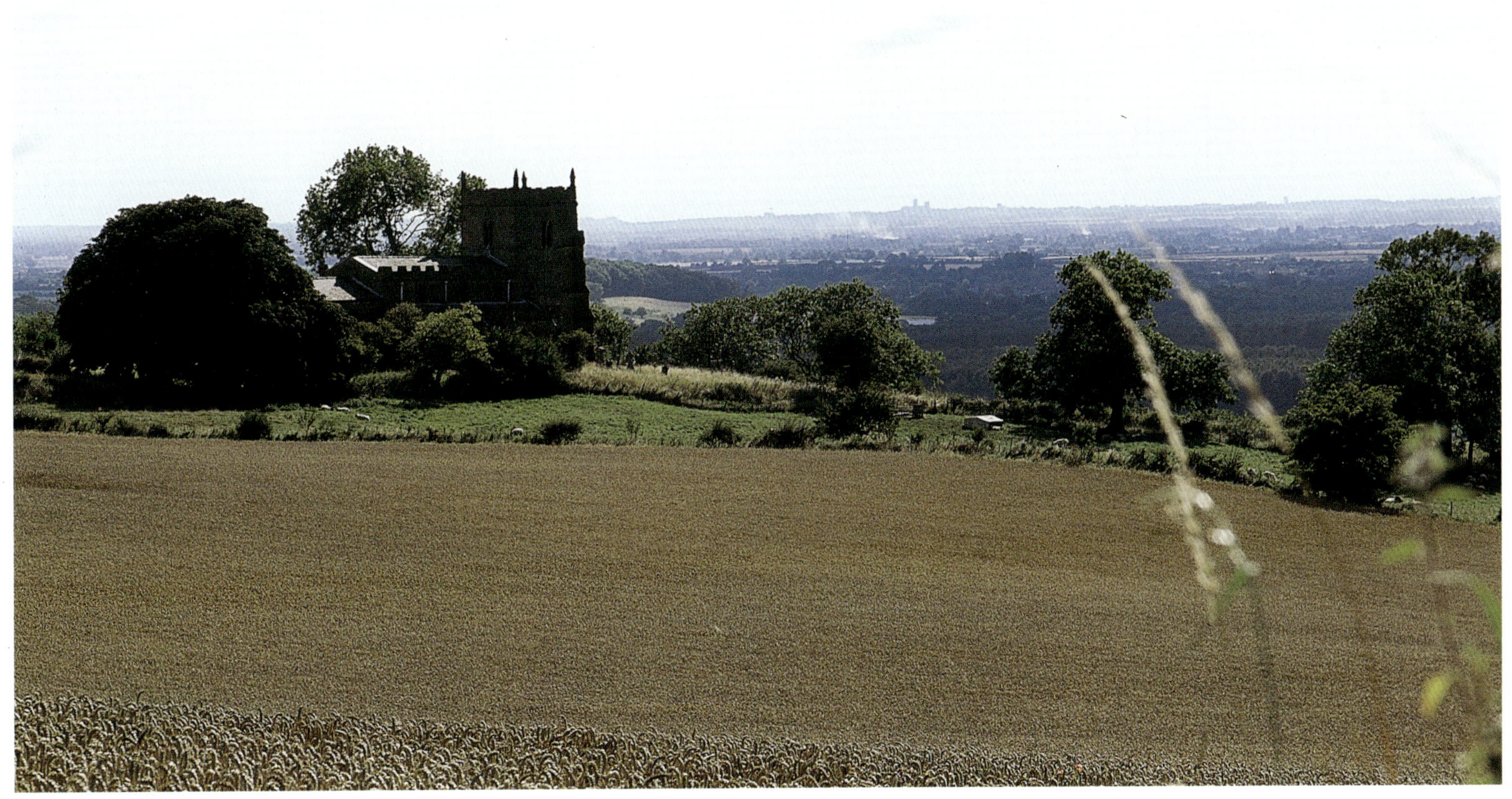

Church of All Saints, Walesby ('The Ramblers' Church') with Lincoln Cathedral on the skyline
Photo: Andrew Tryner, copyright Lincolnshire County Council

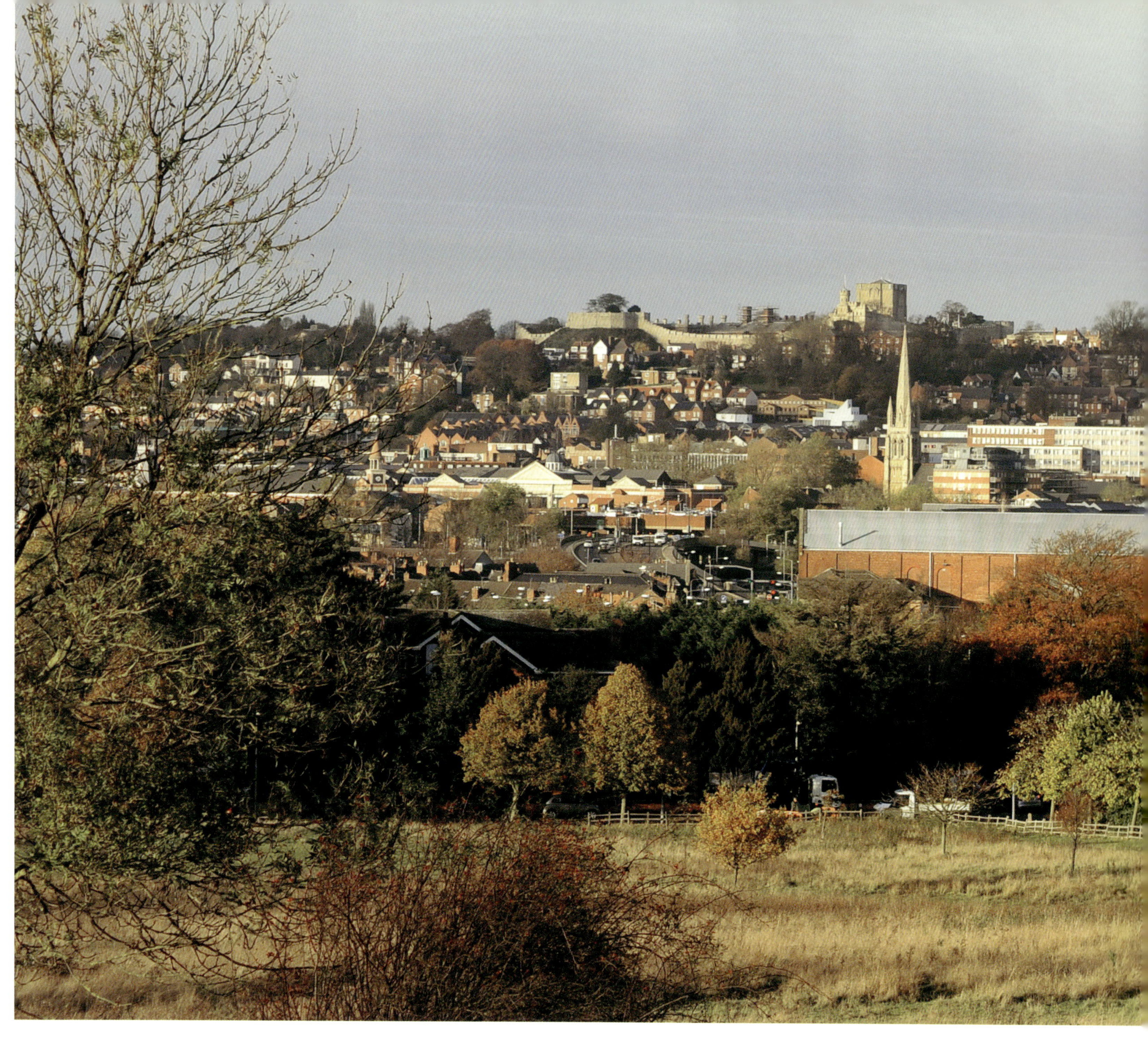

Lincoln Castle and Cathedral from the South Common
Photo: Andrew Tryner, copyright Lincolnshire County Council

size and beauty of its cathedral. Lincoln Cathedral has hosted parliament, welcomed kings, buried queens and withstood armed attack. A medieval audience, visiting a site of pilgrimage that was second only to Canterbury, would have been able to 'read' every element of the building, the carvings and stained glass acting as a book, telling the Christian stories with almost cartoon-like simplicity. Today we see the beauty but have forgotten how to read this Gothic vision.

The Cathedral's sister building, Lincoln Castle, is clearly William's stick, making his 'I'm in charge now' statement. It is a pragmatic building, functional

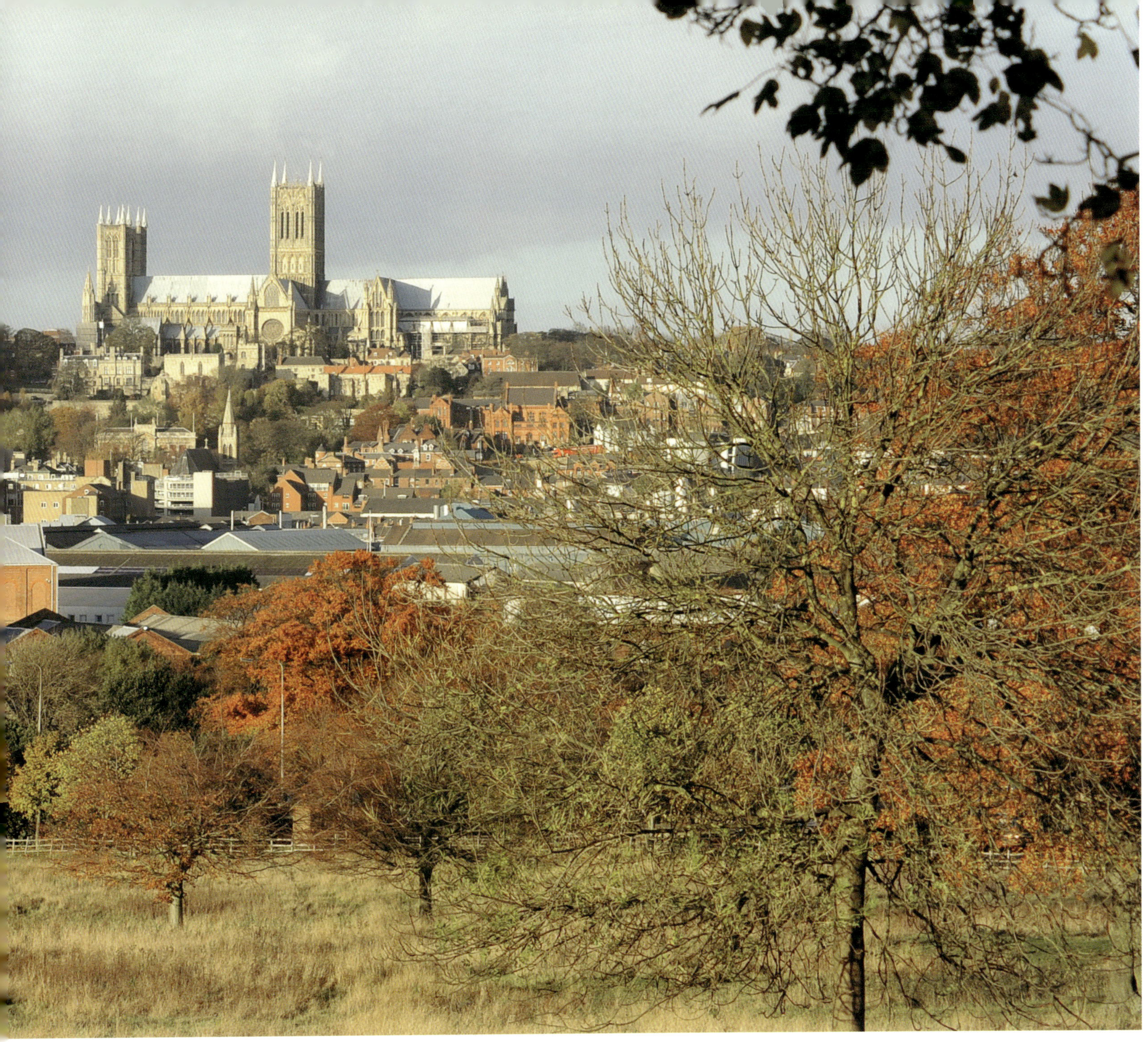

where the Cathedral is beautiful, built using lower-quality stone and having money spent on it only when needed. It was the site of battles and sieges, not to mention some complicated medieval wheeling and dealing. Even right up to the present day it has always been a working building as a centre of administration, justice and punishment, containing a former prison and a working Crown Court.

By 2008 it was clear that although the whole uphill historic quarter required care and attention, it was Lincoln Castle that was in the most urgent need of repair. Not only were its medieval walls in imminent danger of collapse, it was offering a

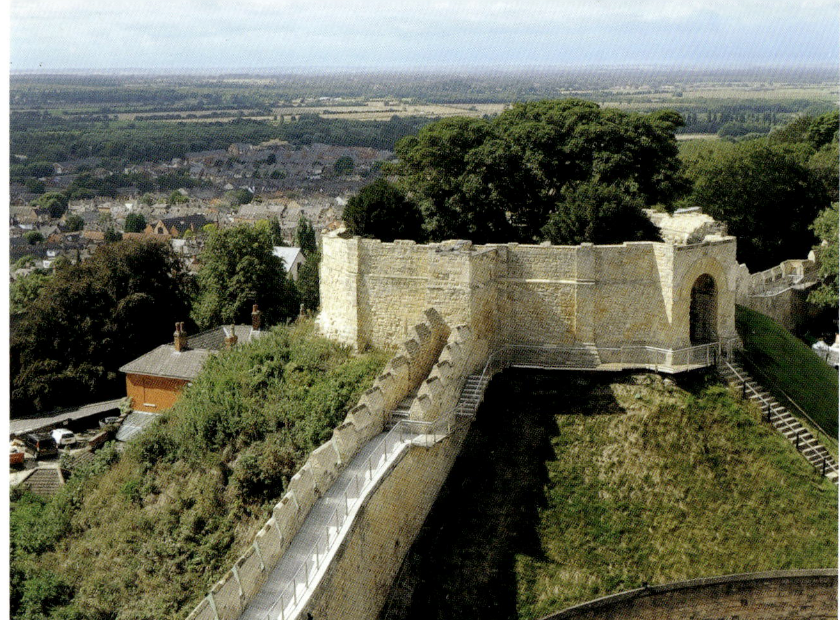

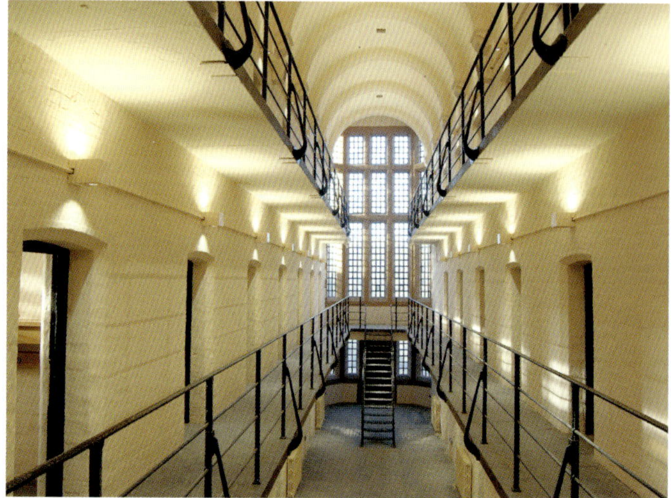

Lincoln Castle, Lucy Tower
Photo: Andrew Tryner, copyright Lincolnshire County Council

Lincoln Castle, Victorian male prison interior
Photo: Andrew Tryner, copyright Lincolnshire County Council

OPPOSITE
William Brown (1788–1859)
***Louth Panorama*, 1844–7**
Detail showing the view eastwards from the top of the church spire
Oil on linen
Louth Town Council

poor-quality visitor experience, with many of its buildings inaccessible to the public. Lincoln Castle Revealed was therefore conceived, a £22m project of restoration and improvement. The castle walls were to be repaired, creating for the first time a complete wall walk circuit and, most startling for a building that dates to 1068, a lift onto the east curtain wall for wheelchair access. The early Victorian prison was to be opened up and, using an extensive archive of prisoner records and staff journals, the stories told of this survivor of the 'separate system' Pentonville model. Lincoln Cathedral's 1215 Magna Carta had been displayed at the Castle for many years, but in an exhibition that really did not match its iconic status; so a new vault and cinema auditorium would be provided, to the highest security and environmental specification, and all in time to celebrate the document's 800th anniversary in 2015. It took three years to prepare the plans for this complicated layer upon layer of buildings and to bring together the necessary funding but, with the award by Heritage Lottery Fund of £12m, work was able to begin on the urgent wall repair in 2011.

Lincoln Castle Revealed has been a very big and expensive project for a rural county like Lincolnshire, continuing despite a difficult economic climate; but its successful completion, together with the 800th anniversary of Magna Carta, means that we have much to mark in 2015. *Lincolnshire's Great Exhibition* emerged as part of that celebratory mood, so that, just as the original Great Exhibition of 1851 brought together artefacts from across Britain and the Empire, so this exhibition was to celebrate Lincolnshire's own heritage. Some of this heritage was spread far and wide, and in some cases its connection with Lincolnshire rather forgotten. This county has a wealth of people who have not only affected and altered the nature of the county but in some instances have made a distinctive contribution to our local and national culture, and also internationally, changing our perceptions of the world around us. Bringing together these significant items has helped tell the story of Lincolnshire, its landscapes and its people. We hope that from this its sense of place will emerge and a feel for what makes Lincolnshire its own dear self.

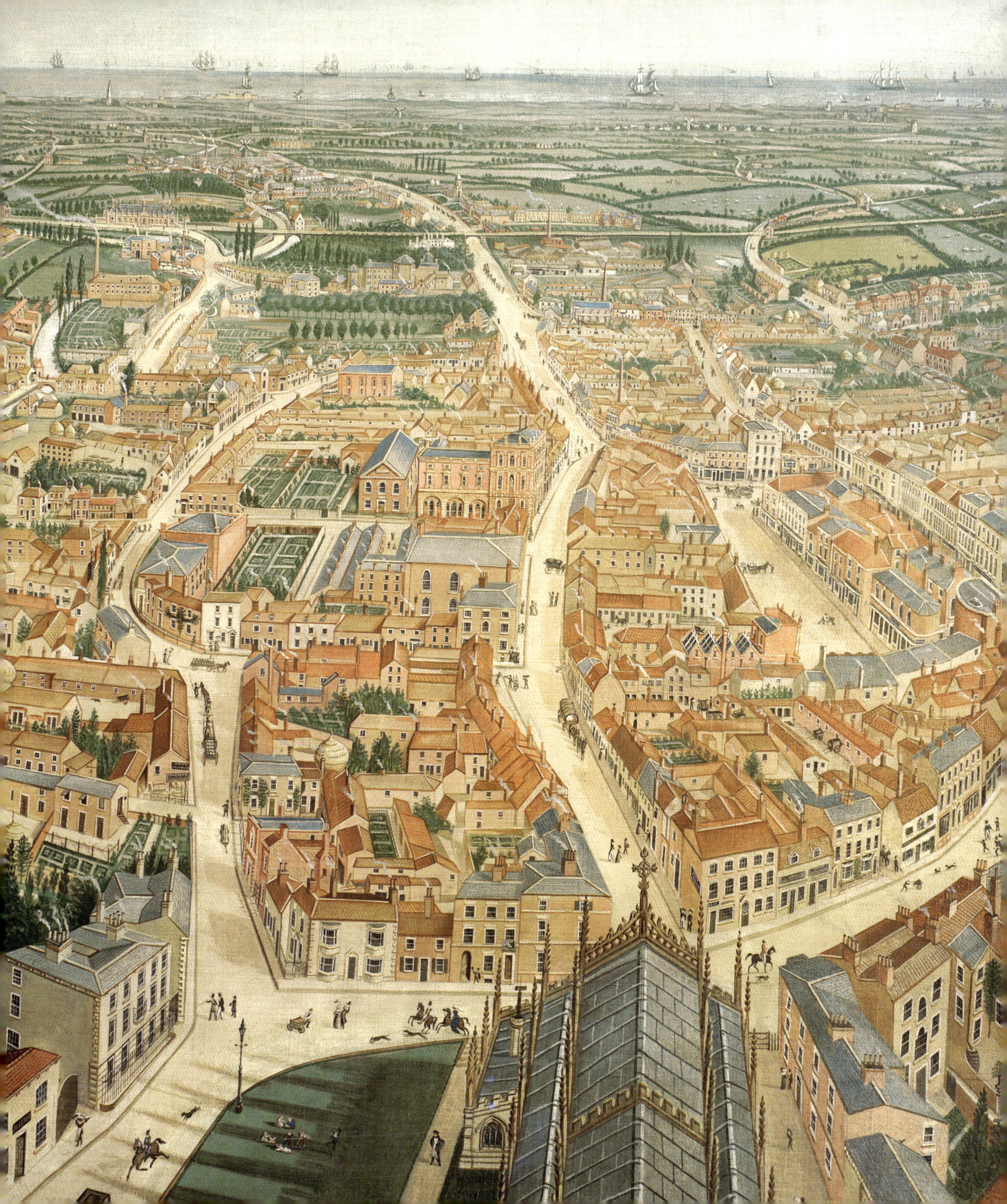

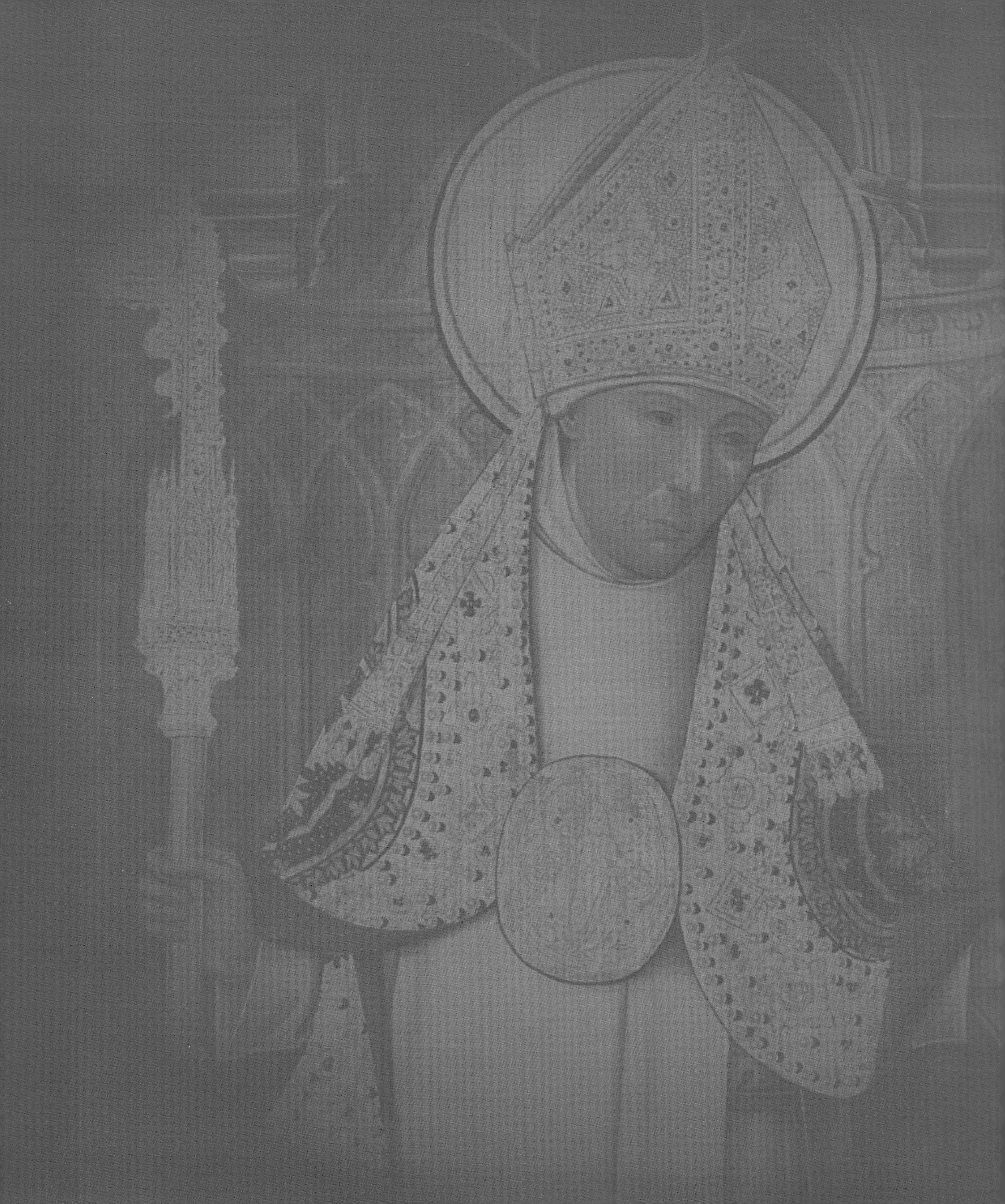

The medieval Church in Lincolnshire: saints and heroes

NICHOLAS BENNETT

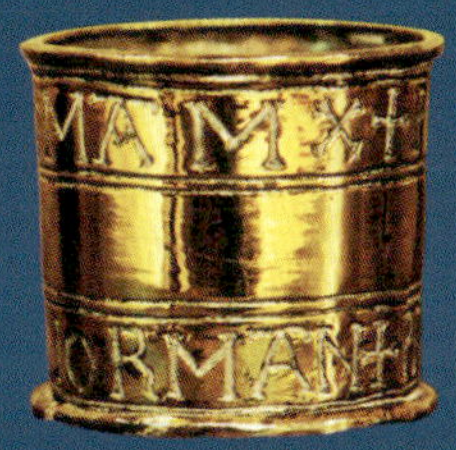

OPPOSITE

Pinchbeck Fen Map, fifteenth century
Detail showing Bourne Abbey and surrounding churches
The National Archives, MPCC1/ 7

BELOW

Church of St Andrew, Sempringham
Photo: Nicholas Bennett

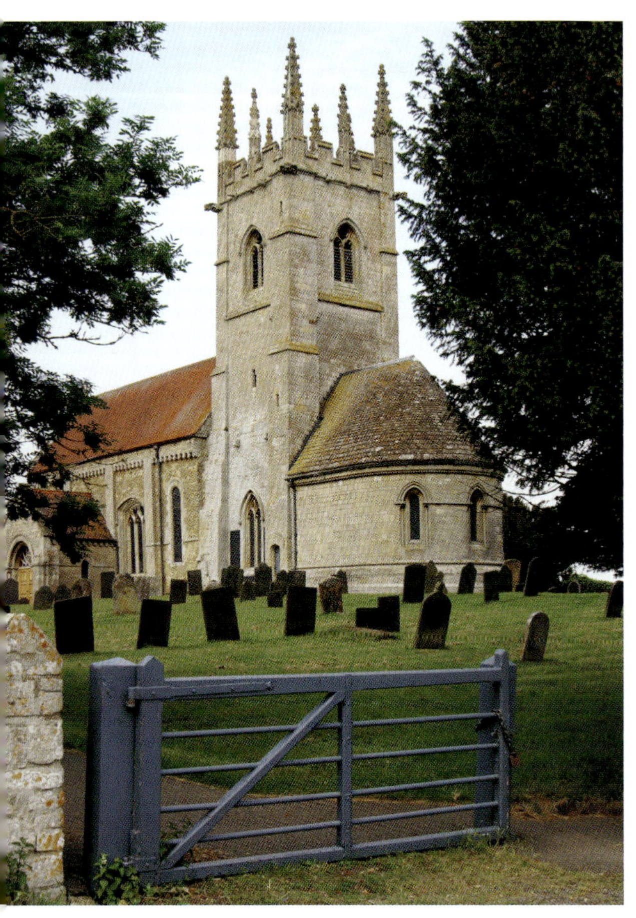

THE Lincolnshire landscape bears eloquent testimony to the all-pervading influence of the Church during the twelfth and thirteenth centuries. From heath and fen, from wold and marsh, the towers and spires of innumerable parish churches serve as a reminder of the ministry of the clergy among their people. In Lincoln itself, magnificent on its hilltop site, is the Cathedral Church of the Blessed Virgin Mary, offering a focal point for the spiritual life of the diocese. This rich tapestry of buildings provided the setting from which five men played a distinguished part in the history of their age.

Gilbert of Sempringham was born in 1083, the son of a Norman knight who had acquired a small estate in Lincolnshire after the Conquest. The young Gilbert suffered from an unspecified physical handicap, which ruled out a knightly career. Instead he embarked on a course of study, probably locally at first and then in France, perhaps at Paris or Laon. On his return to England his father presented him with two Lincolnshire churches, Sempringham and West Torrington. He served in the household of the bishops of Lincoln and was offered an archdeaconry, the first step on a ladder of ecclesiastical preferment. But he chose a different path. Renouncing his wealth, he returned to Sempringham to serve his cure in person.

Here he established a group of holy women, living as anchoresses in a cloister attached to the church. This grew into a religious community devoted to prayer and worship, the daily needs of the household being met by lay sisters, later joined by lay brothers and eventually by male canons. There was still no formal structure to the community when, in 1147, Gilbert travelled to the general chapter of the Cistercians, requesting that his foundation be incorporated into that order. The Cistercians, unenthusiastic about the role of women in the religious life, declined.

Returning to England the following year, Gilbert determined to establish his own order for the Sempringham community. His rule of life for the nuns drew inspiration from the Benedictines, that for the lay brothers from the Cistercians and that for the canons from the Augustinians. From the 1150s a number of 'Gilbertine' houses were founded, mainly in Lincolnshire and, unusually, many of them double houses where canons and canonesses lived parallel but separate lives. The number of foundations grew during Gilbert's lifetime to thirteen. A manuscript missal of the distinctive Gilbertine rite, possibly from the Priory of St Katherine outside Lincoln, survives in Lincoln Cathedral Library.

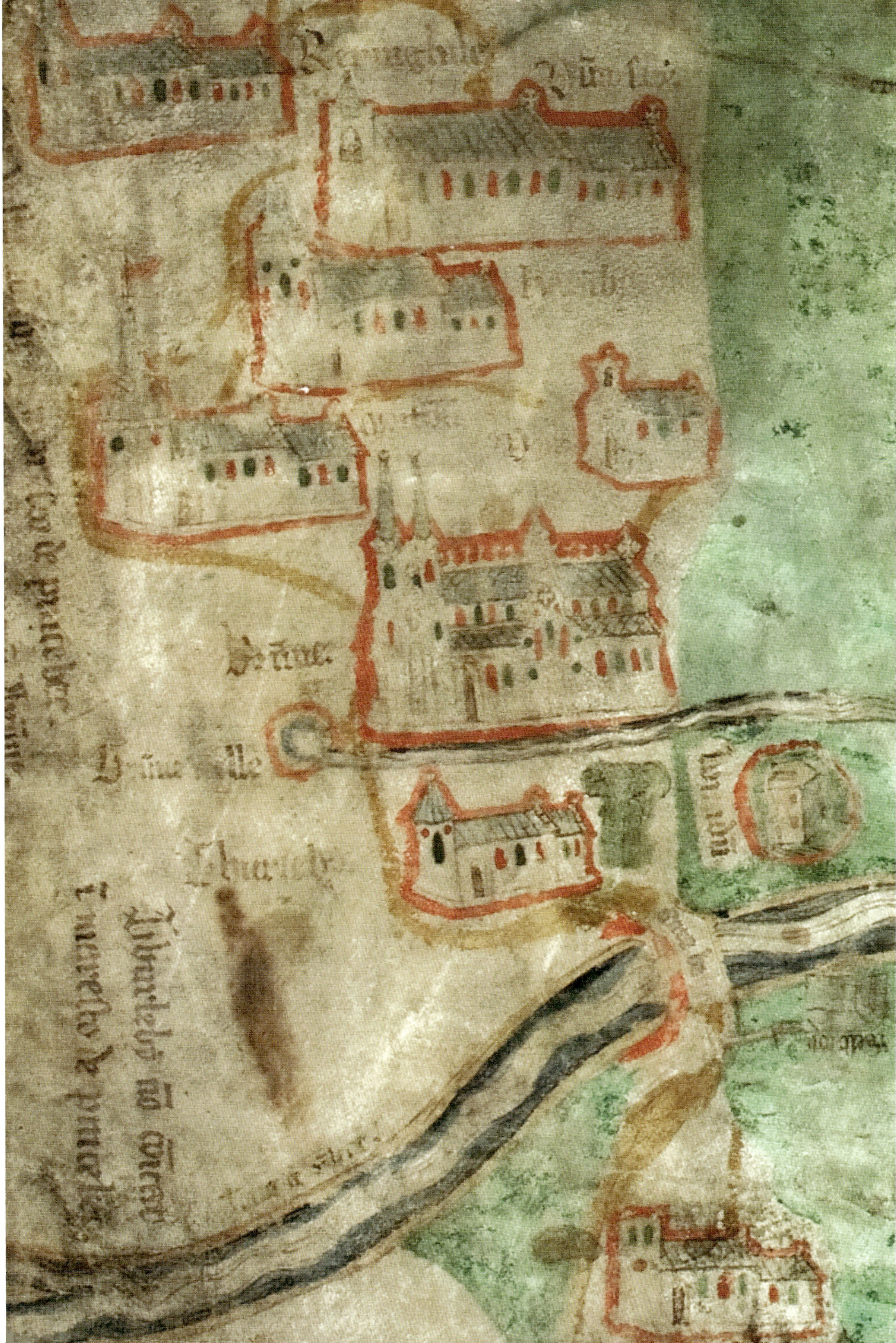

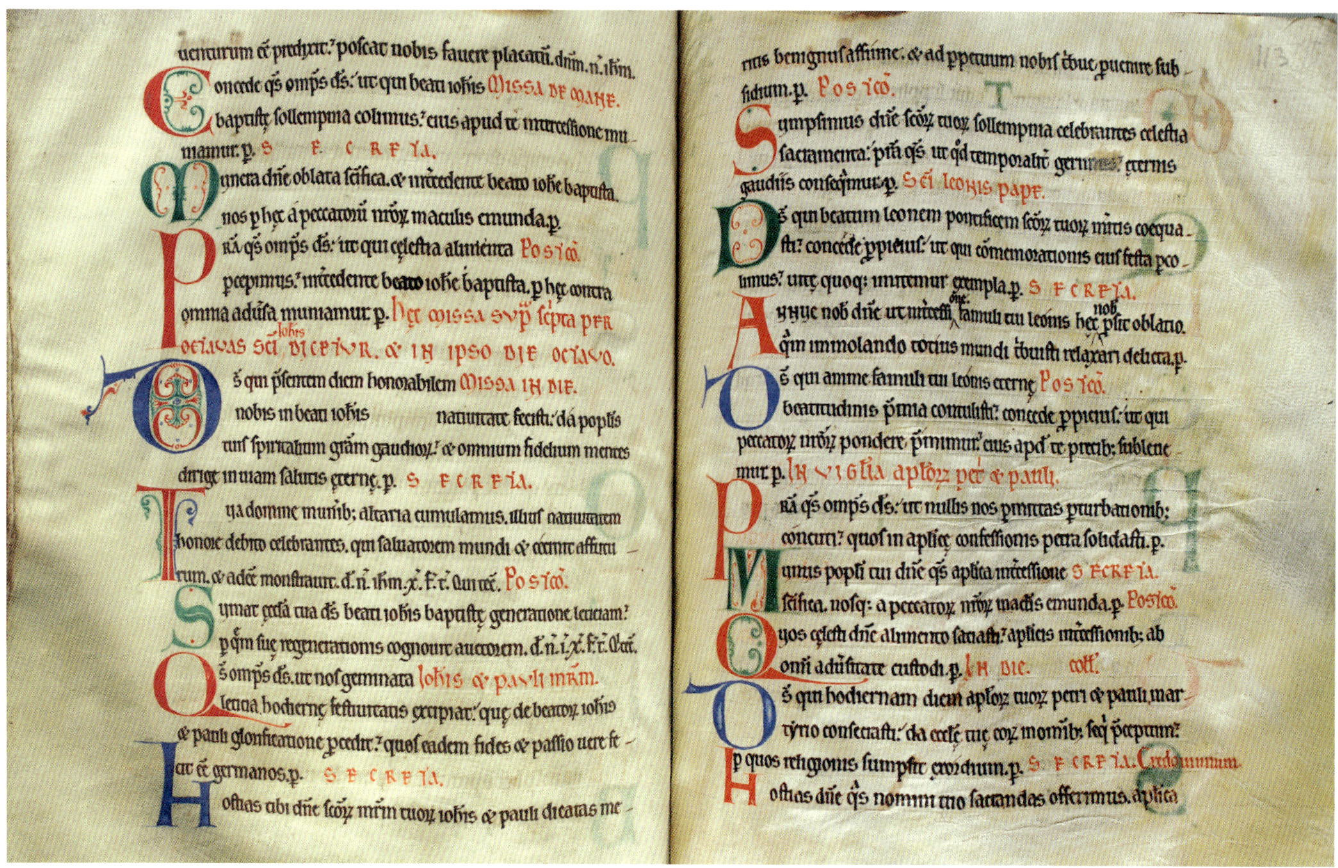

Sacramentary of the Use of the Order of Sempringham, twelfth century
Lincoln Cathedral Library, MS 115

OPPOSITE
Life of Gilbert of Sempringham, early thirteenth century
British Library, Cotton MS Cleopatra B 1, f.32

The first – and only – native English religious order, Gilbert's creation was not without its critics. Those who argued against the concept of men and women religious living in close proximity could point to the notorious scandal at Watton, a double house in east Yorkshire, involving an illicit relationship between a nun and a brother. Then in the 1160s the lay brothers of the order broke out in revolt, partly against the austerity of the Gilbertine rule and partly in protest at the increasing authority of the canons. The resulting dispute, in which Archbishop Thomas Becket, Henry II and Pope Alexander III all became involved, was a serious threat to the continuation of the order. It was eventually resolved in Gilbert's favour.

Gilbert died in 1189 and was buried in Sempringham Priory. His tomb was placed in the wall separating the nuns' part of the church from that of the canons, so that both men and women could have access to it. A detailed file of his life and miracles was collected – the 'Book of St Gilbert' – and this resulted in his canonisation in 1202. Sempringham never became a major pilgrimage destination in the Middle Ages; indeed, its remote situation on the edge of the Lincolnshire fens caused it to be seen as a suitable place for the exile of Gwenllian (died 1337), only child of Llewellyn, the last native Prince of Wales. Nevertheless, St Gilbert and the Gilbertine Order remain a potent influence on spiritual development today and the parish church of Sempringham, close to the site of the destroyed priory, is a visual reminder of Lincolnshire's own religious order.

Vita Gileberti de Sempingham. Baleus in Centur. legendam vocat, nec immerito quidem.

Reuerentissimo domino et patri in Christo Huberto dei gratia Cantuariensi archiepiscopo totius Anglie primati: (a) unus ex minimis fratribus ordinis sancti Gileberti Sempinghamensis. sanctorum meritis et premiis coequari. Diuine gratie largitati tanto nouit pater uenerande prudentia uestra nos debere esse gratiores: quo minus meritis uberiores contulit usus gratiarum. Sicut enim cum gratiarum actione crescunt munera gratie: ita se priuat acceptis. quisquis non pari committitur honore donorum dignitate. secundum illud. Omni habenti dabitur et habundabit: ei autem qui non habet et quod uidetur habere auferetur ab eo. Ad nos communiter iudex serenissime. hanc arbitror spectare rationem. quos extremos tempore. extremos loco. presentes scilicet carne. anglicos natione. ad equalitatem antiquorum deduxit nouissimos: orientalis orbis glorie coequauit diuina bonitas. ab orbe (b) fere remotos. Hec est summi patris dei gratia et uenerabilium patrum nostrorum. sanctorum scilicet insule nostre gloria. quorum alios in omni gradu et utroque sexu martirii decorauit corona: alios uero fidei ueritas et uite sinceritas confessorum Christi sacro numero copulauit. Inter quos diebus nostris in regione nostra post beatum Thome

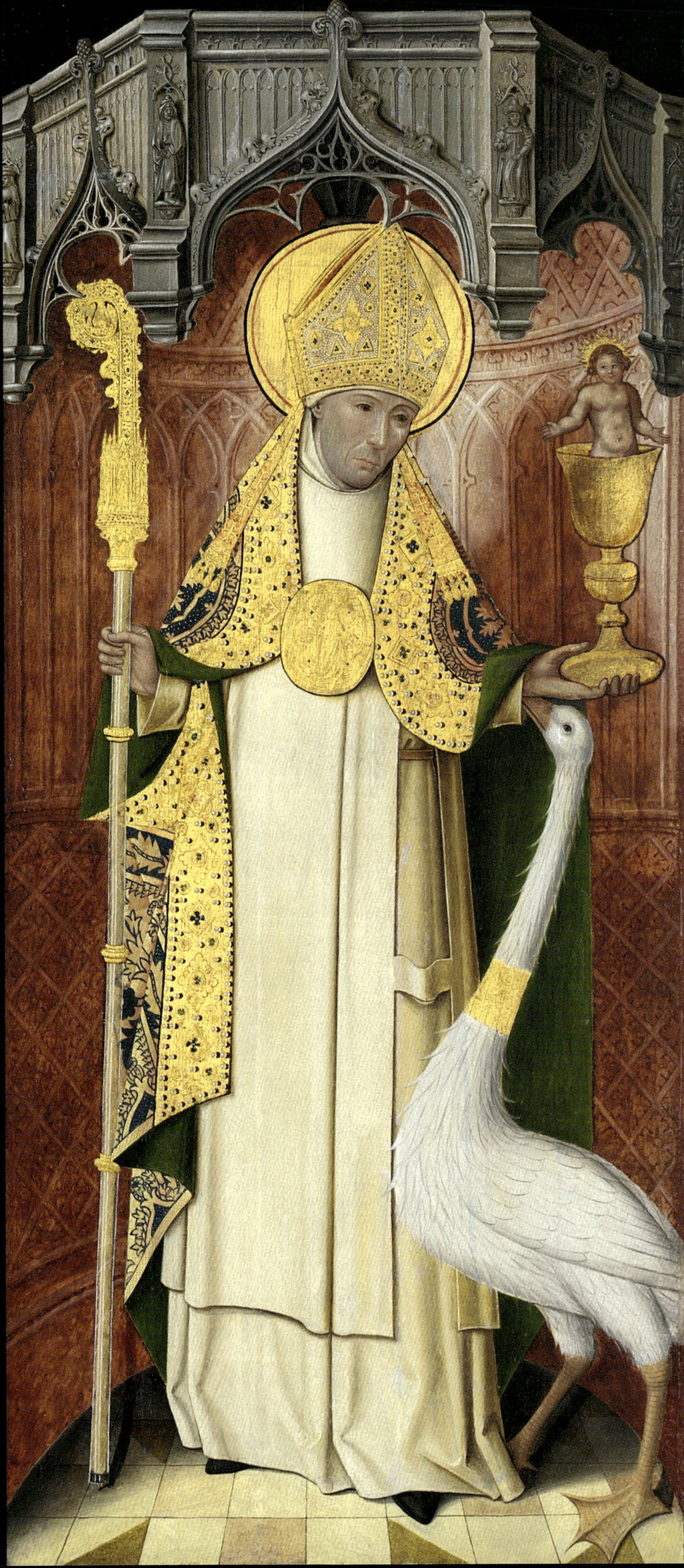

Altarpiece from Thuison-les-Abbeville, 1490–1500
Detail showing St Hugh of Lincoln
Oil on panel
The Art Institute of Chicago,
Mr and Mrs Martin A. Ryerson Collection 1933.1060

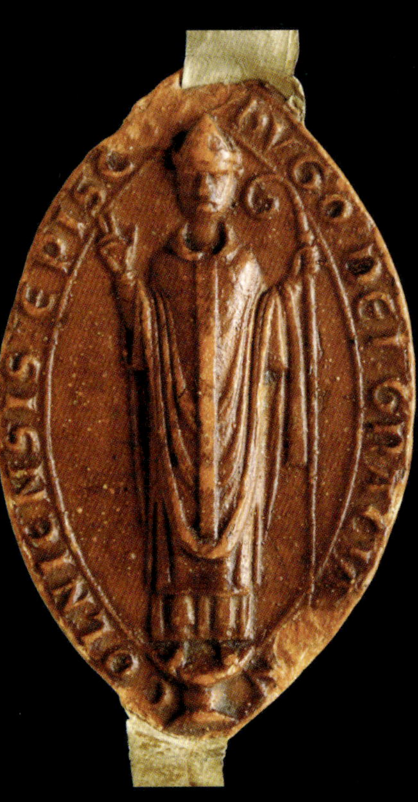

Episcopal seal of St Hugh of Avalon (Bishop of Lincoln 1186–1200), about 1189–93
Red wax, attached to confirmation for Sempringham Priory
Lincoln Cathedral Library

St Hugh of Lincoln with his swan
Medieval sculpture, now in the cloister of New College, Oxford
Photo: Nicholas Bennett

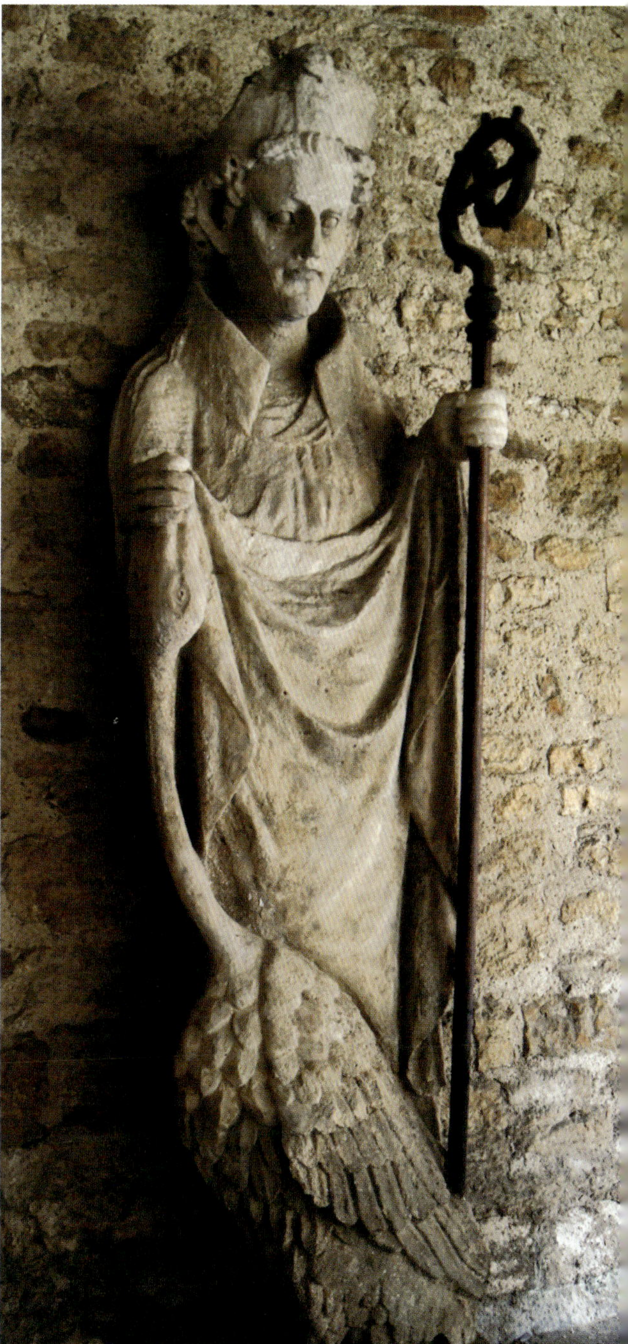

Shortly before Gilbert's death, a modification in the lay brothers' rule of life was enacted before the Bishop of Lincoln. This assembly may well represent the only meeting between two Lincolnshire saints, for the bishop concerned was Hugh of Avalon. Hugh had entered the Carthusian Order in Grenoble and was brought to England in 1179 to become Prior of Witham in Somerset, founded by Henry II as part of his penance following the murder of Thomas Becket. The king was favourably impressed by the new prior and in 1186 he chose him for the vacant bishopric of Lincoln. Hugh refused to accept the office until two conditions were met: that he should be canonically elected by the Lincoln Chapter, and that his monastic superior should consent. As bishop, Hugh had a particular care for his cathedral church, the fabric of which had been devastated by earthquake on Palm Sunday 1185. The bishop inspired the rebuilding of the fabric in the new Gothic style; he is recorded as having assisted in the work by carrying a hod of stone or mortar. Within his diocese he was remembered for his concern for the poor and marginalised, and the care with which he performed the episcopal offices of ordination and confirmation.

Beyond the diocese, Hugh's status as a holy man, one whose austere life was dedicated to God, enabled him to stand up to those in authority. Even the Angevin kings, notoriously quick-tempered, appear to have been unable to withstand Hugh's combination of sanctity, tenacity and teasing wit. When Henry II, having summoned the bishop to explain why he had excommunicated a royal forester, attempted to ostracise him by ignoring his presence and instead stitching a leather bandage to protect a hunting wound, Hugh remarked, 'How you remind me of your cousins of Falaise!' This audacious jest, reminding the king of the low status of his ancestress, the tanner's daughter who was mother of William the Conqueror, shook Henry from his cold fury into irresistible laughter.

The reverence felt towards Hugh during his life was mirrored in the reaction to the news of his death on 17 November 1200. Many accompanied the cortège on its journey from London to Lincoln, where King John and King William of Scotland both helped to carry his body to the grave. Reports of miracles which took place at Hugh's tomb were collected together into a report petitioning the Holy See for his canonisation, which was granted by Pope Honorius III in 1220. The shrine of St Hugh became a significant focus for pilgrimage, resulting eventually in the construction of the magnificent Angel Choir at the east end of

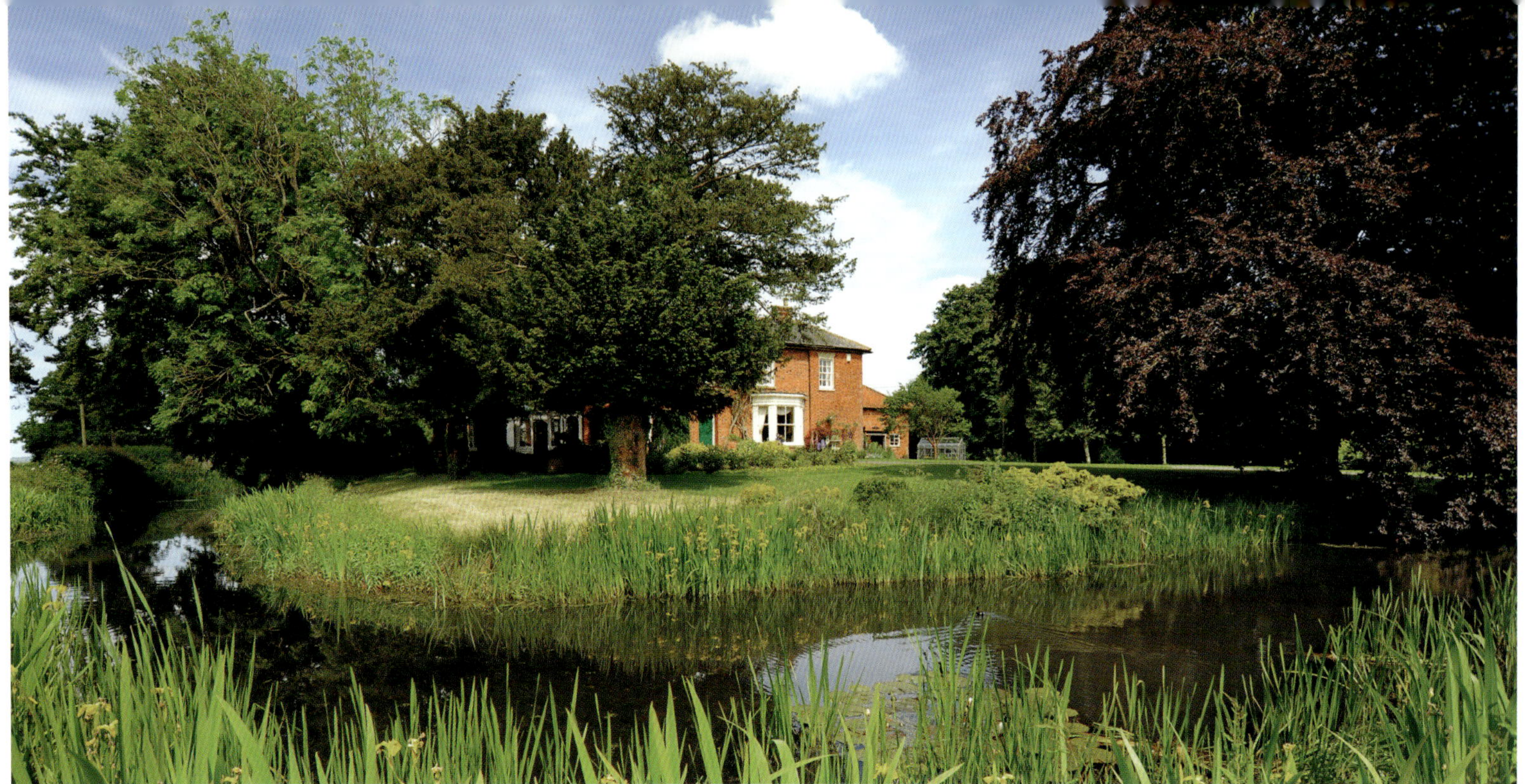

Moated farmhouse at Langton by Wragby
Photo: Andrew Tryner, copyright Lincolnshire County Council

Lincoln Cathedral, dedicated in October 1280 in the presence of Edward I and Queen Eleanor.

The commission that petitioned for the canonisation of Hugh of Avalon was led by the Archbishop of Canterbury, Stephen Langton. Born about 1150, Langton was one (possibly the eldest) of three sons of Henry Langton of Langton by Wragby, a minor landholder in Lincolnshire. A moated farmhouse west of Langton Church may mark the site of his birthplace.

The young Stephen apparently demonstrated early aptitude for scholarship. It is likely that his early education took place in the schools of Lincoln Cathedral, then at the height of its reputation as one of the most influential centres of learning in England. Among the books that the young Stephen Langton would have found at Lincoln were the commentaries of Peter Lombard, the standard theological text book of the time, based on lectures given at the schools of Paris in the 1150s. Langton himself moved to Paris, where he studied and taught.

At Paris, Langton would have known a fellow Englishman, Ralph Niger. Niger's trenchant opinions on kingship, stemming from his outrage at the murder of Archbishop Thomas Becket on the orders of Henry II, can be found in his commentaries on the Old Testament Books of Kings (now preserved in unique copies in Lincoln Cathedral Library). Returning to England after Henry's death, Niger obtained a prebend at Lincoln, where the most significant corpus of his theological writings survives.

Another of Langton's colleagues at the Paris schools was Lothario dei Segni, who was elected Pope in 1198, taking the name Innocent III. When after 1205 the succession to the archbishopric of Canterbury was in dispute between the monks and King John, Innocent used his papal authority to appoint Langton. The king, outraged

Ralph Niger, *Moralia Regum, pars 1*, late twelfth century
Lincoln Cathedral Library, MS 25

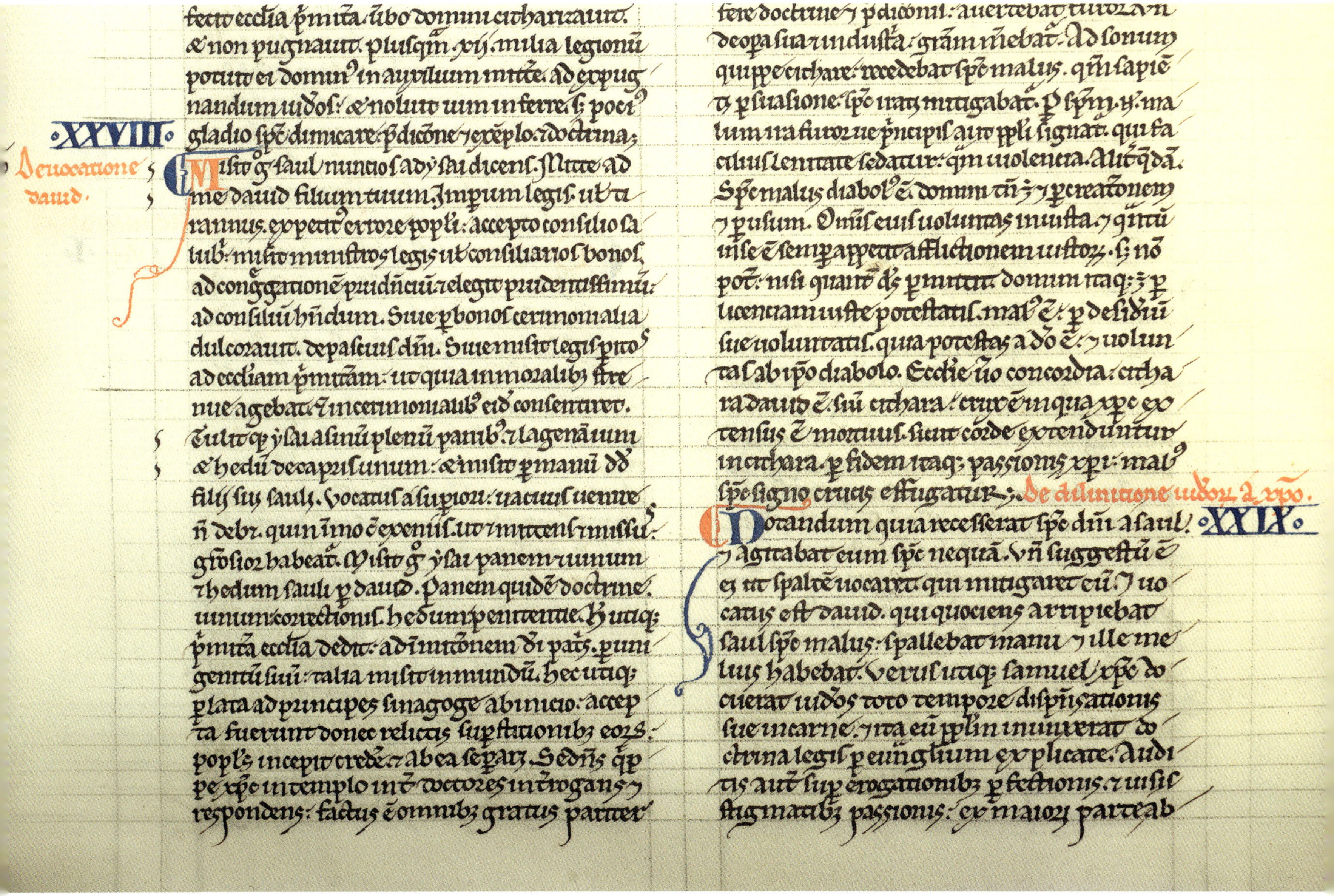

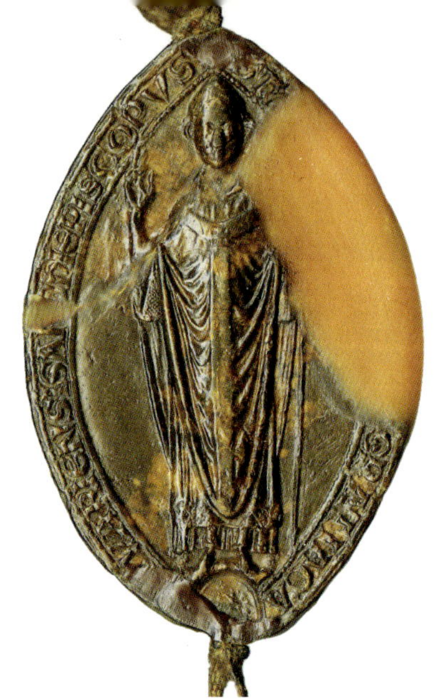
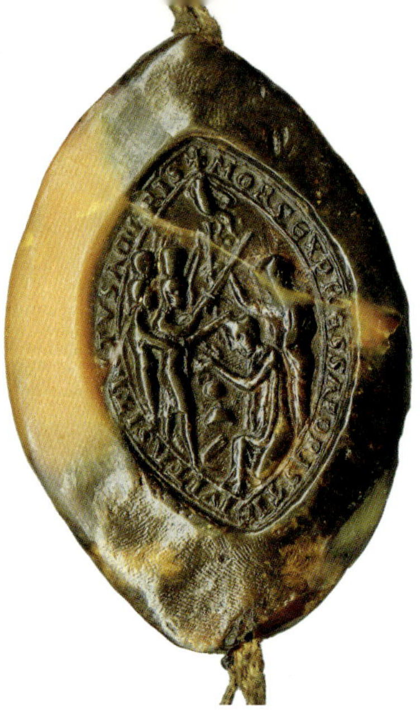

Archiepiscopal seal of Stephen Langton (Archbishop of Canterbury 1207–28), about 1213–15
The National Archives, DL 27/4

OPPOSITE
Stained glass figure of Stephen Langton in the church of St Giles, Langton by Wragby, twentieth century
Photo: Andrew Tryner, copyright Lincolnshire County Council

at what he saw as interference in his authority over the Church in England, refused to recognise Langton's appointment. The archbishop remained in exile in France until 1213. Meanwhile, in 1208 the pope placed England under an Interdict.

King John's submission to the pope in 1213 and the subsequent lifting of the Interdict enabled Langton to return to England, where he played a significant part in the events leading up to the issue of Magna Carta. His influence on the framing of Magna Carta has been a matter for debate among historians. He may have come to see the charter as tainted by the fact that it was forced on the king by the coercion of civil war. Rebellion against a lawful ruler (and John was now reconciled to the Church) went against the teaching of the Bible. However much Langton might sympathise with the rebels, he was unable to support them openly.

Langton did, however, play a significant role in the negotiations, acting as an intermediary between king and barons. He also ensured the inclusion in Magna Carta of clause 1, guaranteeing the freedom of the Church. This clause, significantly, was granted 'to God' rather than (as with the remainder of the charter) 'to all free men'. It refers to the king's grant, 'before the quarrel between us and our barons began', of freedom of elections, making it quite clear that this clause was free from any taint of intimidation. Langton's intention here may have been to protect the liberties of the Church in clause 1, while subtly dissociating himself and his fellow bishops from Magna Carta's later clauses won by coercion and the threat of civil war.

When the settlement between king and barons broke down, Langton's position became untenable. The pope suspended him from office for refusing to excommunicate the rebels and he went abroad to Rome to seek restoration. He did not return to England until May 1218 but thereafter played an important part during the minority of the young king Henry III. In particular, it was Langton's promotion of Magna Carta as a bulwark of good government that led to its definitive reissue in 1225. One of the greatest figures in the firmament of European theologians, Langton played a central part in the crisis of government of early thirteenth-century England.

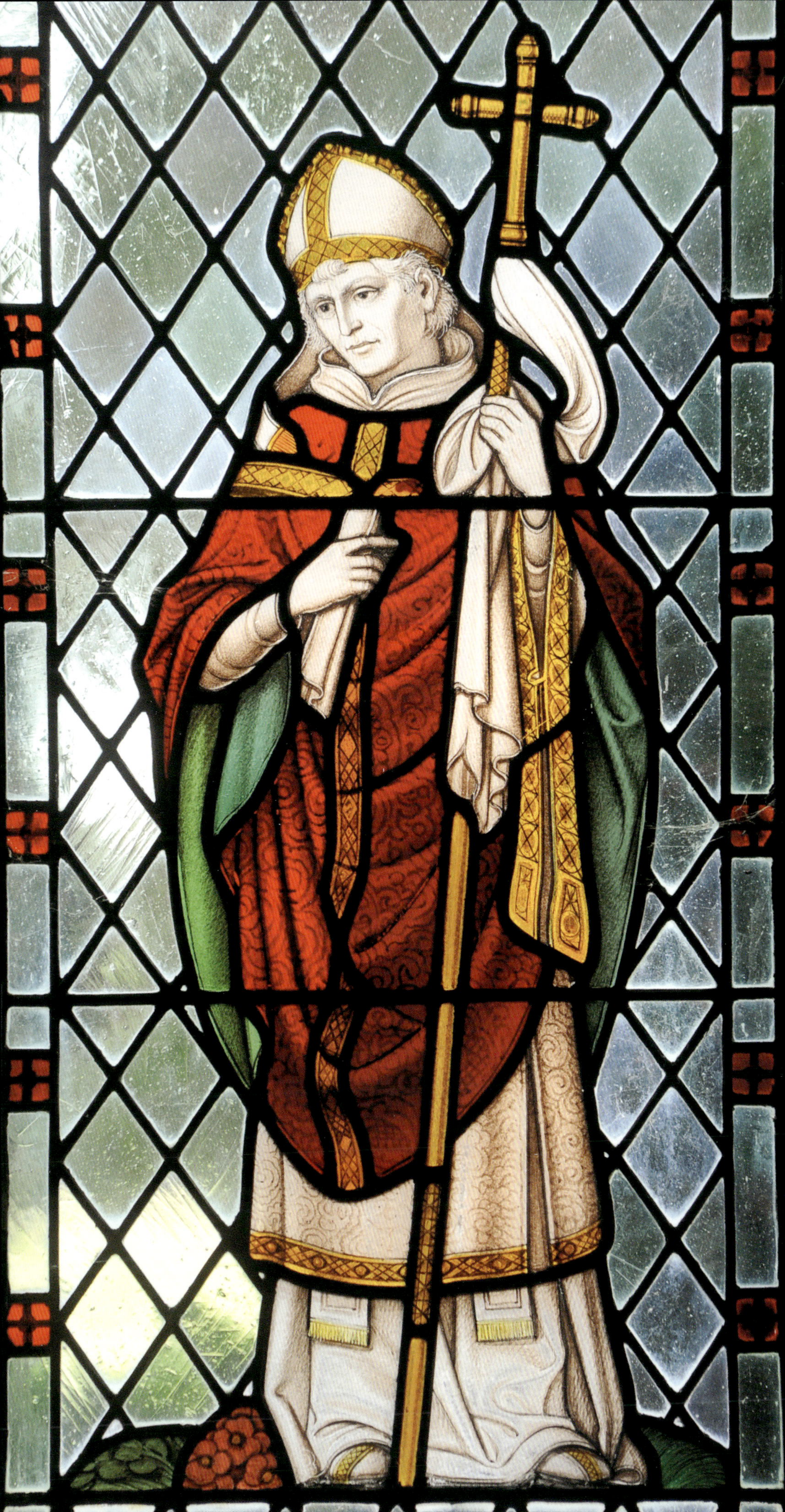

Magna Carta, 1215
Detail of reverse showing the inscription 'LINCOLNIA'
Lincolnshire Archives, D&C A1/1/45

One of the key issues at stake between the king and the English Church was the way in which, on the death or translation of a bishop, successive rulers kept that see vacant for as long as possible while its income flowed into the royal treasury. The diocese of Lincoln had been a notable casualty of this practice. After the death of Bishop Robert Chesney in 1166 the see was effectively kept vacant for almost seventeen years before the election in 1183 of Walter of Coutances. Geoffrey Plantagenet, who held the see for some of the interval, was unable to fulfil the pontifical responsibilities of the bishopric because of his unwillingness to proceed to consecration. It may be, as Hugh's biographer Adam of Eynsham suggested, that Henry II was seeking to make amends for the scandalous length of this vacancy by insisting on the appointment of the conspicuously holy man Hugh of Avalon as bishop.

Nonetheless, subsequent vacancies in the see of Lincoln were by no means brief, nearly three years elapsing between the death of St Hugh and the election of his successor, William of Blois, and a period of similar length after William's own death in 1206. King John was clearly aware, as his father had been, of the financial value of a delay in filling up bishoprics. With the Interdict in force and Archbishop Langton in exile, the king had a free hand in nominating the next Bishop of Lincoln and he eventually chose one of the clerks of his chancery, Hugh of Wells.

The second Bishop Hugh was the son of a citizen of Wells in Somerset. He began his career as a clerk in the household of the bishops of Bath and Wells. On the accession of King John in 1199 he entered the service of the royal chancery and in all likelihood played a significant part in implementing the reforms of Archbishop Hubert Walter, including the institution of systematic registration of chancery records by enrolment. Between 1200 and 1203 he acted as custodian of the vacant see of Lincoln on behalf of the king.

If the king had sought, in proposing one of his loyal clerks to become Bishop of Lincoln, to gain a key ally in his struggle with the Church, he was to be disappointed. Hugh was elected by the Cathedral Chapter in the early months of 1209. The king was excommunicated by Pope Innocent III in November of that year and shortly afterwards Hugh, along with many of his episcopal brethren, made his way to France, where he received consecration from Archbishop Langton on 20 December of that year. He was to remain abroad until the lifting of the Interdict; on 24 May 1213 royal letters were issued to him promising peace to the Church and urging his return to England.

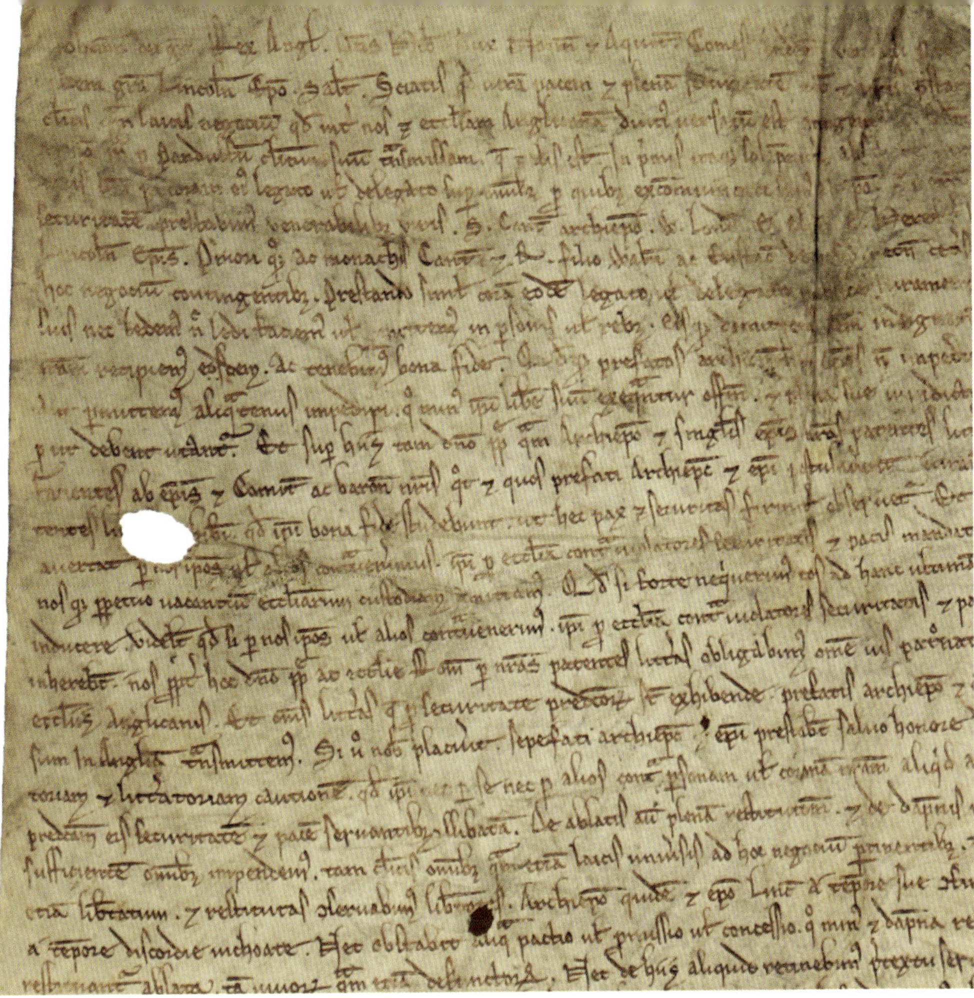

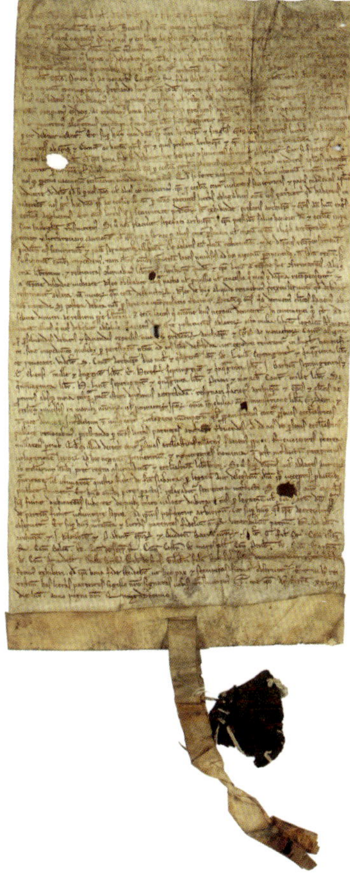

Letters patent announcing that King John has granted peace to the English Church, 28 June 1213

Detail of text above left: 'Know that we have granted peace and security to you … and to all clergy and laity, touching the long dispute between us and the English Church'
Lincolnshire Archives, D&C A1/1/42

Hugh was present at Runnymede in June 1215 during the negotiations between king and barons that resulted in the issue of Magna Carta. It is virtually certain that the celebrated Lincoln copy of the charter, with its twice-repeated endorsement of 'Lincolnia', was the one given to Bishop Hugh for dissemination to his diocese. A list drawn up shortly after Runnymede indicates that thirteen copies of the charter were to be made, and it is likely that these were the copies referred to in the contemporary annals of Dunstable Priory, 'to be deposited for safe-keeping in each bishopric'. It was Bishop Hugh, therefore, who brought the copy of Magna Carta to Lincoln and entrusted it to the Cathedral Chapter to be preserved among the historic archives of the see, where it has remained ever since.

The concern of Hugh of Wells for the preservation of archives, influenced no doubt by his experience in the royal chancery, can also be seen in his introduction, soon after his return to England in 1213, of the systematic registration of episcopal business. The series of parchment rolls which still survive among the Lincoln diocesan records represent the earliest extant bishop's registers in England. They consist of membranes of parchment, on which the bishop's clerks wrote summaries of business transacted, and which were subsequently sewn together end-to-end and rolled up. It is probable that it was the sheer size of the medieval diocese, stretching from the Humber to the Thames and covering eight and a half counties, that provided the spur to such organised record-keeping.

OVERLEAF

Episcopal roll of Hugh of Wells (Bishop of Lincoln 1209–35), about 1214–18

The second entry in this section, for the church of Mavis Enderby, refers to an inquiry into the alleged excommunication of the patron, Henry Malebise, for fighting with the barons against the king. Malebise was able to show that, as he had been stricken with a universal paralysis, he had always remained in the king's peace.
Lincolnshire Archives, DIOC/ROLLS/WELLS/10

et hre facer.

Hug de Elleton clic' psentat' a Priorissa 7 Conventu de Grimelesbau[...]
[...]ustun. sup eade ecclia factam. 7 p confessionem a dnō. W. de Albimac una voce co[...]
dia [...] ecclie est adept'. 7 mandatu est Archido Leic ut custodia ei hre
faciat [...].

Enderby. R. de Malebise clic' psentat' a Witto Malebise pre suo ad Ecclam de Ender[...]
ita [...] sua tindam ab epo si tam do dante uenit. 7 cum examinat' p scolar[...]
epo recipiat. Alioqn. ecclia in manu dni epi capiat'. 7 de numero psent. [...]
7 A. Decan de Bulingbroc. scdm qm omia fuerit liqda. 7 mandatu est [...]

[illegible] Ric de Wideran cliric psentat' ab Abbe 7 conuentu de Egnesham ad Ecclam de [...]
salu [...] iure suo ad psens pmissa psentato pcedit. custodia ei est adept'. salua inst[...]
H. [...] Com Linc p inqsitionem ui factam. reseruata [...] gone de [...] dnō
Archido qd ad psentationem ei ab Abbe 7 conuentu factam 7 de [...] R. . de [...]

p Abbem
[illegible] Magr. Nichol fil Fym psentat' 7 Conuentu Westm ad ecclam [...]
ab Archido Huntigdon sup eade ecclia factam exstit liquida. custodia illi ecc[...]
pdco Archido. ut custodia ei scdm formam pmissam hre facat. Idem [...]
gotio huic i man offic resignauit.

20 Johs capellanus de Mildecumb psentat' p Abbissam 7 conuentu de Godestowe [...]
[illegible] expedito. custodia ipius vicarie est adept'. Consistit aut dca vicaria tu in [...]
ut. dixit in ubo dni se nllm ecclsticum hre bnficiu. 7 mandatu est dco Ar[...]
7 in ea residentia face.

ecc'iam de Wistan'. cu' p' inq'sitoem p' magr'm. R. de Bleis Offic' Archid' Leircestr'
factam. q'd donac'oem illi' eccl'ie domui de Kaukewald' attulit. negociu' p'dcm ee't inexpedito. custo
: Ide' p'mod' ap' Leire ad p'sentac'oem earde' & p' inquisitoem eande' a d'no Ep'o ... & in

odia ei' est adept'. Ita tn' q'd in Octab' pasch' p'x'io sequ'ns p' hac custodia ei t'dita. rediens ad in
tac'oem i litt'atura co'petenciori & psallendi addiscat ... fuerit inuent' idone'. instituc'oem a d'no
n sufficiente' ee. & q'd aliu' p'sentet ad eande'. Facta p' inq'sitione sic ... p' R. de Kaukewell
... ut ei custodia illi' ecc'e h're faceret. secu'du' forma' memoratam.

. de uoluntate. R. de Martiuall' mil' cum dicerat se ius h're p'onand' in eade' ecc'a & c'senciente q
d'no Ep'o. salua & possessione pensionis. Cent' Sol' Matheo de Signesham. de q'a c'stat p' eundem
& aliis quor' interest. Facta p' inq'sitione sic eade' ecc'a p' J. Archid'm Oxon' &c. & sc'psit Offic' eidem
... c'senciente ut ad p'missa p'cedat p'sentato. Ep'i. R. de Windeham eade' ecc'e custodia h're faceret

heneach salua ei & eccl'ie sue debita & antiq' pensione Quinq'ginta Sol' p' annu'. cu' om'ia p' inq'u secundum
adept'. salua d'cis Abbi & conuentui eandem. Lx. Sol' pensione de eade' ecc'a. & mandatu' ...
& vnius Aurei q'm nomine p'sonat' h't i ecc'a de Sutchburg'. p' carta d'ni Ep'i q'm sit eade' ne

aria medietatis eccl'ie de Pateshill'. cu' p' inq'sitoem ab Archid'o Northamt' in facta negociu' ee't in
prato. tm' in mesuagio & attalagio eiusde' medietatis. Ide' q'z capell' req'sit' ab Offic' an ee't b'n'fic
... ut custodia ei h're faceret. Debet au' ide' vicari' i eade' ecc'a in p'p'a p'sona ministrare.

... negociu' factum secu'du' q'm negociu' fuit i expedito. custodia ipius

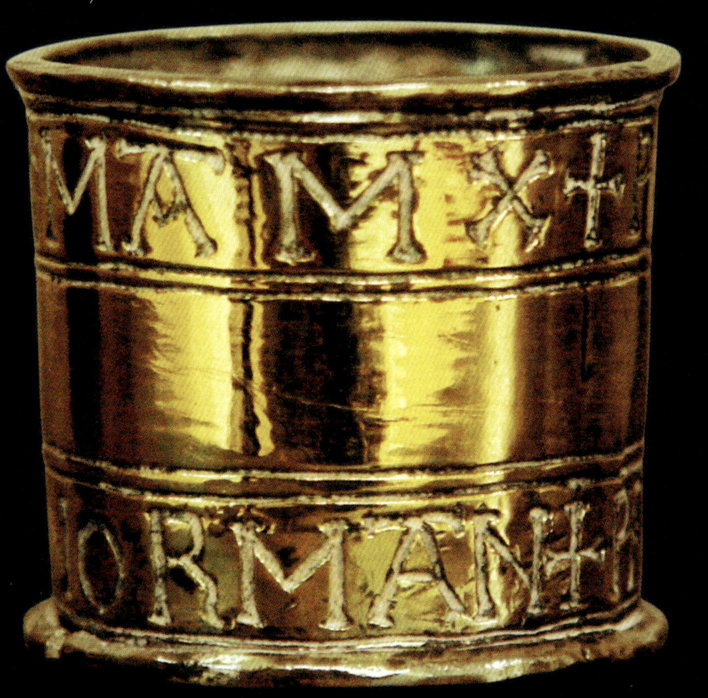
ORMAN+

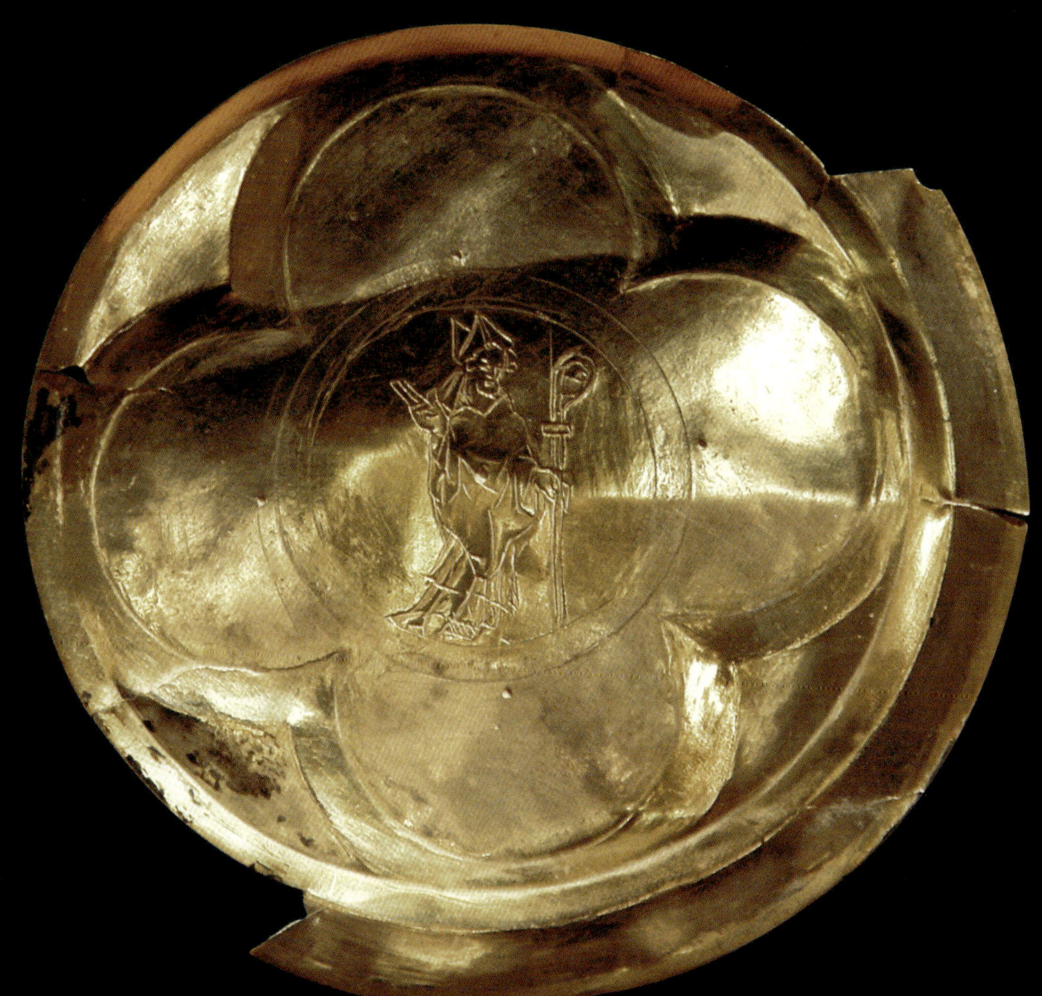

Hoop from the pastoral staff (above) and paten (below) of Robert Grosseteste (Bishop of Lincoln 1235–53)
These were removed from Grosseteste's tomb in 1782
Silver gilt
Lincoln Cathedral

Bishop Hugh's archival innovation was continued under his successor, Robert Grosseteste. Grosseteste was a figure of immense stature in medieval scholarship. He appears to have been born in Suffolk, in humble circumstances; in 1190 he was recorded as a junior clerk in the household of the Bishop of Lincoln, witnessing a charter of St Hugh, and shortly afterwards he received a warm testimonial from no less a scholar than Gerald of Wales, recommending him to the Bishop of Hereford. There is little firm evidence for his biography during the first two decades of the thirteenth century. There are sporadic references to administrative work in Hereford diocese, while later evidence suggests the possibility that he taught at the fledgling University of Oxford and served there as Master of the Schools (an office that evolved into the Chancellorship) in the early years of Bishop Hugh of Wells. At all events, by 1223 he was well known as a scholar and teacher, his written works extending by the beginning of the following decade over the fields of astronomy, chronology, the metaphysics of light, biblical exegesis and pastoral care. It was this last concern that led him to welcome and support the early Franciscans in Oxford and to undertake the offices successively of Archdeacon of Leicester and then, in 1235, Bishop of Lincoln.

Grosseteste's episcopate was dominated by his belief that he held a personal responsibility for the care of the soul of each individual member of his flock. While this duty could be, and was, delegated to others – archdeacons, rural deans and parish priests – it was nevertheless the bishop's duty to carry out visitations in person to ensure that the cure of souls was being performed effectively, and where this was not the case, to take action. In pursuit of this aim he did not spare himself; no aspect of diocesan life escaped his attention. Those seeking ordination or institution to parish churches were examined as to their honesty of life and standard of learning; he embarked on a perambulation of his diocese, in the course of which monasteries were scrutinised and abuses corrected (he deposed seven abbots and four priors), deaneries were visited, the clergy were interrogated, children were confirmed and the Word of God preached. He encouraged the pastoral work of both Dominican and Franciscan orders of friars, and he promulgated a set of statutes for the guidance of the clergy of the diocese, the influence of which is reflected in the number of copies that survive.

Robert Grosseteste died in 1253 and, although he was never officially canonised, his influence as a scholar and teacher remains a powerful one, not least in Lincoln's Bishop Grosseteste University, where his concern for the advancement of education continues today.

Further reading

Brian Golding, *Gilbert of Sempringham and the Gilbertine Order* (Oxford 1995)
James McEvoy, *Robert Grosseteste* (Oxford 2000)
Henry Mayr-Harting (ed.), *St Hugh of Lincoln* (Oxford 1987)
Dorothy Owen, *Church and Society in Medieval Lincolnshire* (Lincoln 1971)

Magna Carta and English liberty
1215–1500

CHRISTINE CARPENTER

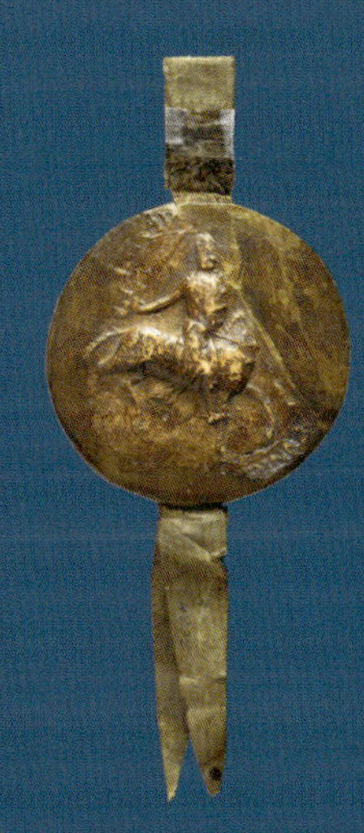

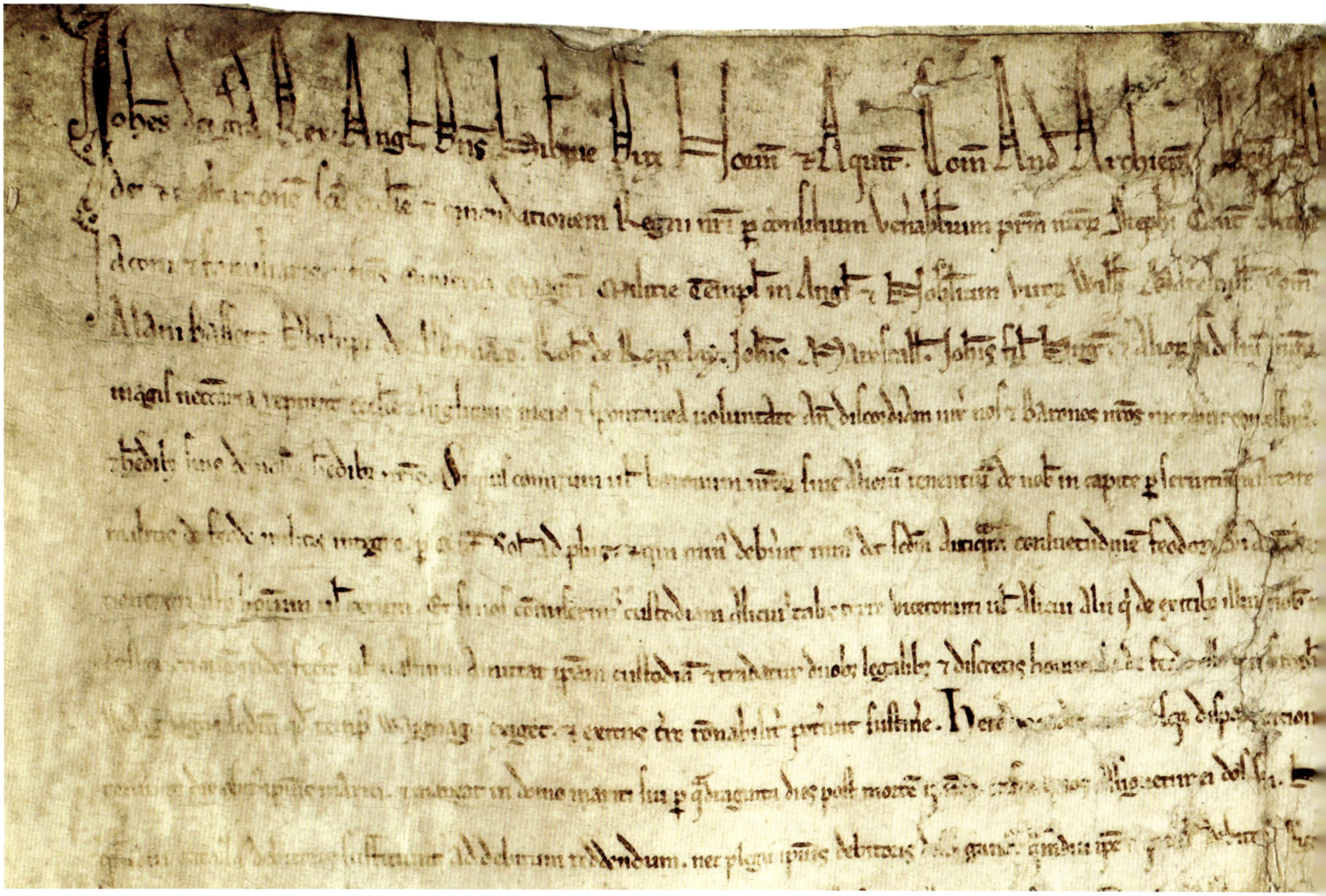

THERE are two contrasting myths about Magna Carta, both still in circulation and both incorrect. The older one belongs to the 'Whig' interpretation of English history that emerged during the nineteenth century. According to this, what was seen as England's exceptional development into a parliamentary democracy headed by a monarch limited by parliament essentially began with Magna Carta. The more recent myth, which appeared between the wars, is that, far from being the foundation of English freedom, Magna Carta was a document designed to protect and enhance baronial privilege.

To understand the true meaning of Magna Carta, we need to examine its origins. Its deeper roots lie in the reign of Henry II (1154–89). He was responsible for the creation of a uniform legal system in England, the so-called 'common law'. This law was designed primarily to protect landed property, the rights associated with it and the income derived from it. Its consequence (perhaps not intended by Henry)

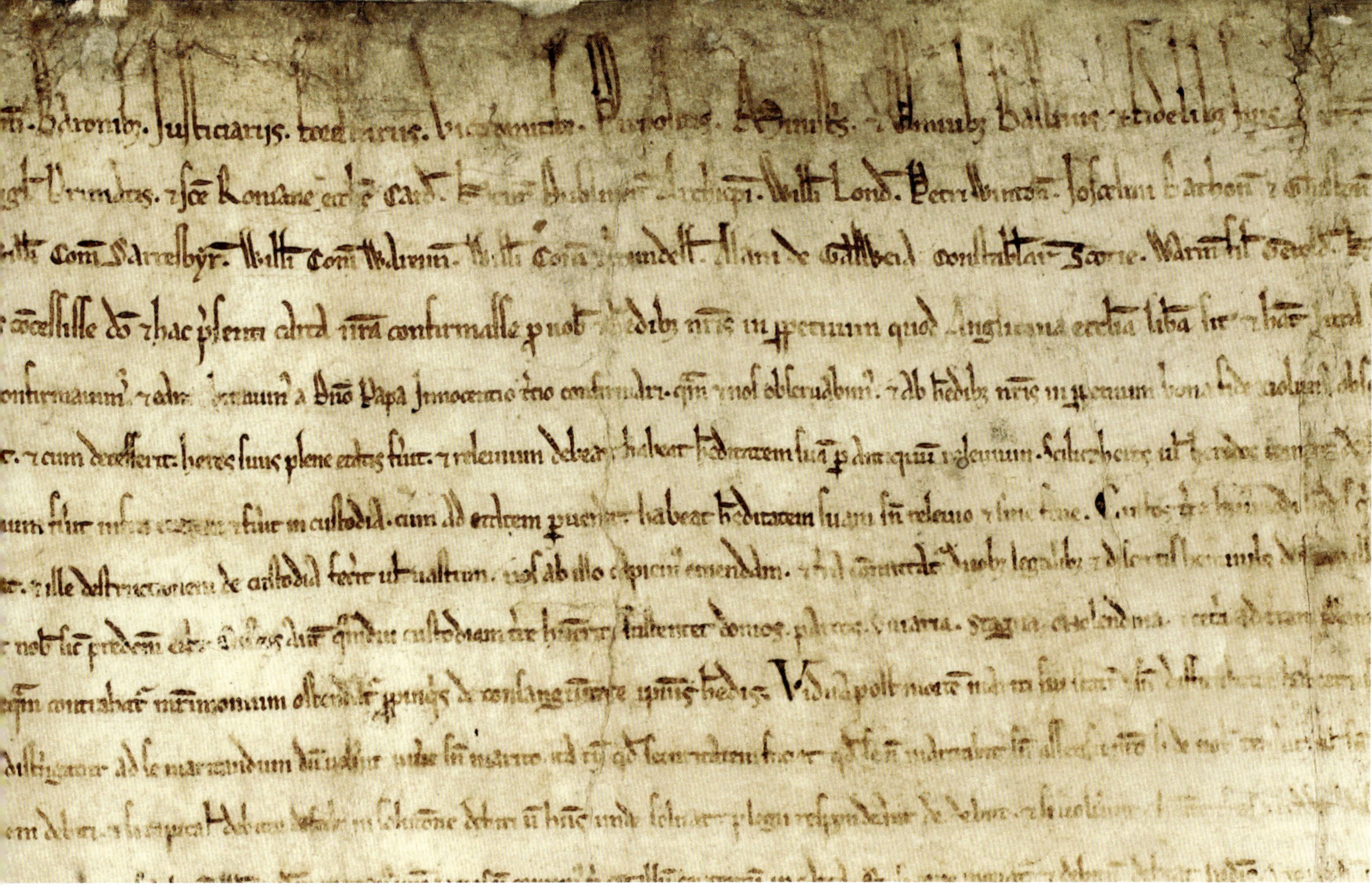

was an enormous enhancement of the king's authority, because the king's law undermined the judicial power of the barons over their knights – their feudal tenants who held land from them and did military service in return – and hence their ability to control what the knights did. If a knight felt that his baronial lord was acting unjustly towards him, he could now go to the king's law for redress. The barons could therefore no longer assume that their knights would support them in a confrontation with the king.

One result of this was that it became easier for the king to force his barons to pay him the large sums in feudal dues – money paid on specified occasions, such as the 'relief' on inheriting their land – which he needed to finance his wars. For Henry had inherited the great French lordships of Normandy, Anjou and Maine and spent much of his reign in France, defending or extending these possessions. That set up a contradiction. The tenant of a baron could use the king's law against his lord, taking

Magna Carta, 1215
Detail of the opening of the charter, showing the king's titles and salutation
Lincolnshire Archives, D&C A1/1/45; on loan to Lincolnshire County Council

Charter of Henry II giving the church of Langford (Oxon) to Lincoln Cathedral, 1155–8
Lincolnshire Archives, D&C A1/1/35

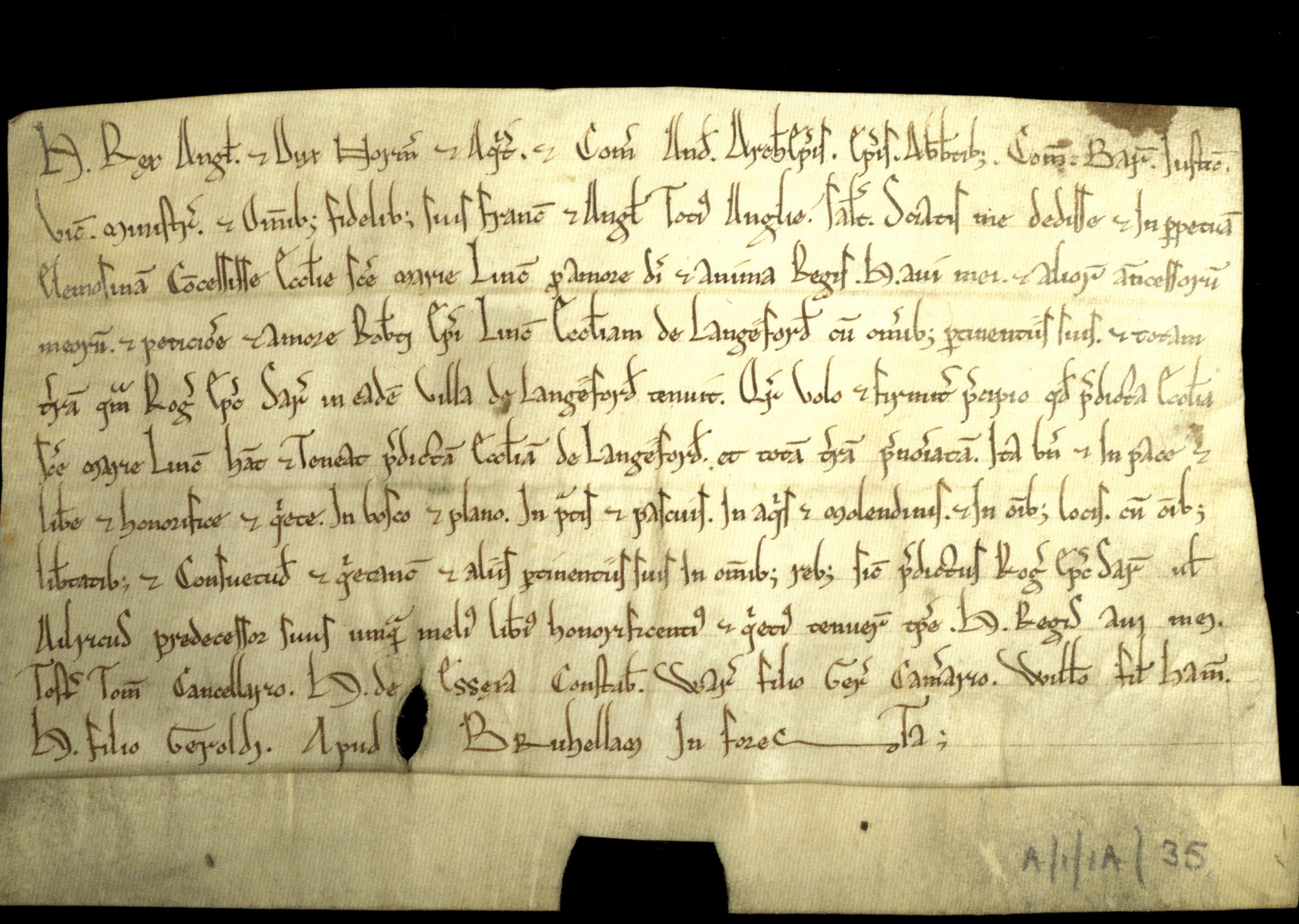

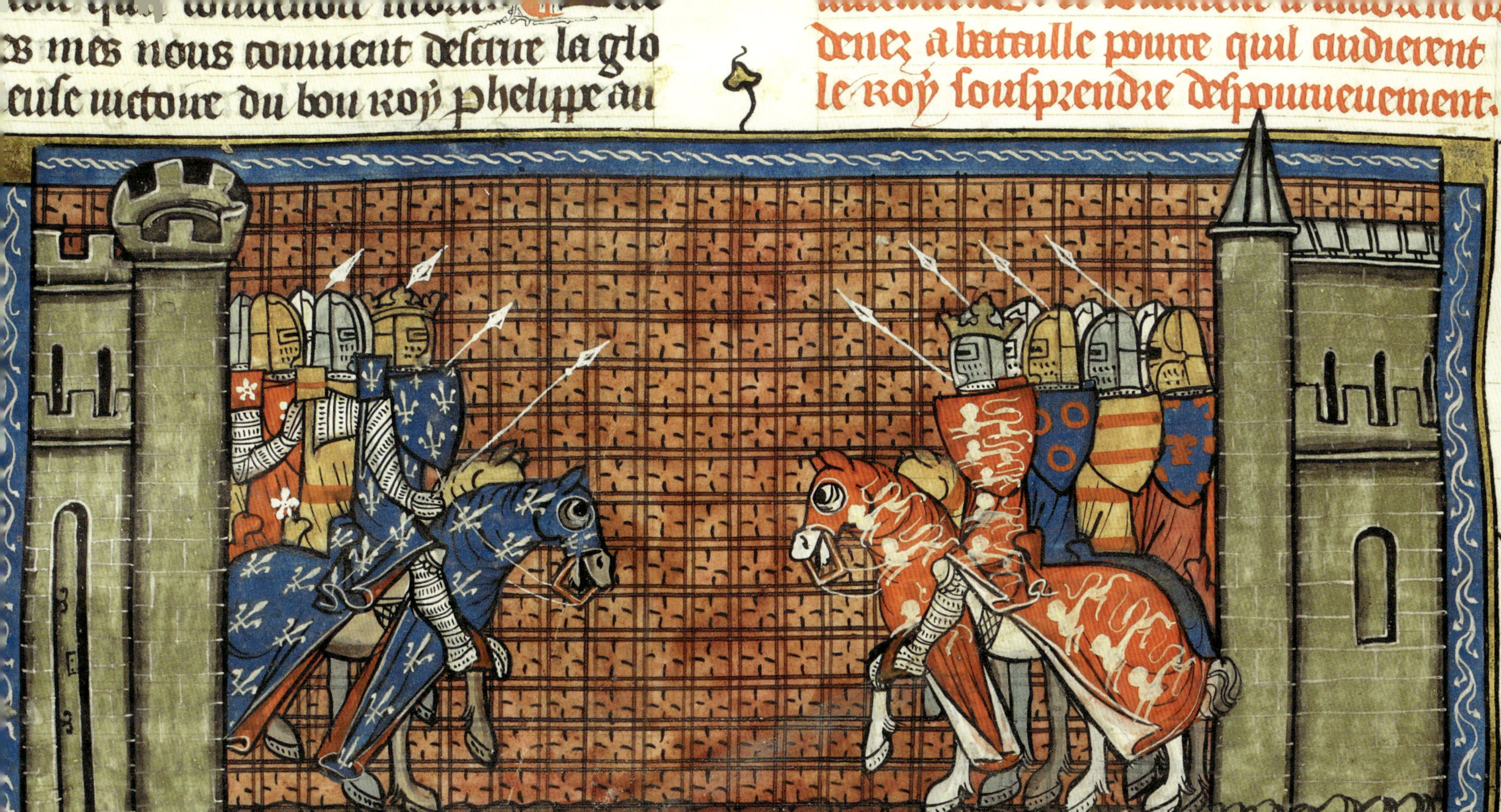

him to court if he believed the lord was asking too much in feudal dues or if the lord took his land. The baron, however, could not use the law against his own lord because he was a tenant of the king, and the king controlled the law. The king became used to taking money from his barons for the privilege of having their cases heard in his courts, or in large fines if they had offended him and, because he was head of the legal system as well as their feudal lord, there was no redress against him.

All this came to a head under King John (reigned 1199–1216). John was an able and clever king but lacked the kingly virtues. He did not trust his barons and, by the end of his reign, gave his trust almost entirely to the foreign mercenaries, many of them low-born, who both filled his household and took many of the key governing posts. Crucially, he was a much less successful soldier than his father or his brother, Richard I (reigned 1189–99). In 1204 he lost Normandy to King Philip II of France (reigned 1180–1223) and in 1214 the coalition of continental allies he had built up to help him regain Normandy was defeated decisively by Philip at the battle of Bouvines.

This coalition had been financed by John using vast sums of money he had accumulated between 1204 and 1214. He was mostly exploiting the same financial resources as his two predecessors but on a far bigger scale than before. For instance,

Grands Chroniques de France, 1332–50
Detail showing the armies of King John and Philip Augustus of France approaching each other
British Library, Royal MS 16.G.VI, f.376v

Great Seal of King John, formerly attached to the Articles of the Barons, 1215
British Library, Add MS 4838

he charged reliefs of several hundred pounds, sometimes several thousand, at a time when even a great baron might have an annual income of only £500 to £700 a year. John took large fees to have his barons' cases heard in his court and used his law against them to levy very large fines. While both Henry II and Richard I had placed considerable financial burdens on the kingdom, they had been successful soldiers, had largely got on well with their barons and had been abroad for large parts of their reign, so the heavy hand of their personal rule had been felt only intermittently. John, by contrast, was in England continuously from 1204 and the culmination of this period of iron-fisted rule was the wasting of all the money accumulated in that time through the failure at Bouvines. The knights too had suffered under John, especially from his efforts to exploit the law for profit, notably the forest law, which levied large fines for a host of offences committed by anyone whose lands lay within the boundaries of the very extensive royal forests.

The battle of Bouvines led almost immediately to the rebellion that brought about Magna Carta, issued by King John on 15 June 1215. Why is this document so special? The answer is that it was the outcome of wholly new circumstances. All landowners in England now needed the power of the king and the king's law to keep the peace in England and their property secure. The barons could not, as they had done before, replace an over-powerful king with a weak one or simply shut his power out, and nor would their feudal tenants, the knights, have permitted them to do so, since they benefited greatly from their access to the common law. Yet without the knights' support the barons would not have had the military might to force the king to come to terms. While all landowners wanted an effective king, they wanted one who would not exploit them viciously as John had done.

The answer was to state what the king might or might not do in a document to which he was forced to agree; a document which endorsed much of the existing governmental structure, especially the legal system. While Magna Carta was a mixture of great statements of principle and clauses that dealt with immediate issues (such as John's mercenaries and the hostages he had taken during the rebellion), its underlying principle was that the king himself should be subject to the law that he had imposed on his people. This was summed up in the famous clauses 39 and 40 (still on the statute book), which respectively prohibited the king

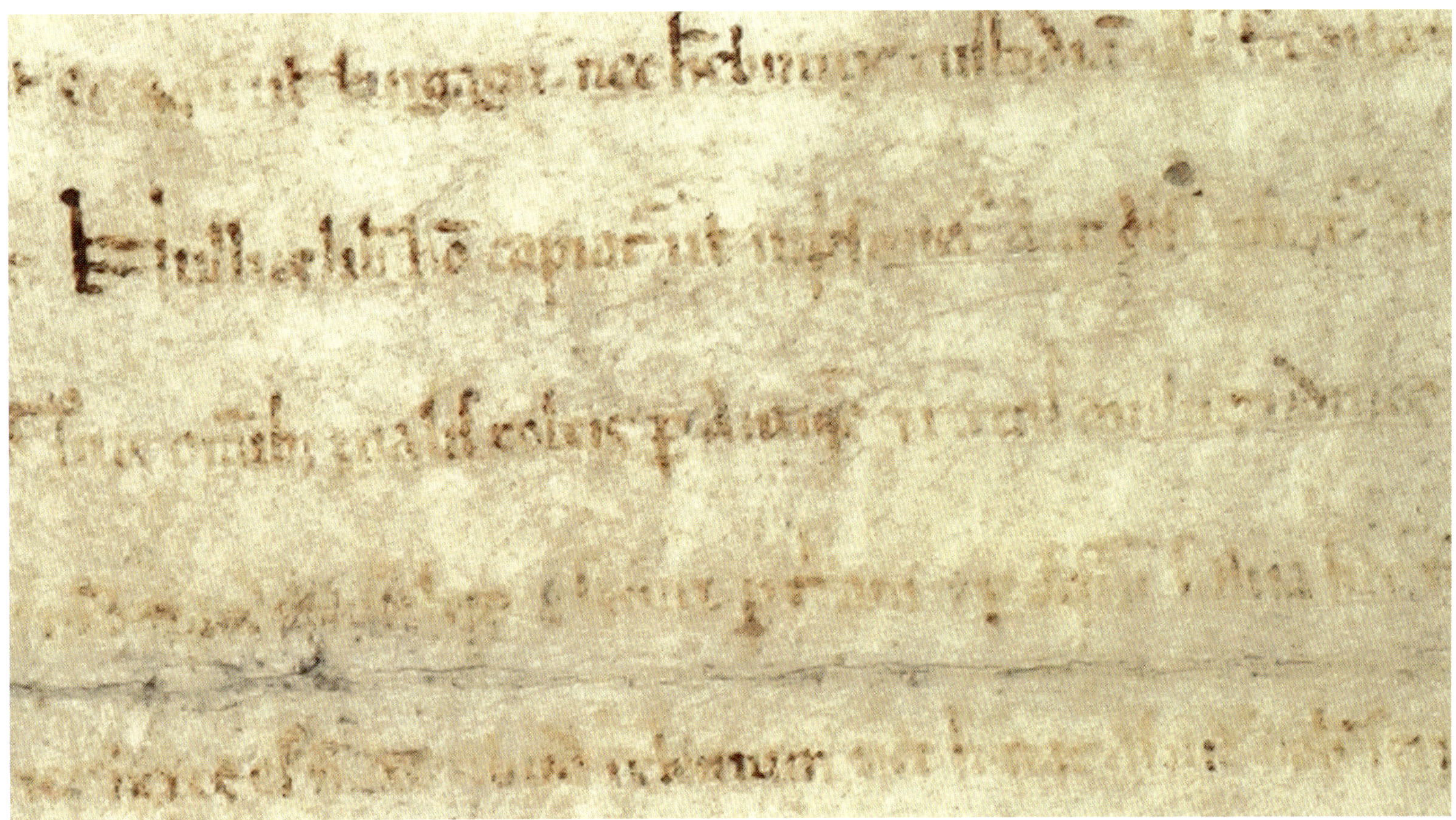

from acting without due process of law and from selling, denying or delaying justice. If subjects were not permitted to take each other's land and money illegally, neither was the king. The barons, whose knightly tenants had been protected by the law while they themselves had had no corresponding protection against the king, were the obvious beneficiaries.

However, these principles applied not only to barons and knights but to all men and women who were permitted to use the king's law. These were termed 'freemen', and freemen who used the king's courts also included townsmen and even some prosperous peasants. Magna Carta was granted to all freemen and was therefore never a purely baronial document. The charter also protected the liberties of the Church, which had, if anything, been even more ruthlessly exploited than lay landowners. Stephen Langton, Archbishop of Canterbury, played a role in its framing but its ideology would have been understood by all landowners. John soon rejected the charter and appealed to the pope to release him from it but he died in 1216, in the midst of the Civil War that followed. The battle of Lincoln Fair of 1217 was the decisive engagement of this war. In 1216 the men who were ruling on behalf of John's young son, Henry III, reissued Magna Carta in his name and in 1217, in their treaty with the rebels, it was reissued again, along with a separate Forest Charter. By this everyone acknowledged that the game had changed: kings should no longer attack their free subjects' rights.

Magna Carta, 1215
Detail of clause 39: 'No free man shall be taken or imprisoned ... except by the lawful judgement of his peers or by the law of the land'
Lincolnshire Archives, D&C A1/1/45; on loan to Lincolnshire County Council

OVERLEAF
Magna Carta, 1215
Detail of clause 1: 'That the English Church shall be free'
Lincolnshire Archives, D&C A1/1/45; on loan to Lincolnshire County Council

...tuitu dei et pro salute anime nostre et omnium antecessorum...

...Walteri Wigorn. Willelmi Coventr. et Benedicti Roffen. episcoporum...

...Senescalli Pictavie. Petri filii Hereberti. Hugonis de Nevill...

...omnes suas illesas; et ita volumus observari; quod apparet ex eo q...

...omnia liberis hominibus regni nostri pro nobis et heredibus nostris in perpetuum omnes...

...per centum libras... heres vel heredes baronis de baronia integra...

...in capite, de warda heredis... rationabiles consuetudines...

...[illegible]...

...[illegible]...

...[illegible]...

...[illegible]...

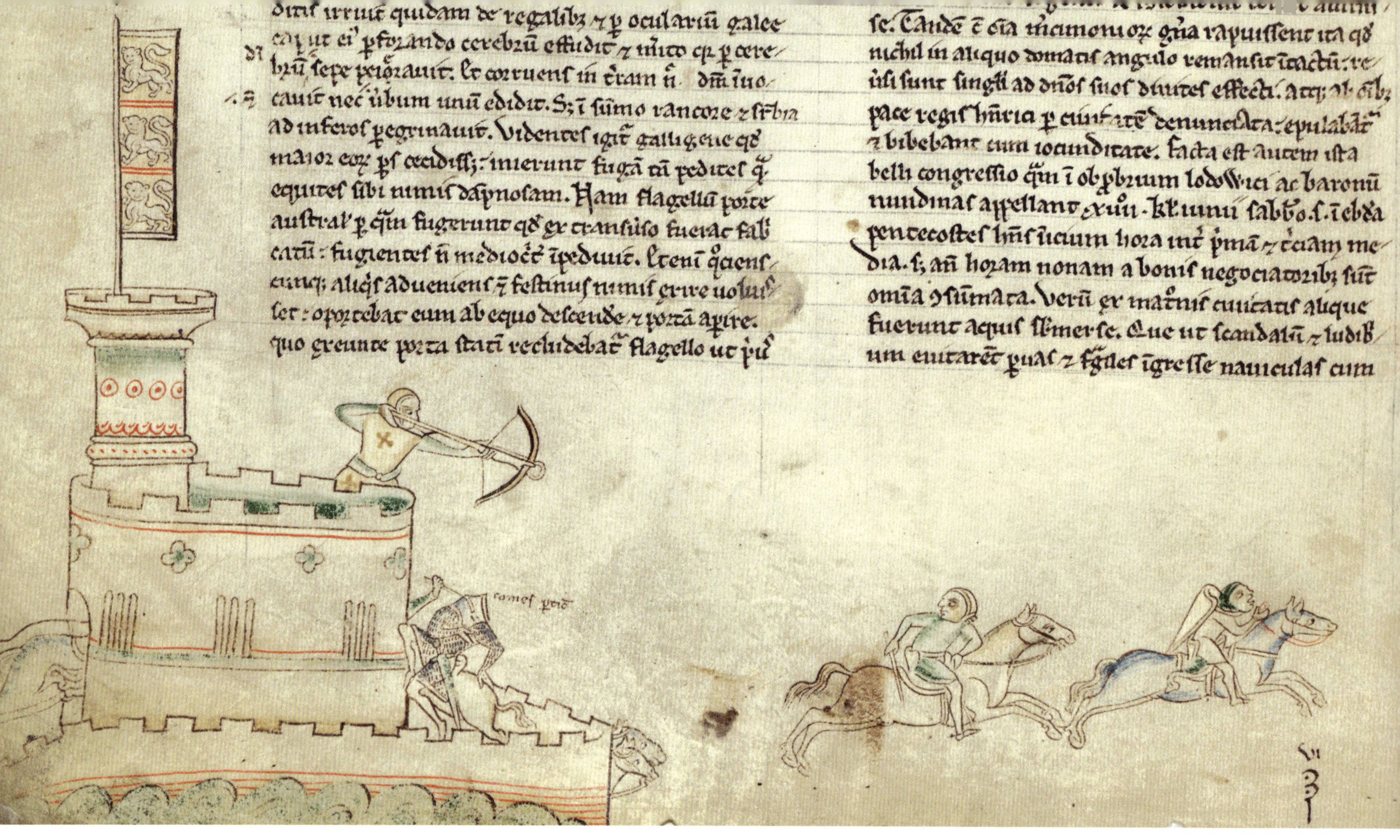

Matthew Paris (died 1259)
***Chronica maiora** II*,
thirteenth century
Detail showing the battle of Lincoln Fair, 1217
Corpus Christi College, Cambridge, Parker Lib MS 16II, f.55v

Magna Carta thus marked a watershed in English politics and political thought. After it, no king could ride roughshod over the law or take the lands, goods or money of the freemen, which the law protected, without a strong chance of meeting organised resistance. There was now a clear understanding of how to resist such a king and a clear ideology underlying resistance. But what Magna Carta did not do was subject the king to the sort of restraints that might be seen as the beginning of parliamentary monarchy. Indeed, the two clauses that demanded the king take advice were removed from the reissue. And there was good reason for this: so great were the king's powers, especially over property, that the barons feared control of the king by one of their number almost as much as they feared an over-powerful king. It was in fact the committee of twenty-five barons, set up to ensure that John kept his word, whose divisive actions helped bring about the Civil War. So enforcement remained a problem, especially as the growing power of the Crown, fighting ever more complex and expensive wars in France and the British Isles, and supervising an expanding legal and peacekeeping system at home, emphasised the need for a dominant king. Another problem was to find a means of financing these wars, now that Magna Carta's decisive restriction of the king's feudal dues and of the money he could make by exploiting the law had gravely reduced his income. While the essential message of Magna Carta was clear, there

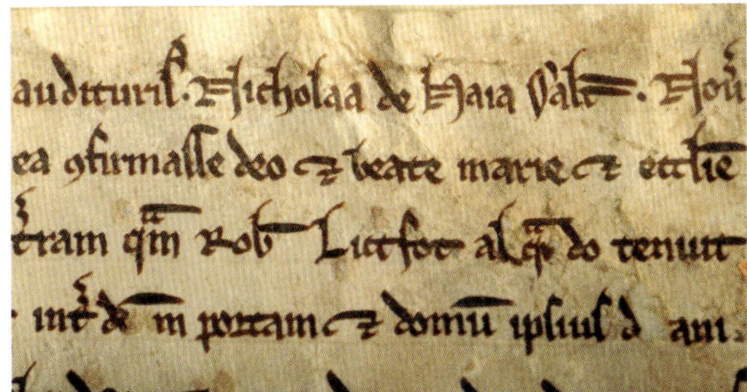

Nichola de la Haie (died 1230)
Charter granting to Lincoln Cathedral land adjoining the Eastgate in Lincoln (detail), 1224–7
Lincolnshire Archives, D&C Dij/81/2/33

was still plenty of room for the king to find new sources of income that had not been specifically prohibited by the charter.

The next two reigns, those of Henry III (1216–72) and Edward I (1272–1307), would be crucial for the consequences of Magna Carta. In 1225 Henry III's minority government reissued the Magna Carta and the Forest Charter once more, in what were to be their definitive forms. When in the late 1220s and early 1230s Henry acquired his full powers as king, he found indeed that he could no longer resurrect the arbitrary kingship of his father, but that did not prevent him and his advisers attempting to find other ways to raise money. Several of these entailed exploiting the legal system, including even the forest law, but the focus now had to be on taking money from the knights and (as ever) the Church: the ready pickings from the barons were no longer available. In 1258 the knights rebelled against his demands, in a movement that was clearly inspired by Magna Carta, but, although the barons led the revolt, their motive was much more about Henry's personal failings. They had had enough of his incompetence as king, manifested in his capricious favouritism and, especially, in his misconceived and very expensive foreign policy. The knights joined the barons because they now had to pay for this incompetence.

The result was the creation of a council to control the king and his expenditure, and force good advice on him. Although this council was answerable to the enlarged version of the king's normal council that had begun to emerge in the 1230s under the name of 'parliament', there was no wish on the barons' part to put the king under permanent conciliar or parliamentary control. The barons wanted to end Henry's expensive foreign entanglements, while the knights, whose support was needed for a rebellion against the king, were trying to force upon the barons root-and-branch reform of a system in which they felt both the barons and the king were exploiting them. Accordingly the barons, as soon as they could, drifted back to Henry's side and allowed him to begin to dismantle the supervisory system they had set up. Simon de Montfort, who has a key but misconceived place in the Whig history of parliament as the supposed leader of the movement from 1258, then staged his own rebellion. In truth, he only became the leader in 1263, once the original baronial movement had effectively ended. He did indeed exploit the knights' feeling that they had been abandoned but he acted chiefly from a complex mixture of personal greed and ambition, hatred of Henry, and a crusading zeal to cleanse the realm in God's name, a fervency that was alien to his fellow barons and probably to most of the

Rochester Chronicle, 1355
Detail of marginal drawing showing the dismemberment of Simon de Montfort after the battle of Evesham (1265)
British Library, MS Cotton Nero D.II, f.177

knights who fought for him. He certainly did want to dictate to the king, and he envisaged dictating to Henry's successor as well, but, although nominally part of a new controlling council, he effectively set himself up as king. A figure now isolated from the political mainstream, he met his end at the battle of Evesham in 1265.

Henry III's son, Edward I, was a hugely able ruler who fulfilled all the expectations of his landed subjects: a successful warrior, the bringer of peace to a divided kingdom, law giver and law enforcer. His success even permitted him to get away with taking some baronial estates to endow his large family, in ways that clearly breached Magna Carta. However, he still had to solve the conundrum, which Magna Carta had created, of how to finance his wars, at a time when warfare was becoming ever more expensive. He had the sense to realise that the knights would no longer stand for the exploitation that had caused them to rebel under Henry III, and that the only way forward was to establish a system of national taxation. This avoided the problem that Magna Carta had prohibited the appropriation of freemen's property, because it was based on consent, a consent given by a body that represented all the king's subjects, which was, of course, parliament.

Parliamentary taxation had already been used by Henry III but he had found it difficult to persuade his subjects to agree to it and had had to reissue Magna Carta in return, in recognition that his requests were in breach of the charter. Edward I succeeded where his father had failed, in part simply by being a king whom his subjects admired and trusted, but also by greatly reducing his resort to all the other resources that his father had exploited. He was able to establish the principle that if he showed necessity, parliament was obliged to consent. Since necessity was defined as defence, which in practice included offensive wars, he did not have to bargain with parliament over taxation. However, in the 1290s, when he found himself at war with both Scotland and France, he overreached himself, exacting too much in taxation while exploiting all the other powers at his disposal to raise men and money. This resulted in a series of parliamentary crises in which he was forced to reissue both the charters.

It was under Edward I's grandson, Edward III (reigned 1327–77), that these issues were resolved, as the king worked out how to finance the Hundred Years War, the most expensive and long-drawn-out war to date. He began, in 1337, in the same vein as his grandfather, taxing heavily and exploiting every other avenue that was open to him. That led to a major parliamentary crisis in 1340–1, in which he too

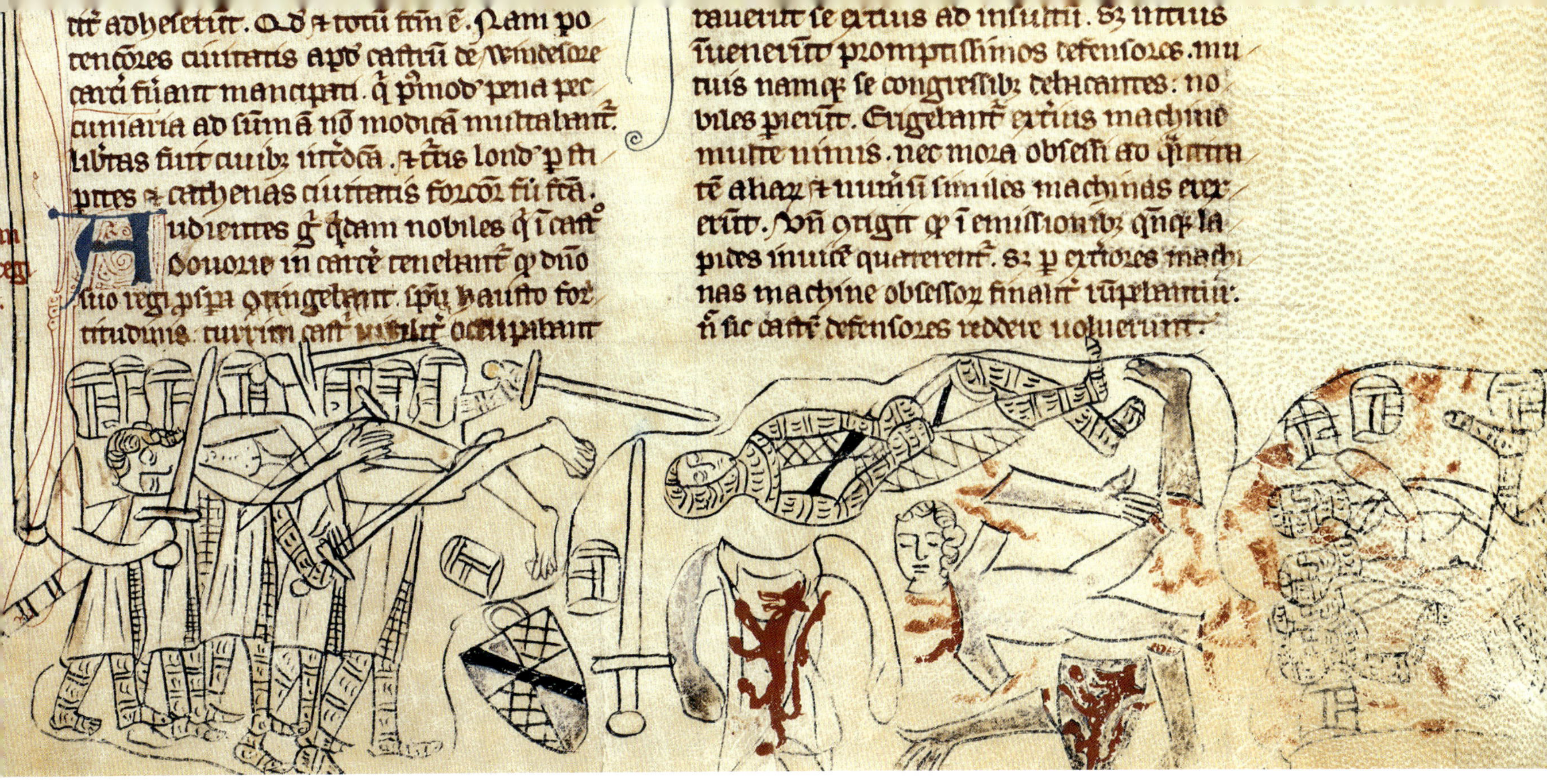

was forced to reissue Magna Carta. But after this salutary lesson Edward never again taxed so heavily and, over the course of the reign, all the other sources of money and troops were reduced, modified or brought under parliamentary control. Well before the end of the reign, parliamentary taxation had become the uncontested and accepted means of financing wars, and all further parliamentary conflicts over taxation were about whether the money had been well spent, not about the principle. Since kings could now raise the money they needed without breaching Magna Carta, and had long accepted that they could no longer routinely use the law as they wished, Magna Carta largely disappeared as an active element

The Charter of the Forest, 1217
Detail of the opening of the charter
Lincolnshire Archives, D&C A1/1/46; on loan to Lincolnshire County Council

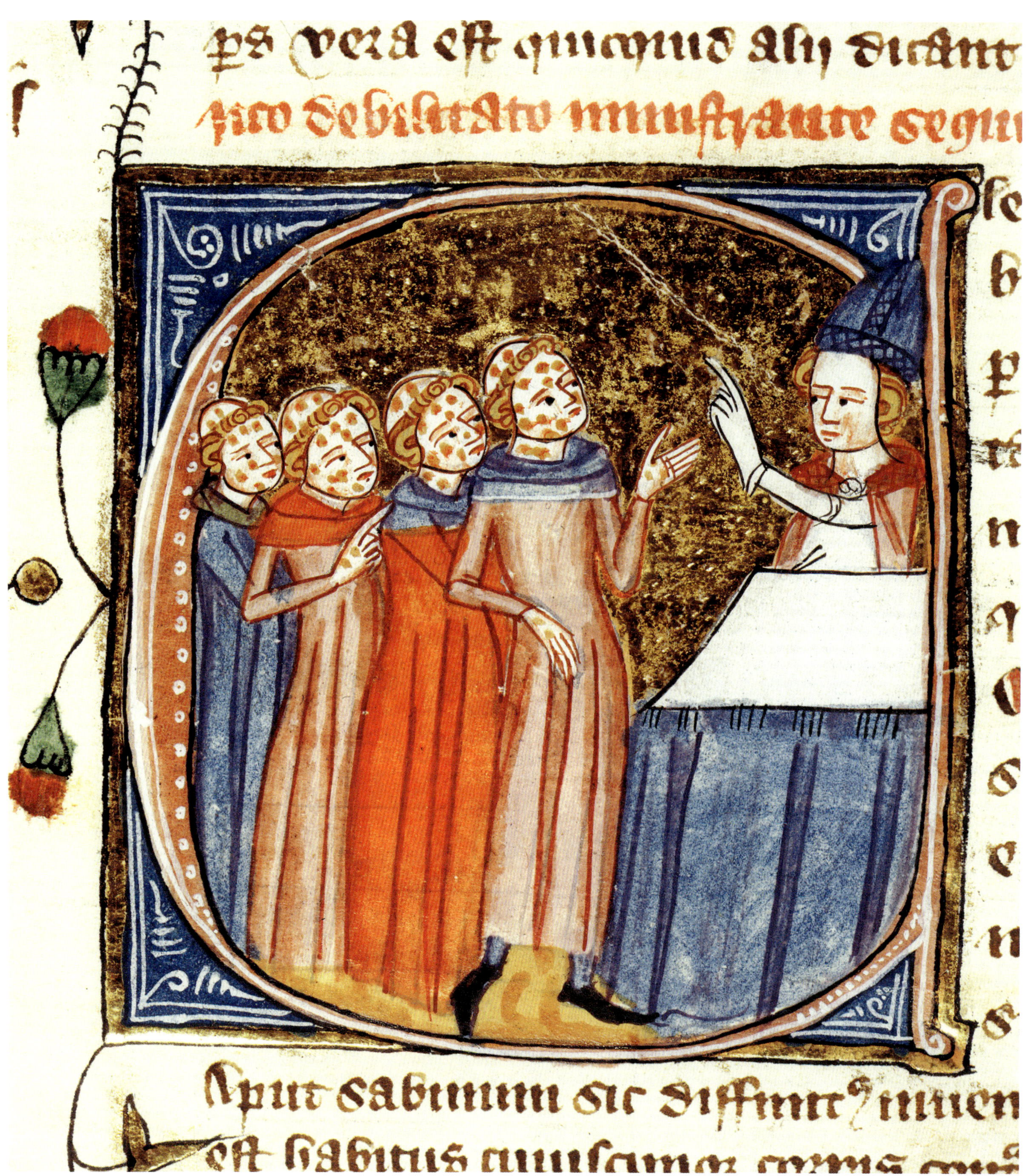

James le Palmer (died about 1375)
***Omne Bonum*, 1360–75**
Detail showing diseased clerics receiving instruction from a bishop
British Library, Royal MS 6.E.VI, f.301

in English politics. But the charter was still very much to hand to be used as part of the condemnation of kings who bucked the trend by abusing or overriding the law and attacking their subjects' property, notably Richard II (reigned 1377–99), whose deposition articles cite clause 39 of Magna Carta.

However, the charter still had a significant part to play in the emergence of lower-class politics in town and country. The Black Death of 1348–9 and subsequent outbreaks of plague, by hugely reducing the population, led to all peasants achieving de facto freedom, since they could afford to reject land that carried servile status. It also meant that the wages of labourers in town and country rose considerably. From 1349, the king's law was used in an attempt to keep wages down, to the benefit of landowners and urban employers. Then, from 1377, the government levied a series of poll taxes. These were designed to tax the wealth of peasants and labourers, which, as their lords and employers perceived it, had come at the expense of their betters. From the perspective of the peasants and labourers, who now increasingly saw themselves as freemen, able to use the king's law, these stratagems exploited the law against them and took their property, since, as far as they were concerned, they had not consented to the taxes. It is telling therefore that, when they rebelled in 1381, they demanded 'a charter under [the king's] great seal', surely a reference to Magna Carta.

Magna Carta was indeed a crucial episode in the growth of English liberty but not in the way the Whigs would have it. It did not lead directly to a parliamentary check on royal power but, in placing the king beneath his law, it ensured that there was a means to resist the king thereafter and a clear ideology concerning the limits of his power. It did, however, play a key role in the emergence of parliament because it ultimately forced kings to fund war through taxation, taken with assent, and that assent was given in parliament. But neither was it a self-serving baronial document. The 'freemen' to whom it was granted never comprised the barons alone and ultimately included all the king's subjects. Thus, in contrast to continental countries, the nobility were not a legally privileged class but part of that body of freemen who used and were subject to the king's law and, like all his subjects, paid the king's taxes. While the law initially defended land, it ended up defending everyone's person, rights and property. In 1500 there was still a long way to go before royal power was permanently contained and the rights of all the inhabitants of England equally respected and protected but, thanks to Magna Carta, the foundations were there.

Further reading

Sir James Holt, *Magna Carta* (Cambridge 2003)
Nicholas Vincent, *Magna Carta: A Very Short Introduction* (Oxford 2012)

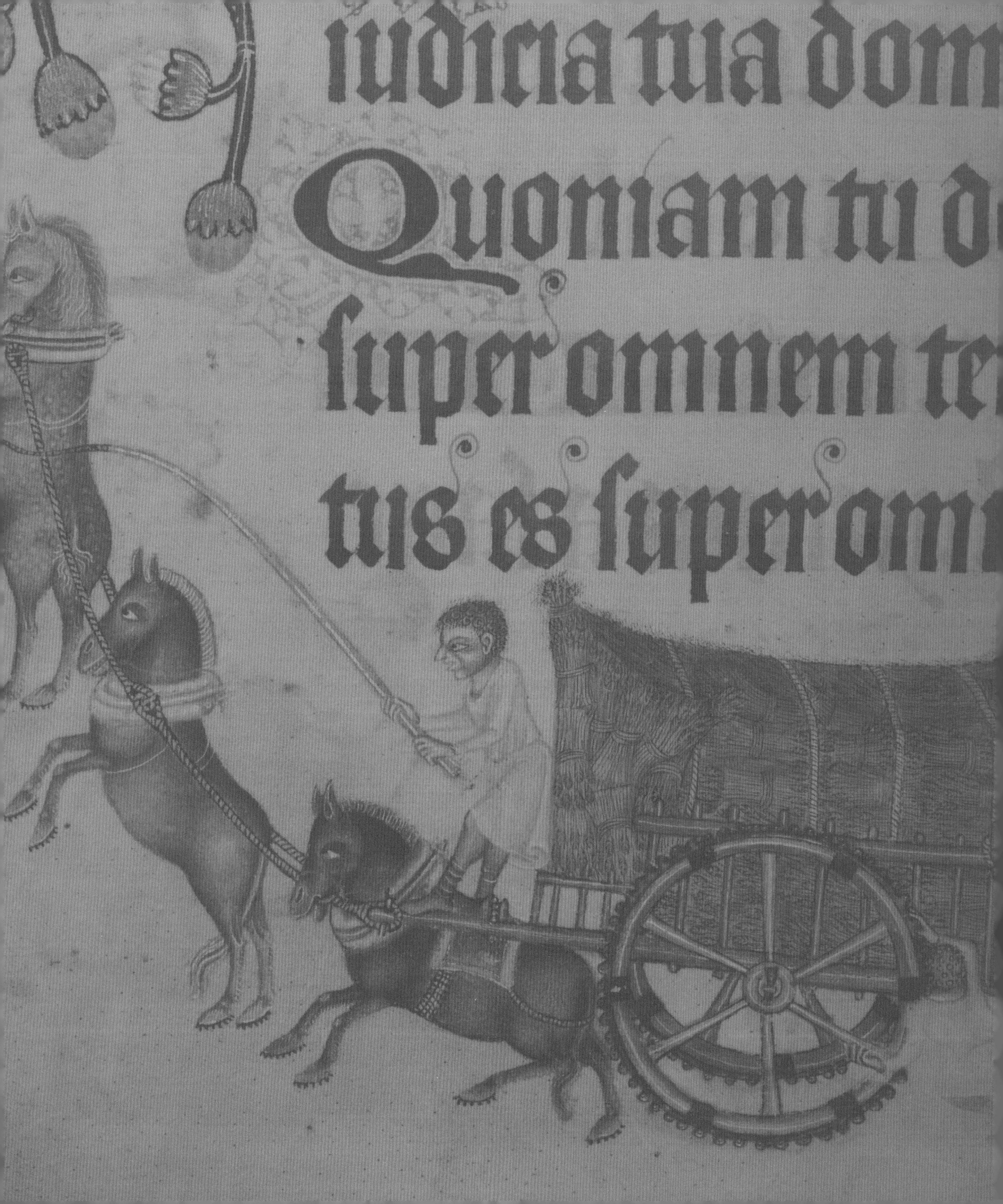

iudicia tua dom

Quoniam tu d

ſuper omnem te

tus es ſuper om

The Luttrell Psalter

KATHLEEN DOYLE

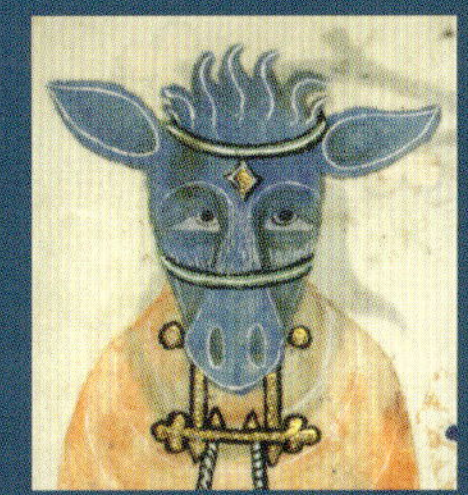

THE LUTTRELL PSALTER has been called 'arguably the most famous fourteenth-century English illuminated manuscript' (Freeman Sandler 2008). It is rightly celebrated for its extensive and compelling marginal imagery, which includes scenes from rural life and huge, bizarre hybrid creatures. These images ornament a copy of the Book of the Psalms that also includes traditional biblical illustrations of its text.

Psalters

The Psalms were at the heart of medieval spirituality. Not surprisingly, therefore, manuscripts containing them in one form or another are the most common type of book to survive from the Middle Ages. In most medieval psalters, the Psalms are preceded by a calendar that provides information about saints' days and other holidays. The most important feasts are often listed in red ink, as in the Luttrell Psalter, the basis for our 'red letter' days. The calendar in the Luttrell Psalter includes a number of English saints and has a 'Lincoln flavour', with saints relevant to the area around Lincoln, such as Hugh (Bishop of Lincoln), Guthlac (of Crowland), Botulph (commemorated in Boston), Wilfrid and Frideswide (Freeman Sandler 1986; Brown 2006). After the Psalms proper, the Psalter includes the Canticles, or biblical passages characterised as songs, as is also typical in medieval psalters. It then features further litanies and prayers, thereby creating a Christian devotional book from a collection of songs originally written in Hebrew and constituting part of the Jewish sacred text. At the end of the volume is an incomplete copy of the Office of the Dead, prayers (drawn from the Psalms and other biblical books) to be said for the souls of the deceased.

The manuscript is written in Latin, in a translation traditionally ascribed to St Jerome, one of the four Fathers of the Western Church, who died in AD420. Over a period of nearly twenty-five years St Jerome worked on translations of biblical texts from Hebrew and Greek into the Latin vernacular, and completed three versions of the Psalms. The translation included in the Luttrell Psalter is the Gallican, known as such because it was adopted in Gaul, in contrast to the Roman version used in Italy and England in the early Middle Ages.

In size, the Psalter is a very large format even now (355 x 245 mm) and it was once much larger. Throughout the book there is evidence of cropped images

The Luttrell Psalter, about 1325–40
Opening of the Book of Psalms: Psalm 1, '*Beatus Vir*' ('Blessed is the man that hath not walked in the counsel of the ungodly'). The bas-de-page scene depicts the Virgin and Child.
British Library, Add MS 42130, f.13r

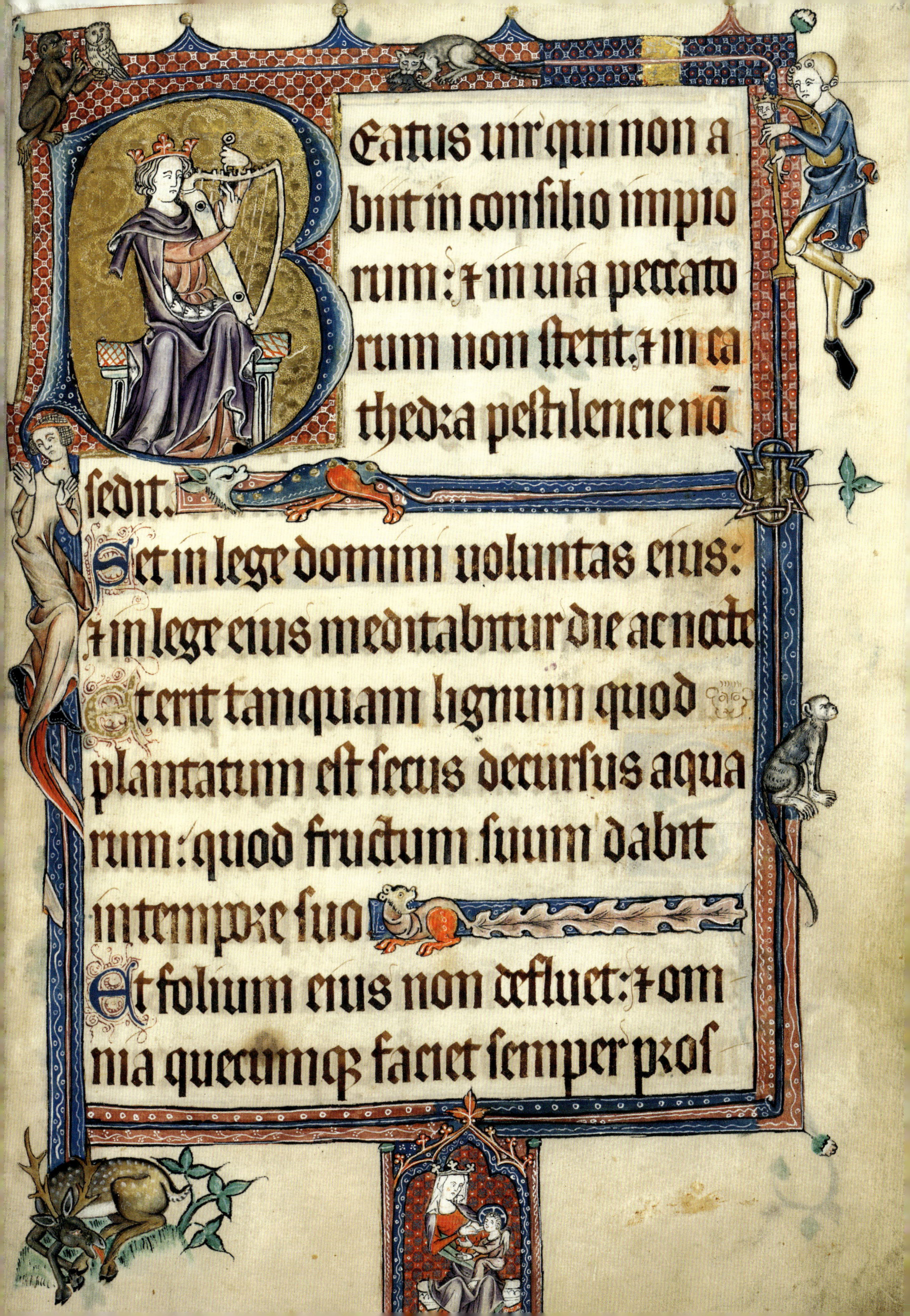

Beatus uir qui non a
biit in consilio impio
rum: ⁊ in uia peccato
rum non stetit, ⁊ in ca
thedra pestilencie nō
sedit.

Set in lege domini uoluntas eius:
⁊ in lege eius meditabitur die ac nocte
Et erit tanquam lignum quod
plantatum est secus decursus aqua
rum: quod fructum suum dabit
in tempore suo

Et folium eius non defluet: ⁊ om
nia quecumque faciet semper pros

The Luttrell Psalter, about 1325–40
A jester: detail of historiated initial from the opening of Psalm 52, '*Dixit insipiens*' ('The foolish body hath said in his heart, "There is no God"')
British Library, Add MS 42130, f.98v

indicating that all of the outer edges have been severely trimmed, presumably during rebinding(s). The Psalter is heavy, too, even without an original binding, so it is clear that it was not designed as a hand-held devotional book to be used by one person. Indeed, the Luttrell Psalter would have been much easier to handle (and still is) when placed on a lectern or desk of some sort. The text is large (the smaller letters are about 10 mm high) and is extremely legible, with very few abbreviations. These factors, together with the size of some of the decoration (explored below), suggest that the Luttrell Psalter may have been intended for communal reading or use.

Psalter decoration

Although the Psalter may be best known for its marginal illustrations, it also includes decoration in the text itself, characteristic of luxury copies of the Psalms. Thus most Psalms in the book begin with large initials in colours and gold, decorated with plant forms, animals or hybrids, faces, or more elaborate scenes such as figures in prayer (for example Psalms 41, 87, 104 and 112). Even larger initials occur at the major divisions of the Psalter, which are derived from the groups of Psalms recited each day (and at Sunday vespers) in monastic practice, and these are placed at the beginnings of Psalms 1, 26, 38, 52, 68, 80, 97 and 109 (using the Vulgate numbering). Ultimately these groups echo the Psalmist's reflection that 'Seven times a day do I praise thee' and 'At midnight I will rise to give thanks unto thee because of thy righteous judgements' (Psalm 119: 164, 62). In the Luttrell Psalter, as in many English psalters, these eight liturgical divisions are combined with another, earlier system of division, the so-called 'three fifties', dividing the Psalms into three sections of fifty Psalms, yielding ten major divisions altogether (Psalm 1 being part of both systems).

At these major divisions, and in some of the other Psalms, the initials are 'historiated', that is, they are populated with narrative or figurative scenes. The subjects featured became somewhat standardised over time within certain regions, and were generally related to the first lines of the text itself, a commentary on it, or the Psalm's heading or title. For example, the initial for Psalm 52, beginning '*Dixit insipiens in corde suo non est Deum*' ('The foolish body hath said in his heart, "There is no God"'), often includes an image of a jester or fool, as is the case in the Luttrell Psalter. Similarly, the initial 'C' for Psalm 97,

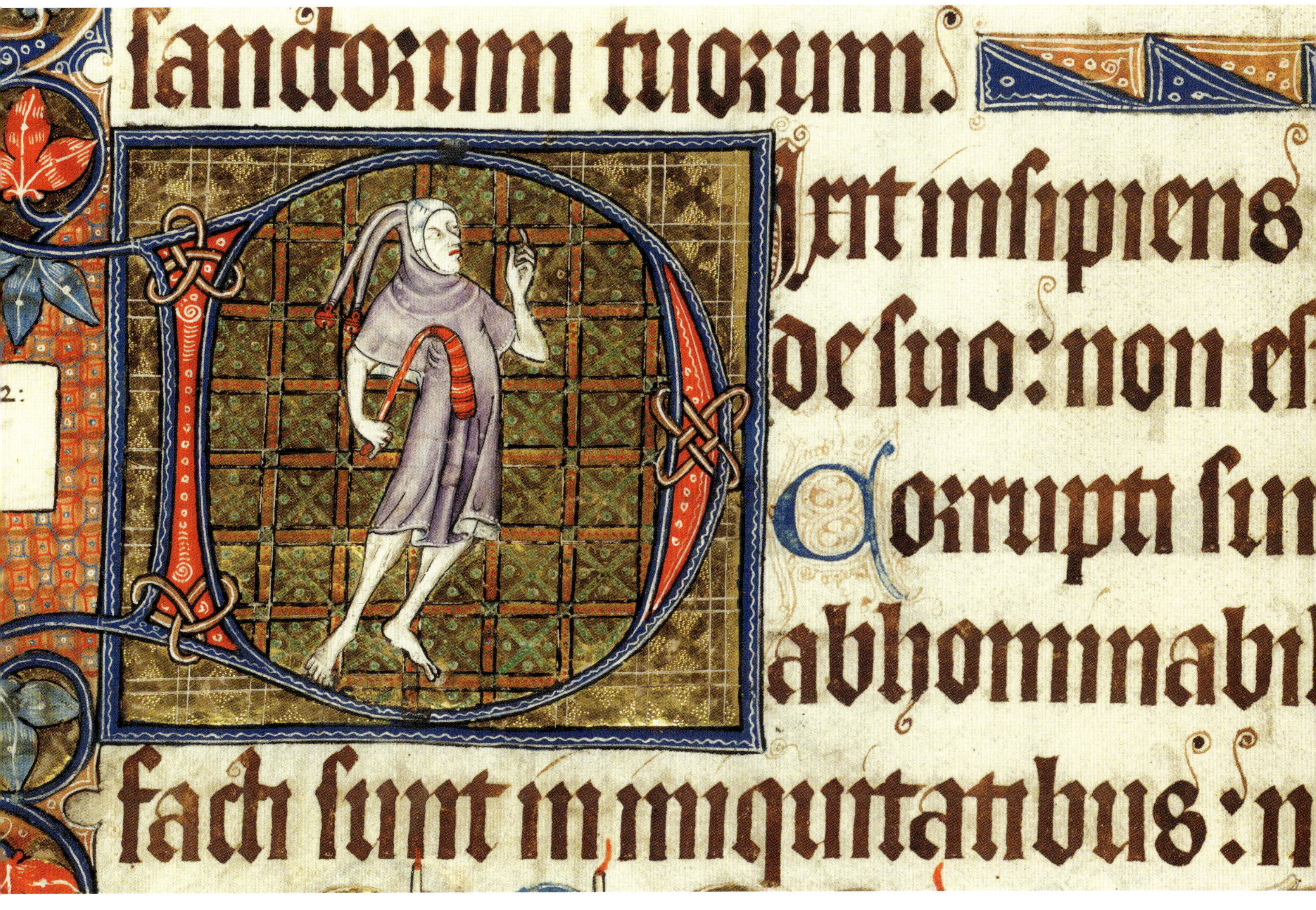

illustrating the verse '*Cantate Domino canticum novum quia mirabilia fecit*' ('O sing unto the Lord a new song, for he hath done marvellous things'), includes monks singing together from a choir book, complete with noted music on staves, placed on an eagle-headed lectern.

Scenes from the life of David, the supposed author of the Psalms, are a common subject for the initials. In most medieval psalters the most elaborate decoration is reserved for Psalm 1 and features an image of David playing the harp, an appropriate motif for the beginning of this book of David's songs. The Luttrell Psalter includes this image, as the largest initial in the manuscript: David sits in the large 'B' beginning the first Psalm, '*B[eatus] vir qui non abiit in consilio impiorum*' ('Blessed is the man that hath not walked in the counsel of the ungodly').

OVERLEAF

The Luttrell Psalter, about 1325–40
David tuning his harp: detail of historiated initial from the opening of Psalm 1, '*Beatus vir*'
British Library, Add MS 42130, f.13r

The Luttrell Psalter, about 1325–40
Five clerks chanting around a lectern with a psalter: detail of a historiated initial from the opening of Psalm 97, '*Cantate Domino*' ('O sing unto the Lord a new song')
British Library, Add MS 42130, f.174r

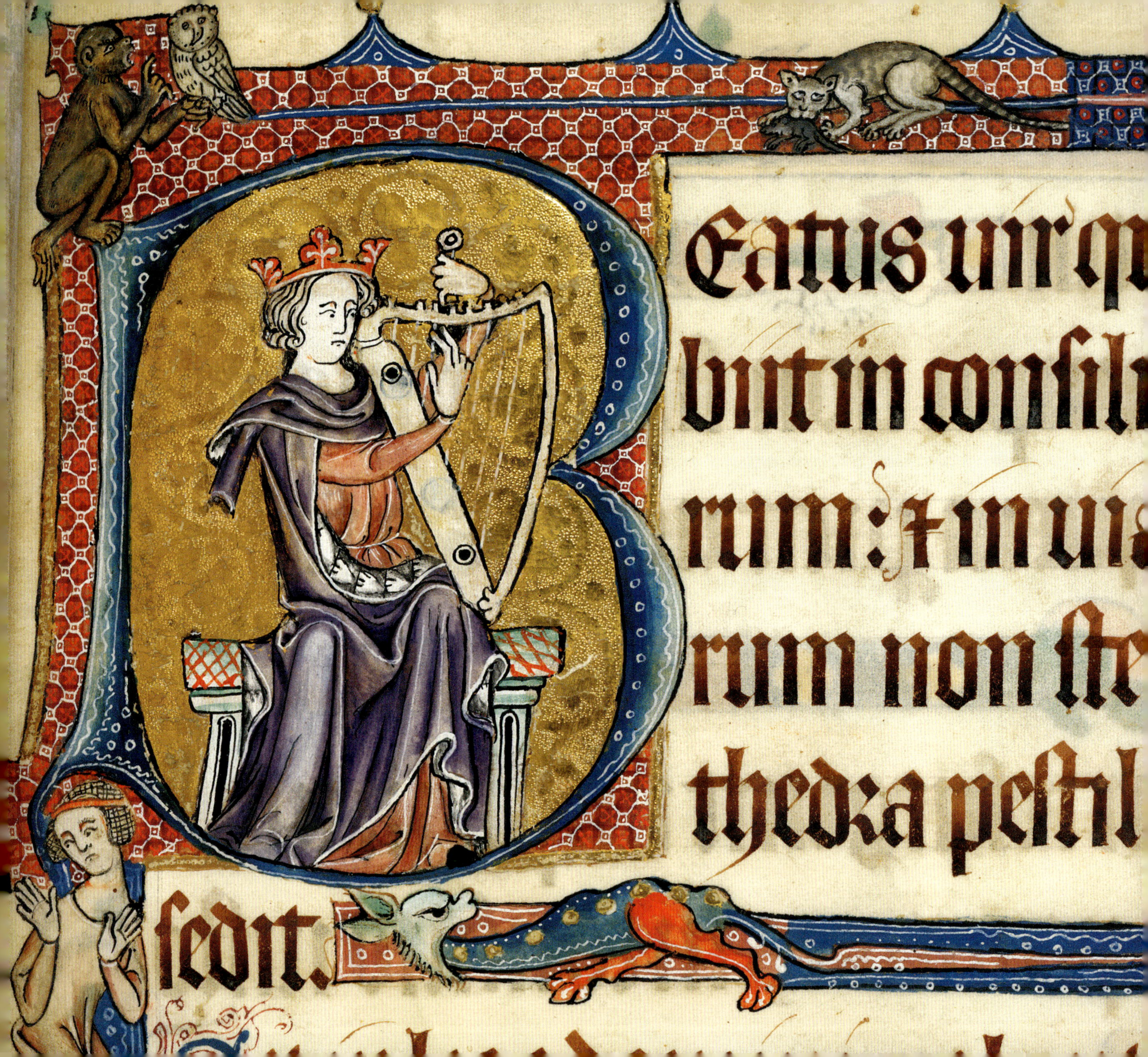
Eatus uir q
biit in consil
rum: ⁊ in ui
rum non st
thedra pestil
sedit.

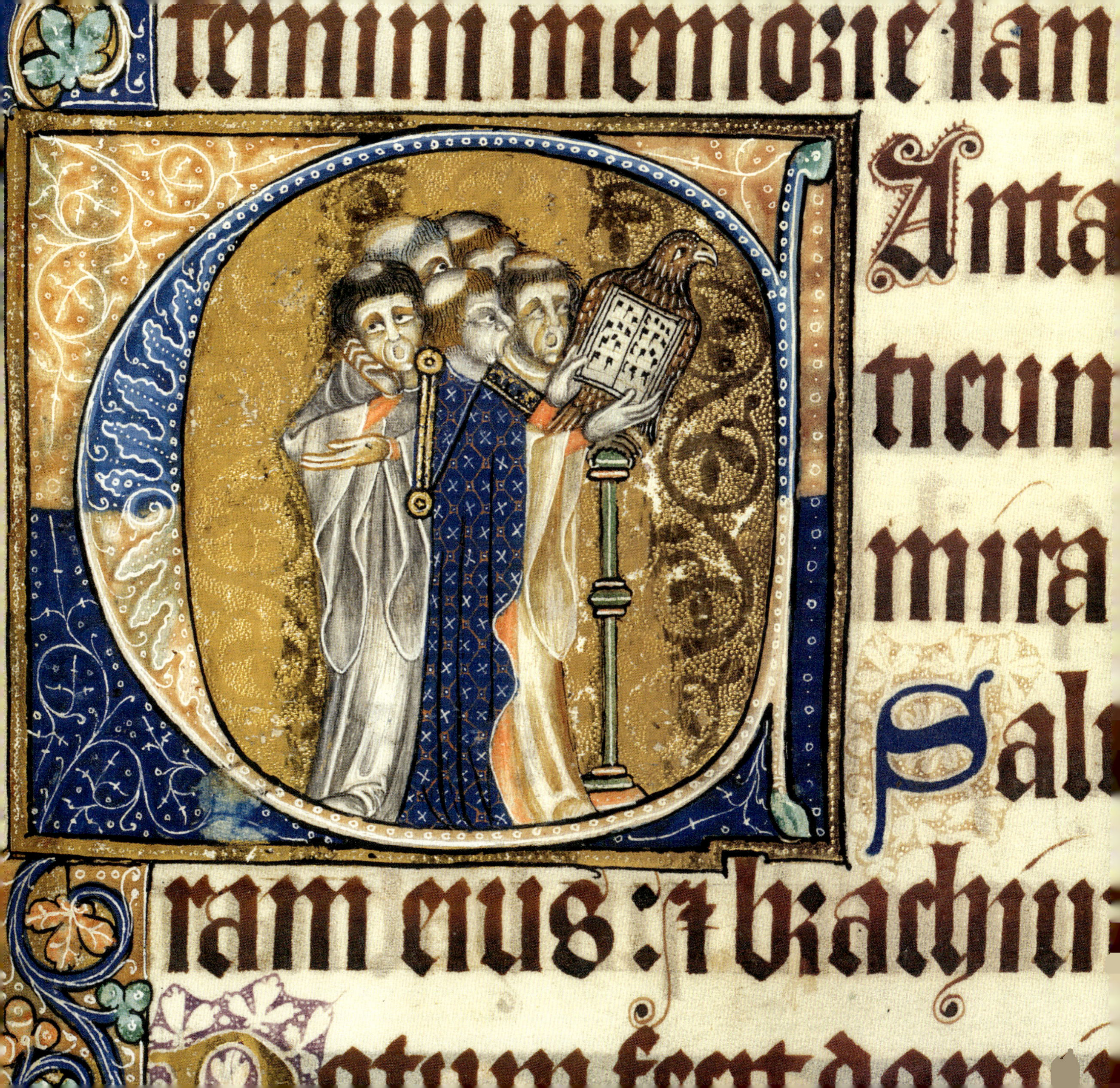
temini memorie san
Canta
mira
Sal
ram eius: & brachiu

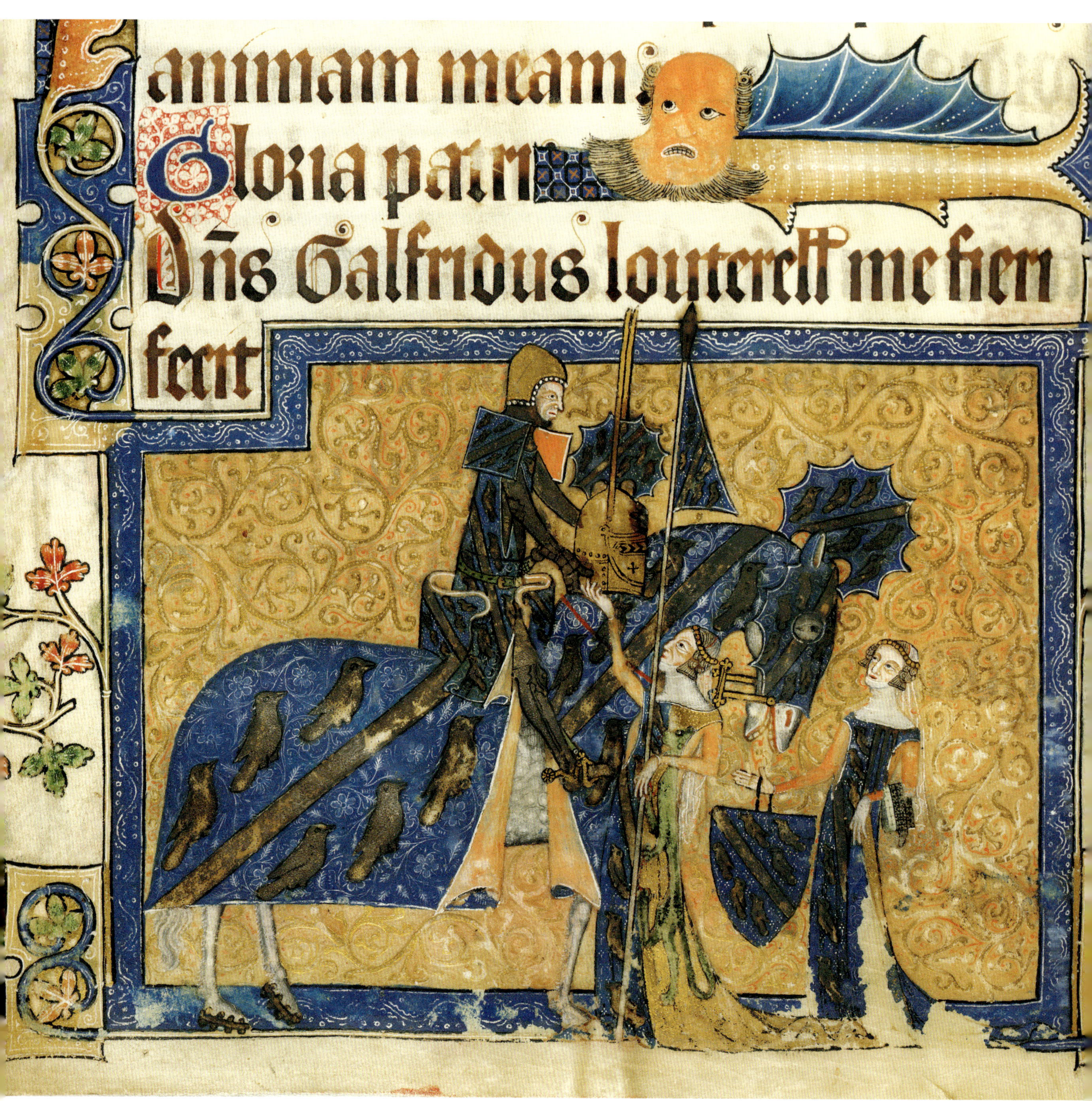
animam meam.
Gloria patri
Dñs Galfridus louterell me fieri
fecit

The Luttrell Psalter, about 1325–40
Sir Geoffrey Luttrell mounted and armed, attended by his wife Agnes and his daughter-in-law Beatrice, with the heraldic devices of their three families. Above them is the inscription '*Gloria patri. Dominus Galfridus louterell me fieri fecit*' ('Glory to the Father. Sir Geoffrey Luttrell caused me to be made')
British Library, Add MS 42130, f.202r

Patron

What is more unusual about the decoration of the Luttrell Psalter is the prominent inclusion of an image of the patron of the manuscript, together with an equally conspicuous inscription identifying him, written by the original scribe. Both are inserted into the middle of the biblical text. The inscription and the image come at the end of Psalm 108. Psalm 109, the last of the major Psalm divisions, begins at the top of the facing page. The additional language reads: '*Gloria patri. D[omi]n[u]s Galfridus louterell me fieri fecit*' ('Glory to the Father. Sir Geoffrey Luttrell caused me to be made'). Directly below, and fitted around the last word of this declaration, is an image of a man on horseback, with two women: one handing the knight his helm and the other holding a shield with the Luttrell family arms of six silver birds on a blue background separated by a diagonal stripe (in heraldic terms, *azure, a bend [sinister] between six martlets argent*). The heraldry on the gowns of the two women provides a date range for the making of the manuscript and allows the relevant Geoffrey Luttrell (there were several) to be identified. The first woman wears a gown with a large green lion on a gold background (the Sutton family arms are *or, a lion rampant vert*). This is Lady Agnes, née Sutton (died 1340), the wife of Sir Geoffrey Luttrell (1276–1345) of Irnham, Lincolnshire. Next to her is Beatrice, the daughter of Sir Geoffrey Scrope of Masham, who was betrothed to the Luttrells' son, Andrew, in 1320 (her dress has a gold stripe, reflecting the Scrope arms of *azure, a bend or, a label of five points argent*). Most scholars identify the mounted knight as Sir Geoffrey himself.

Marginal imagery

While the text seems to have been written by only one scribe, the illustrations appear to be the work of several different artists. Medieval manuscripts were produced in gatherings, or booklets, usually of eight to twelve leaves, that were then sewn together to form the completed manuscript. In the Luttrell Psalter the gatherings are all of twelve leaves (except for the one ending with the image of the Luttrell knight, which has only ten). This is relevant because the type of illustration varies considerably from gathering to gathering, which suggests that different sections were parcelled out to different artists for decoration.

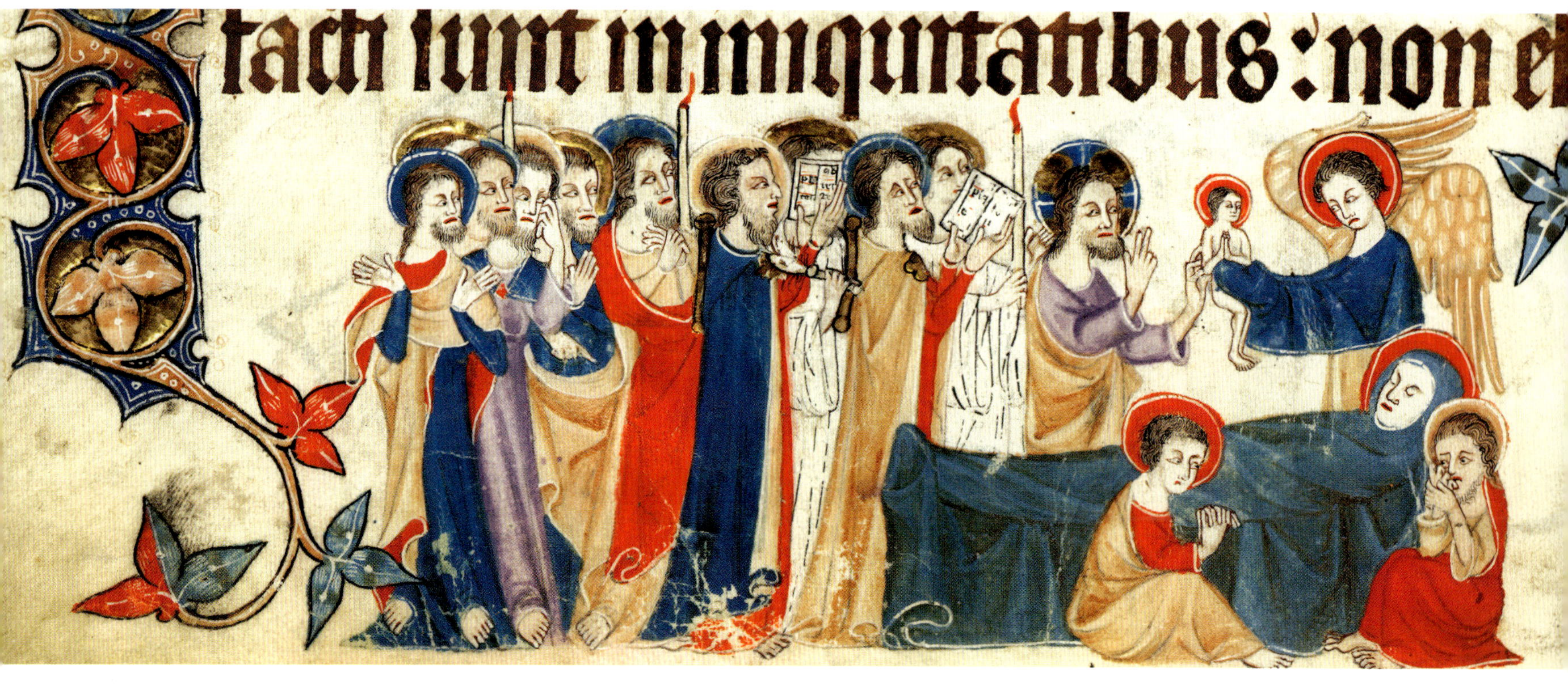

The Luttrell Psalter, about 1325–40
Bas-de-page scene depicting the death (Dormition) of the Virgin Mary, her body surrounded by eleven Apostles singing, while an angel presents her soul (in the form of a small child) to her Son in heaven
British Library, Add MS 42130, f.98v

Further, the subject of the marginal imagery also shows a high degree of variation in different parts of the book. So, for example, virtually all of the overtly religious imagery occurs only in the first sections. In these earlier gatherings there are images of various saints (gatherings 2, 4–5 and 7–9) and a long sequence of forty-eight continuous marginal scenes of the life of Christ and of the Virgin, and of various saints, prefaced by two standing bishops (folios 85–108 verso). One of these is the Dormition of the Virgin, a scene of the Apostles gathered around the deathbed of the Virgin at the moment of her death (here with her soul being handed to Christ by an angel), which appears in the lower margin of Psalm 52. The next group of gatherings (10–13), and those at the end of the book (19–26) are usually described as unfinished, because they feature virtually no decoration whatever in the margins.

It is only with the central group of gatherings of seventy folios that the marginal imagery of hybrid creatures, animals, and people engaged in various activities threatens to overwhelm the written text with its vibrancy and profusion (gatherings 13–18). Each of these pages includes figurative decoration in the lower margin, or bas-de-page, and many include additional figures in the other margins and/or the 'line-fillers' – literally, the rectangular decoration filling up lines when the text does not reach the outer margin. The decoration here features detailed depictions of 'medieval rural life', such as ploughing, sowing, reaping, cooking and feasting, and various creatively constructed hybrid creatures consisting of bizarre animal and animal-human combinations. In most instances these types of image appear together on the same page, often with the hybrids in the outer margins growing out of the foliate borders. The marginal imagery does not

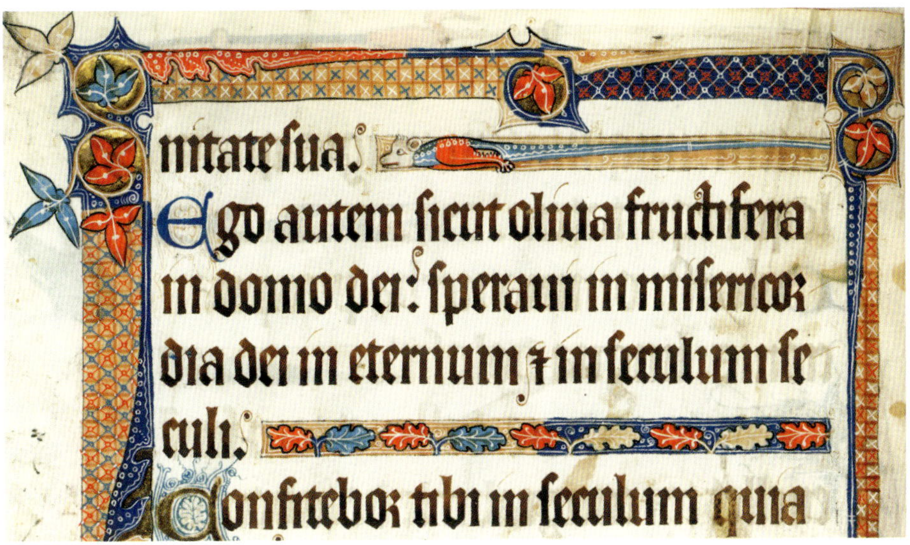

The Luttrell Psalter, about 1325–40
Detail of Psalm 51, '*Ego autem sicut oliva fructifera*' ('As for me, I am like a green olive tree in the house of God'), showing characteristic line-fillers of hybrid creature and foliage
British Library, Add MS 42130, f.98v

illustrate the text of the Psalms (which is Psalms 77: 61–118: 30 in this section) in the same way as the historiated initials do, except in isolated examples.

Amongst the images are two sequences that run across the lower margins of several pages. The first is a series of eight scenes of ploughing and harvesting (folios 170–3), ending with the multicoloured horses drawing a cart. Next there are four scenes of food preparation culminating in a feast attended by two friars, three men and two women, with the Luttrell heraldry of silver birds on a blue background behind the diners (folios 206 verso –208). Presumably this is a scene of the Luttrell family at table. In addition to these sequences, which appear to be unrelated to the Psalm texts, there are many other individual scenes, such as bear-baiting (folio 161), a man hawking with a falcon (folio 163), the city of Constantinople, labelled '*Constantinus nobilis*' (folio 164 verso) and a mill complete with fish traps in the water (folio 181). It has been suggested that these marginal scenes should be taken 'at their face value, as representations of episodes of daily life as it was lived in England early in the fourteenth century' (Backhouse 2000). As a result, these images have been widely mined for details of contemporary dress, practice and cultivation of the land, and are frequently reproduced, even appearing in a twenty-minute film that can be seen on YouTube (Loven 2008).

Other images are much more difficult to characterise or even label, as they consist of extremely varied and variegated creatures, often sprouting from or transforming into a foliate border. A good example may be seen in the outer margin above the cart hauling away the sheaves, an upright hybrid with a blue horse head, human arms and hands, and spotted orange legs, whose 'tail' ends with red and

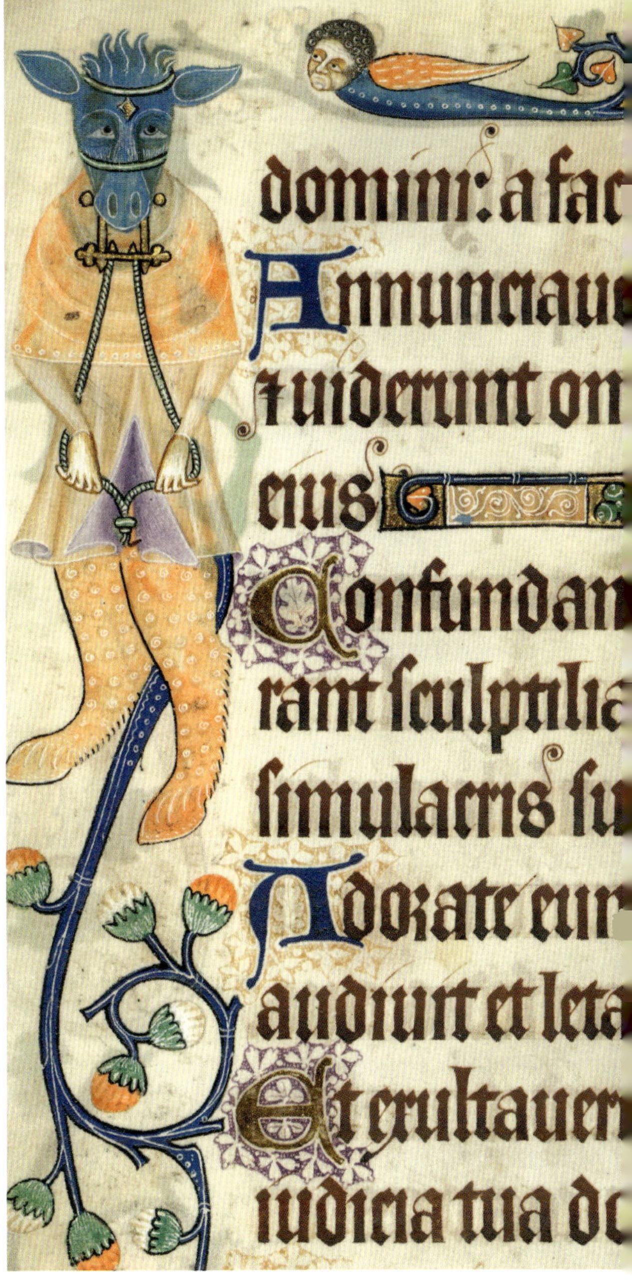

The Luttrell Psalter, about 1325–40
Hybrid creature with a horse's head, human arms, orange spotted legs and a blue tail
British Library, Add MS 42130, f.173v

OVERLEAF
The Luttrell Psalter, about 1325–40
Bas-de-page scene depicting a harvest cart drawn uphill by three horses
British Library, Add MS 42130, f.173v

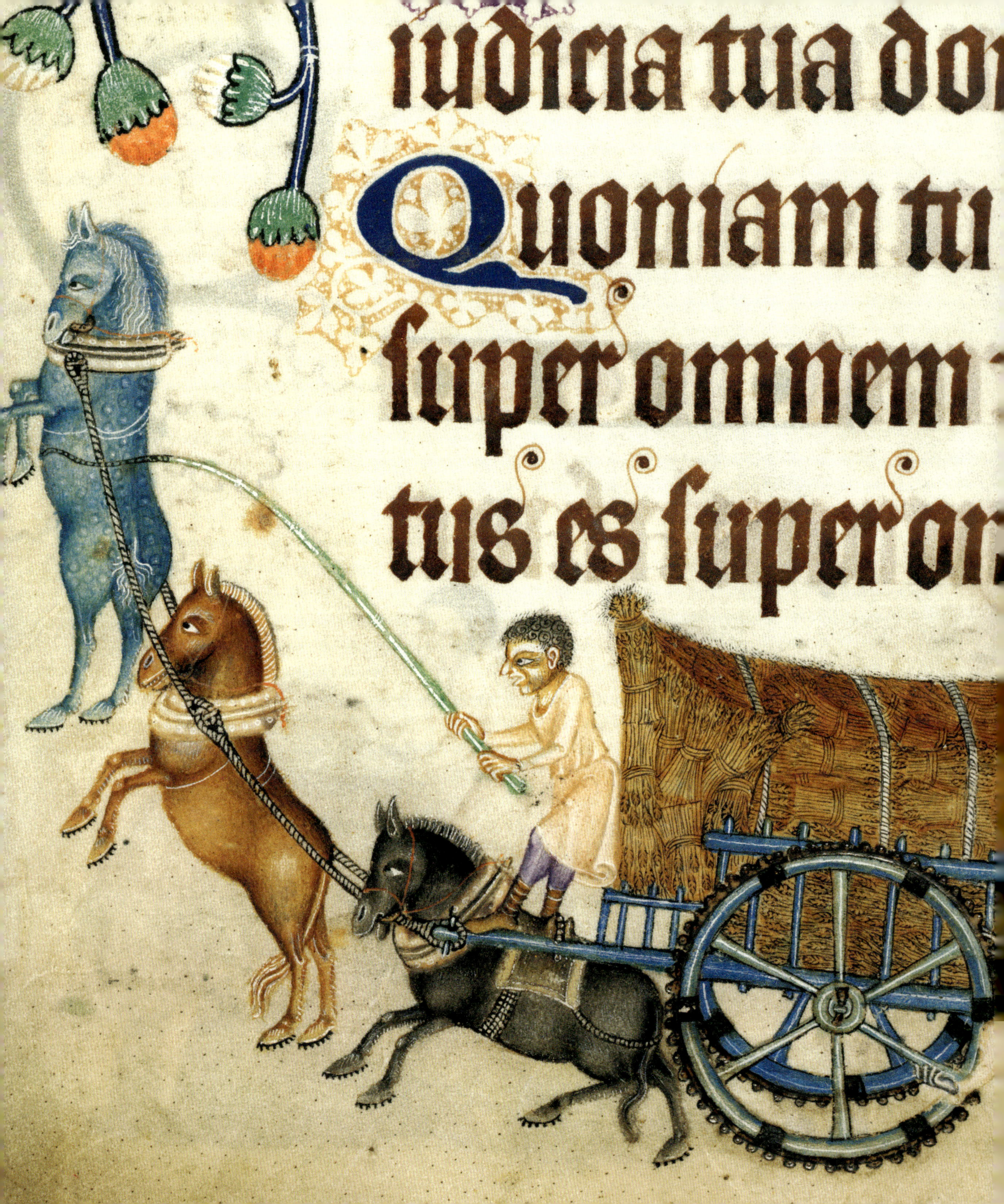
iudicia tua do
Quoniam tu
super omnem
tus es super o

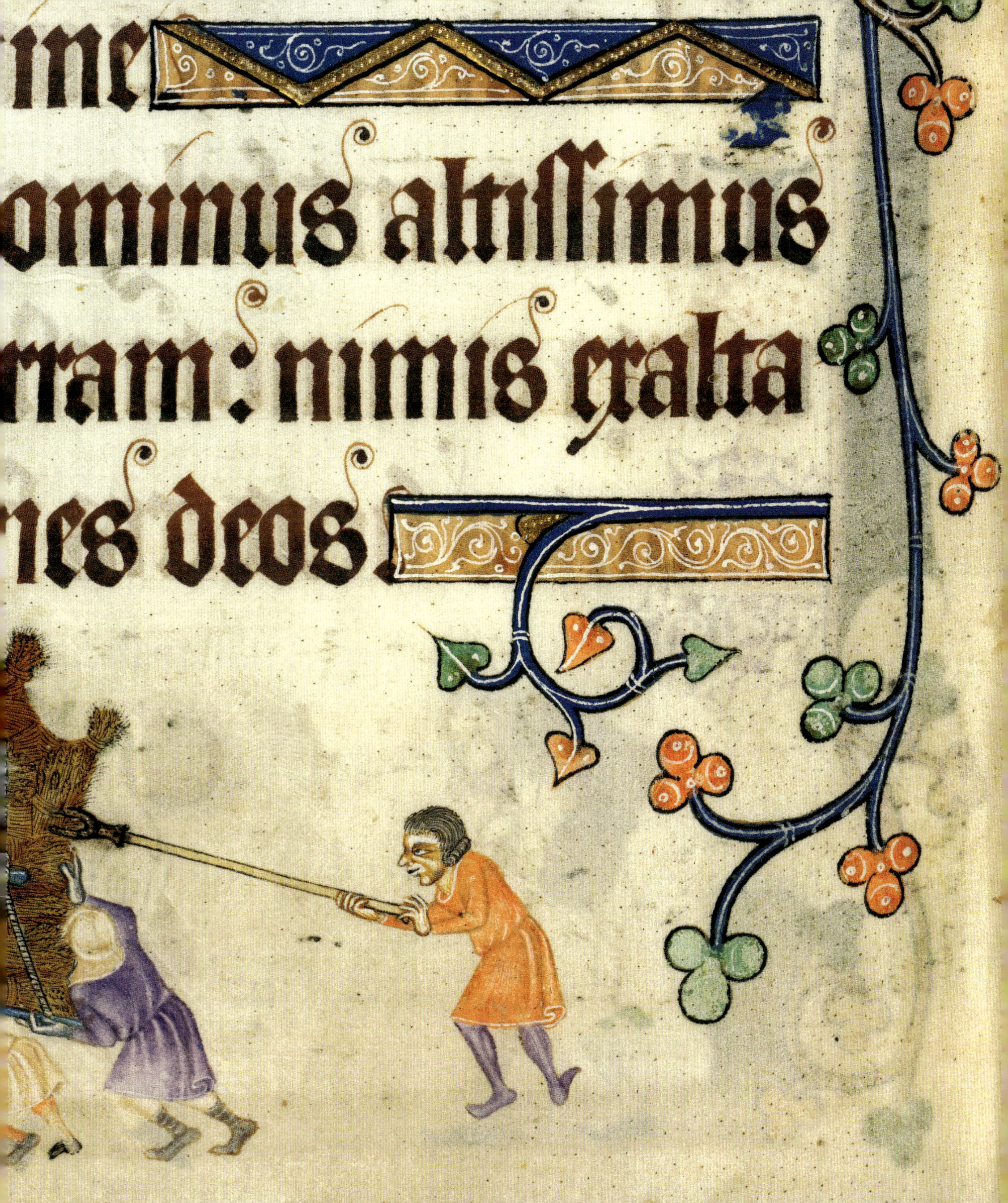
ine
ominus altissimus
rram: nimis exalta
nes deos

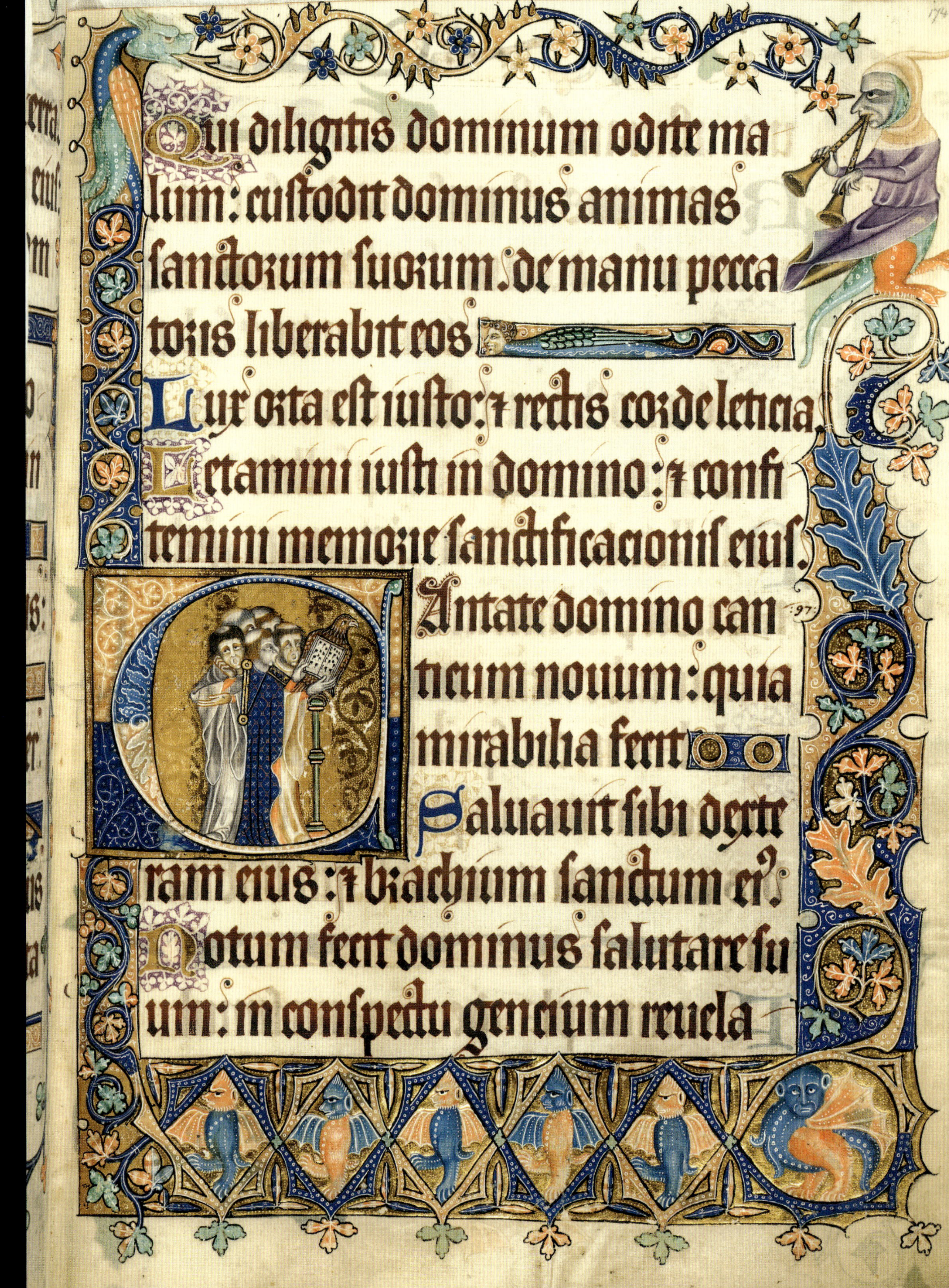
174

Qui diligitis dominum odite ma
lum: custodit dominus animas
sanctorum suorum. de manu pecca
toris liberabit eos
Lux orta est iusto: et rectis corde leticia.
Letamini iusti in domino: et confi
temini memorie sanctificacionis eius.
97 Cantate domino can
ticum nouum: quia
mirabilia fecit
Saluauit sibi dexte
ram eius: et brachium sanctum eius.
Notum fecit dominus salutare su
um: in conspectu gencium reuela

The Luttrell Psalter, about 1325–40
Opening of Psalm 97, '*Cantate Domino*', the beginning of one of the major divisions of the Psalter, marked with a historiated initial and a decorative border featuring a grotesque playing a double pipe
British Library, Add MS 42130, f.174r

white flower buds. However, sometimes these marginal images or line-fillers correspond to a word or phrase in the text, in what have been called 'word pictures' (for over forty suggested examples see Freeman Sandler 1996, with additional ones proposed in Camille 1998). In these instances a particular word is illustrated by a picture representing it, usually in very close proximity, but often without reference to the meaning of the Psalm verse. Instances of this type of decoration include the image of a pelican picking at its breast with three chicks in a nest (folio 178), directly beside the word '*pellicano*' ('I am become like a pelican in the wilderness'), and a little bird below, adjacent to the word '*passer*' ('a sparrow that sitteth alone upon the house-top', Psalm 101: 7–8; see Freeman Sandler 1996). Enthusiastic debate about this approach, and the meaning of the marginal images more generally, is ongoing.

Conclusion

The development of marginal imagery unconnected with the text was an English innovation, and it became particularly pronounced in the fourteenth century (Freeman Sandler 1986). Without question, the Luttrell Psalter is one of the high points of this type of decoration. In this book the hybrid creatures and various rural scenes are given prominence equal to (or even greater than) than the more clearly religious ones that also decorate or illustrate the text. As a result, the Psalter commissioned by Sir Geoffrey Luttrell remains a moving testament to the enduring importance and fascination of this fundamental biblical book.

References to the Psalms are to the Vulgate numbering. English Psalm quotations are from the Book of Common Prayer version.

Further reading

The entire manuscript is available freely online with a zoom feature, description and full bibliography, on the British Library's Digitised Manuscripts website, http://www.bl.uk/manuscripts/.

Janet Backhouse, *The Luttrell Psalter* (London 1989)

Janet Backhouse, 'The sale of the Luttrell Psalter', in *Antiquaries, Book Collectors and the Circles of Learning*, eds R. Myers and M. Harris (Winchester 1996)

Janet Backhouse, *Medieval Rural Life in the Luttrell Psalter* (London 2000)

Michelle Brown, *The Luttrell Psalter: A Facsimile with Commentary* (London 2006)

Michelle Brown, *The World of the Luttrell Psalter* (London 2006)

Michael Camille, *Mirror in Parchment: The Luttrell Psalter and the Making of Medieval England* (London 1998)

Nick Loven and the Lincolnshire Heritage Filmmakers, The Luttrell Psalter film (2008)

E.G. Millar, *The Luttrell Psalter* (London 1932)

Lucy Freeman Sandler, *A Survey of Manuscripts Illuminated in the British Isles, 5: Gothic Manuscripts 1285–1385*, 2 vols (London 1986)

Lucy Freeman Sandler, 'The Word in the text and the image in the margin: The case of the Luttrell Psalter', *Journal of the Walters Art Gallery*, 54; *Essays in Honour of Lilian M.C. Randall* (1996)

Lucy Freeman Sandler, '*The World of the Luttrell Psalter* by Michelle P. Brown' (review), *Catholic Historical Review*, 94 (2008)

Kathryn A. Smith, 'Margin', *Studies in Iconography*, 33 (2012)

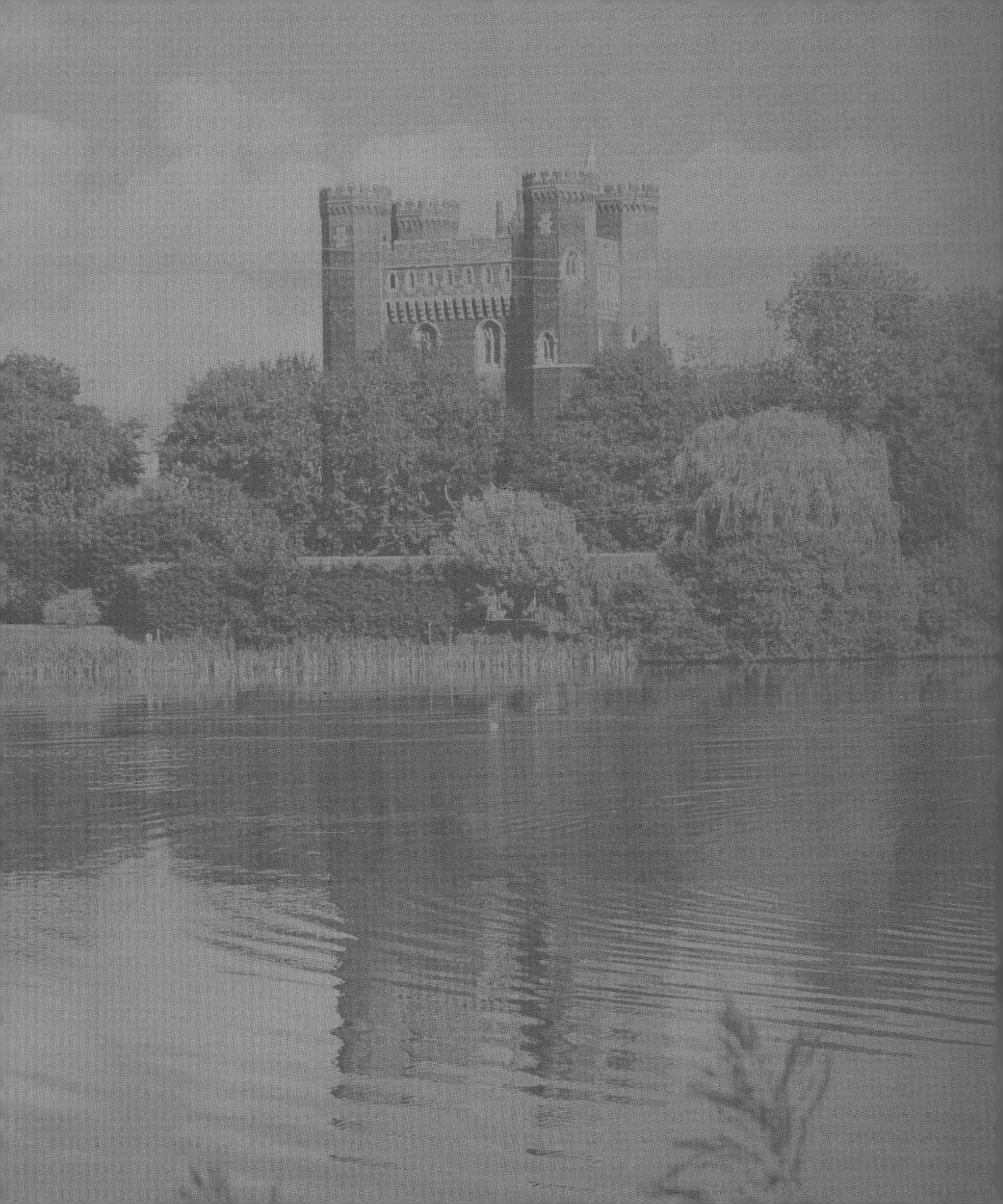

Lincolnshire's landed elite
1215–2015

RICHARD OLNEY

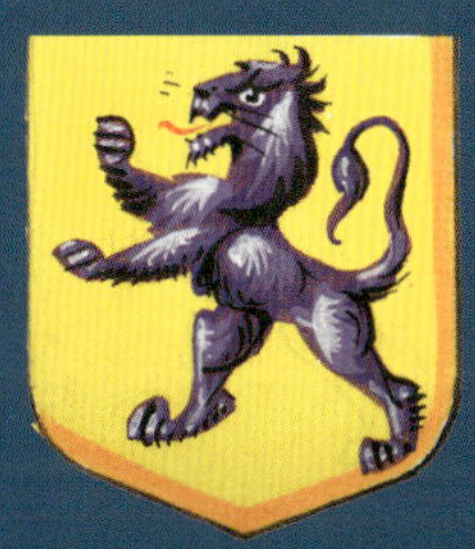

MAGNA CARTA can be seen as an episode in the long tussle between the medieval English monarchy and its leading subjects, men who were concerned above all to preserve or reclaim their liberties and privileges. These men had extensive estates and many adherents in their localities. Yet England was not just a conglomeration of baronial fiefdoms. It was a country that required to be governed; and a key element in the medieval and early modern system of government was the county. The king needed loyal representatives in each county, preferably men of standing and influence, and the counties themselves needed channels of communication with the central government at Westminster – in other words, friends at court.

Seen from Westminster, however, Lincolnshire was in some ways a problematic county, difficult to control and sometimes downright troublesome. This was partly a factor of its distance from the capital and its poor communications, but it was also in some measure due to its sheer size. It was second only in that respect to Yorkshire, and like Yorkshire it was internally divided. At the centre of Lincolnshire lay Lincoln, in the early Middle Ages a thriving city, the site of a strong castle and the seat of a powerful bishopric. But from about a century and a half after Magna Carta its commerce began to decline. It had already lost some of its strategic importance and perhaps it always lacked the dominant position in the county enjoyed by, for instance, Leicester in Leicestershire or Norwich in Norfolk.

Patterns of land ownership also had their effect. In a predominantly rural and agricultural county the owners of broad acres were bound to occupy a prominent position, but it was difficult for any one owner to exert a pull across the whole shire. A nobleman whose word was law in northern Lindsey might have little clout in Kesteven or Holland. The great tenants-in-chief, moreover, generally had large estates outside the county and might reside on their Lincolnshire properties for only a short period of the year. There was a limit to the local loyalty that such remote figures could command.

As for the lesser barons and knights, the gentry of the shire, they were more likely than the magnates to be resident, but as time went on they tended increasingly to congregate in the more desirable districts. Kesteven became more gentrified; the gentry were less evenly spread in Lindsey; and Holland became a region dominated by small yeoman proprietors. This uneven distribution had implications for local government, when in the later Middle Ages central

Christopher Saxton (1542/4–1610/11)
Map of Lincolnshire from the 'Burghley Atlas', 1576
Detail showing the castles of Bolingbroke and Tattershall, with Lord Burghley's annotations marking gentry seats including Heneage of Hainton
British Library, Royal MS 18.D.iii, f.117

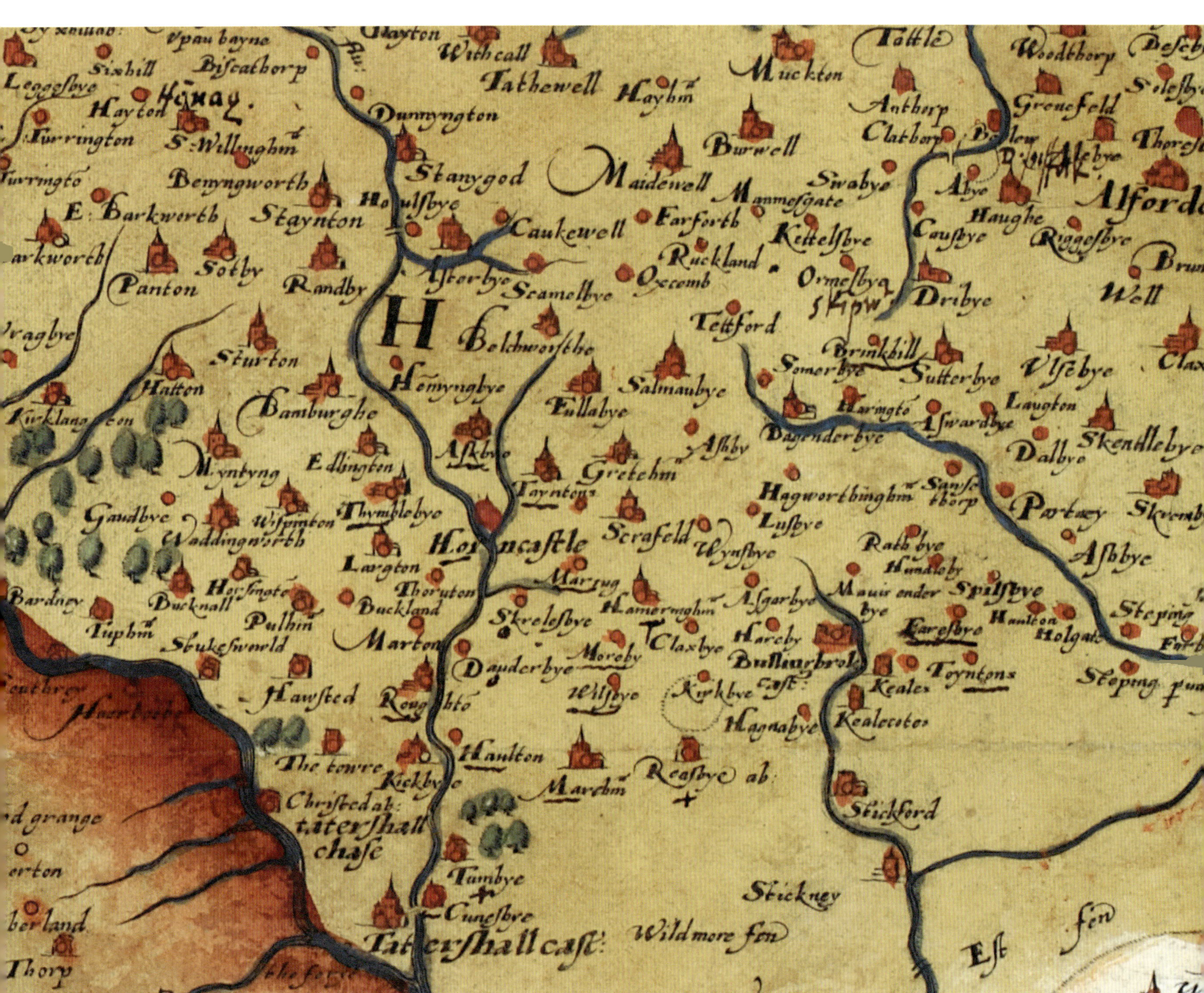

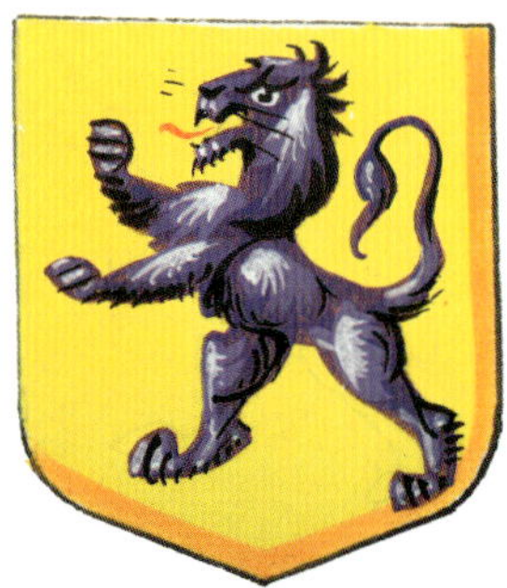

Shield of John de Lacy
Illustration from *Lincolnshire Church Notes made by Gervase Holles* (copy made for J.L. Ffytche of Thorpe Hall, Louth)
Lincoln Cathedral Library, MS 309

Bolingbroke Castle
Photo: Andrew Tryner, copyright Lincolnshire County Council

government came to rely on the resident gentry for the day-to-day administration of justice in the county.

A brief survey of Lincolnshire's landed elite in the centuries following Magna Carta may serve to illustrate some of these points. In June 1215 the Lincolnshire baronage was well represented at Runnymede, and the list of twenty-five barons appointed to enforce the charter contained one name that was to acquire particular significance for the county. John de Lacy, described as constable of Chester in 1215, was later to succeed to Lincolnshire estates that included Lincoln and Bolingbroke castles. He was created Earl of Lincoln in 1232 and his family continued to hold a dominant position in the county for the rest of the thirteenth century.

On the death of the 3rd Earl in 1311 the Lacy estates passed to the house of Lancaster, and in the latter part of the fourteenth century it was John of Gaunt, Duke of Lancaster, who led the Lincolnshire nobility. But he had vast estates elsewhere – even the former Lacy estates had their caput or administrative centre at Pontefract rather than Bolingbroke – and he could not have spent much time in the county. The local tradition that he built a palace at Lincoln is a myth. When his son Henry of Bolingbroke gained the throne as Henry IV, the Lancaster estates became

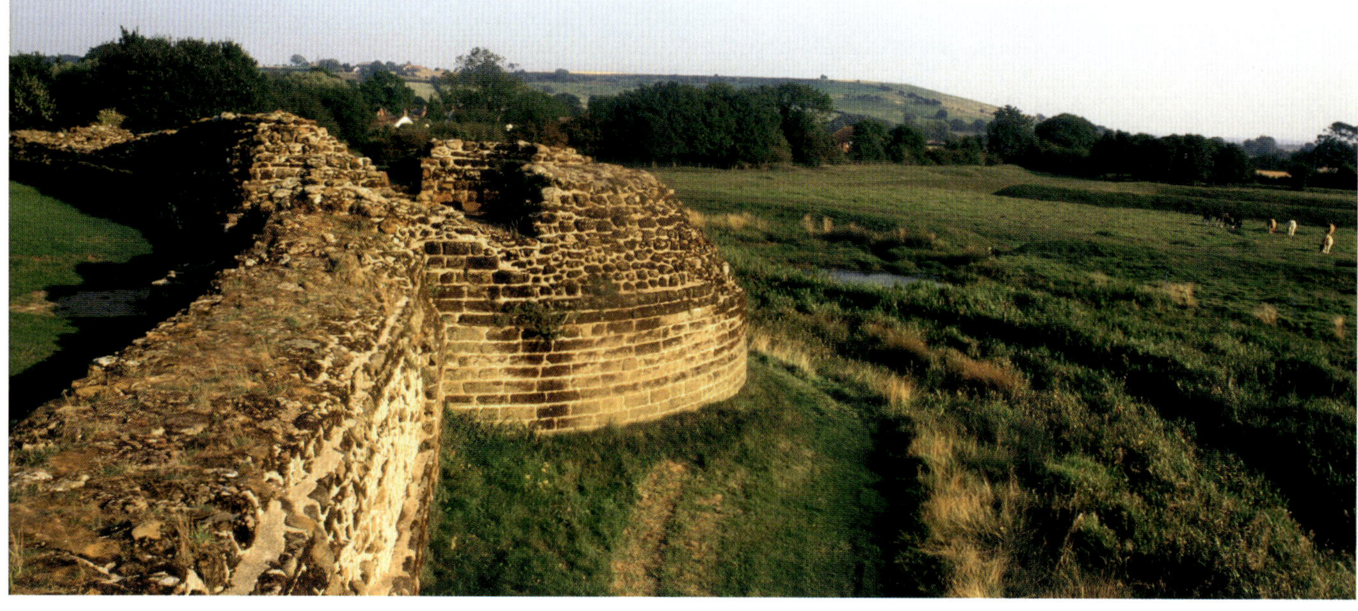

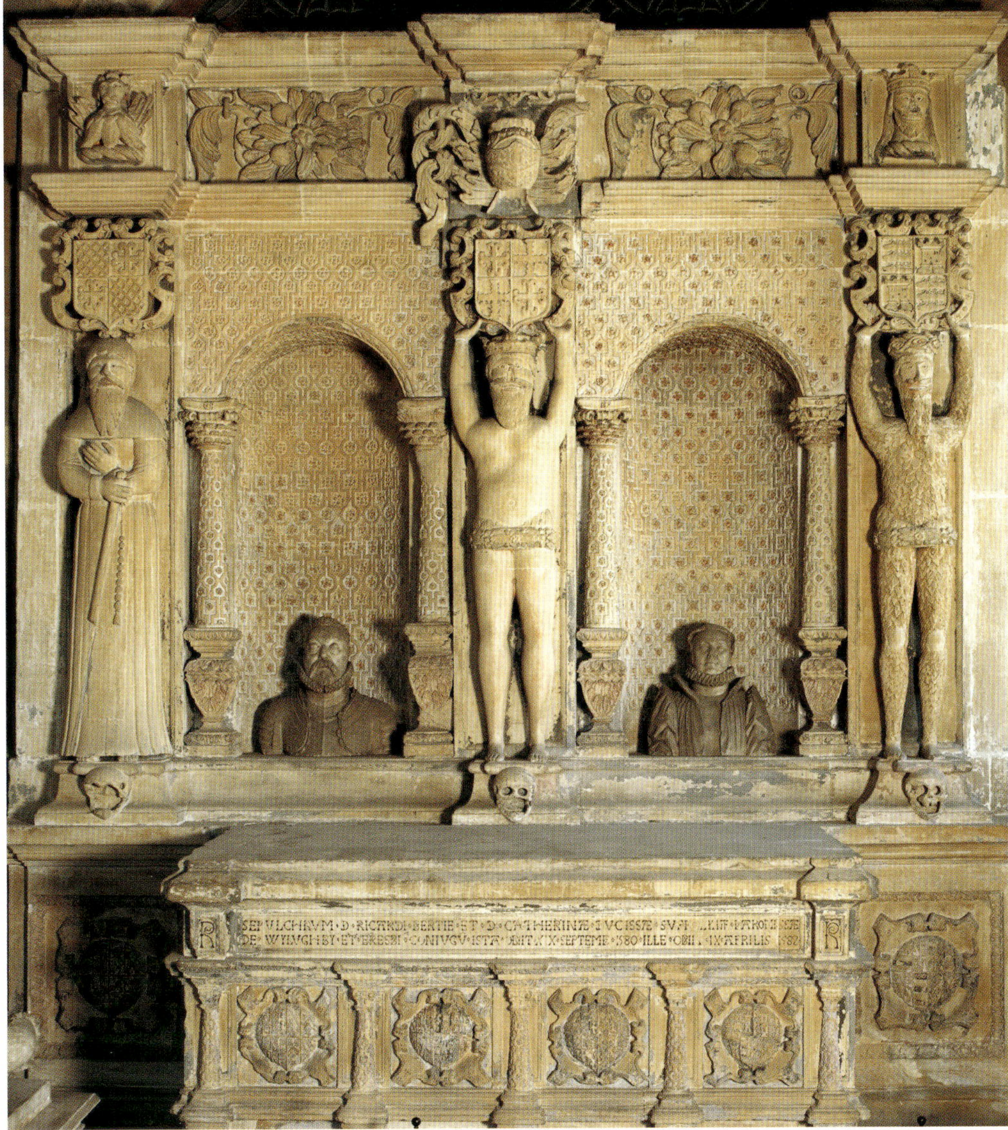

Tomb of Richard and Katherine Bertie (died 1580 and 1582), St James' church, Spilsby
Photo: Andrew Tryner, copyright Lincolnshire County Council

part of the patrimony of the Crown, although they have always been separately administered. Some centuries later, in 1831, Lincoln Castle was purchased from the Duchy by the county; but in 1873 Queen Victoria still owned nearly a thousand Lincolnshire acres and remained Lady of the Manor of Bolingbroke, although the castle there had long been demolished.

Back in the early fourteenth century, when the Lacys were giving way to the Lancasters, Lincolnshire was producing its most distinguished indigenous noble family. The Willoughbys of Willoughby, near Alford, inherited the seat and estate of Eresby, near Spilsby, and were summoned to parliament as Barons Willoughby de Eresby from 1311. In the next two centuries they continued to make their way up the ranks of the county, although from time to time the barony passed through the female rather than the male line. In 1533 or 1534 Katherine Willoughby, daughter and heir of the 9th Baron, married Charles Brandon, 1st Duke of Suffolk and

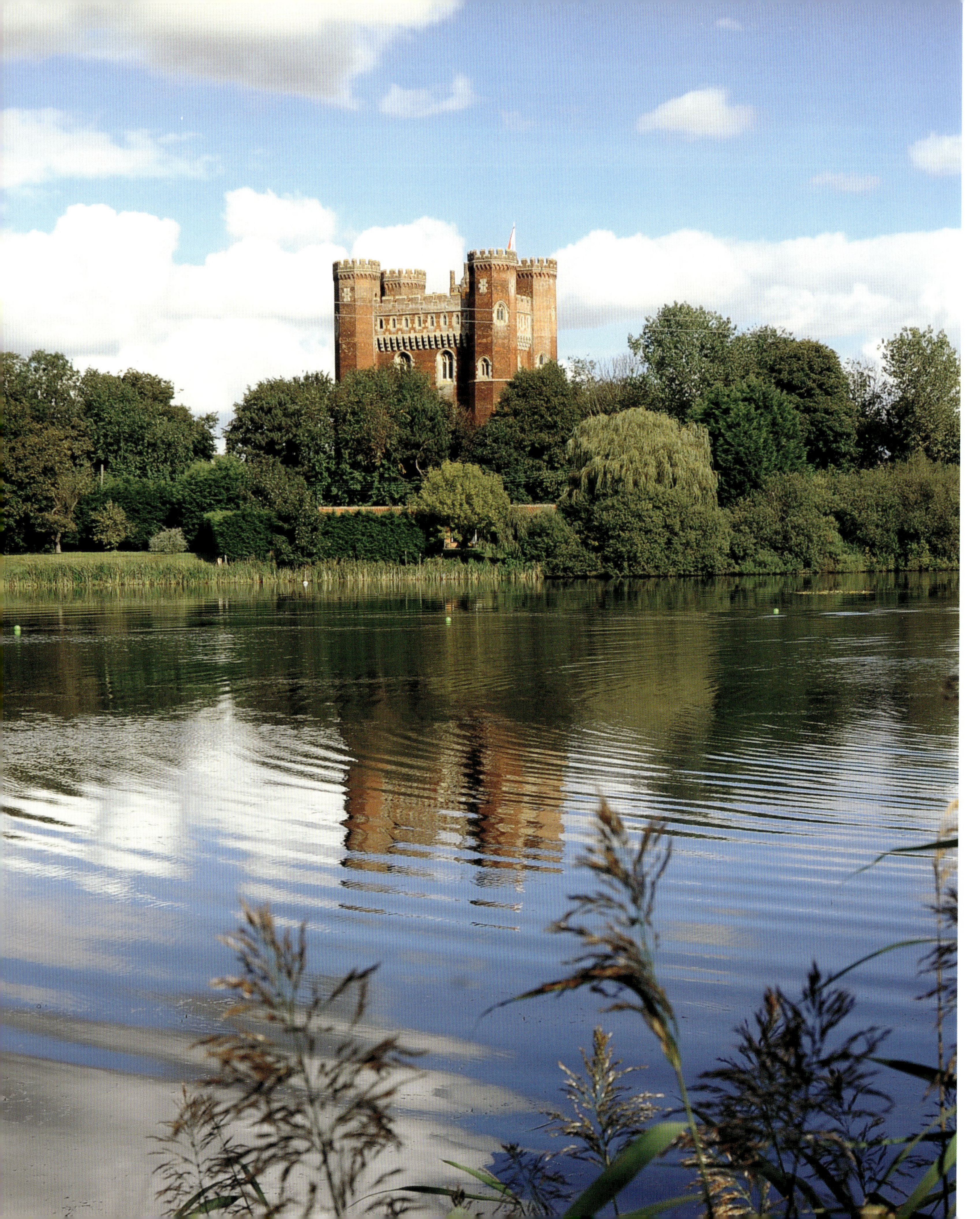

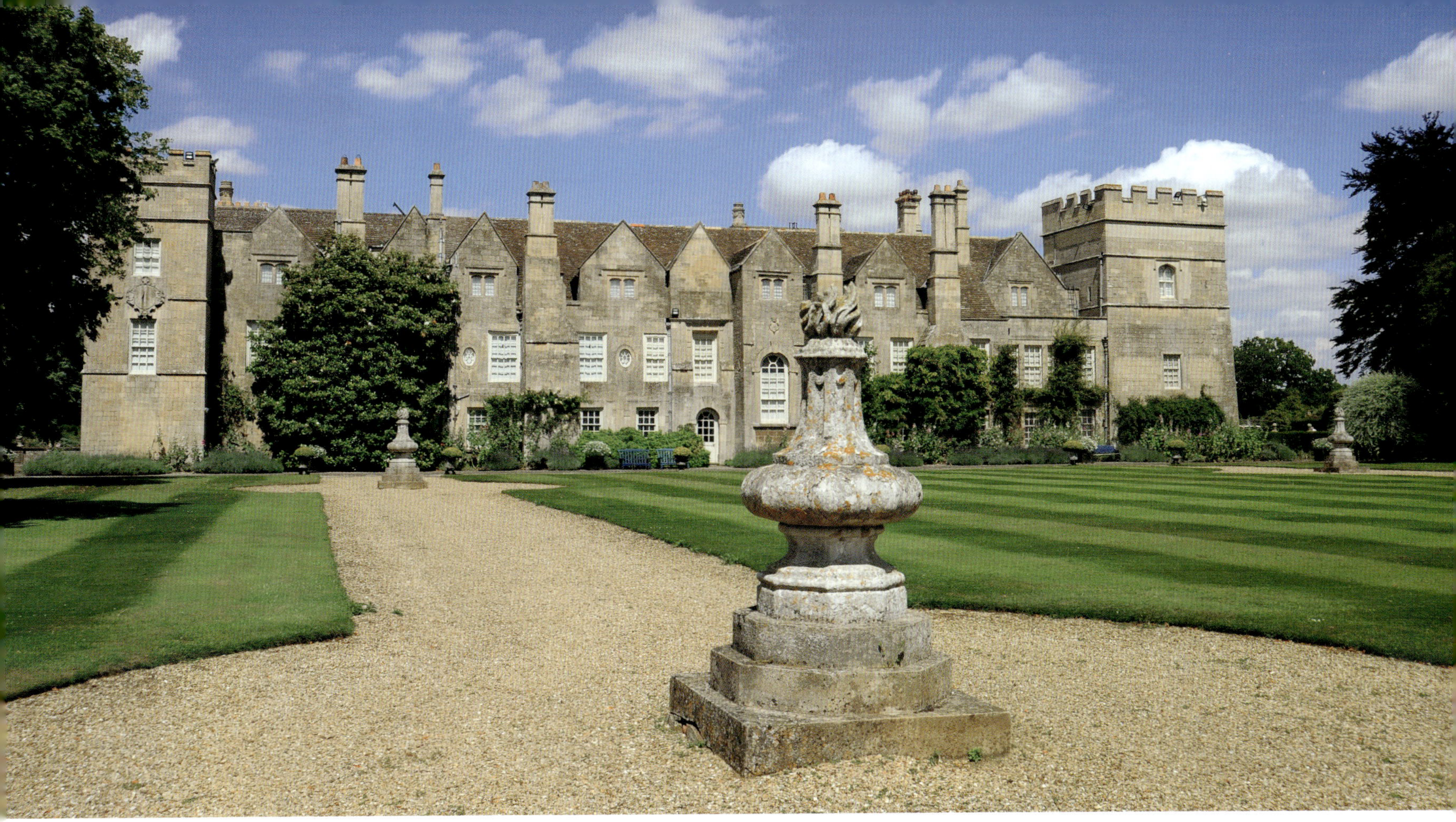

Grimsthorpe Castle: south front
Photo: Andrew Tryner, copyright Lincolnshire County Council

OPPOSITE
Tattershall Castle
Photo: Andrew Tryner, copyright Lincolnshire County Council

brother-in-law of Henry VIII. Already a large landowner elsewhere, Suffolk built up considerable holdings in Lincolnshire and the couple made Grimsthorpe, near Bourne, their principal seat, hastily giving it a make-over in preparation for a royal visit in 1541.

Only ten years later Suffolk died without a male heir, and much of his own property in the county was sold. His widow, however, then married Richard Bertie, and it was to their descendants that the Eresby and Grimsthorpe estates passed. Suffolk's death meanwhile had created a vacancy in the leadership of the county, which was filled by Edward, 9th Baron Clinton. Like Suffolk, Clinton had married into the Lincolnshire aristocracy and, like him, he became a major landowner in the county. He was created Earl of Lincoln in 1572 and two years later acquired Tattershall, the splendid castle that had been erected by Ralph, Lord Cromwell in the mid fifteenth century and had later been one of the Duke of Suffolk's possessions.

When this Earl of Lincoln died in 1585 there was another hiatus. This time the Crown had to look beyond the borders of the county to find a nobleman influential enough to fill the recently created office of Lord Lieutenant, the king's representative as military leader of the shire. Between 1585 and 1629 the choice fell principally on the Manners family, earls of Rutland, who had long owned Lincolnshire property but whose imposing castle at Belvoir, near Grantham, lay in Leicestershire. (The Manners family had inherited Belvoir from the family of Ros, who had been among

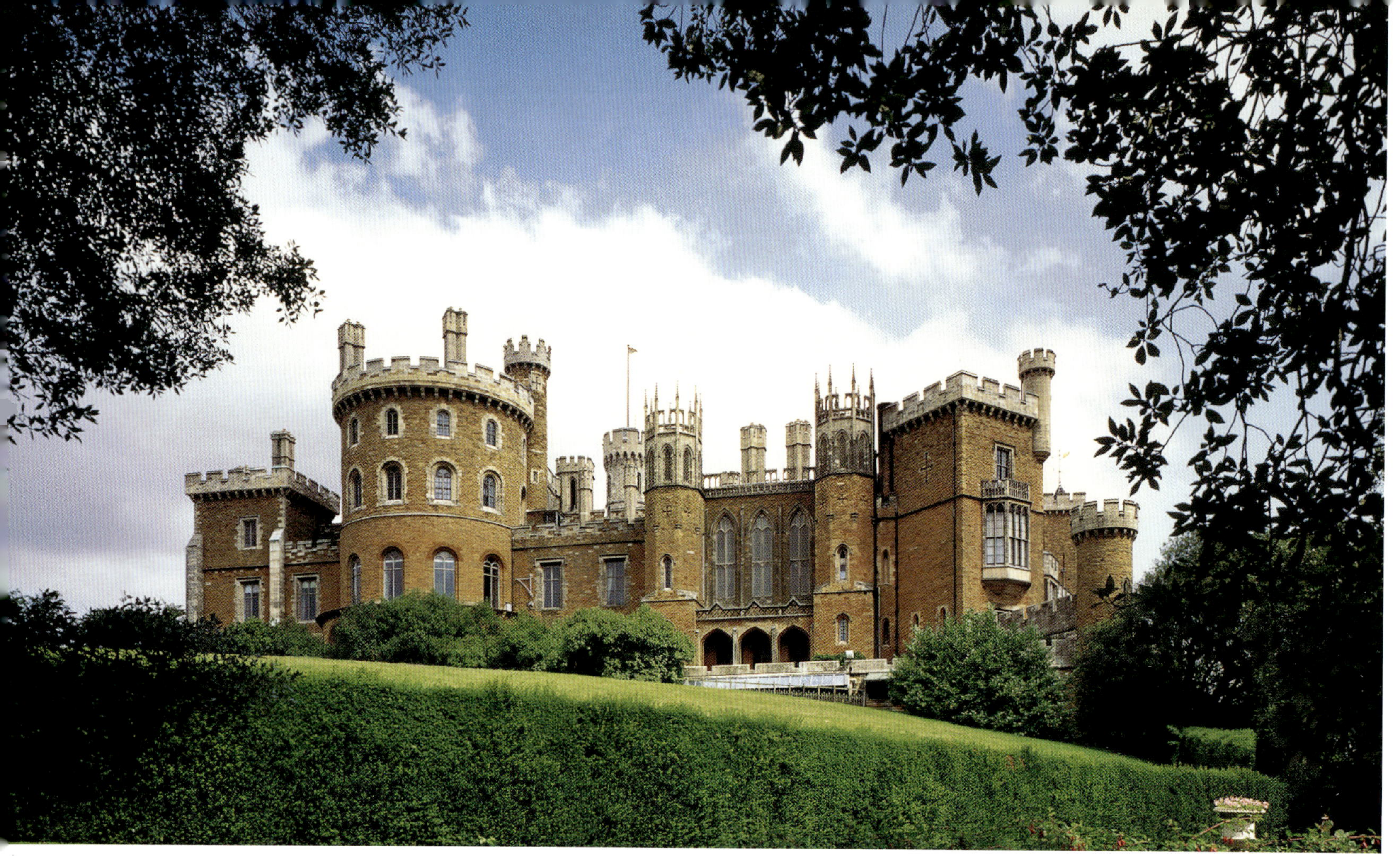

Belvoir Castle
Photo: Andrew Tryner, copyright Lincolnshire County Council

OPPOSITE
John de Critz the elder (about 1552–1642)
***William Cecil, Lord Burghley (1520–98),* about 1590**
Oil on canvas
Hatfield House

the barons of 1215.) Between 1587 and 1598, when there was no member of the Manners family suitable to act as Lord Lieutenant, the office was filled by no less a person than Lord Burghley, whose seat at Burghley near Stamford was, again, just outside the county.

In the early seventeenth century the Clintons were in decline but the Bertie family was now ready to assert its primacy as the largest resident landowner in Lincolnshire. Katherine Willoughby's grandson, Robert Bertie, was created Earl of Lindsey in 1626 and held the lieutenancy from 1629 until his death in 1642. At the Restoration the 2nd Earl, Montagu Bertie, succeeded to the office, and thereafter it stayed in the family for the next century and a half. During this period Grimsthorpe remained the principal seat and its occupant was raised to the dukedom of Ancaster in 1715. In 1779, however, there was another failure in the male line. The dukedom went to an uncle, but when he died without issue in 1809 the lieutenancy passed out of the family.

The new Lord Lieutenant was John Cust, 2nd Baron Brownlow, who was made an earl in 1815 and held the lieutenancy until his retirement in 1852. The Custs traced their family back to the Middle Ages in the Parts of Holland, but they moved decisively up the social scale only in the seventeenth century and reached the uppermost echelon of the county in the eighteenth, when they inherited the

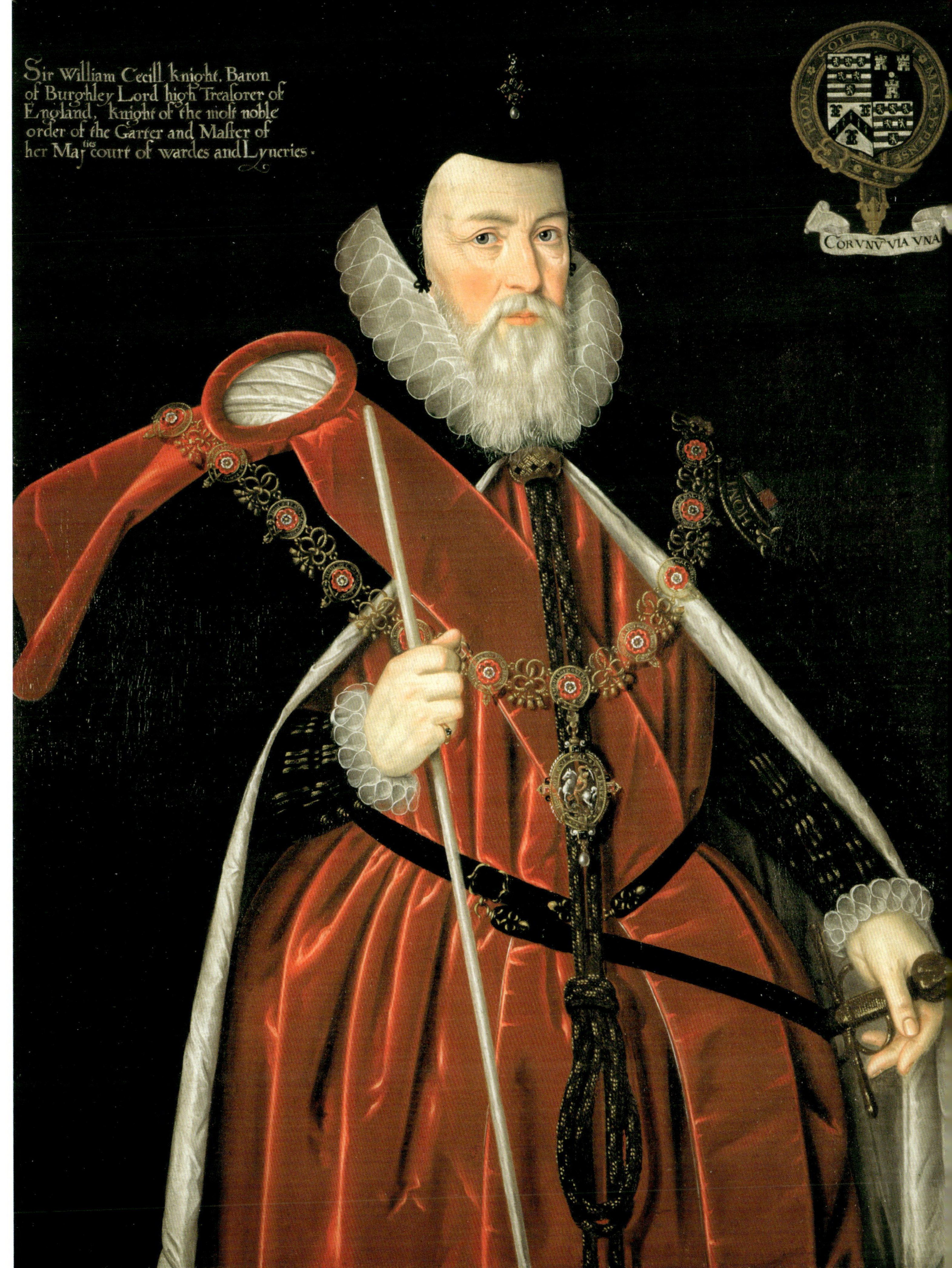
Sir William Cecill knight, Baron
of Burghley Lord high Treasorer of
England, knight of the most noble
order of the Garter and Master of
her Maj[ties] court of wardes and Lyveries.
HONI SOIT QUI MAL Y PENSE
CORVNV VIA VNA

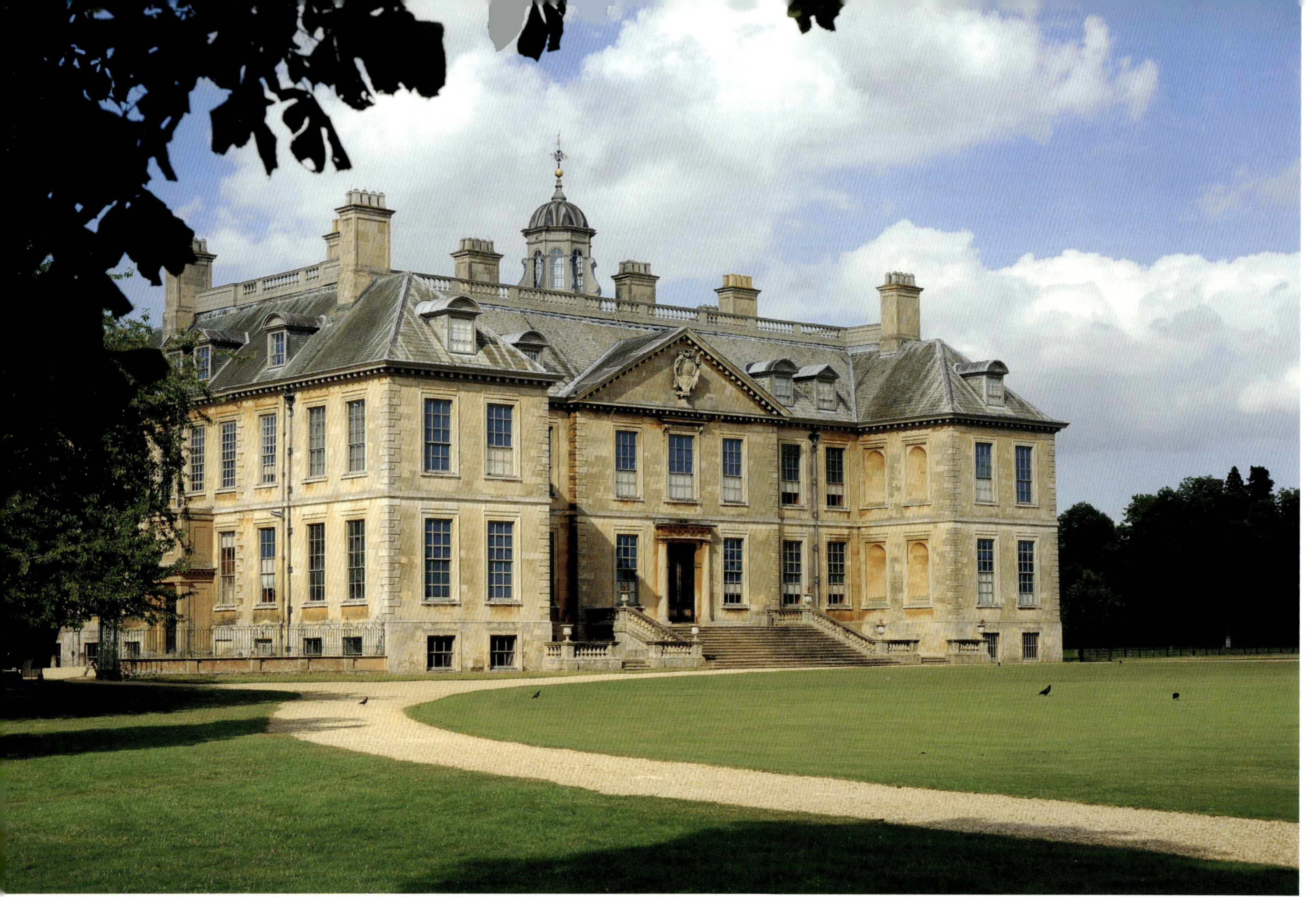

Belton House
Photo: Andrew Tryner, copyright Lincolnshire County Council

handsome seat of Belton, near Grantham, from the Brownlow family. Sir Brownlow Cust was created Baron Brownlow in 1776, in recognition of his father's services as Speaker of the House of Commons. In 1809 the 2nd Baron was an obvious choice of Lord Lieutenant for the government of the day. He was resident in the county, owned property in all three of its divisions, was likely to be a better man of business than his predecessor, and was a good Tory to boot.

Party politics continued to influence the choice of Lord Lieutenant in the mid nineteenth century. In 1852 Brownlow was followed by the Conservative Lord Granby, who conducted Lincolnshire's county business from Belvoir Castle until he resigned on succeeding his father as 6th Duke of Rutland in 1857. The lieutenancy was then given to Lincolnshire's leading Liberal peer, Charles Anderson-Pelham, 2nd Earl of Yarborough. The Pelhams had waited some time for this distinction. They had been major landowners in north Lindsey since the late sixteenth century, had achieved a peerage in 1794, and by the mid nineteenth century had built up an immense estate around their seat at Brocklesby. At over 50,000 acres it was equal in size to the county holdings of the Custs and the Willoughbys put together.

Burghley House
Photo: Andrew Tryner, copyright Lincolnshire County Council

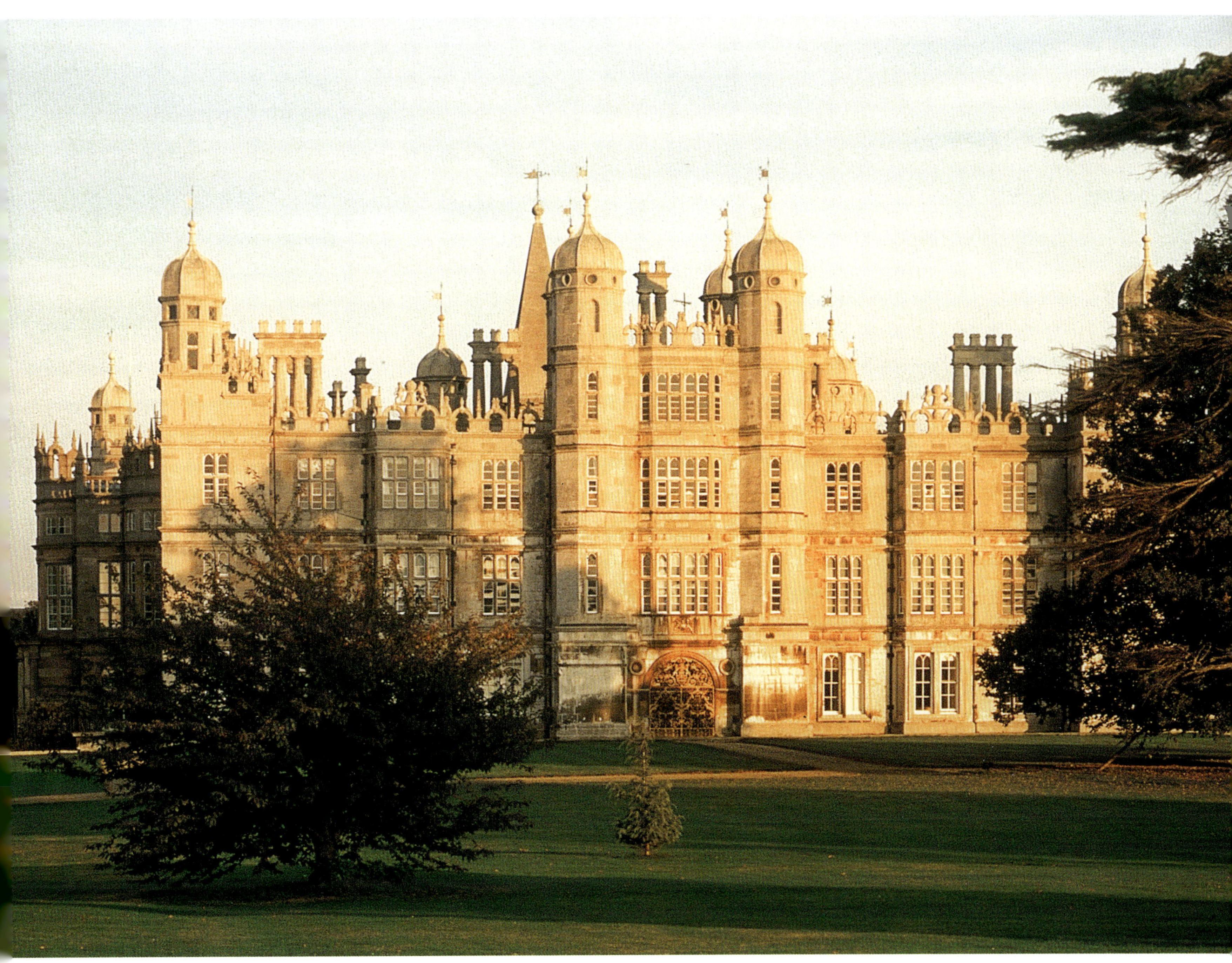

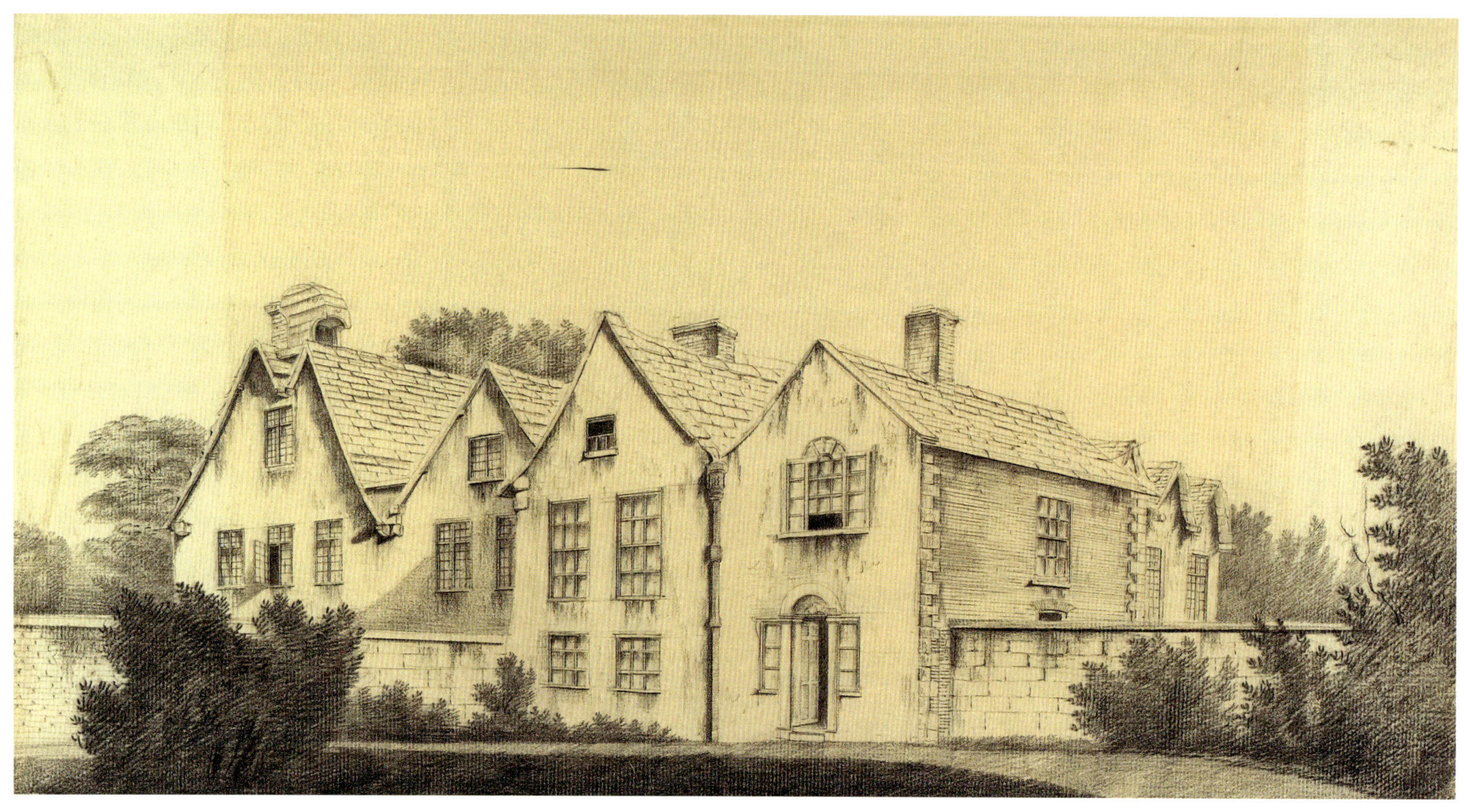

Jean-Claude Nattes (about 1765–1839)
Scrivelsby Hall, 1792
Drawing
Lincolnshire Libraries

OPPOSITE
The King's Champion Saddle, about 1760, probably used by John Dymoke at the Coronation of George III, 1760
Leather, covered with red silk velvet, ornamented with silver-gilt lace, braid and fringe
Private collection

Yarborough held the office for only five years. On his death in 1862 it went to another Liberal peer, Lord Aveland. The head of the Heathcote family, he held considerable property in Kesteven, acquired since the early eighteenth century, and his wife was the elder sister of the unmarried Lord Willoughby de Eresby of the day. Less ideally, he had no Lincolnshire seat of his own, the Heathcote house being Normanton in Rutland. As it turned out, his reign was as short as those of his two predecessors and when he died in 1867, under a Conservative government, it was back to the Brownlows.

For the next hundred years and more the lieutenancy remained with the same three families. The 3rd Earl Brownlow was followed in 1921 by the 5th Earl of Yarborough, in 1936 by the 6th Baron Brownlow (the earldom having expired with the 3rd Earl), and in 1950 by Lord Willoughby de Eresby, shortly to succeed his father as 3rd (and last) Earl of Ancaster. His grandfather, the 2nd Baron Aveland, had inherited both the Heathcote and Willoughby estates, and had been created Earl of Ancaster in 1892. Lord Ancaster was a greatly respected figure in the county, and the last Lord Lieutenant to be appointed from its old magnate families.

A word, more briefly, about the families who ranked below the great nobles, but on whom the county depended for many of its magistrates, members of parliament and other office-holders. In the Middle Ages the family most closely comparable to the Willoughbys in point of lineage and longevity were the Dymokes. In the fourteenth century they succeeded to Scrivelsby, near Horncastle,

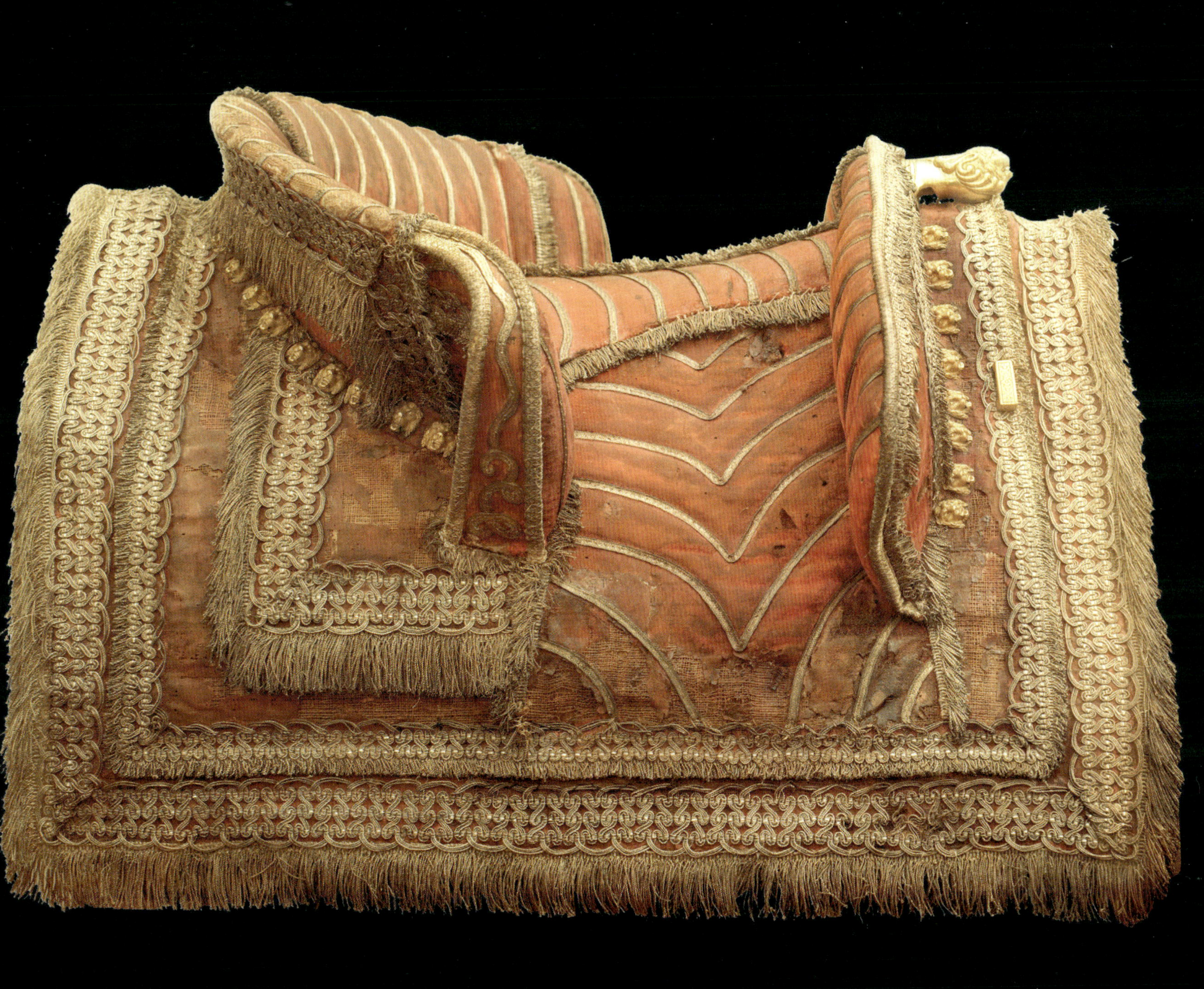

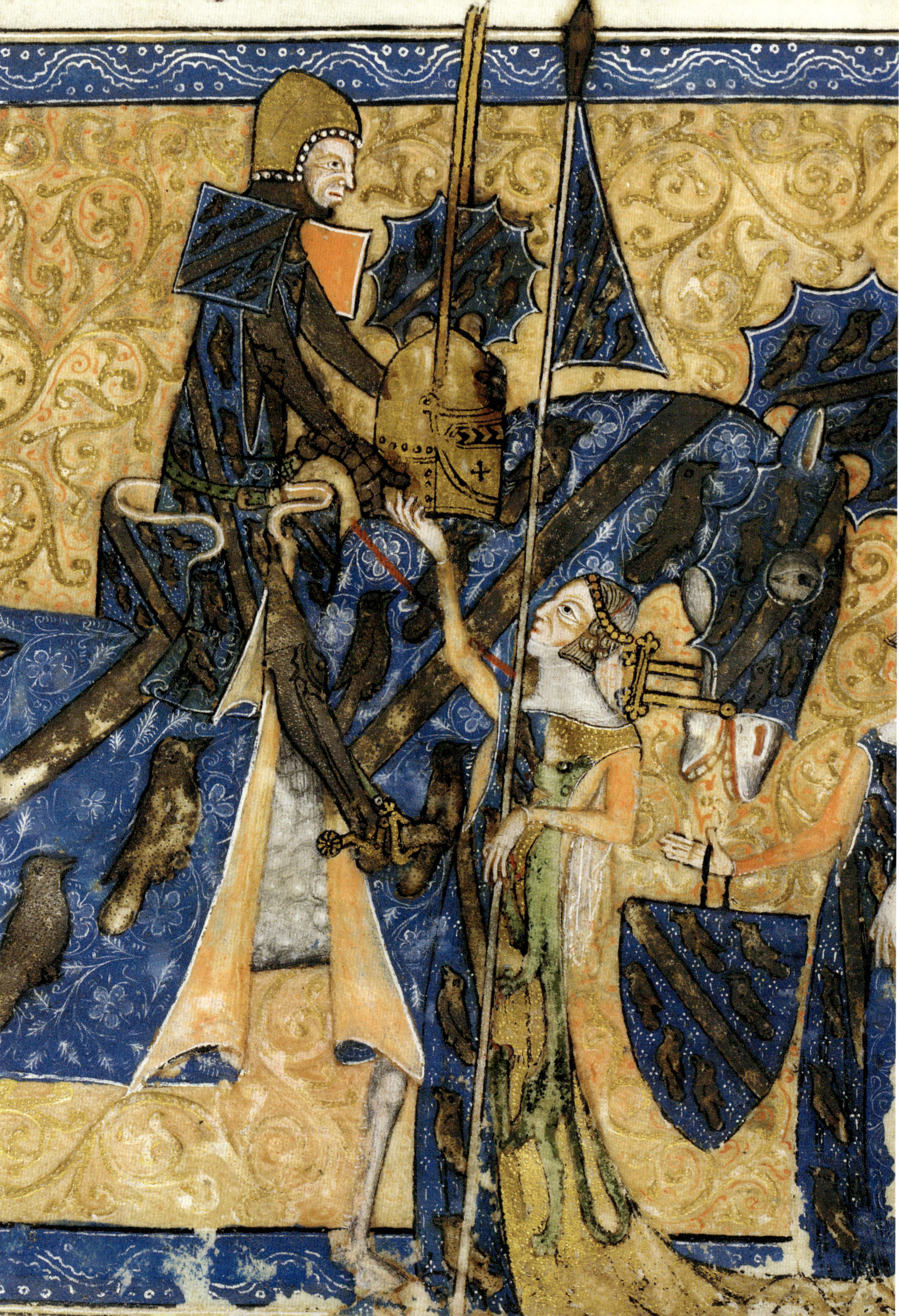

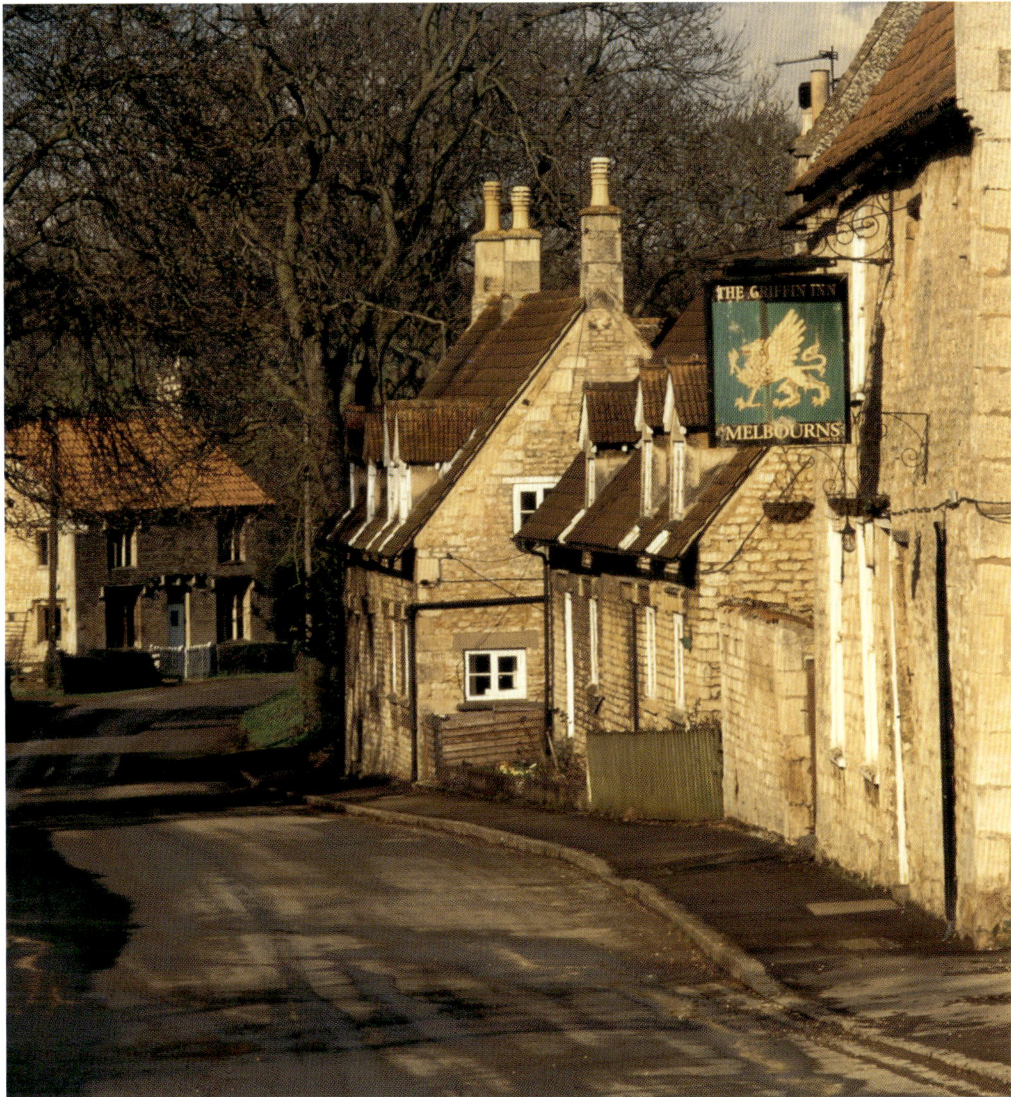

OPPOSITE

The Luttrell Psalter, about 1325–40

Sir Geoffrey Luttrell of Irnham and his wife Agnes (née Sutton)

Illuminated manuscript

British Library, Add MS 42130, f.202r

LEFT

Irnham village street

Photo: Andrew Tryner, copyright Lincolnshire County Council

part of the extensive estates of the Barons Marmion; they established their right to hold that manor from the Crown by attending the coronation as the sovereign's champion, ready to defend the royal title against all challengers. Perhaps generally too ready to resort to arms, the Dymoke family found itself on the losing side at various times of unrest and rebellion. It was the Civil War that finally caused the family's descent into the ranks of the lower gentry, though not its disappearance from the landed classes altogether.

Perhaps equally prominent in their day, though not nearly as long-lived as a gentry family, were the Luttrells. They inherited Irnham in south Kesteven from the Paynell family in the thirteenth century, and it was Sir Geoffrey Luttrell the third, soldier, landowner and supporter of the House of Lancaster, who commissioned the Luttrell Psalter (pp.64–79). The Irnham Luttrells were extinguished in the early fifteenth century, but at much the same period a junior branch began its long tenure of Dunster Castle in Somerset.

The Heneage Jewel, about 1595
Locket of enamelled gold, table-cut diamonds, Burmese rubies and rock crystal, enclosing a miniature of Queen Elizabeth I, painted by Nicholas Hilliard (1542–1619) and given by the Queen to Sir Thomas Heneage (about 1532–95), Vice-Chamberlain of the Household. It remained in the possession of the Heneage family until 1902.
Victoria and Albert Museum

Like the Willoughbys but unlike the Luttrells, the Heneages and the Monsons originated within the county. The Heneages have lived at Hainton, near Wragby, since the fifteenth century, and rose in the sixteenth through government office and (like the Duke of Suffolk) the acquisition of ex-monastic lands. By the nineteenth century they had a well-managed estate of over 10,000 acres in Lindsey. Edward Heneage, a Liberal and later Unionist politician, held the very appropriate office of Chancellor of the Duchy of Lancaster in Gladstone's 1886 ministry and received a peerage in 1894.

The Monsons were living in the Market Rasen district in the fourteenth century and built up estates in Lindsey, eventually settling at Burton-by-Lincoln. They made good local marriages in the sixteenth century, with members of the Tyrwhitt and Hussey families, secured a baronetcy in the early seventeenth, and joined the peerage as Barons Monson in 1728. Heavy sales in the early nineteenth century reduced their estates in the county from around 20,000 acres to under 7,000, but they made a recovery under the 7th Baron, who married the widow of the 2nd Earl of Yarborough and was made Viscount Oxenbridge in 1886.

This account has perforce ignored a number of old-established county families such as the Welbys and Thorolds, not to mention somewhat newer but very substantial ones such as the Chaplins, Vyners and Turnors. Like the county magnates, these families were in a flourishing state in the mid nineteenth century, and several held over 10,000 acres. But magnates and gentry alike were to suffer from two periods of agricultural depression, in the late nineteenth century and then again between the two World Wars. Even the Ancaster estate contracted: outlying properties were sold and Normanton was given up and demolished. Some gentry families sold up altogether, their estates being bought by absentee owners or large farmers.

The reasons for these changes were not just economic. County society was being transformed. New wealth, both urban and industrial, challenged the old, and deference went out of fashion. By the late twentieth century Lincolnshire was a different county from that over which the old magnate families had presided for so long. The histories of those families, however, remain inextricably connected with the history of Lincolnshire as a whole. And a great deal of that history is embedded in the family archives that in so many cases have been deposited in Lincolnshire Archives and elsewhere, and generously made available to the public.

Further reading

Sir Francis Hill, *Medieval Lincoln* (Cambridge 1948)

Sir Francis Hill, *Georgian Lincoln* (Cambridge 1966)

Richard Olney, *Lincolnshire Politics 1832–1885* (Oxford 1973)

Richard Olney, *Rural Society and County Government in Nineteenth-Century Lincolnshire* (Lincoln 1979)

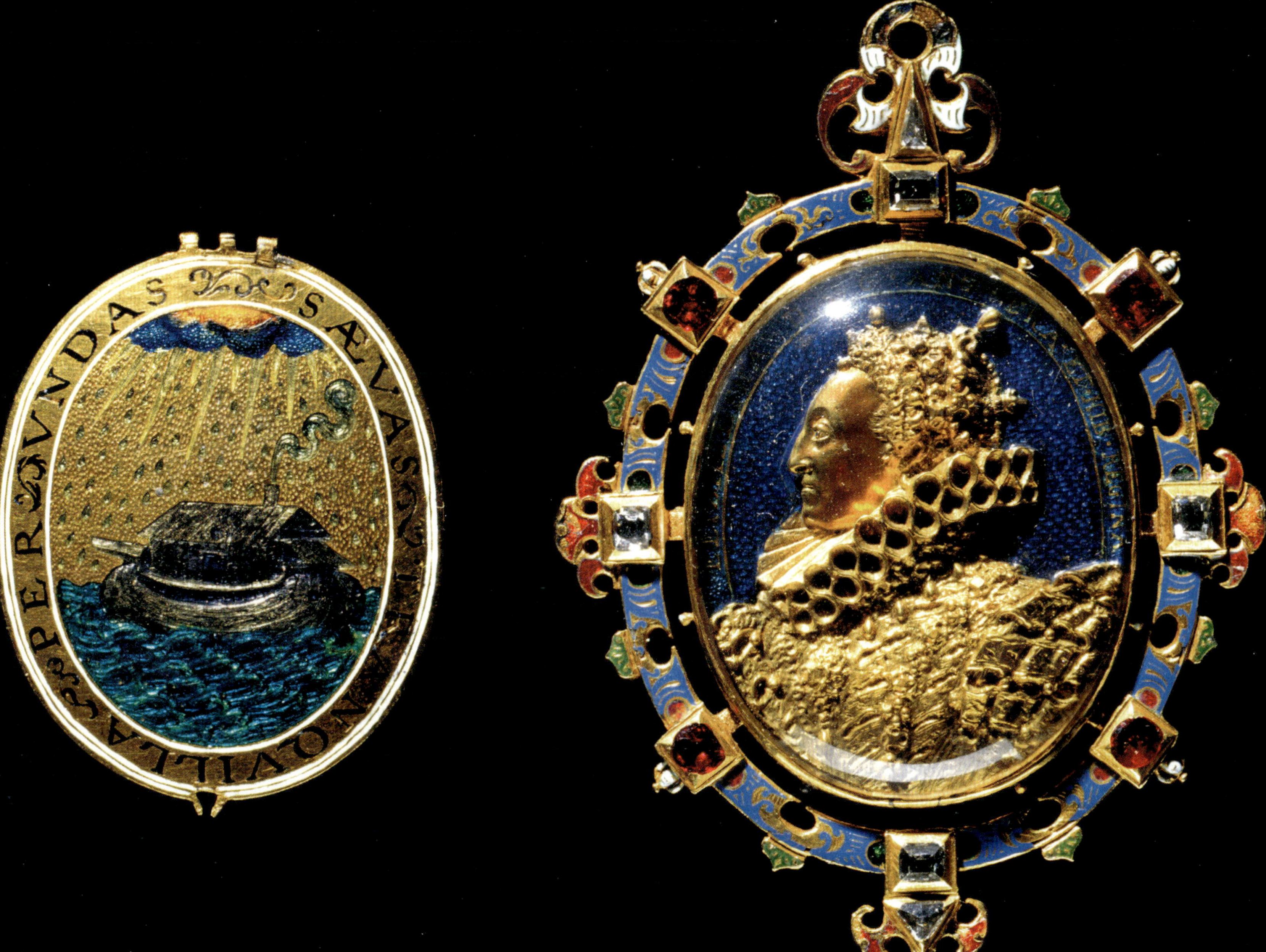
SÆVAS
PER VNDAS
NQVILLA

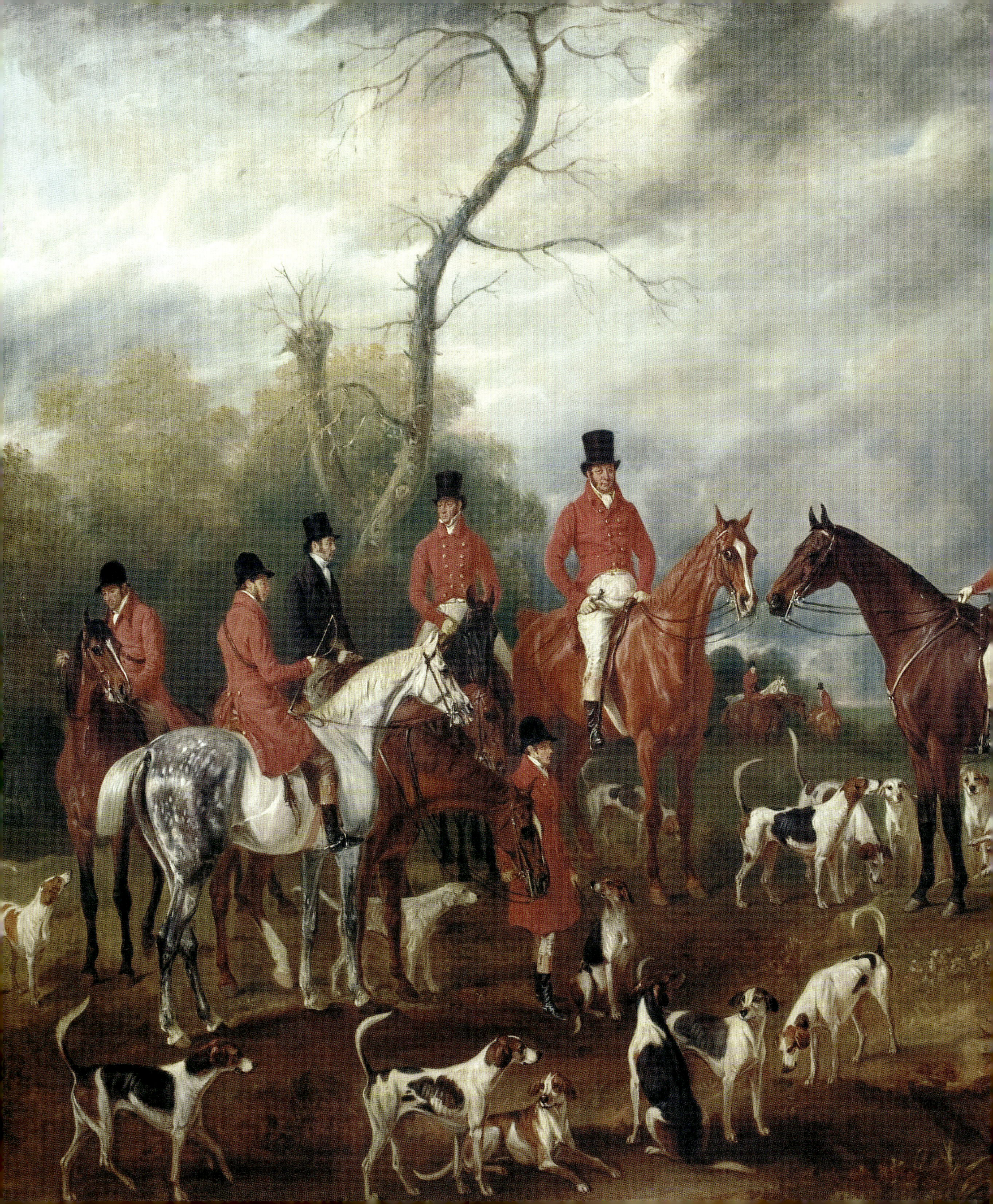

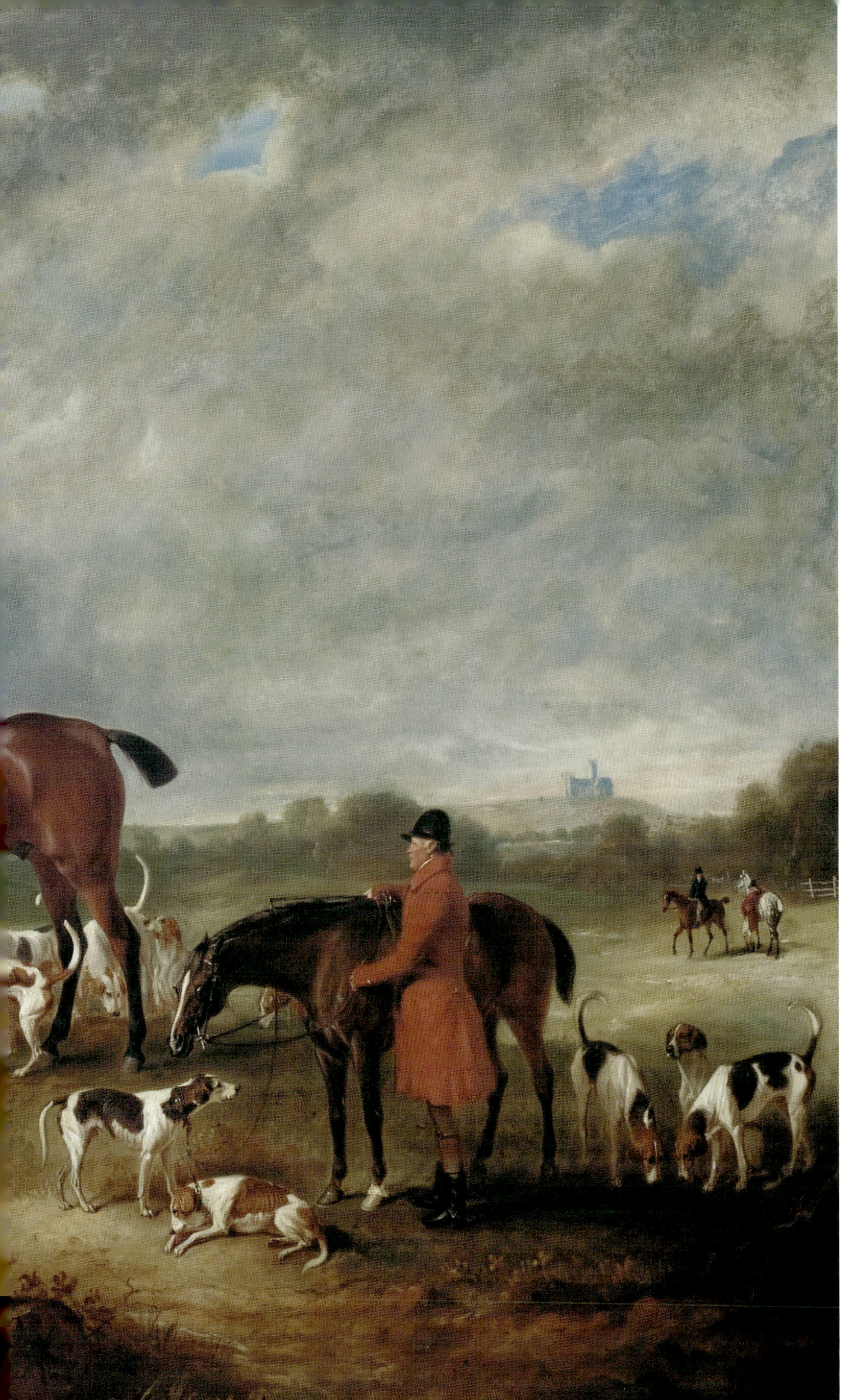

John Ferneley (1782–1860)
***The Burton Hunt*, 1830**
Oil on canvas
Usher Gallery, Lincoln

[illegible] are very rare – for in [illegible]

Some found on Marbles at Palmyra.

Also from Mr Hall a Member of the S A

Celts or Celtic Speares

Aldborough in Yorkshire were not long

those brass Instruments commonly called Celts

or Speare points wch were of Gold enam

Red. if so then probably the Whole wh

was in might be in this forme & for the

hunting or perhaps both. They w

Imagine the Ring at the Side of the C

a Belle. the Revd Mr Jo Lawrence in his New

Gardening fo. 192. 193 gives the figure of on

near Sunderland, Durham, wch he supposes

Battle Ax.

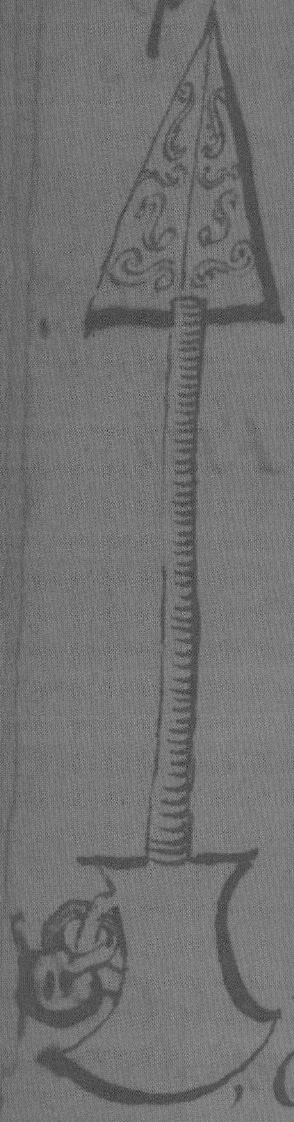

vide ad calcem Vol. 1. Lelandi Itin: Ed: Hearn

Lelandi Collect: P. 37. Ricus Rawlinson LLD. SR & A·S· S

Celtum antiquum romanum, Nullum habebat foramen,

Cuneus sive metallum netum annecteretur: utrinq tamen ad concavitas

Aeneus hunc infirmum ex extremitatem fissum ad utilitate ut mallei vi

facilius, expeditius q scinderet

East India Forts

Read proposals from Messrs Lambert

publishing their 6 Views of Forts in th

to ye East India Company to be Engrav

The history and achievements of the Spalding Gentlemen's Society

DIANA AND MICHAEL HONEYBONE

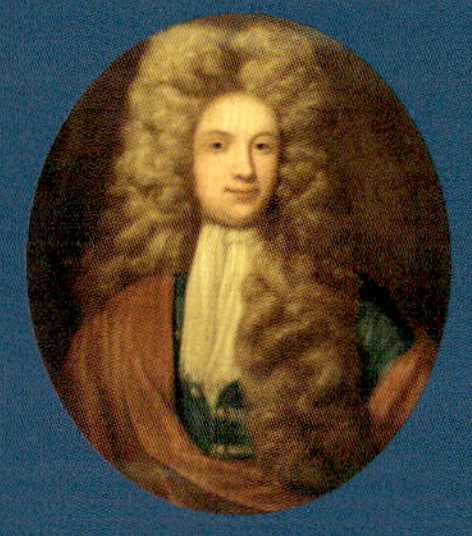

ON THE WALL of the Gentlemen's Society Museum in Spalding hangs a framed facsimile of Magna Carta, engraved in 1733. This engraving by John Pine was presented to the Society in December of that year by its Secretary and founder, the lawyer and antiquary Maurice Johnson. The Society's library possesses another beautiful creation by Pine, the two-volume edition of the poems of Horace, presented by the 2nd Duke of Buccleuch, grandson of the Duke of Monmouth, who was the Society's patron from 1743 to 1751 and Maurice Johnson's schoolfellow at Eton.

These two remarkable examples, from the Society's archive and library, epitomise its nature and activities. Founded in 1710 and flourishing today with over three hundred members, it exists, as its first minute book states, for 'supporting mutual Benevolence and ... Improvement in the Liberal Sciences and Polite Learning'. The Society, often referred to as the SGS, is the only British provincial learned society that has remained in existence for over three centuries. We can follow its regular meetings, with only a short break between 1875 and 1889, through the copious entries in the minute books and treasurers' accounts, and the hundreds of letters that are among the treasures of its archive.

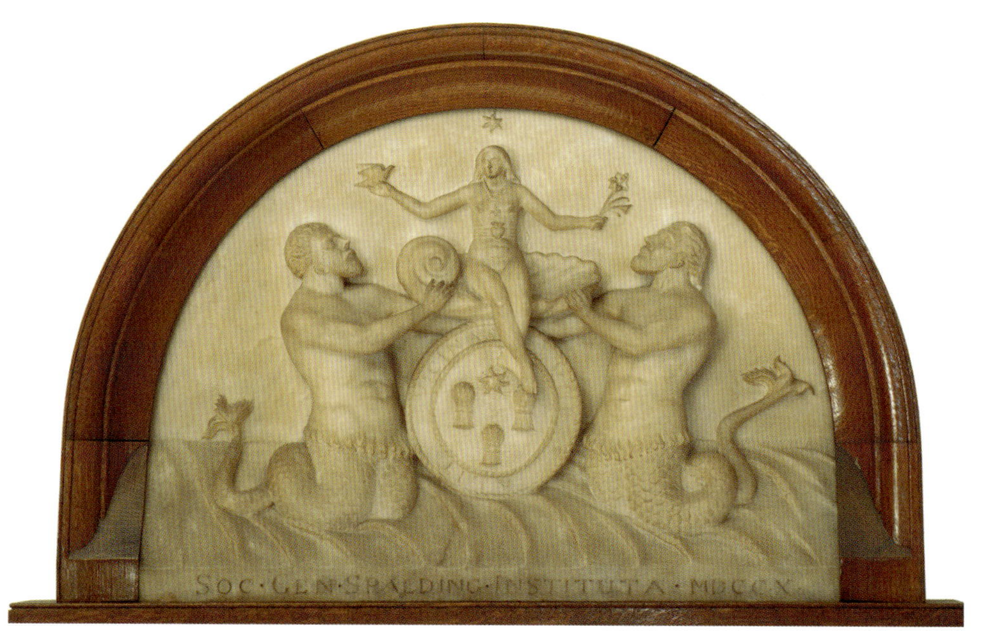

Coat of arms of the Spalding Gentlemen's Society designed by Maurice Johnson, 1746
Two tritons holding a shell on top of a shield bearing a star above three sheaves of corn, with a naked young woman seated on the shell, wearing a heart on a belt, a dove in her right hand and a flower in her left.
Spalding Gentlemen's Society

OPPOSITE
Spalding Gentlemen's Society Minute Book
Detail recording the meeting of 14 June 1733, at which an engraving of Magna Carta was shown to the Society
Spalding Gentlemen's Society, MB 1, f.88v

Fordham Bp. of Ely, & Pr & Convent of Ely, the sd. S. John Colvill
a his Wife – John Duke of Lancaster & Blanch his Wife &
late Countess of Derby.

Armes as Illumined twice at the beginning which Sr.
Colville Says he caused to be painted there —

The Notarial Mark on the back of Sr
Sr John Colvilles papal dispensation

An Account of the Copy of
King John's Magna Charta.
now engraved on a very large
Copper Plate & published
to perpetuate It.

West of the Innr Temple a Secr of that Soc. shewd Them
y of King John's Magna Charta On Vellum, done fro
preserv'd out of the Fire of the Cotton Library. by order of
gh Chancellor & Speaker of the House of Comons & Ld. C.J. of
ate, & the Armes of the Noble Men, Trustees for Its Perfor
emblazond in the Margin in Gold and proper Colours.

The Reverd the Presidt in the Chair & Eight other Regular Memb
& Mr Lawrence an Honorary Member Mr Calamy Jun permitt
to be present

awrence Shewd the Soc. Several Microscopical Observations with the

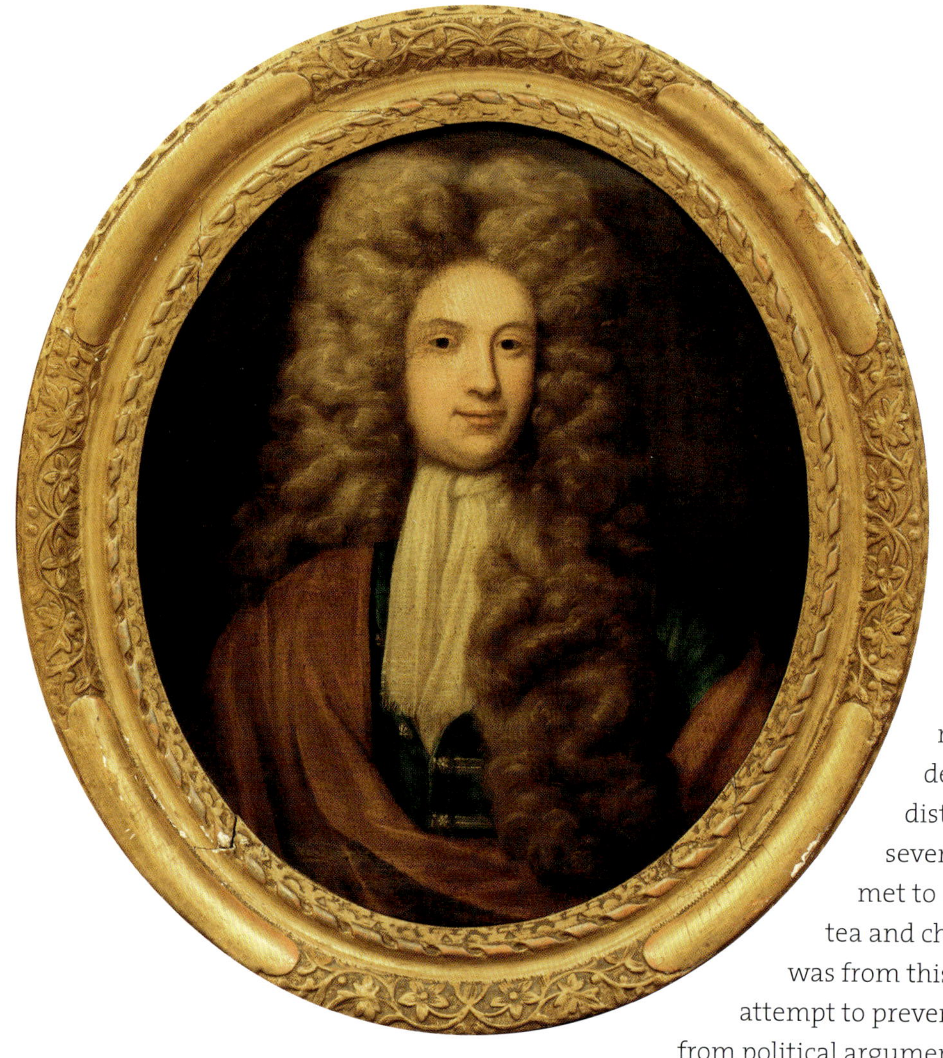

Unknown artist
***Maurice Johnson as a Young Man*, about 1710**
Oil on canvas
Spalding Gentlemen's Society

The purpose of this chapter is to record the events of its long history and achievements and to place it in the context of learned societies over the past three hundred years. The early eighteenth century, a notably sociable time, saw the invention of social groups known as 'literary societies', which meant at the time those concerned with literary or intellectual matters. At their heart lay social politeness, deemed essential following the terrible disturbances of civil war and revolution in seventeenth-century Europe. People, particularly men, met to drink the fashionable new beverages of coffee, tea and chocolate and to talk on almost every subject; it was from this background that the SGS grew. In a deliberate attempt to prevent unpleasantness and disruption resulting from political argument, two London men introduced a new form of literature, the magazine of essays designed to encourage courteous or polite discussion. First, Joseph Addison created the *Tatler* (1709–11) a title chosen to suggest gossip but in fact designed to calm extreme sentiments. This was followed by the *Spectator* (1711–14), co-founded by Addison and his friend Richard Steele.

Such journals became the staple reading matter of the SGS. Both Addison and Steele gave their approval to the foundation of the 'Gentlemen's Society', which gathered at Younger's Coffeehouse in Spalding to read the *Spectator* and discuss the essays it contained. 'Papers were taken in so long as they medled not with Politicks', wrote Johnson in the Society's Minute Book.

Johnson, a barrister, was also determined to put into practice a Parliamentary statute of 1708, the Parochial Libraries Act. The Society's Rules and Orders of 1742 state as one of its objects the 'raising and preserving & rendering of general Use a Publick Lending Library pursuant to the statute of the 7th of Queen Ann'. Accordingly, the SGS set about saving the Spalding Parochial Library, still accessible today in a splendid bookcase in the Society's rooms. Discovering that the Spalding Grammar School possessed only one book, Johnson rectified that by building up a school library. Most importantly, he developed a magnificent library

Hilkiah Burgess (1776–1868)
***Spalding Grammar School*, 1820**
Watercolour
Spalding Gentlemen's Society

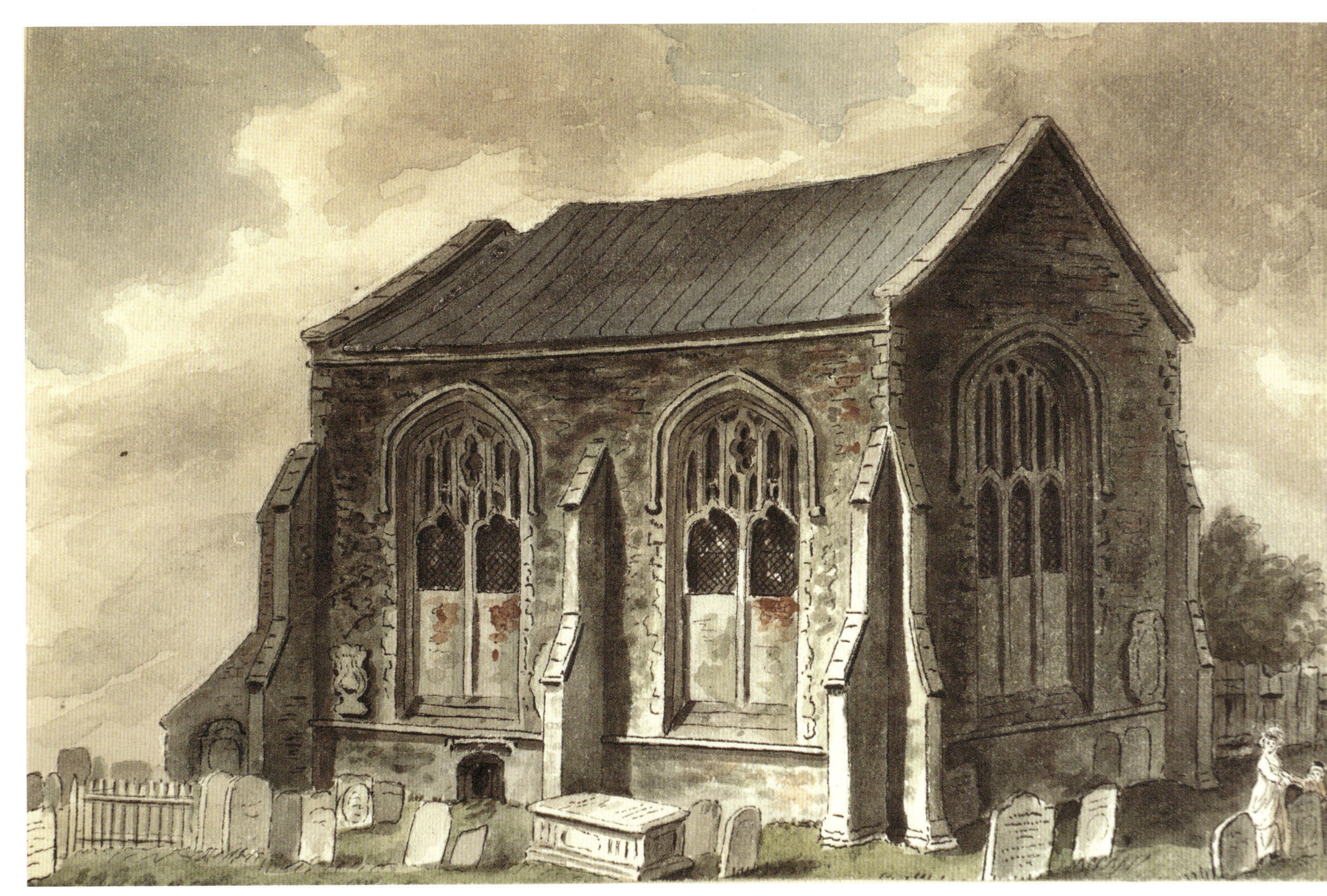

Unknown artist
***The Society's Meeting Room at Mr Cox's Rooms*, Spalding, about 1851**
Print
Spalding Gentlemen's Society

OPPOSITE
Spalding Gentlemen's Society Minute Book
Detail recording the meeting of 25 December 1735
Spalding Gentlemen's Society, MB 1, f.96

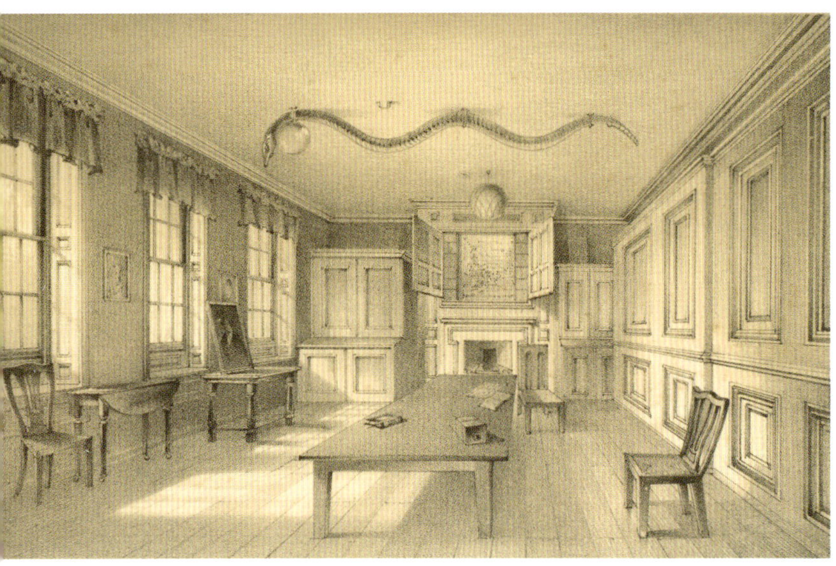

of over a thousand volumes for his Society by donation and purchase. Johnson ensured the library's survival by making, in his will, a legal connection between the salary of the Grammar School headmaster and the maintenance of the Society's library. Today the Headmaster of Spalding Grammar School is still ex officio the Society's Librarian.

The Society as originally constituted had two types of member. Regular members paid monthly subscriptions and were expected to attend the weekly Thursday meetings. Extra-regular or honorary members, often living too far away to attend, were asked to subscribe a book to the library and to contribute to the Society's proceedings through correspondence. Highly significant intellectuals participated in this way, most notably Sir Isaac Newton and Sir Joseph Banks (pp.138–44) in the eighteenth century and Alfred Lord Tennyson (pp.162–77) in the nineteenth. Johnson proudly listed two Presidents of the Royal Society, Sir Hans Sloane and Martin Folkes, as members. Folkes was also President of the Society of Antiquaries. A number of members of both these national societies were corresponding members of the SGS.

What did the SGS do in its early years? One way to understand this is to list the activities of a typical meeting, such as those recorded on 25 December (Christmas Day) 1735. A civil servant at the Tower of London, William Bogdani, sent an account of the formation of pearls. The SGS curator, local surgeon Michael Cox, described an operation to extract a knife blade from a man's thigh. The Society was shown a beautiful example of Chinese writing, still in its archive today. Johnson read an account of the Runic alphabet by the Swedish natural philosopher Anders Celsius, also a member, and showed drawings of 'celts or celtic spears', which were then copied into the minute book. The Society discussed a proposal they had received for publishing six views of forts in the East Indies; finally, Johnson exhibited a cast of the seal of the medieval Gaywood Hospital, Norfolk, and a 1662 Court of the Exchequer writ for the suppression of smugglers.

These weekly meetings took place in the Society's Spalding meeting rooms. When Younger's Coffeehouse proved too limited, the Society moved to the Town Hall and then to a rented building surviving from the medieval priory. In the 1740s

Runic Alphabets

Mr Johnson Secr. comd to the Soc. Mons. Celsius professor of Upsal in Sweden & Member of the ~~Royal Soc.~~ Antiquarian Society Lond. his Runic Alphabets both of ye Vulgar & Helsingic Character wch latter are very rare – & as Mr B Bell has observed not much unlike some found on Marbles at palmyra.

Celts or Celtic Speares

also from Mr Hall a Member of the sd Antiq. Soc. That at Aldborough in Yorkshire were not long since found some of those brass Instruments comonly called Celts & with them 2 Cuspides or Speare points wch were of Gold enamelled with Green & Red. if so then probably the whole when the Woden Shaft was in might be in this forme & for the uses either of War or hunting or perhaps both. They who think thus do Imagine the Ring at the side of the Celt was for the hanging a Bell. the Revd Mr Jno Lawrence in his New System of Agriculture & Gardening fo. 192. 193 gives the figure of one found at Bp Weremouth near Sunderland, Durham, wch he supposes to have been a Danish Battle Ax.

vide ad calcem Vol. 1. Lelandi Itin: Ed: Hearnii, et Praefat: suam ad Lelandi Collect: P. 37. Ricus Rawlinson LLD. SRS A. L. Socu secum Oxonium advexit Celtim antiquum romanum, Nullum habebat foramen, uti nec Ansam qua sive filum, sive metallum netum annecteretur. Utrinque tamen est Concavitas quaedam, quae manubrium hunc in finem ax extremitatem fissum adulit(?) ut mallei vi seu Lapidem, seu lignum facilius, expeditiusque scinderet

Cuneus Aeneus

of this Forme

East India Forts

Read proposals from Messrs Lambert & Scott painters for publishing their 6 Views of Forts in the East India, belongs to ye East India Company to be Engraved by Mr Gerd Vandergucht –

Seale of Gaywood Hospital devoted to St Mary Magdalen by Som: good Penitent.

He also Shewd the Society a fine Cast of a Large Circular Seale representing a Woman in a pensive posture, with Rays around her head, with a Crucifix before her, a Book in her Right hand, her Left on her Brest, & a Small Urne or Vessell called alabastrinum how this being usualy mad: of it (illegible) on a Table, around

✠ SIGIL·HOSPITII·SCÆ·MARIÆ·MAGDALENÆ. IN·GAYWOOD. NORF. –

Writ of Assistants for Suppress Smugglers hereabouts

And from the Coadjutor to this Soc. Wm Dodd Deputy Customer of Spalding) a Writt of Assistants under the Seale of the Court of Excheqr authorizd by 13 & 14 Car. 2. Cap XI. S 5. and Sent him & Mr Gatehouse ye Dep: Comptr for the Suppression of Smugglers –

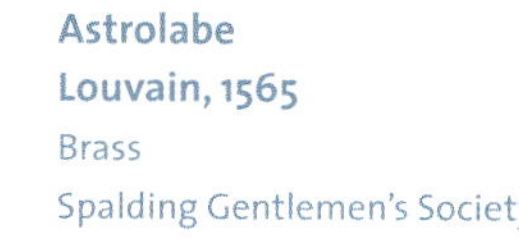

Astrolabe
Louvain, 1565
Brass
Spalding Gentlemen's Society

the Society moved to Holyrood or Gayton House, next door to Johnson's home, Ayscoughfee Hall. After 1755 it set up in rooms owned by Michael Cox, on the other side of the river, where it stayed until 1875, becoming mainly a book-lending society with lectures from time to time. Following a short hiatus of fifteen years, the Society was brilliantly revived from 1889 by Dr Marten Perry, a doctor at Spalding Hospital, who in 1910 organised the construction of the present Society building, designed to provide a meeting place, library and museum. The regular weekly meetings were re-established and continue to this day.

All this time, from 1712 to 1910, the Society's collections of artefacts, archives and books had, amazingly, survived as distinct catalogued collections. The original library, though today still separately housed in a splendid bookcase, is now augmented by several other collections, notably those of the Spalding Mechanics' Library and Newark Lending Library, both obtained in the early twentieth century. The present museum retains some of the original eighteenth-century items, such as a 1761 reflecting telescope and an armillary sphere given in 1751 by Thomas Hawkes of Norwich, and has been added to by extensive donations of fascinating items relating to the history of Spalding and its surroundings.

One eighteenth-century feature of the Society has sadly diminished: its music concerts. For twenty years in the 1730s and 1740s, musical members gave an annual anniversary concert. On 31 August 1738 'The Gentlemen of the Musical meeting … performed a Consert of Musick … both Vocal and Instrumental with which & Wine, Teas & Coffee the Ladies and Gentlemen who favourd the Society with their company at Mr Everards were treated by the Society as Usual upon this Occasion'. They listened to music by Dionisio Zamparelli, Pietro Antonio Locatelli and George Frideric Handel, and songs set by the Society's own composer, Dr Musgrave Heighington of Yarmouth.

Whilst the music may have diminished, over the years the Society's archives have become more and more extensive, including hundreds of letters, an outstanding series of minute books, many manuscript dissertations and a detailed set of

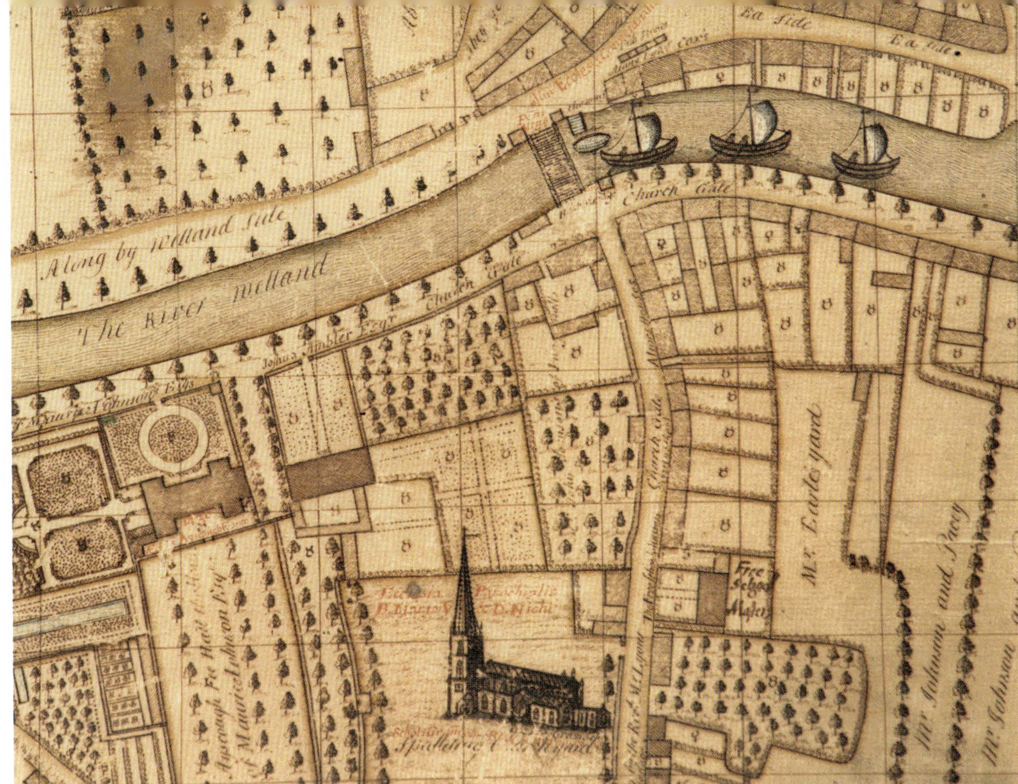

John Grundy (1696–1748)
Map of Spalding, 1732
Detail showing the parish church and Ayscoughfee Hall, home of Maurice Johnson
Ink on paper
Spalding Gentlemen's Society

treasurer's accounts from 1720 to 1813. To these have been added, during the twentieth century, archive collections such as that relating to local Methodism and a remarkable range of charters deposited when the Society became a local repository for national records in the 1920s. In addition to these, the Society holds large collections of stamps, coins, specimens of natural history and military memorabilia, together with a series of prints, maps, posters and drawings. Although some items of the original collection, such as the *hortus siccus* (dried garden) of preserved plants, have not survived, it still reflects the original intention of its creators; like its contemporary in Oxford, the Ashmolean Museum, it was intended as a place for active study. It would be difficult to find its equal among provincial societies.

It is now increasingly appreciated that the Society's collection is outstanding and work is under way to maintain the archives using the most effective modern techniques. Plans are under discussion to digitise vital items such as the minute books, so preserving the originals and making the texts electronically available to a wider public.

The fortunes of the Spalding Gentlemen's Society have fluctuated over three hundred years. Although it has diminished in activity from time to time, it has never ceased to exist, preserve its collections and add to them. There have always been those on hand, like the Revd J.H. Marsden, Secretary in the 1830s, and Marten Perry, President in the 1900s, to revive its fortunes. Diligent curators, presidents and councils have maintained the buildings and their contents. Today a keen body of men and women (for women were admitted as members in 2007, as Maurice Johnson had originally hoped in the 1730s) work together to keep this astonishing collection, make it available for the public and preserve it so that it, and the Society, can continue into the twenty-first century. Maurice Johnson would have approved.

Further reading

Michael Honeybone, 'Sociability, Utility and Curiosity in the Spalding Gentlemen's Society, 1710–1760', in *From Natural Philosophy to Natural Science, 1700–1900*, eds D.M. Knight and M.D. Eddy (Aldershot 2005)

Diana and Michael Honeybone (eds), *The Correspondence of the Spalding Gentlemen's Society, 1710–1761* (Lincoln Record Society 99, 2010)

Diana and Michael Honeybone (eds), *The Correspondence of William Stukeley and Maurice Johnson, 1714–1754* (Lincoln Record Society 104, 2014)

Dorothy Owen (ed.), *The Minute-Books of the Spalding Gentlemen's Society, 1712–1755* (Lincoln Record Society 73, 1981)

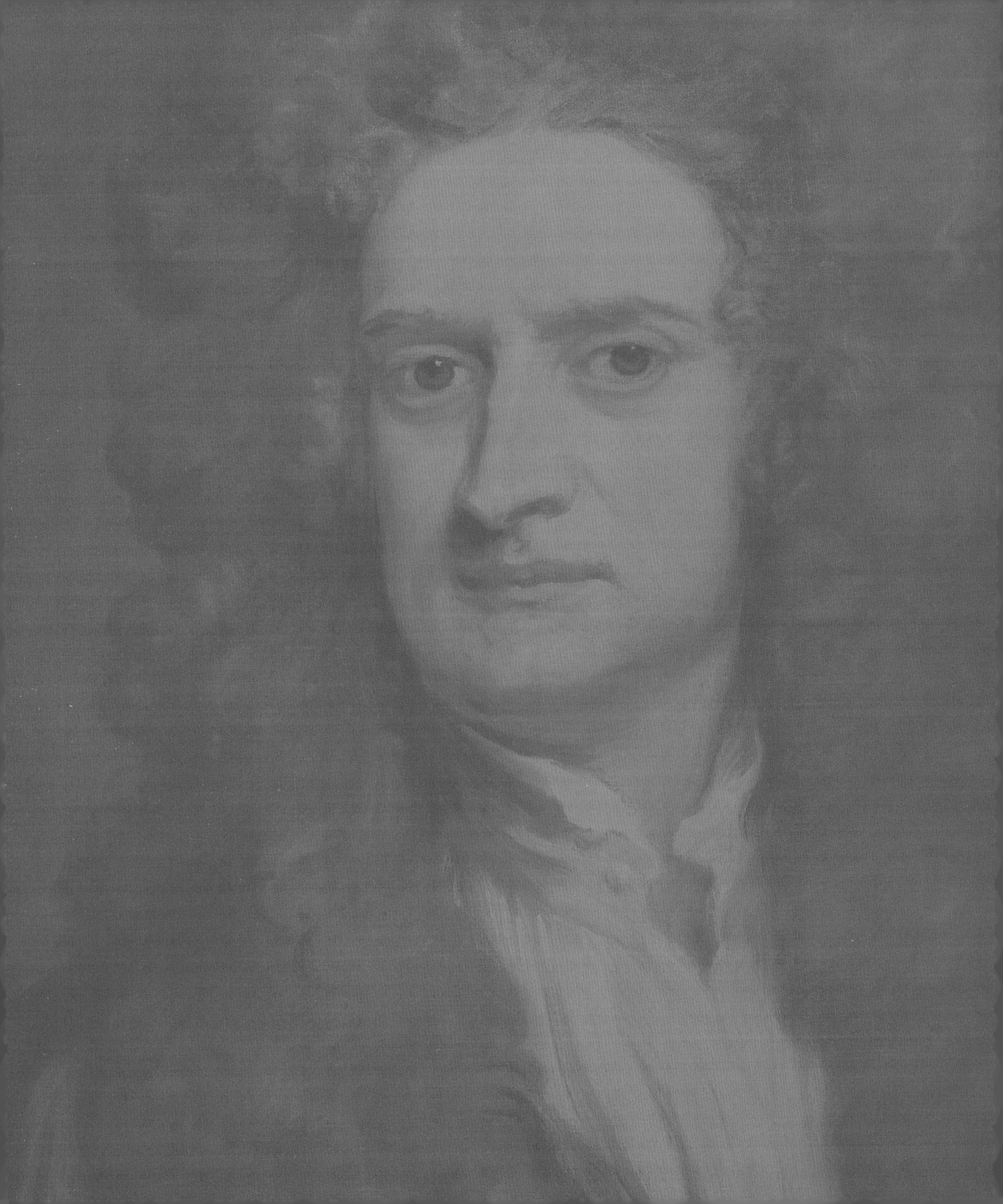

Lincolnshire's greatest mathematicians

MARK HOCKNULL

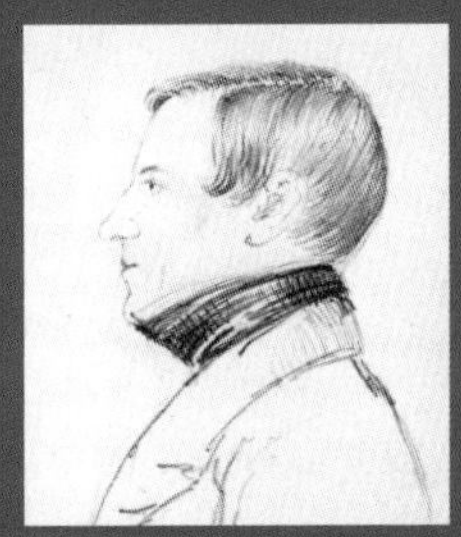

ON THURSDAY 5 FEBRUARY 1835 a nineteen-year-old Lincoln-born man delivered an address to the Lincoln Mechanics' Institute entitled 'On the Genius and Discoveries of Sir Isaac Newton'. The address was delivered at an event to mark the gifting of a bust of Newton to the Mechanics' Institute by Lord Yarborough and took place in Grey Friars' Chapel before a capacity audience of members of the Institute and prominent citizens of Lincoln. Every Victorian schoolboy knew that Sir Isaac Newton was a mathematical genius without rival and most would have been able to give a basic account of Newton's central discoveries in mathematics and natural philosophy. Indeed, the young man's address, as befitted that of a nineteenth-century Englishman, lauded Newton as the inventor of differential calculus and praised him as the possessor of a 'calm, patient, all-surmounting genius'. Both the age of the speaker and his command of his subject matter were sources of amazement to the audience. He carried his appreciation of Newton's work beyond the general account, even to the extent of offering a critique or evaluation of the weaknesses of Newton's approach to mathematical language. The young man went on, nine years later, to win the Royal Society's first-ever Gold Medal for Mathematics for a paper he wrote describing a new method for solving differential equations that he had recently discovered. The young man's name was George Boole. Whilst Newton is rightly remembered today as the discoverer of the inverse square law of gravitation, and for his invention, along with the German mathematician Gottfried Leibniz, of calculus, George Boole is more often forgotten than honoured today. Yet his contributions to mathematics and to modern life are no less significant than those of Newton himself. It is Boolean mathematical logic, with its binary system of 'on or yes' (1) and 'off or no' (0) that underpins today's computer technology and there is scarcely an electrical device that does not deploy the now near-universal symbol of 1 and 0 on its power switch.

Isaac Newton was born on Christmas Day 1642 according to the calendar in use in England at the time, though throughout the rest of Europe the date was 4 January 1643. A tiny and sick baby, as he described himself in later life, it was thought at the time of his birth that he would be unlikely to survive. His father, also called Isaac, a yeoman farmer who had inherited the Manor at Woolsthorpe, had died three months before his birth. His mother, Hannah Ayscough, was a member of the lower gentry. Whilst his mother had received a rudimentary education, his father was illiterate and unable to sign his own name. Newton would almost

Woolsthorpe Manor
Photo: S. Haimes

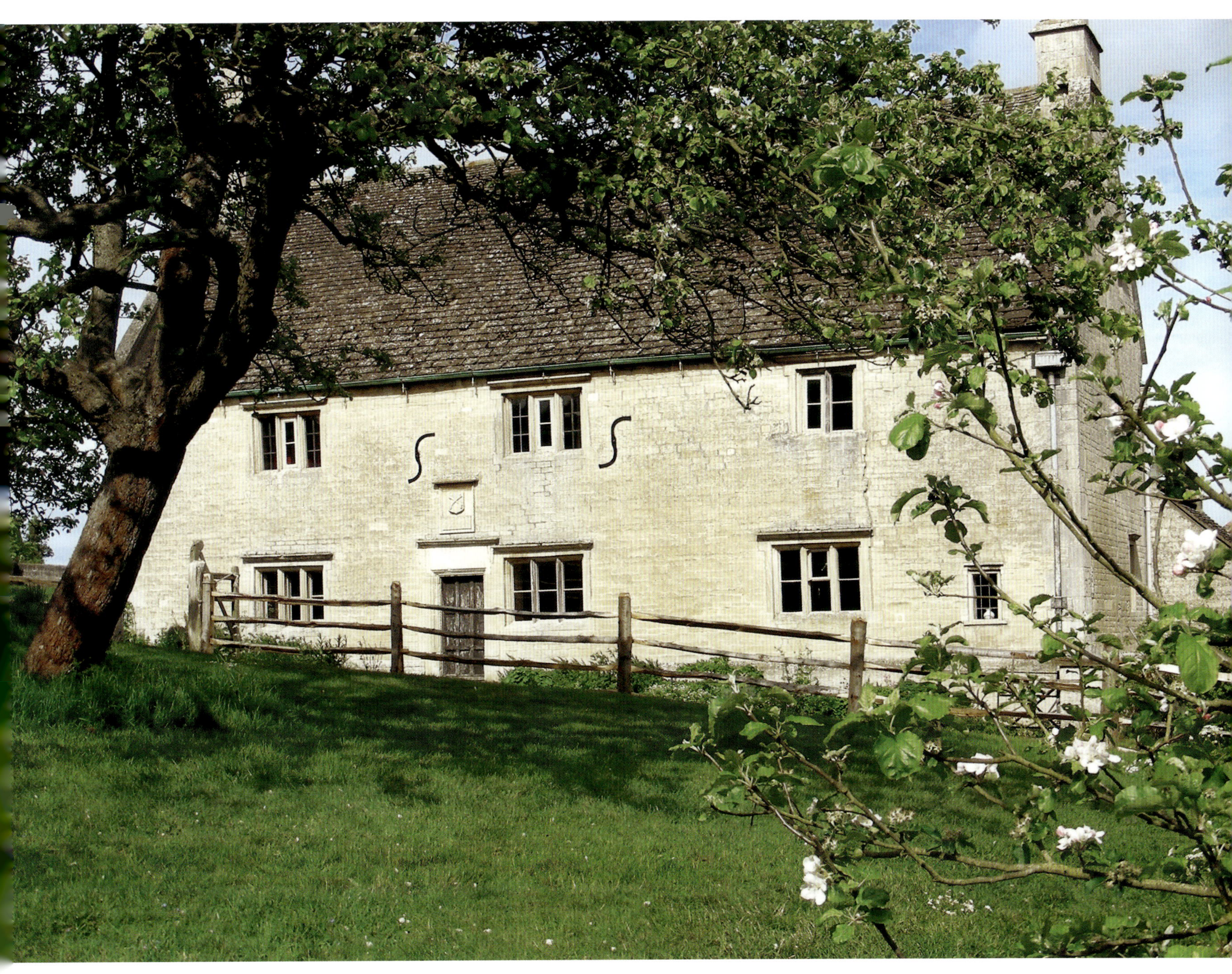

The alleged inscription by Sir Isaac Newton (1642–1727) into the windowsill of the library at Grantham grammar school
Photo: Andrew Tryner, copyright Lincolnshire County Council

BELOW
Trinity College Cambridge, 1690
From *Cantabrigia Illustrata* by David Loggan (1634–92)
Woolsthorpe Manor, Grantham

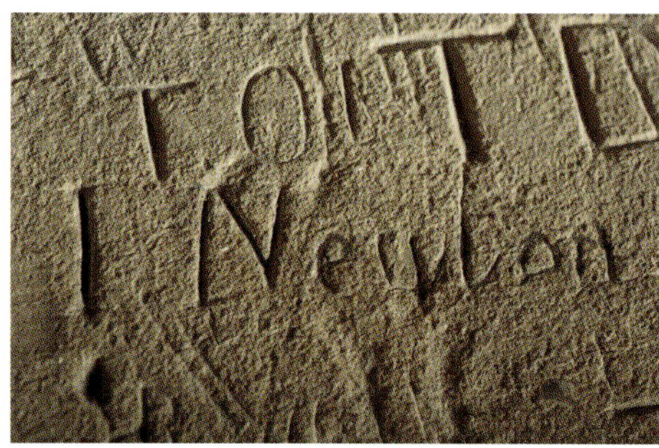

certainly have been destined for the life of a yeoman farmer himself, had it not been for the intervention of Henry Stokes, Headmaster of Grantham Grammar School, which Newton attended as a teenager. Stokes spotted the boy's potential and prevailed upon his mother to allow him to continue his education. William Stukeley, Newton's biographer, observes of Newton that 'philosophy absorbed all his thoughts' and his mother is said to have been 'not a little offended by his bookishness'. From Grantham, Newton went to Trinity College, Cambridge, arriving in there on 5 June 1661 and occupying the position of 'subsizar'. This was a lowly

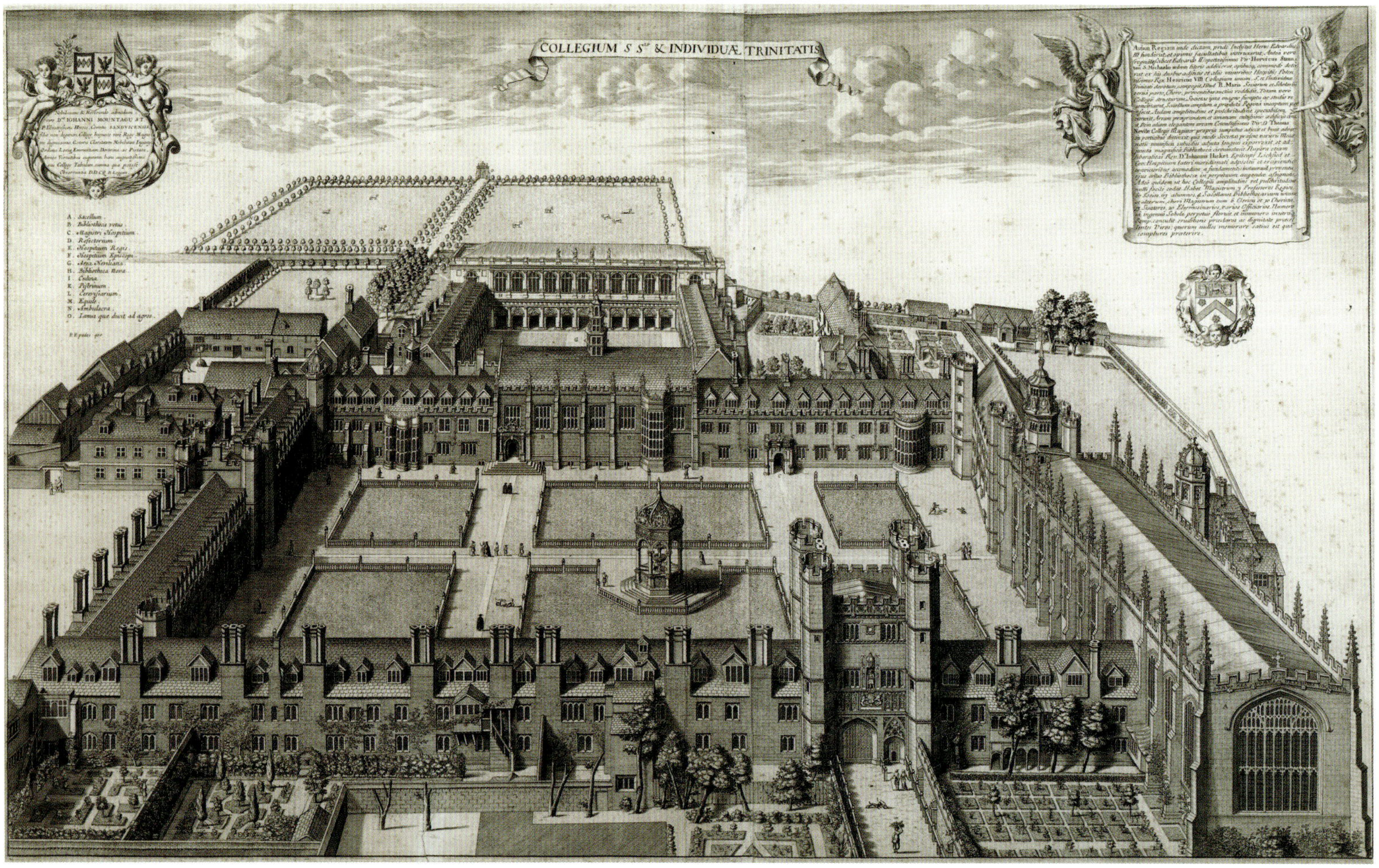

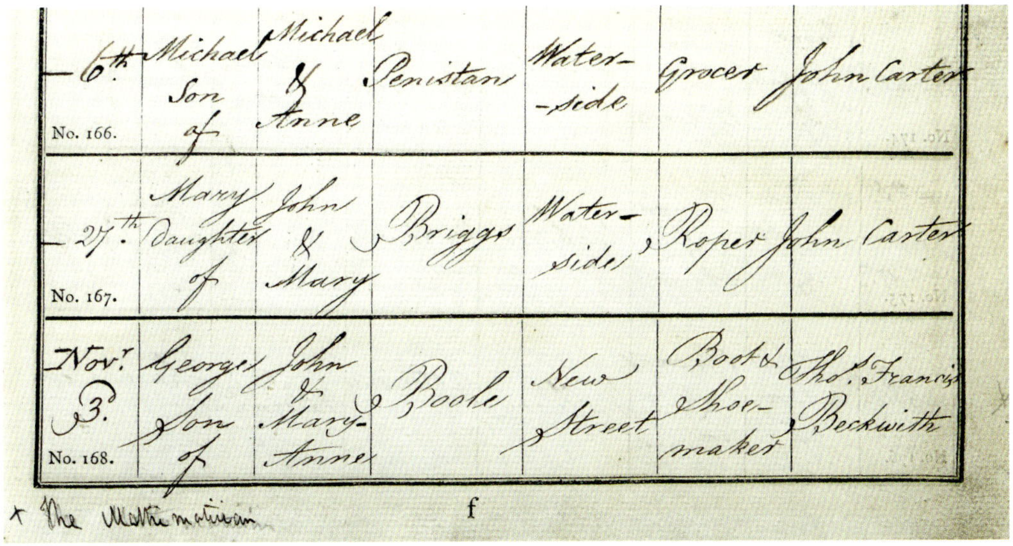

George Boole's baptism record in the register of St Swithin parish, Lincoln
Lincolnshire Archives, St Swithin's Par 1/7, p.21

status, for in effect subsizars were servants to the fellows and wealthier students. Considering the wealth that his mother had at her disposal, this almost menial role occupied by her son in his early years at Cambridge is a little strange, indicative perhaps of a desire not to encourage Newton's academic side or possibly even of resentment at his removal from the management of the farm at Woolsthorpe. We know from Newton's own account of his life that he had a difficult relationship with his mother during his teenage years. Perhaps this is connected with his status upon arriving in Cambridge.

George Boole was born on 2 November 1815. He was the first-born of a struggling shoemaker, John Boole, a man more interested in creating scientific instruments than in making and repairing shoes. As a consequence, young George was forced to leave school before the age of sixteen and never became an undergraduate. He taught himself languages, mathematics and natural philosophy. After his father's business failed, George Boole supported the family by becoming an assistant teacher. By 1834, still aged only nineteen, Boole founded his own school in Free School Lane, Lincoln, and later, in 1840, at No. 3 Pottergate. The young Boole had established himself as a well-respected local schoolmaster with sufficient income to support his family. Not content with this reasonably comfortable and respected position, Boole began to produce some original mathematical work. He was almost certainly facilitated in this by his capacity for languages that enabled him to read European mathematicians in their own tongue and thus benefit from insights that were unavailable to many a professional British-educated mathematician of the nineteenth century. This was the source of one of his critiques of Newton in that first public lecture, for at the time European mathematicians used a set of symbols in calculus different from those deployed by Newton. Boole preferred the European system, because it made manipulating its symbols easier to follow in logical sequence. This system, rather than Newton's own, is now almost universally adopted.

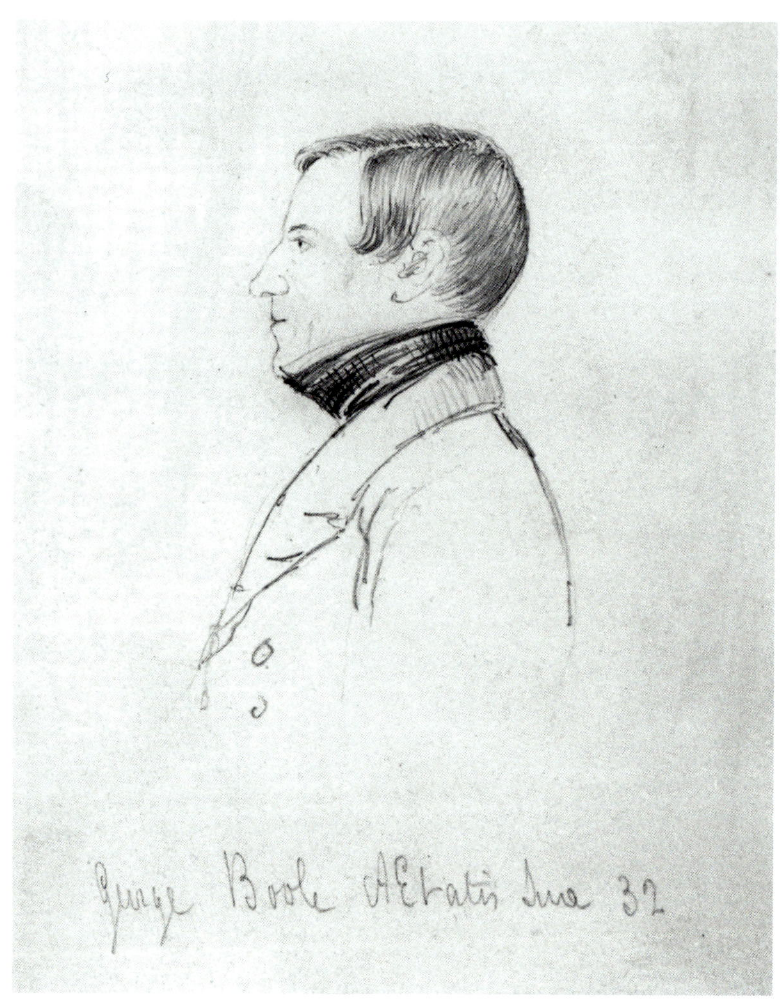

Unknown artist
***George Boole (1815–64)*, 1847**
Pencil on paper
National Portrait Gallery, London

The year 1846 proved a turning point for Boole. Up until this time his responsibilities to his family had been his priority but increasingly he felt the pull of mathematics and the desire to make this his profession. Already in possession of the Royal Society's Gold Medal for mathematics, Boole resolved to apply for a professorship at one of the Queen's Colleges then being founded in Ireland. With the support of many of his mathematical friends in Cambridge, and to the pride and delight of the citizens of Lincoln, who held a public dinner in his honour and presented him with a silver inkwell, Boole was appointed to the professorship at Cork in August 1849, taking up the appointment in November of the same year.

There is an element of the autodidact in Newton's mathematical education and career also. At first his education was the standard one for a Cambridge undergraduate, including a substantial amount of theological literature as well as the works of Aristotle. It seems, however, that Newton supplemented this with a much deeper study of mathematics than was provided for in the standard seventeenth-century curriculum. Records of his time at Cambridge suggest a much more carefree life than that lived by George Boole. A small notebook he kept as an undergraduate reveals how he spent both time and money. As well as the usual things required by a seventeenth-century student, Newton purchased a watch and a chessboard and pieces, and paid an annual subscription of sevenpence for access to the tennis court. Surviving records also indicate that Newton was unique among undergraduates in that he quickly began to lend money to his fellow students, many of whom occupied a higher rank in the university hierarchy than Newton himself did. He graduated as a Bachelor of Arts in 1664. Plague devastated Cambridge from the middle of 1665 and Newton, along with many others was forced to flee, returning in 1666. The following year he was elected minor fellow of Trinity College and in 1669 he became the Lucasian Professor of Mathematics. Like Boole at this age, Newton was reading the leading mathematicians of his day, mastering their arguments and inventing refinements and improvements to their methods, extending the field and thus contributing to new knowledge. Both men, however, were interested in much more besides mathematics.

Sir Isaac Newton (1642–1727)
Manuscript notebook, 1665–8
Fitzwilliam Museum, Cambridge, MS 1-1936

William Stukeley (1687–1765)
Manuscript Life of Newton, 1752
Royal Society, MS 142, f.15

Robert French (1841–1917)
***Queen's College, Cork*, published about 1880–1900**
National Library of Ireland

Sir Godfrey Kneller, Bt (1646–1723)
***Sir Isaac Newton*, 1702**
Oil on canvas
National Portrait Gallery, London

From the mid 1660s Newton conducted a series of experiments with light and established his chromatic theory showing that white light is composed of different colours, as seen in the rainbow. His work on optics was finally published in 1704, the year after he was elected President of the Royal Society. Perhaps more surprising, though, is Newton's deep interest in alchemy. By the late seventeenth century many despised alchemy's quest to turn base metal into gold as hopeless and without foundation. Nevertheless, many of the techniques of alchemy continued to be part of the chemist's repertoire and Newton remained committed to a programme of alchemical research, both in terms of experimentation and in working on many of the somewhat esoteric texts of the alchemical tradition, throughout much of his life. Many of the results of this programme formed the basis of a correspondence with Robert Boyle, though Newton was never explicit about his research to Boyle, who was deeply suspicious of alchemy. Newton's deep interest in the subject reflects not only the range of topics to which he was willing to give careful consideration, but also the absence of modern boundaries between scientific and other forms of knowledge. In the seventeenth century the emerging Natural Philosophy tradition was just beginning to define itself more clearly and Newton played a significant role in that emergence, laying the foundation stone for several branches of modern physics. The terms 'science' and 'scientist' were very much the invention of the nineteenth century.

Boole's interest, too, extended beyond mathematics. His private papers held by University College, Cork, contain lectures he delivered on the possibility of life on other planets, as well as a thorough study of the origins and evolution of religious myths. He was of the view that no mathematical theory could ever be regarded as satisfactory unless it could also be regarded as containing beauty. Boole's biographer links this sense of the aesthetic to Boole's love of poetry, both as a reader and writer, but hastily adds that Boole could not be regarded as a great poet. Boole also showed a passing interest in phrenology, homeopathy and mesmerism, amongst other things. In the early nineteenth century these were regarded as part of mainstream science and so, just as in Newton's time, the boundaries between science and other branches of inquiry were far from being rigidly

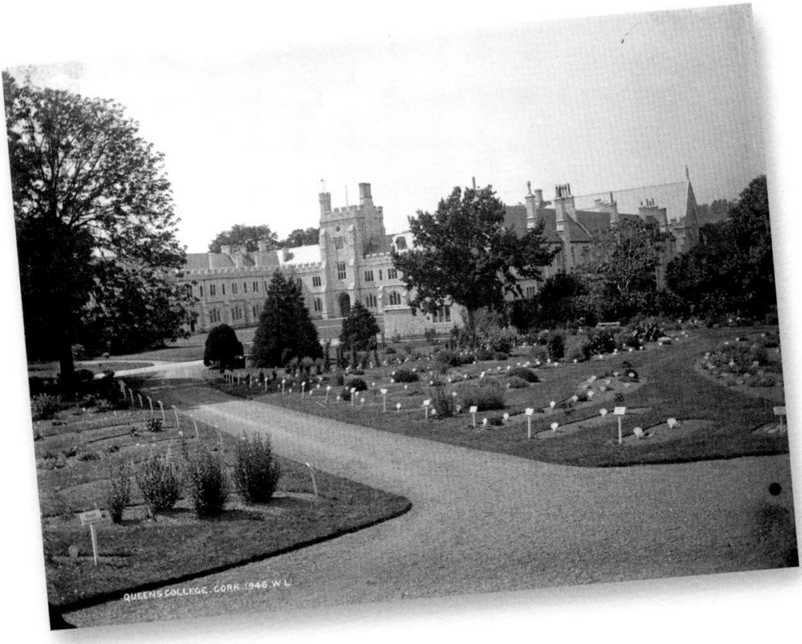

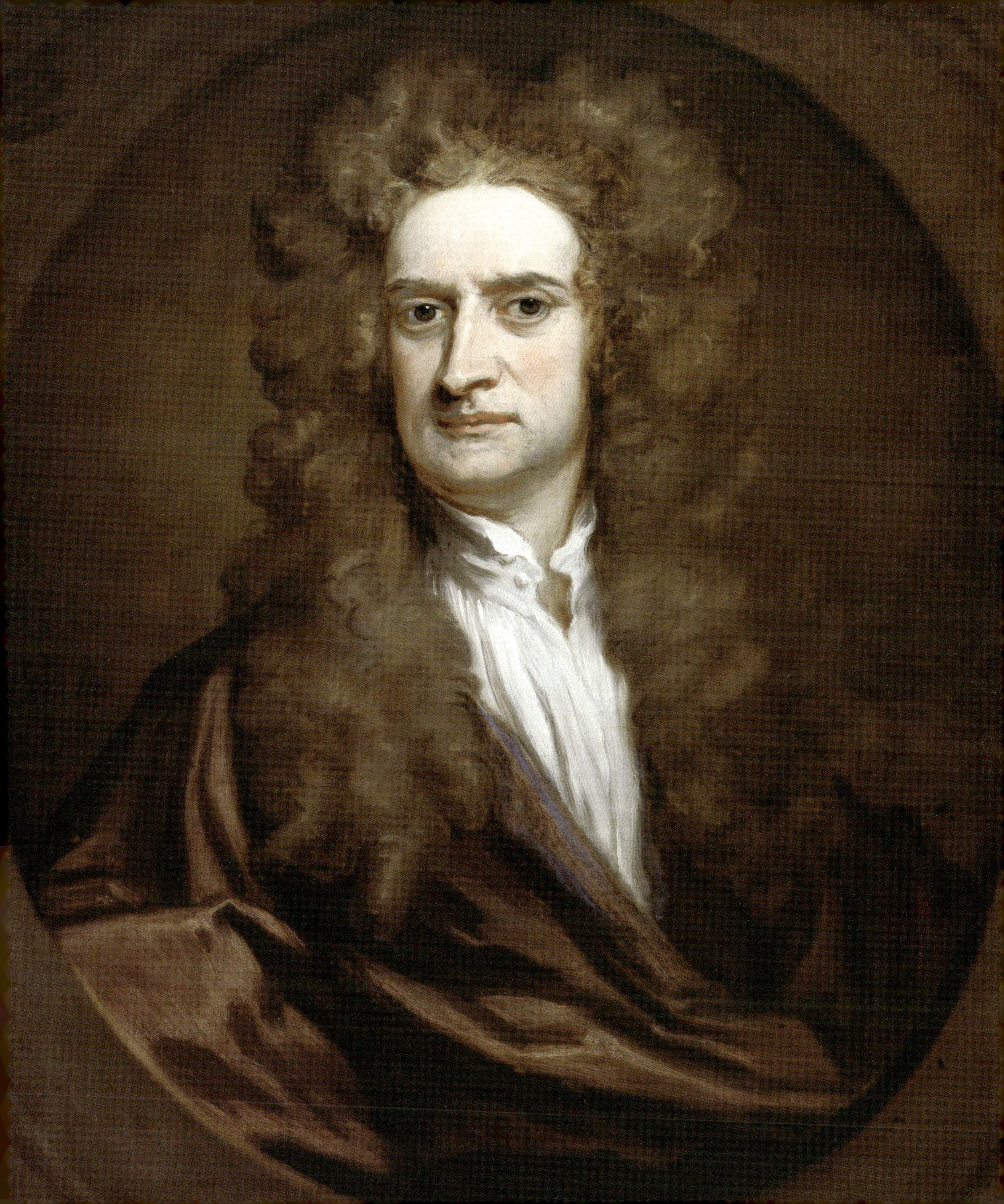

defined. Perhaps this is most clearly shown in the case of Boole in his magnum opus, *The Laws of Thought* (1854), which set out for the first time the Boolean logic that has become so instrumental in shaping the world of the twenty-first century. He devoted chapter XIII to an analysis of the arguments of two philosophers, Baruch Spinoza and Samuel Clarke, for the existence of God. At the end of the chapter Boole concludes that the a priori demonstration of the existence of God is a futile activity, doomed to failure because the finite cannot contemplate the infinite.

It is remarkable that Boole even attempted to apply his method of logical analysis to the question of the existence of God. But as we have noted already, the boundaries that we perceive between different areas of human endeavour were often absent in earlier times. This is particularly true when it comes to science and religion. In the twenty-first century these are two very distinct areas of human activity and studying their relationship is a discrete activity in itself, of interest to relatively few people. In both the seventeenth and the early nineteenth centuries the situation was very different and it was simply assumed that science was studying God's world and thus its discoveries were of profoundly religious significance. Both Newton and Boole were intensely religious men, but the exact nature and content of their beliefs is difficult to pin down. More is known about Newton in this respect than of Boole, though interestingly, Boole's biographer, Des MacHale, himself a mathematics professor at Cork, remarks that it is impossible to separate Boole's mathematics from his religion. What little we know of Boole's religious beliefs comes from the writings of his wife, Mary Everest Boole.

As a student in Cambridge, Newton would have studied the Bible, Christian doctrine and the writings of the Church Fathers as part of the undergraduate curriculum. As a result of these studies he became convinced that the doctrine of the Trinity, which states the equality of the three persons of the Father, the Son and the Holy Spirit in the one God, was a corruption introduced into the Christian faith in the fourth century. For Newton, the heart of this corruption of the truth was the physical identity of Christ with God; Newton believed that Christ was neither truly human nor God but a different kind of being altogether, empowered and enabled by God to bring about human salvation. His heterodox beliefs help to explain why it is that Newton received special dispensation allowing him to become a Fellow of Trinity College without the need for ordination in the Church of England. Such an ordination would have required him to give public assent to the doctrines of the

Louis François Roubiliac (1702–62)
***Sir Isaac Newton*, about 1741**
Marble
Private collection

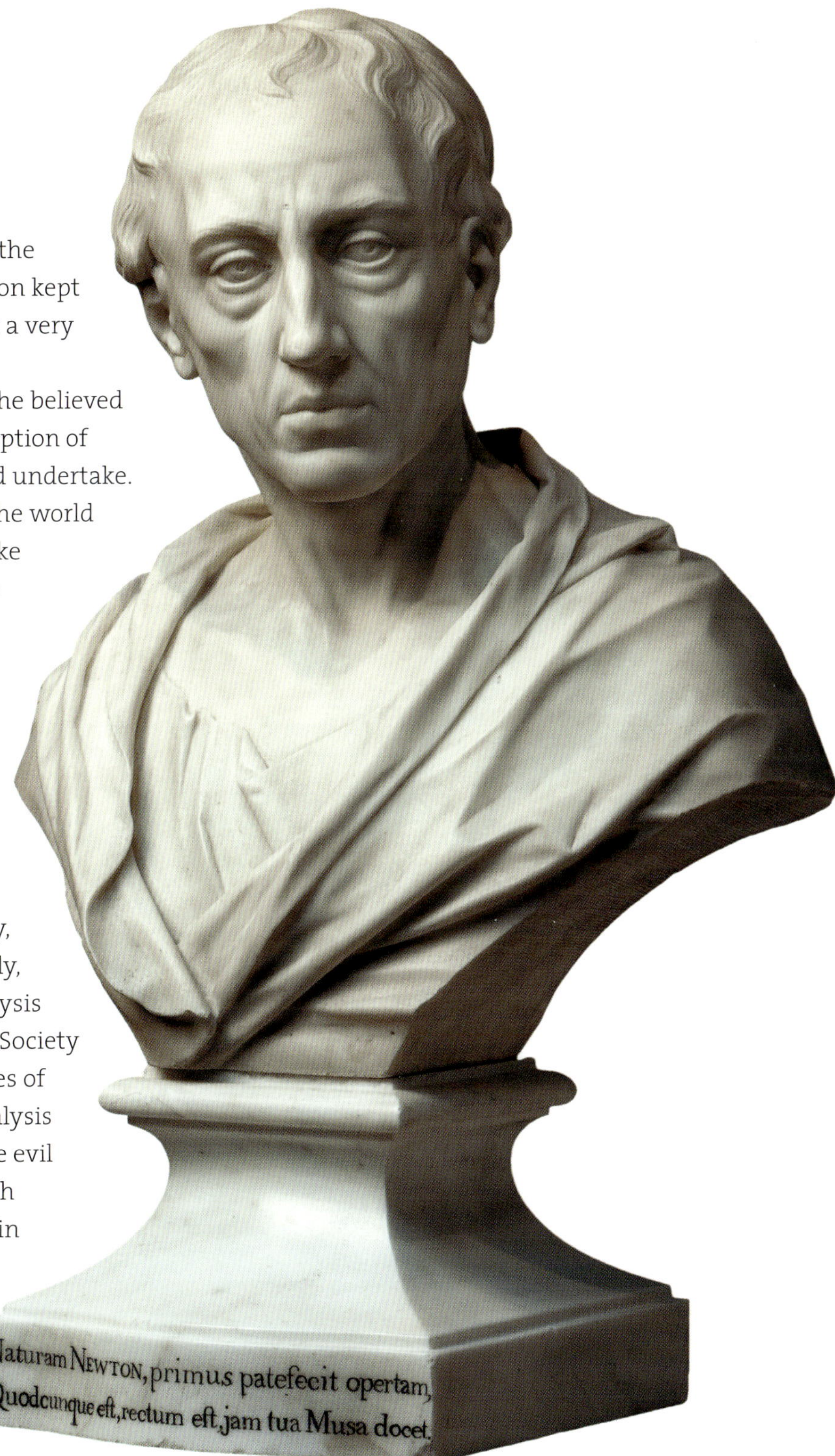

Church, including that of the Trinity, which he did not believe. In the late seventeenth century there were severe penalties on the statute books for those denying Anglican orthodoxy, and Newton kept his true religious beliefs hidden during his lifetime from all but a very few trusted fellow believers.

Newton's beliefs were complex and highly esoteric, but he believed that he was called by God to discover the truth about this corruption of Christianity, and that it was the most important work he would undertake. This sense of call and the desire to explain the ways of God to the world was something shared by George Boole some 150 years later. Like Newton, Boole was baptised by the Church of England and, like Newton, he came to reject the doctrine of the Trinity and the divinity of Christ. Boole was perplexed by the sheer variety of religious beliefs, finding this difficult to reconcile with the concept of the unity of God, a concept that for him was paramount. He came to believe that though all the monotheistic religions bore witness to the truth of God, none of them had captured what he considered to be 'pure religion'. The various doctrines of different faiths needed sifting and analysing in order to distil the truth they contained. In this way, true apprehension of God was to be found for Boole. Accordingly, he sought to use his methods of logical and mathematical analysis in this task. Amongst Boole's papers in the archive of the Royal Society are handwritten exercises in logic in which he subjects passages of Scripture to this kind of analysis. He also attempts a logical analysis of the problem of evil, ending with the conclusion that absolute evil does not exist. This may well be the first attempt at an approach to the problem of evil that came to dominate much discussion in the philosophy of religion in the twentieth century.

Both Newton and Boole are key figures in the development of science in general and mathematics in particular. Both led remarkable lives and, though coming from very different backgrounds and separated in time by almost a century, shared many things in common.

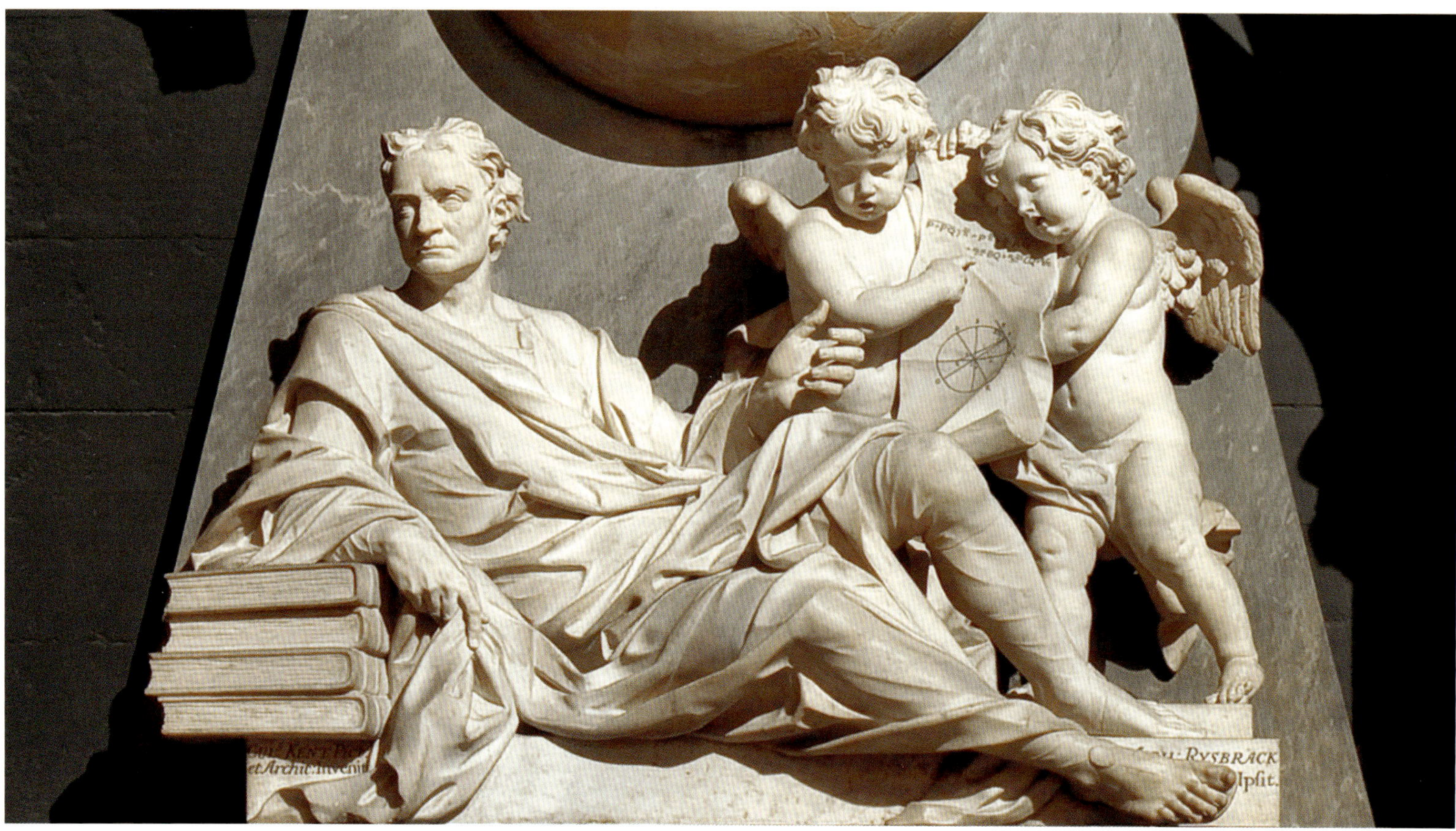

John Michael Rysbrack (1694–1770)
Tomb monument of Sir Isaac Newton (1642–1727), 1731
Marble
Westminster Abbey

OPPOSITE
Memorial window for George Boole (1815–64), Lincoln Cathedral, 1866
Photo: James Newton

Perhaps chief amongst their shared experience was the desire to understand and to explain as clearly and as precisely as possible the world around them. History has treated both men rather differently. While Newton's reputation remains as high today as it ever was, Boole remains more obscure and unknown, even within the mathematical community. Newton died on 20 March 1727 at the age of eighty-four and was buried in Westminster Abbey. His monument stands in the nave of the Abbey, against the choir screen. Boole died of pneumonia on 8 December 1864, aged just forty-nine. He is buried in the parish church of St Michael Blackrock, his home parish, four miles outside Cork. A simple stone inscribed with his name and dates marks his grave, though there is also a memorial to him inside the church. He is commemorated, too, in a stained-glass window in Lincoln Cathedral.

The real legacy of both men, however, lies not in buildings or monuments but in the world their ideas have shaped. Much of how we live and what we take for granted today can be traced back to the pioneering work of these two Lincolnshire scientist-mathematicians.

Further reading

Rob Iliffe, *Newton: A Very Short Introduction* (Oxford 2007)
Des MacHale, *The Life and Work of George Boole: A Prelude to the Digital Age* (Cork 2014)

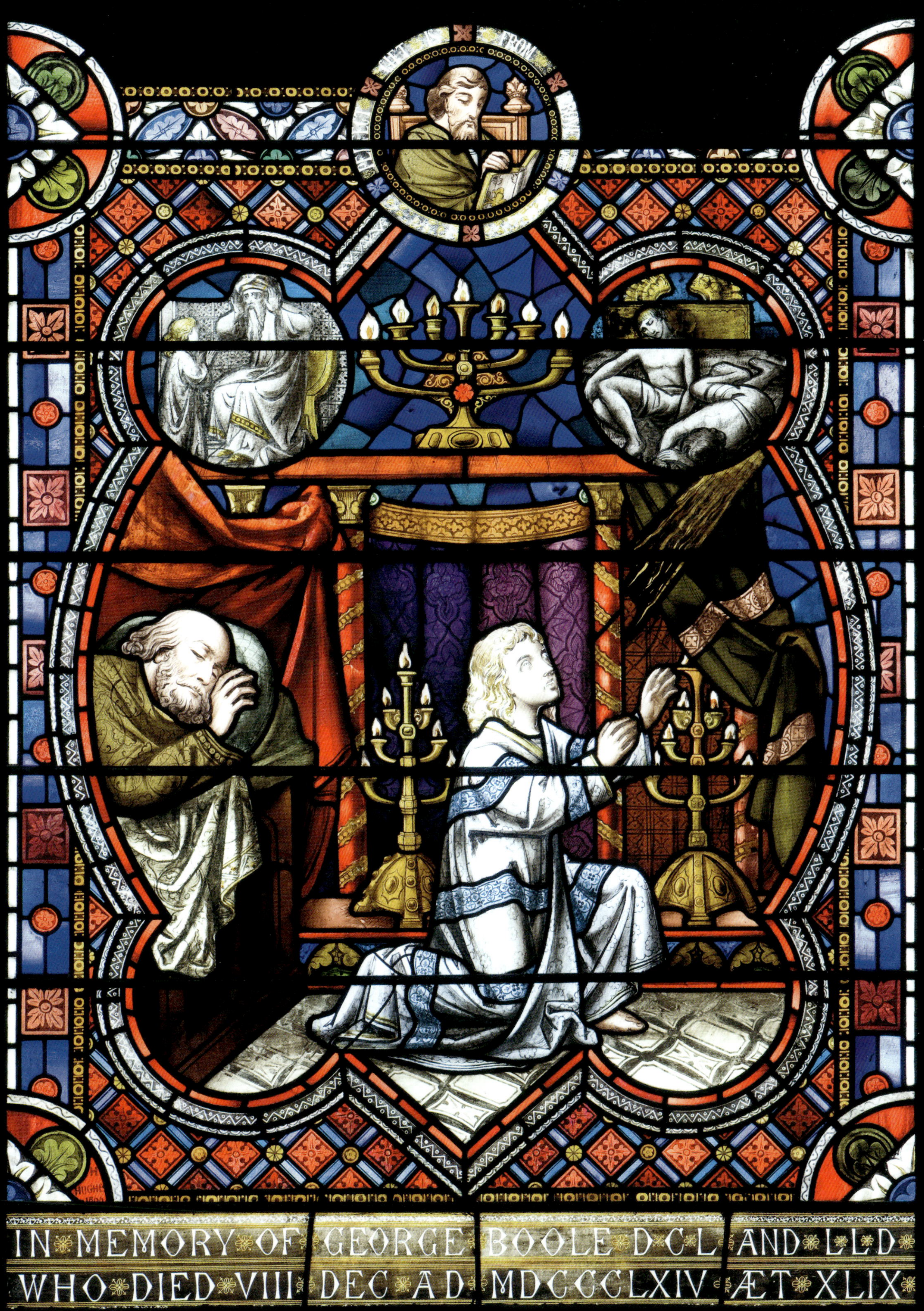
IN MEMORY OF GEORGE BOOLE D C L AND L L D
WHO DIED VIII DEC A D MDCCCLXIV ÆT XLIX

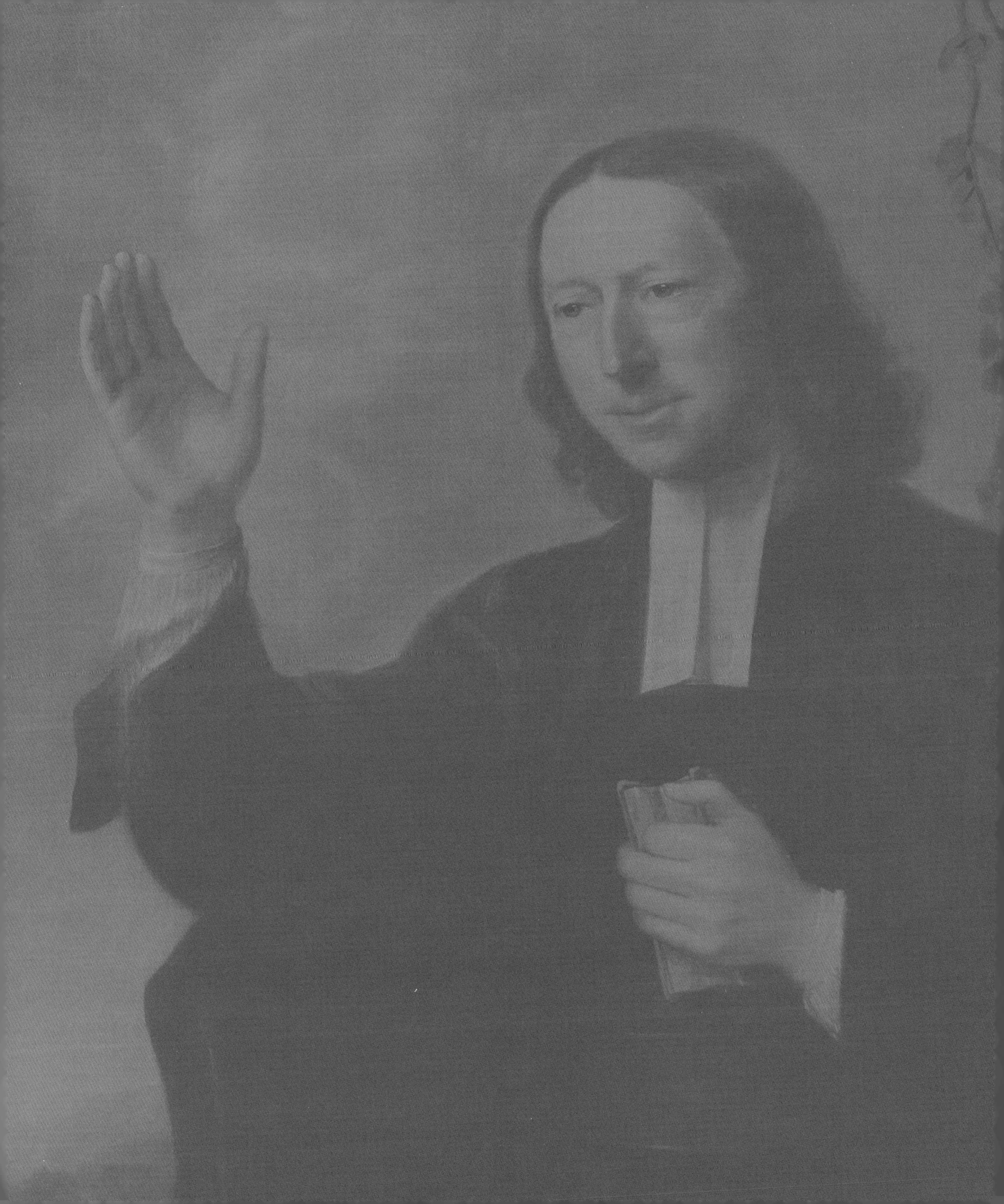

John Wesley: a Lincolnshire lad

LORD GRIFFITHS OF BURRY PORT

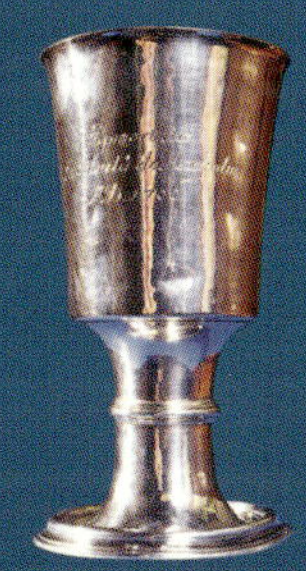

JOHN WESLEY and all but one of his siblings were yellowbellies (born in Lincolnshire) – eighteen of them were born either in the village of South Ormsby or else in the little town of Epworth, situated in what is now the unitary authority of North Lincolnshire. In those days the district was known as the Isle of Axholme, an inland island surrounded by rivers, streams, bogs and meres. The Rector of Epworth and his wife, parents of those children, were not Lincolnshire folk at all. They were Londoners, both the offspring of clergymen who had been ejected from their livings in 1662 for refusing to agree to the Act of Uniformity that sought to impose order on a Church of England still fighting for its identity in the aftermath of the Reformation a century earlier.

The rector, Samuel Wesley, was well connected but his friends in high places were unable to secure a comfortable living for him. It was traditionally thought that it was Queen Mary II, impressed by a flattering poem Samuel had written for her, who offered him Epworth, but more recent research suggests that it was her husband, William III. In any case, though an improvement on the very primitive (and poorly paid) parish of South Ormsby, it was far from the kind of place he had longed for. He and Susanna, his wife of ten years, arrived in Epworth in 1697 with four small children. They settled into a parish that was replete with difficulties. While Susanna seemed constantly to be giving birth (only ten of her children survived into adulthood), Samuel was coping with serious problems, some of them of his own making. He remained in Epworth until his death in 1735.

Crowle Waste
Photo: Lincolnshire Wildlife Trust

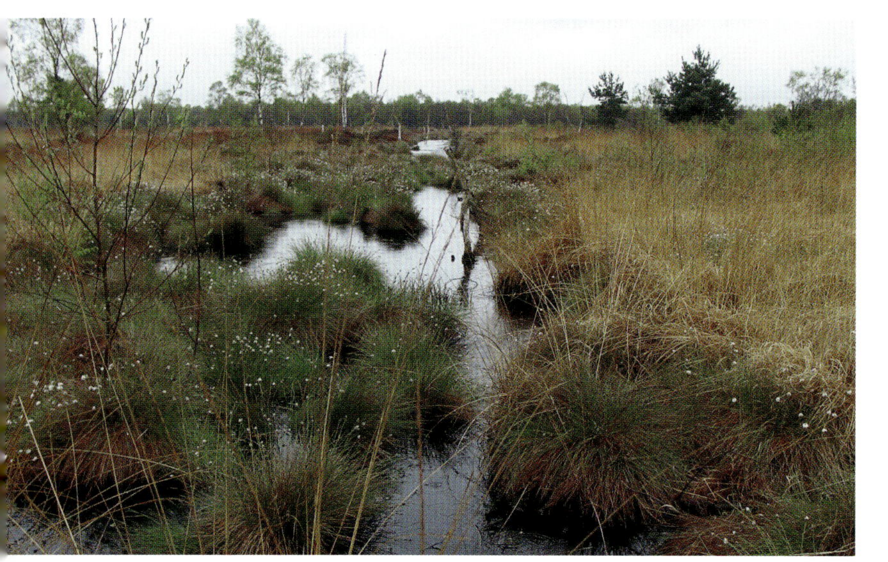

During the Civil War (1642–51) the people of the parish had sided with parliament against the king, and for a very good reason. Their whole way of life had been destroyed by the decision to drain the land in order to turn it over to agriculture. A brilliant Dutch engineer, Sir Cornelius Vermuyden, had been commissioned to undertake this work, carried out in 1627–9. It may have been a logical (and even desirable) thing to do but, at a stroke, it extinguished a traditional system of husbandry. An ancient deed had conferred on the commoners the right to forage, to gather reeds, take fish and fowl and other wildlife for food. With the draining of the land, all this was lost. So too was such traditional employment as that done by swanniers and

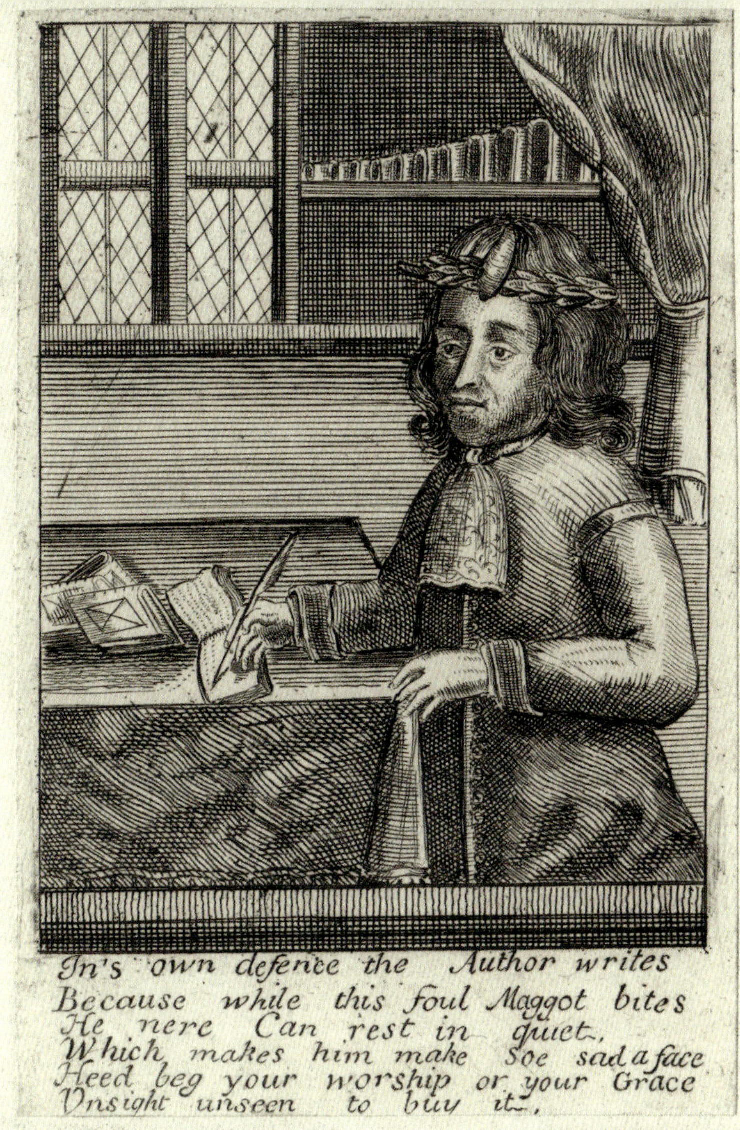

Unknown artist
Samuel Wesley the Elder (1662–1735), late seventeeenth century
Etching
National Portrait Gallery, London

ferry operators. Annual otter hunts on the River Trent came to an end and a great deal of local culture was lost. We can hardly wonder at the resentment this caused. It festered well into the new century and Samuel Wesley, a High Tory and Crown appointee, would undoubtedly have been on the receiving end of much of this from the very moment he arrived.

Samuel Wesley did nothing to assuage the villagers' discontent. In the rowdy (and contested) election of 1705, he played an active part in supporting the Tory candidate. He wrote tracts that were highly critical of dissenting groups. They, in turn, vented their spleen on the rector, 'drumming, shouting and firing pistols and guns' under the rectory windows, threatening to 'squeeze his guts out' if they caught him and even issuing threats to his children. Their animals were stabbed and there is a distinct possibility that it was a mob of dissenters that set fire to the rectory in 1702 and 1709. It was during the second of these that John Wesley, then a small boy aged six, was rescued from the flames by a human ladder formed under his bedroom window. He saw the hand of God in this miraculous escape; it led him to describe himself as a 'brand plucked from the burning'.

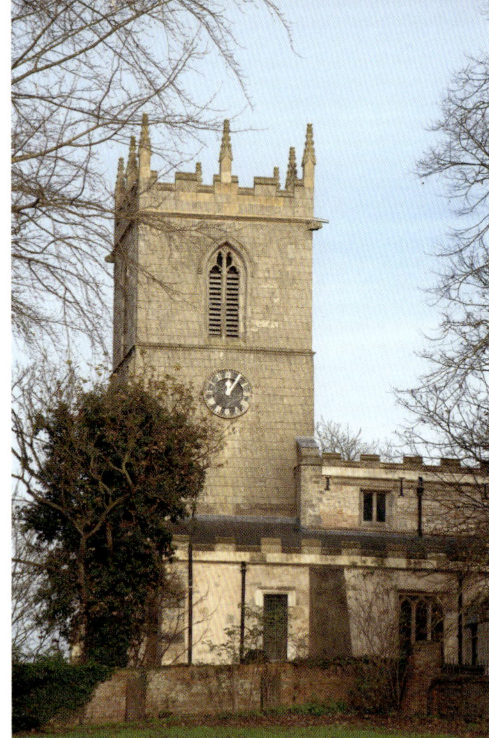

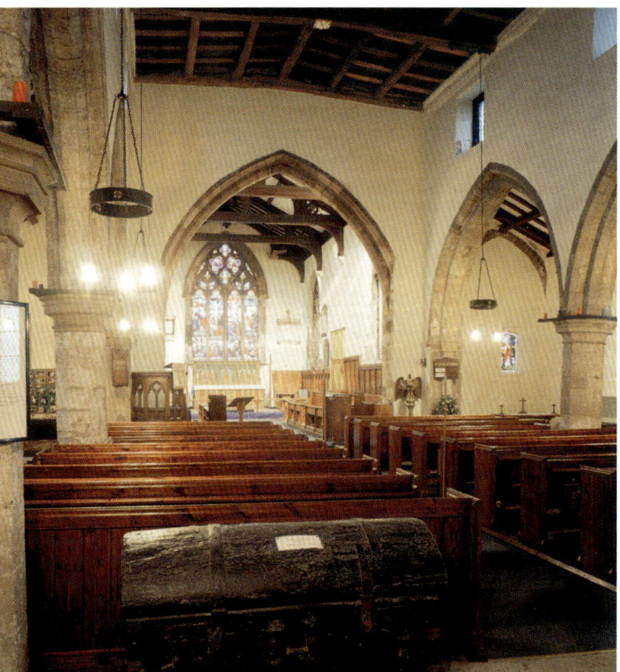

Epworth Church, exterior
Photo: Andrew Tryner, copyright Lincolnshire County Council

Epworth Church, interior
Photo: Andrew Tryner, copyright Lincolnshire County Council

Three Wesley boys survived into adulthood. All of them were sent to London for their formal education as soon as they were old enough, but not before they had all received a rigorous formation at the hands of their truly remarkable mother, Susanna. It was she who taught them to read, to keep their promises, to confess their faults. She believed that it was vital to 'break the wills' of her children as early as possible. Only then, she believed, could the slower process of understanding be developed. This seems to have worked well enough.

In 1714, armed with a letter of introduction from the Duke of Buckingham, John began his life at Charterhouse. His brother Charles was later to attend Westminster School, where the eldest brother, Samuel, had become a teacher. John and Charles went on to Christ Church, Oxford, where they excelled at their studies. John graduated in 1724 and, after his ordination as deacon in the following year (he was ordained priest in 1728 at the hands of the Archbishop of Canterbury), he was elected to a fellowship of Lincoln College, a position he kept until his marriage in 1751. By this time Samuel, the eldest son, had taken a position in Tiverton and remained there with his wife and children for the rest of his life. He was conscientious in his desire to keep a watchful eye on his younger siblings and also on the needs of his ageing parents. He became critical of the 'methodistical' development of his two younger brothers and put a lot of pressure on John to return to Epworth to help his father and, eventually, to take over the parish from him, something John resolutely refused to do.

The direct association of the Wesley family with Lincolnshire ended with Samuel's death in 1735. By that time, the seeds of what was to become Methodism had been planted. Charles Wesley and a group of his Oxford friends formed an association that was often referred to as 'The Holy Club'; John Wesley was drawn into this and gave it shape. Its timetabled activities – study, prayer, prison visiting, fellowship – led bemused observers to describe those who attended it as 'Methodist' because they went about their lives so methodically. This intense devotional activity made the brothers aware of a need on both their parts for some deeper inner awakening, which, though they were both ordained, seemed still lacking to them. Later, John was to describe himself at this stage in his life as an 'almost Christian'.

The two brothers accompanied General James Oglethorpe to America, where he was in the process of founding the colony of Georgia. Despite their woeful failure in this venture, John and Charles became mightily impressed by the spiritual depth of some

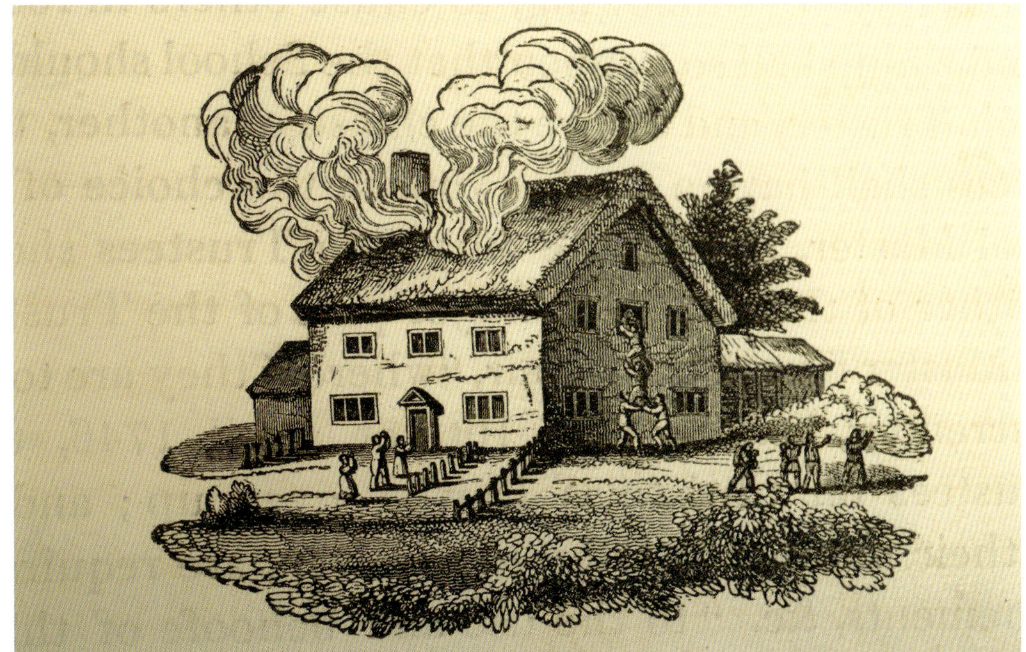

Epworth Rectory on fire in 1709
Vignette from W.B. Stonehouse, *The History and Topography of the Isle of Axholme* (1839)
Lincoln Cathedral Library

Moravian fellow-travellers. They also witnessed the cruelties of American slavery and thus began a lifelong passionate disapproval of it. John's very last letter was written to William Wilberforce in 1791, just days before his death, in which he urged the young MP to continue with his efforts to banish 'the execrable villainy' of slavery.

The search for an inward confirmation of the Christian principles to which their lives were so obviously dedicated reached a climactic moment in May 1738, when both brothers underwent a profound conversion experience. 'I felt my heart was strangely warmed', John wrote in his journal, 'and I received an assurance that God had forgiven my sins, even mine.' Charles burst into song: 'My chains fell off, my heart was free; I rose, went forth, and followed thee.' After a brief flirtation with Moravianism, John Wesley decided to launch a Methodist society. He rented a ruined foundry at Moorfields in East London, did some hasty repairs and began his work there towards the end of 1739. Methodism was now born. It was never intended to be a schismatic body, a new church. Those who attended its meetings were urged to see them as complementary to the services of the parish church. And this continued to be the stance of John and Charles Wesley until their dying day. Events were, however, to point in other directions.

The 'Foundery' (*sic*) stood just two hundred yards to the south of the New Chapel which replaced it in 1778. It is now called Wesley's Chapel and I have been its minister for the last nineteen years. All the distinctive hallmarks of Methodism can be traced in what was happening there. The message being preached was aimed at everyone without distinction; even 'harlots and publicans and thieves' could enter into a gracious relationship with their Maker. There could be no question of mere pietism – it would be a case of 'practical divinity' and there would be perceptible outcomes. Members visited people on 'death row' in nearby Newgate

William de Fawdrey of London
Epworth Chalice, 1706
Inscribed 'Epworthia Insula Axholme AD 1706'
St Andrew's Parochial Church Council

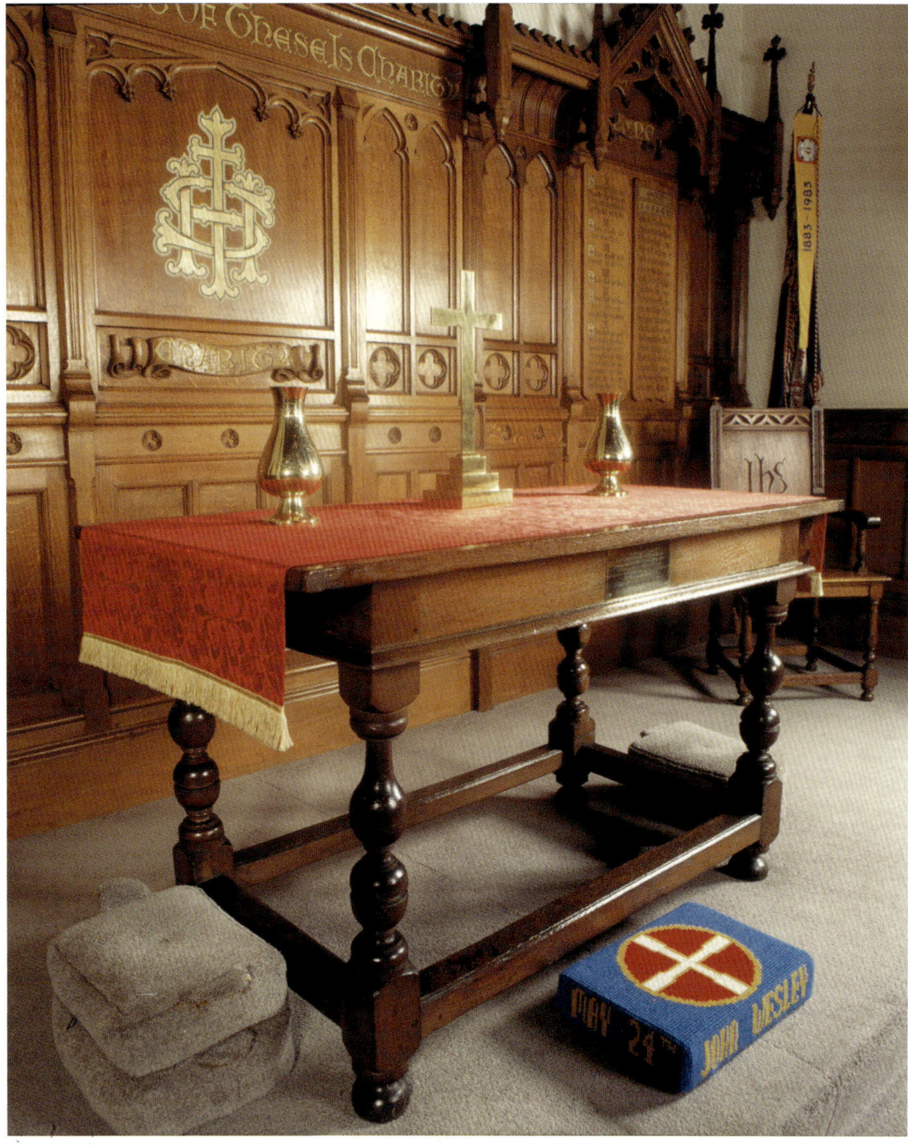

Communion table in the Wesley Memorial Methodist Church, Epworth
Photo: Andrew Tryner, copyright Lincolnshire County Council

Prison and even, on occasion, accompanied them on the grisly ride across town to the gibbet at Tyburn. A ragged school, for girls and boys, functioned at the Chapel, with the children from the surrounding Moorfields slums clothed and fed according to need. A prototypical health service was established that was free at the point of use. There was a 'revolving loan fund', a micro-finance project to help people with their cash flow problems or else to offer some venture capital to those wanting to establish a business. Elderly and indigent people were housed and fed. This extraordinary programme stands as a reminder not only to non-Methodists but also to subsequent generations of Methodists of the core values (and practices) of Methodism.

Soon John Wesley was travelling the length and breadth of the country. Bristol, Newcastle and London became his staging posts. In the course of his ministry he is said to have travelled (on horseback) 250,000 miles, an average of 5,000 miles per annum. He made thirty-three visits to Ireland and included the Channel Islands in his itinerary. He would preach anywhere he could get a hearing – market places, inns, fields, private homes. He confided to his journal that, in putting himself around like this, he had 'submitted to become more vile'. Indeed, Wesley's populist activities were frowned upon initially by members of his own class. The year 1745 saw the arrival of Bonnie Prince Charlie and the last stutterings of Jacobite rebellion. The Methodist insistence on an activist faith led some to suspect the Wesleys of endangering public order. Indeed, John was the subject of a cartoon where he was labelled 'a Jesuit fox'.

Little could stop the spread of Methodism, however, and it eventually gained a national character. It might have remained what it was always intended to be, a renewal movement within the Church of England. But events in America changed all that.

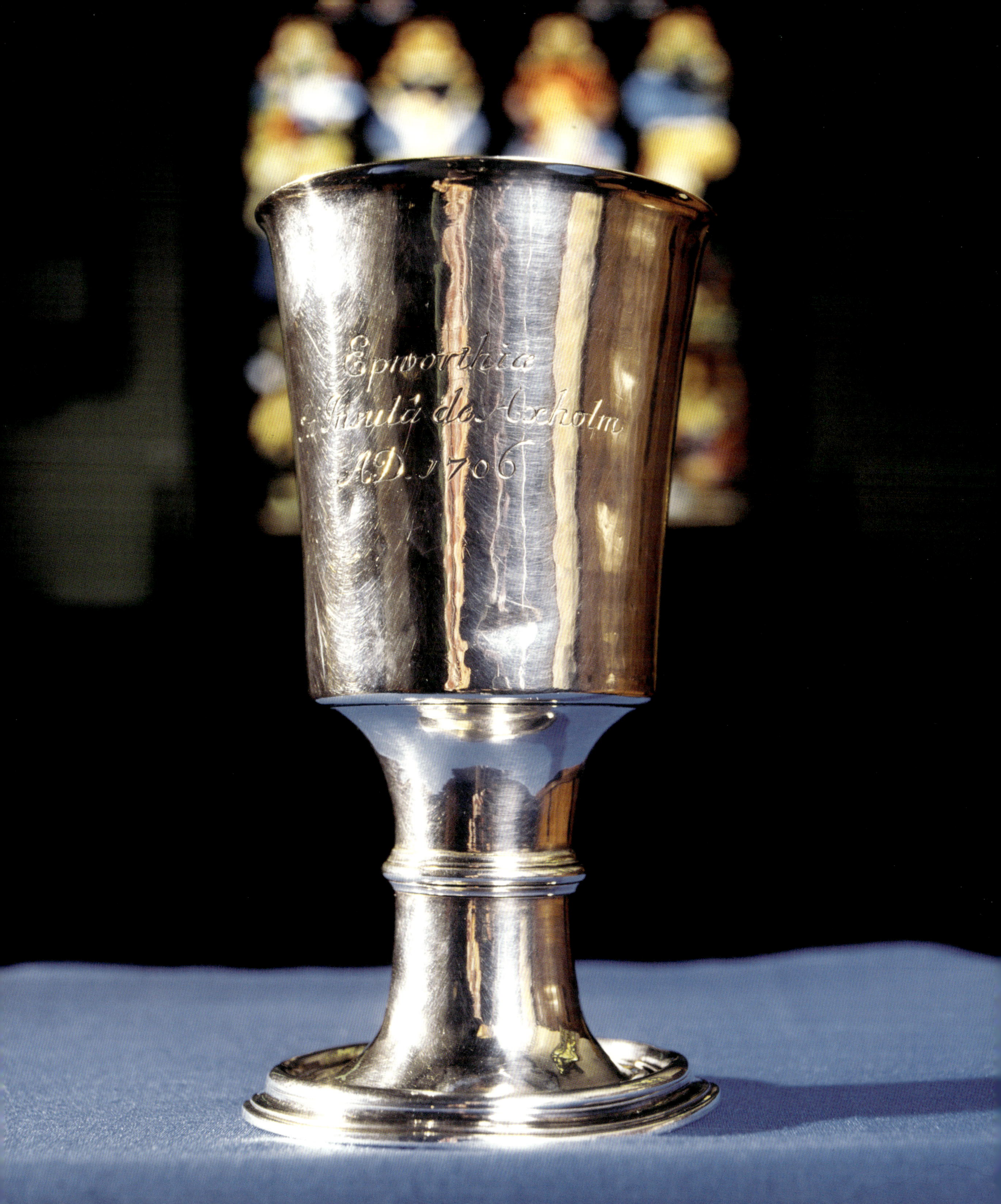
Epworthia
Insulá de Axholm
AD 1706

Charles Wesley (1707–88)
'Love Divine, all Loves excelling'
From *Hymns for those that seek, and those that have redemption in the blood of Jesus Christ* (Bristol 1747)
British Library

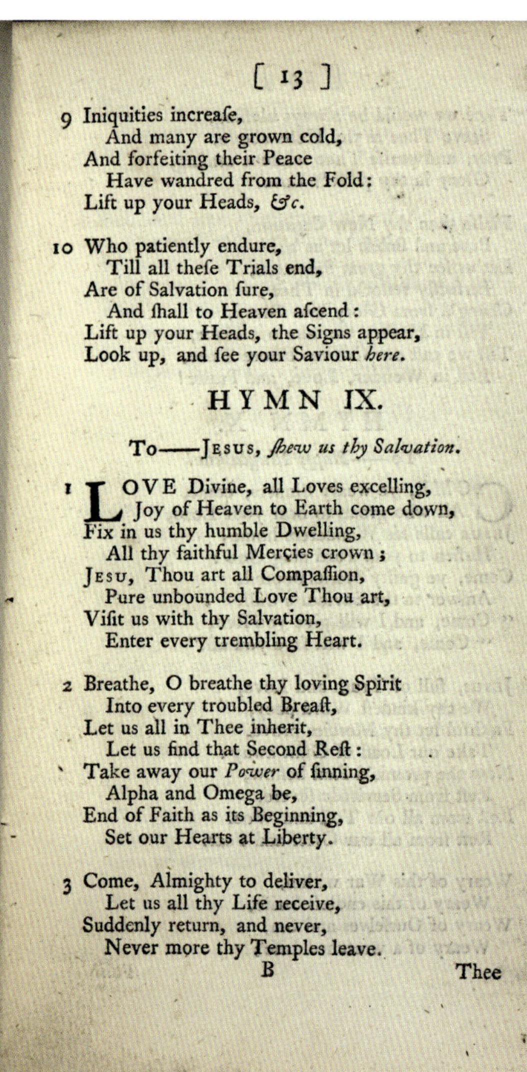

[13]

9 Iniquities increaſe,
And many are grown cold,
And forfeiting their Peace
Have wandred from the Fold:
Lift up your Heads, &c.

10 Who patiently endure,
Till all theſe Trials end,
Are of Salvation ſure,
And ſhall to Heaven aſcend:
Lift up your Heads, the Signs appear,
Look up, and ſee your Saviour *here*.

HYMN IX.

To——JESUS, *ſhew us thy Salvation.*

1 LOVE Divine, all Loves excelling,
Joy of Heaven to Earth come down,
Fix in us thy humble Dwelling,
All thy faithful Mercies crown;
JESU, Thou art all Compaſſion,
Pure unbounded Love Thou art,
Viſit us with thy Salvation,
Enter every trembling Heart.

2 Breathe, O breathe thy loving Spirit
Into every troubled Breaſt,
Let us all in Thee inherit,
Let us find that Second Reſt:
Take away our *Power* of ſinning,
Alpha and Omega be,
End of Faith as its Beginning,
Set our Hearts at Liberty.

3 Come, Almighty to deliver,
Let us all thy Life receive,
Suddenly return, and never,
Never more thy Temples leave.
B Thee

'Patrick Bull' (pseudonym)
***A wolf in sheep's cloathing: or, an old Jesuit unmasked. Containing an account of the wonderful apparition of Father Petre's ghost, in the form of the Rev. John Wesley. With some conjectures concerning the secret causes that moved him to appear at this very critical juncture*, 1775**
British Library

A
WOLF IN SHEEP's CLOATHING:
OR,
AN OLD JESUIT UNMASKED,
CONTAINING AN ACCOUNT OF
THE WONDERFUL APPARITION
OF
FATHER PETRE's GHOST,
In the Form of the Rev. JOHN WESLEY.
WITH
SOME CONJECTURES CONCERNING THE SECRET CAUSES THAT MOVED HIM TO APPEAR AT THIS VERY CRITICAL JUNCTURE.

MELIUS ET FORTIUS——
RIDICULUM ACRI——
——HIC NIGER EST,
HUNC TU, ROMANE, CAVETO.

By PATRICK BULL, Esq;

DUBLIN PRINTED, LONDON RE-PRINTED,
And Sold by MARY TRICKETT, (No. 9.) BROADWAY, BLACK-FRIARS; and by the Bookſellers at the ROYAL EXCHANGE.
[Price 1s. 6d. a Dozen, or 10s. per Hundred.]

The American victory in their war for independence left the Church there in complete disarray. The Bishop of London was nominally the Bishop of America too and he was certainly not going to send priests to the upstart revolutionaries who had defeated the king's armies. John Wesley wrote to him a number of times, pleading with him that the pastoral needs of the people of America overrode all other considerations. But the bishop was adamant. So John Wesley took action. Invoking a precedent from the fourth-century Alexandrian church, he set pastors apart, or ordained them, for service in America. He authorised his right-hand man, Dr Thomas Coke, to travel to Baltimore to ensure an orderly transfer of power to the leader of the American Methodists, a man named Francis Asbury. Their famous meeting on Christmas Day 1784 marks the beginning of the Methodist Episcopal Church of America. This act did more to separate Methodists and Anglicans than any other and was a decisive step along the way to the creation of a Methodist Church in Britain.

Nathanial Hone (1718–84)
***John Wesley (1703–91)*, about 1766**
Oil on canvas
National Portrait Gallery, London

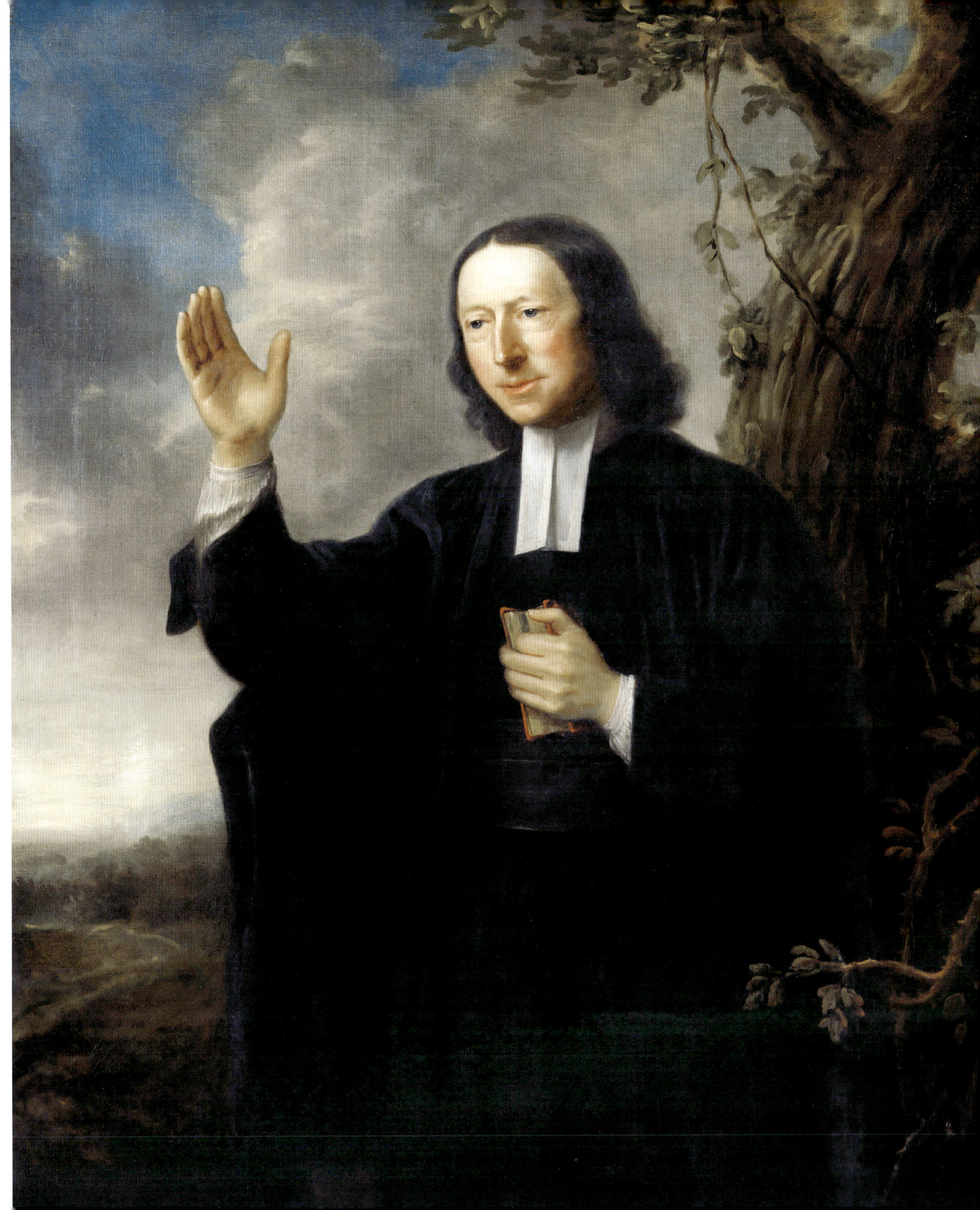

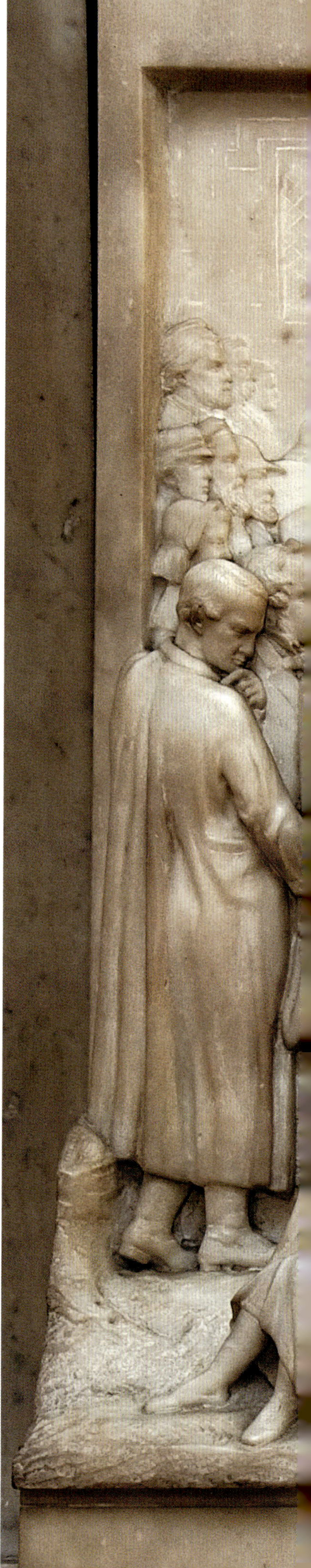

John Adams-Acton (1830–1910)
Memorial to John (1703–91) and Charles (1708–88) Wesley, 1876
Detail of relief, depicting John preaching from his father's tombstone in Epworth churchyard
Westminster Abbey

Charles Wesley died in 1788. The 'sweet singer of Methodism' had contributed an armoury of hymns to his people, enabling them to sing their theology and learn their catechism through song. John Wesley died three years later. He had acquired the status of Grand Old Man by then and his movement had already spread into the West Indies, parts of West Africa and continental Europe.

Roy Hattersley, in his recent biography of John Wesley, is quite astringent in his assessment of Wesley's character, which he does not find very attractive. But he makes a strong case to suggest that the work begun by Wesley in the eighteenth century became one of the shaping influences on nineteenth-century Britain. The development of trade unionism, the birth of the Labour Party, the rise of benevolent capitalism, a devotion to social enterprise, a commitment to education and learning, all of which can be traced to the age of Wesley, flourished mightily in the century following his death. Methodism has continued to grow. It has become a worldwide communion and currently numbers in excess of seventy million.

Let me end as I began, in Lincolnshire. In 1742, long after his family's connection with the county had come it its end, John Wesley entered Epworth on one of his preaching tours. In common with so many others at that time, the rector refused him permission to preach in the parish church. So he jumped on to his father's tomb, which became the platform from which he began to preach. A large crowd soon gathered. And Wesley was able to reveal the energy, imagination and determination that were the hallmarks of his entire ministry. He had (literally) a field day and the event became part of the Wesley legend.

Towards the end of his life, he paid his last visit to Epworth and seems to have been overcome by nostalgia. He quoted the Latin poet Ovid and offered his own translation:

The natal soil to all how strangely sweet!
The place where first he breathed who can forget?

A Lincolnshire lad to the end!

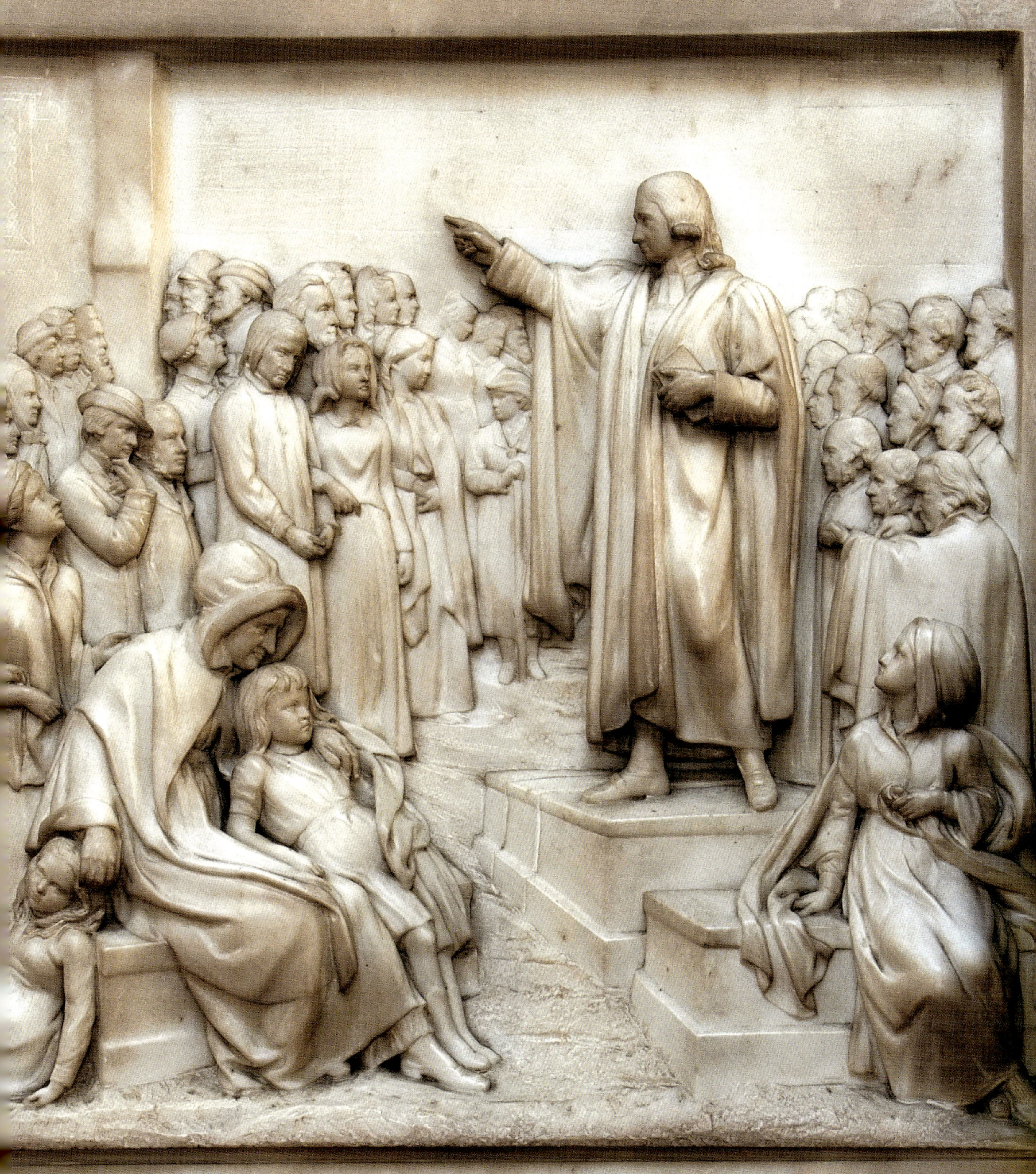

LOOK UPON ALL THE WORLD AS MY PARISH."

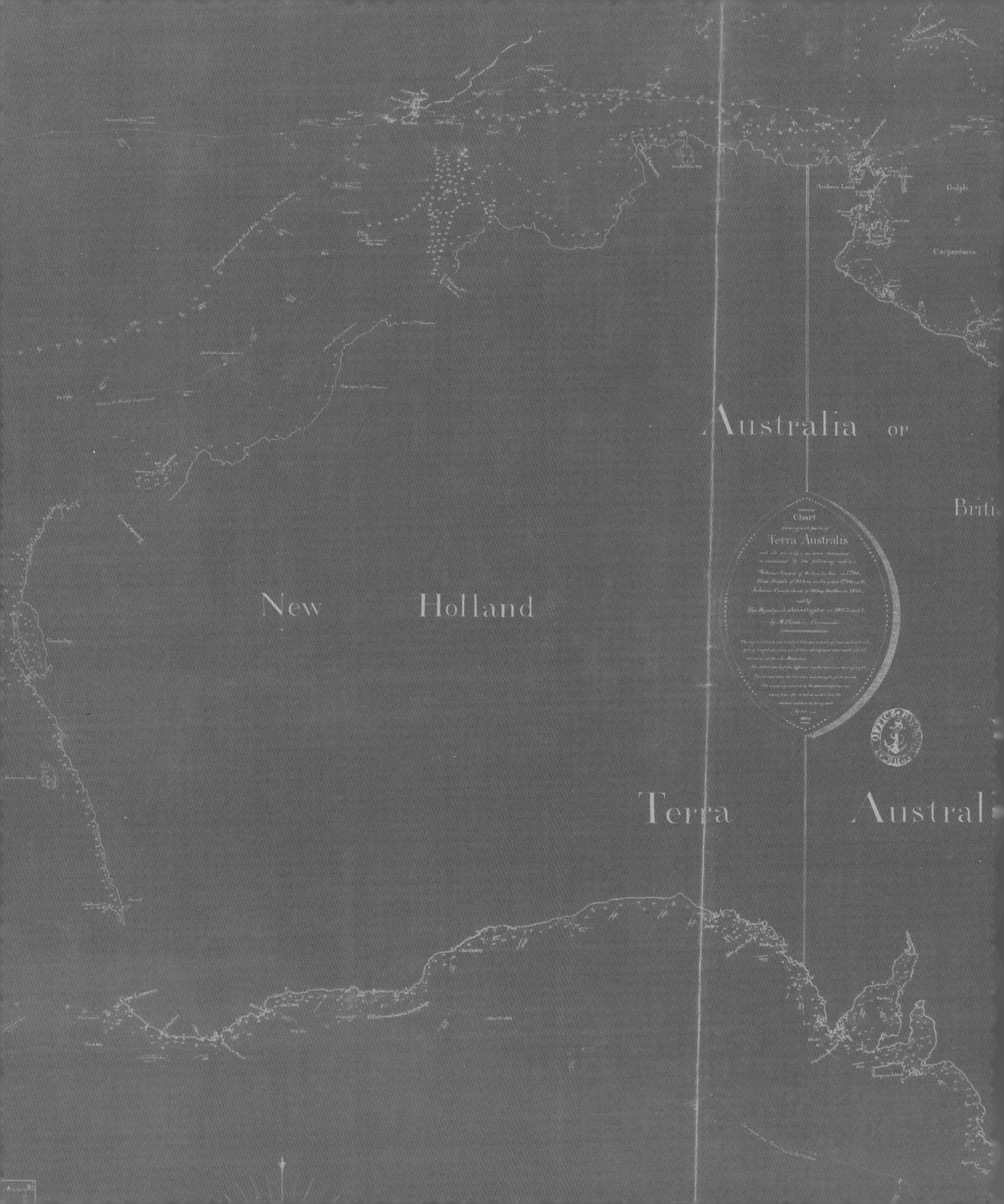

Gulph

of

Carpentaria

Australia or

Briti

Chart

Terra Australis

New Holland

Terra Australi

The Lincolnshire explorers of Australia

JOHN SIMONS

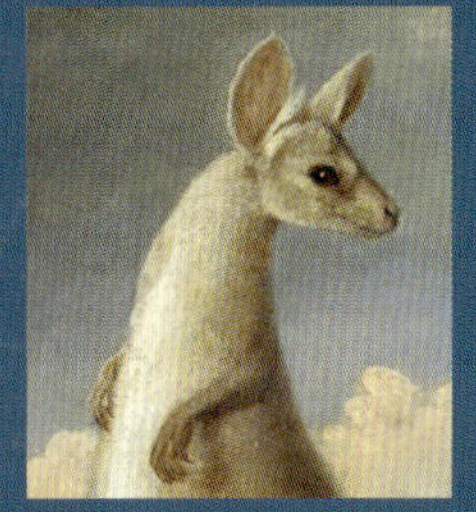

Sir JOSEPH BANKS (born in Horncastle in 1743), George Bass (born in Aswarby in 1771) and Matthew Flinders (born in Donington in 1774) are the three Lincolnshire men to whose endeavours are owed the opening up of the natural history and cartography of Australia. To their names may be added that of Sir John Franklin (born in Spilsby in 1786), whose more famous exploits took place in the Arctic but who sailed as a midshipman with Flinders (who was his uncle) and served (not entirely successfully, as his humanitarian beliefs did not suit the time and place) as Lieutenant-Governor of Van Diemen's Land (now Tasmania) from 1836 to 1843; Robert Merrick Fowler (born in Horncastle in 1778), who was Flinders's second-in-command, memorialised in South Australia's Fowlers Bay (*sic*) and went on to be a Rear Admiral; and Samuel Ward Flinders (born in Donington in 1782), who accompanied his brother Matthew to Australia and had a naval career in his own right.

OPPOSITE
Benjamin West (1738–1820)
***Sir Joseph Banks (1743–1820)*, 1771–2**
Oil on canvas
Usher Gallery, Lincoln

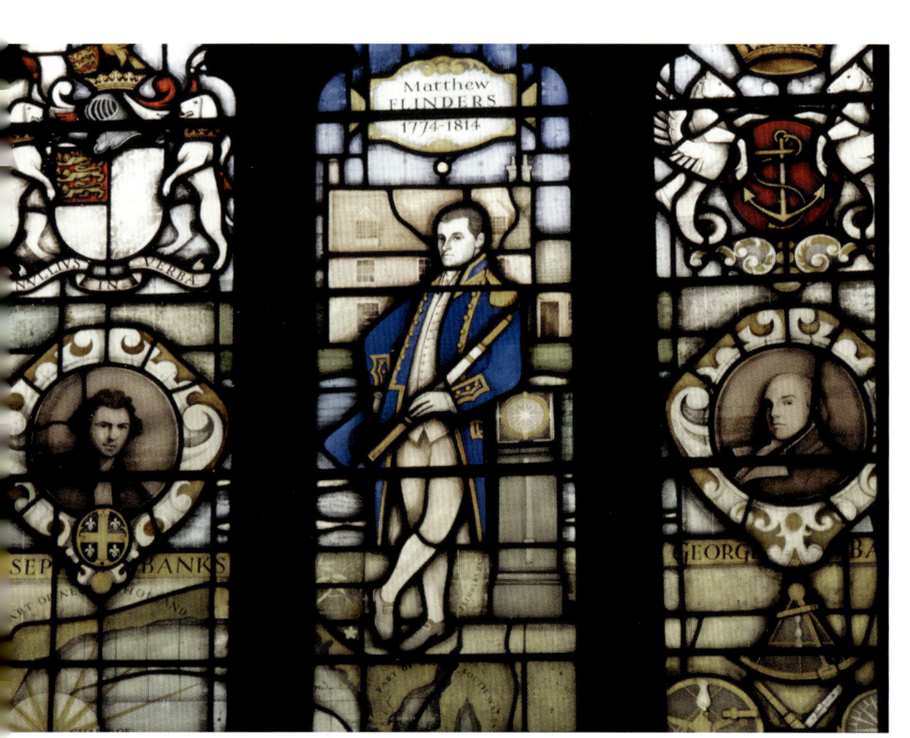

Church of St Mary and the Holy Rood, Donington
Detail of stained-glass window depicting Matthew Flinders (1774–1814), with Sir Joseph Banks (1743–1820) and George Bass (1771–1803)
Photo: Andrew Tryner. Copyright Lincolnshire County Council

However, it was Banks, Bass and Flinders who made the biggest contributions. Today these men are chiefly remembered for their voyages, whereas the enormous advances they made in natural history are not so well acknowledged, except perhaps in the case of Banks. This is a pity and this neglect leads to a misunderstanding of just how important studies and collections of flora and fauna were to early colonial enterprises. Sir Stamford Raffles, who founded both Singapore and London Zoo, summed it up well in his analysis of the importance of the Malay Peninsula:

> *It has always appeared to me that the value of these countries was to be traced rather through the means of their natural history rather than the dark recesses of Dutch diplomacy.*

Accordingly, this short essay will explore the contributions of these three great Lincolnshire men to the introduction of Australian nature to Europe.

Banks sailed with Captain Cook on the voyage of HMS *Endeavour* (1768–71) and acted as the expedition's chief naturalist, ably assisted by Daniel Solander. It is often forgotten that the purpose of Cook's first major voyage was

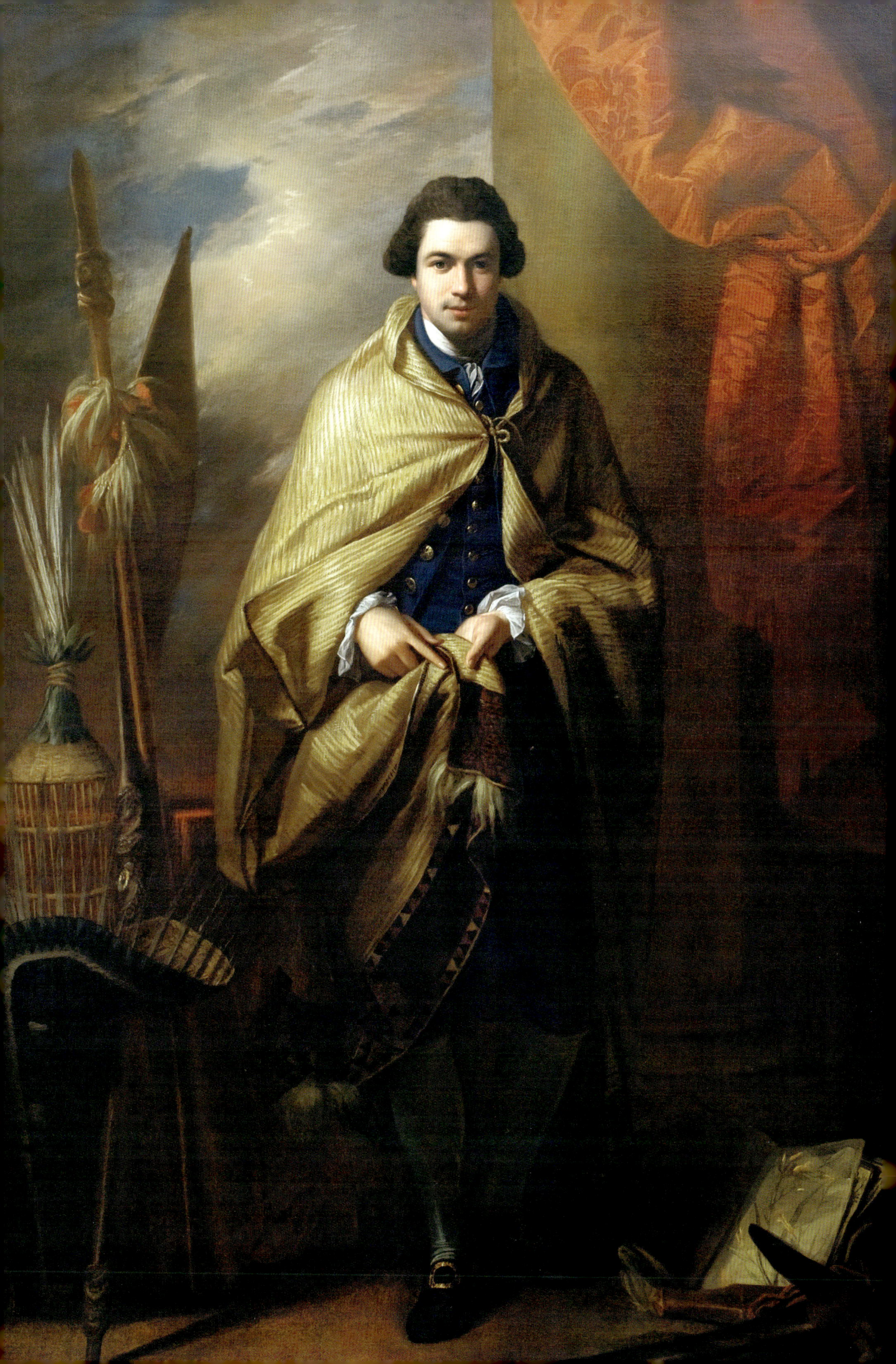

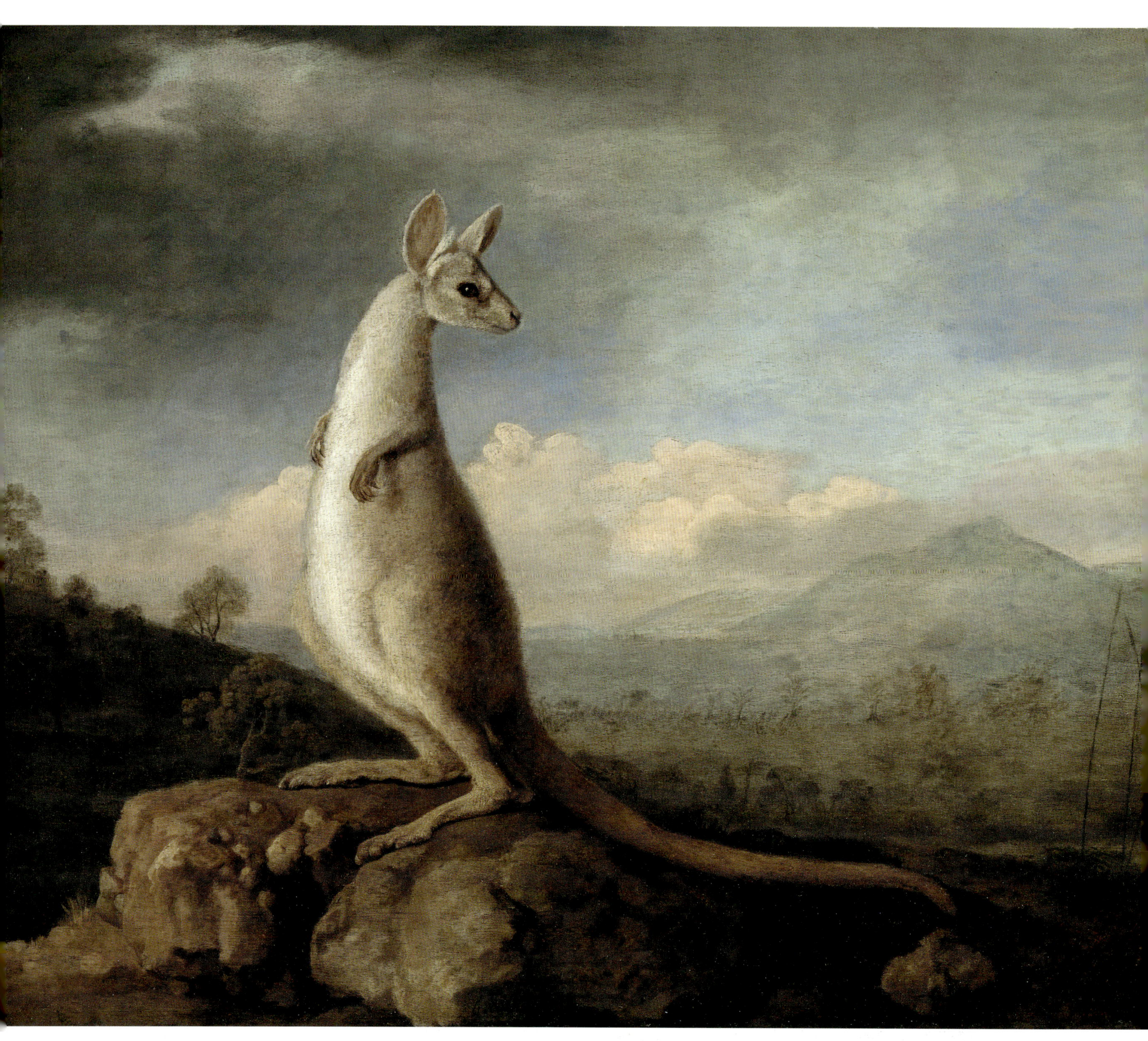

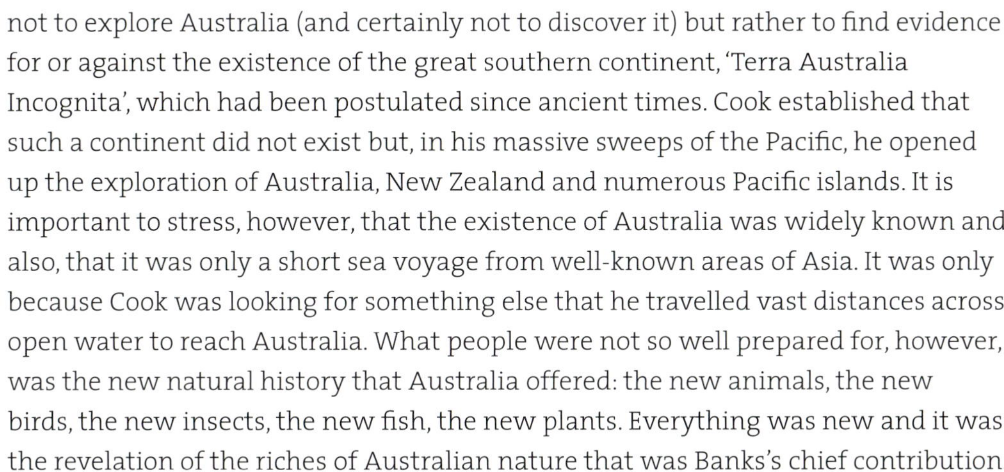

George Stubbs (1724–1806)
***The Kongouro from New Holland*, 1772**
Oil on panel
National Maritime Museum, Greenwich

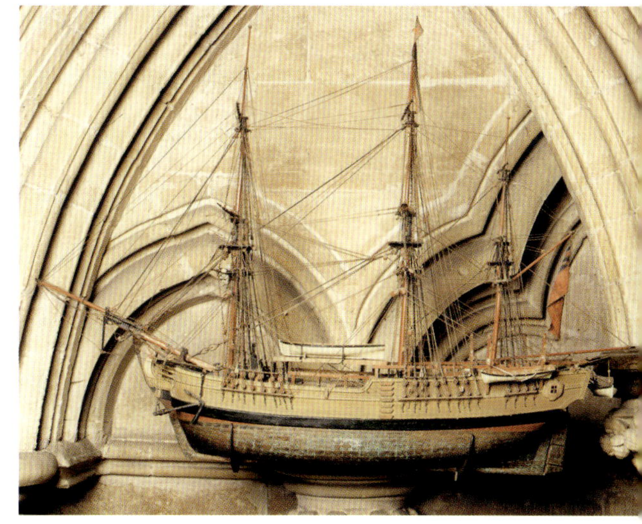

HMS *Investigator*
Model displayed in the Seamen's Chapel of Lincoln Cathedral
Photo: Andrew Tryner. Copyright Lincolnshire County Council

not to explore Australia (and certainly not to discover it) but rather to find evidence for or against the existence of the great southern continent, 'Terra Australia Incognita', which had been postulated since ancient times. Cook established that such a continent did not exist but, in his massive sweeps of the Pacific, he opened up the exploration of Australia, New Zealand and numerous Pacific islands. It is important to stress, however, that the existence of Australia was widely known and, also, that it was only a short sea voyage from well-known areas of Asia. It was only because Cook was looking for something else that he travelled vast distances across open water to reach Australia. What people were not so well prepared for, however, was the new natural history that Australia offered: the new animals, the new birds, the new insects, the new fish, the new plants. Everything was new and it was the revelation of the riches of Australian nature that was Banks's chief contribution.

Banks brought back huge collections from Australia, as well as scientific manuscripts and the drawings of the expedition's artists Sydney Parkinson, Herman Spöring and Alexander Buchan, all of whom died on the voyage. This collection enabled the natural history of Australia to be studied in Europe. Although organisational issues meant that a full catalogue was never published, the collection seems to have comprised roughly 30,300 plant specimens, including 1,400 previously unknown. We can gauge some idea of the collection by comparing it with the specimens, numbering between 100,000 and 200,000 (with 2,000 previously unknown), brought back to Paris in 1804 by the ships of the French explorer Nicolas Baudin. Certainly Banks was responsible for the introduction of some 7,000 exotic species (not all Australian) into England. He paid from his own considerable wealth to have 734 plates engraved but these were not published in full until 1990, and then in a very limited deluxe edition.

Within a few years, live specimens started to arrive in England. Banks kept kangaroos on his estate at Revesby and had sufficient stock by 1789 to send a spare to France to support zoological studies there. However, the traffic in animals was not all one way: Banks's championing of the merino sheep and his activity in bringing this wonderfully productive breed from England enabled the first flush of Australian prosperity when the nation 'rode on the sheep's back' to wool-generated wealth.

Banks was also influential in the mounting of Flinders's voyage on HMS *Investigator*. This led to the circumnavigation of the Australian mainland and the production of the most important early map. Flinders's 1804 chart was not only the first map to show the complete coastline of Australia; it was also the first to name the continent 'Australia'. Although Flinders did not coin this word, it gained popularity and was commonly used by the great Governor of New South Wales, Lachlan Macquarie, whose recommendation of 1817 that this name should be officially adopted was ratified in 1824.

The story of Flinders's epic voyages, his incarceration on Mauritius by the French and his early death is well known. What is perhaps less celebrated is his contribution to the understanding of Australian natural history. Thanks to the influence of Banks, the *Investigator* was well crewed with naturalists and artists. Robert Brown, Peter Good, John Allen and John Crosley provided the scientific support, while Ferdinand Bauer and William Westall were the illustrators. Bauer's illustrations were of the highest quality, but a combination of lack of money and Bauer's perfectionism meant that his work was not finally published until 1997. Bauer brought back with him more than 1,600 drawings of plants and over 300 of animals. Especially important were those made during a visit to Norfolk Island and an expedition into the Blue Mountains of New South Wales. Brown collected over 3,000 plants and numerous animal, bird and mineral specimens and these were published in his *Prodromus Florae Novae Hollandiae et Insulae Van Diemen* (1810).

Flinders had made a previous journey to Australia on HMS *Reliance*, and his exploration of the coastline in the two small boats called *Tom Thumb* and the *Norfolk* also yielded important scientific knowledge. On these voyages Flinders was accompanied by his friend George Bass. Bass distinguished himself on the second *Tom Thumb* voyage by finding (in the area of modern Sydney now known as Cowpastures) some of the precious herd of cattle that had been brought over by the First Fleet in 1788 but had wandered off due to a combination of bad weather and poor oversight. It is amazing that by the time Bass found them they had been gone seven years; this perhaps tells us just how fearful were the early colonists of straying too far from their main settlements. The rediscovery of the lost herd made a major contribution to the sustainability of the fledgling colony, which was, in its earliest days, in constant risk of failure due to malnutrition.

Bass also essayed a voyage of his own when he sailed in an open whaleboat down the coast of New South Wales to a point in what is now Victoria, not far from the eventual site of Melbourne. This expedition proved that Tasmania was wholly separated from the Australian mainland (early maps show it as a kind of peninsula)

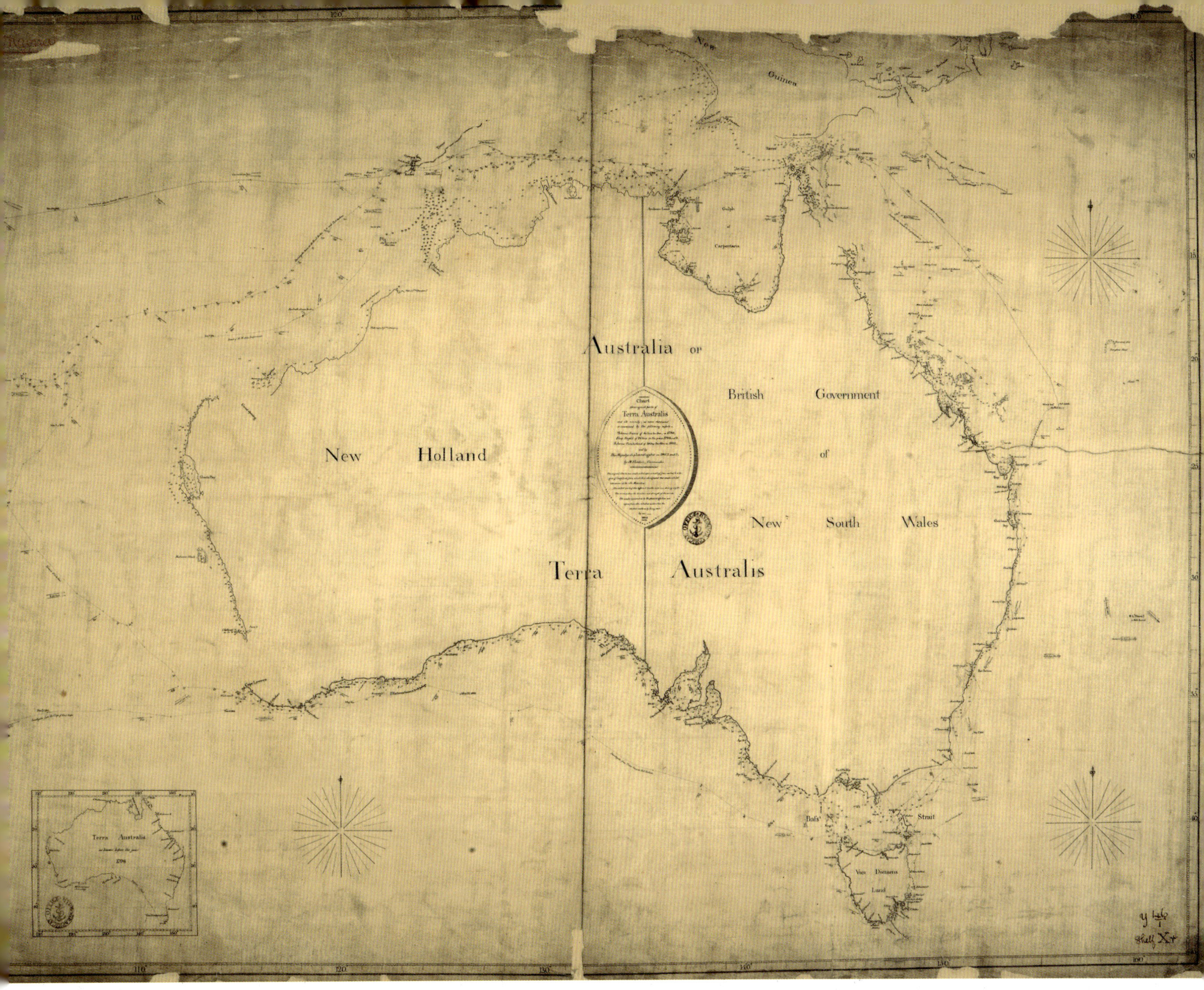

and the strait Bass sailed now bears his name. On this journey Bass also explored the area around Kiama and made extensive notes on its natural history and, especially, a study of a remarkable geological feature, the Kiama Blowhole.

But it was on Flinders's *Norfolk* voyage that Bass made his most lasting contribution when he became the first European to encounter and describe a wombat. His description is worth quoting at length as it offers a marvellous illustration of the concise accuracy of eighteenth-century naturalism and a reminder that the author was describing an animal that few, if any, of his readers would ever see:

Matthew Flinders (1774–1814)
Chart showing such parts of Terra Australis and its vicinity, as were discovered or examined by the following vessels: Schooner Francis in 1798, Sloop Norfolk in 1798 and 9, Schooner Cumberland in 1803 and HMS Investigator in 1801, 2 and 3 by M Flinders, Commander, 1804
The National Archives, ADM 352/477

Aswarby: birthplace of George Bass (1771–803)
Photo: Andrew Tryner. Copyright Lincolnshire County Council

OPPOSITE
Helena G. de Courcy Jones (active 1919) after an unknown artist
***Matthew Flinders (1774–1814)*, about 1919**
Watercolour
National Portrait Gallery, London

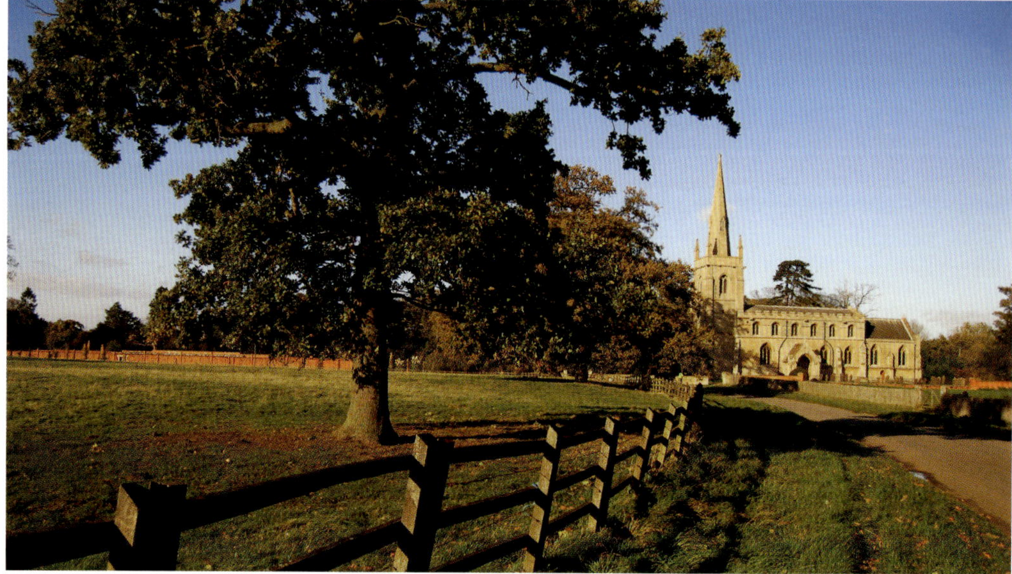

The wombat is about the size of a turnspit dog. It is a squat, short-legged and rather inactive quadruped with an appearance of great stumpy strength. Its figure and movements, if they do not resemble those of the bear at least remind one of that animal ... The head is large and flattish and when looking the animal full in the face, seems independent of the ears, to form nearly an equilateral triangle. The hair on the face lies in regular order, as if combed.

Later Flinders would present Marquess Wellesley, Governor-General of Bengal and Governor of Madras, with a wombat – arguably the first Australian of any kind to set foot on the subcontinent. The circumnavigation of Tasmania by the *Norfolk* also furnished Bass with the opportunity to collect and study the local flora, and he sent samples of those plants that he had not encountered in New South Wales back to Joseph Banks.

Of these three great Lincolnshire explorers only one, Banks, ended his life in his home country at a ripe old age. He has an unmarked grave in the Hounslow parish of Heston (he was most concerned that he be buried without ceremony or memorial). Bass was last seen in 1803, when his ship the *Venus* dipped under the horizon en route from Sydney to Chile. He was buried at sea, in the southern ocean. Flinders died in London at the age of forty, his health broken by his gruelling voyages, the day after his masterpiece, *A Voyage to Terra Australis*, was published. Sadly he had lapsed into his final unconsciousness by the time the first copies were rushed to his house. In many ways the most important of the early explorers but perhaps the least remembered, Flinders now lies somewhere beneath platform 15 of Euston Station.

These are the men who between them named and mapped Australia and brought the enduring knowledge of its flora and fauna to the attention of the wider world. Any single one of these achievements would be worthy of memorial.

The Historic Lincoln Trust is most grateful to Macquarie University, Sydney, for a generous grant enabling the Flinders Map to be displayed in *Lincolnshire's Great Exhibition*.

Further reading

Martyn Beardsley and Nicholas Bennett (eds), *The Diary and Accounts of Matthew Flinders* (Lincoln Record Society 95, 97, 2007–9).
Tim Flannery (ed.), *The Explorers* (Melbourne 1998)
Matthew Flinders (ed. Tim Flannery), *Terra Australis* (Melbourne 2001)
Patrick O'Brian, *Joseph Banks* (London 1987)
John Simons, *Rossetti's Wombat* (London 2008)
John Simons, *Kangaroo* (London 2013)

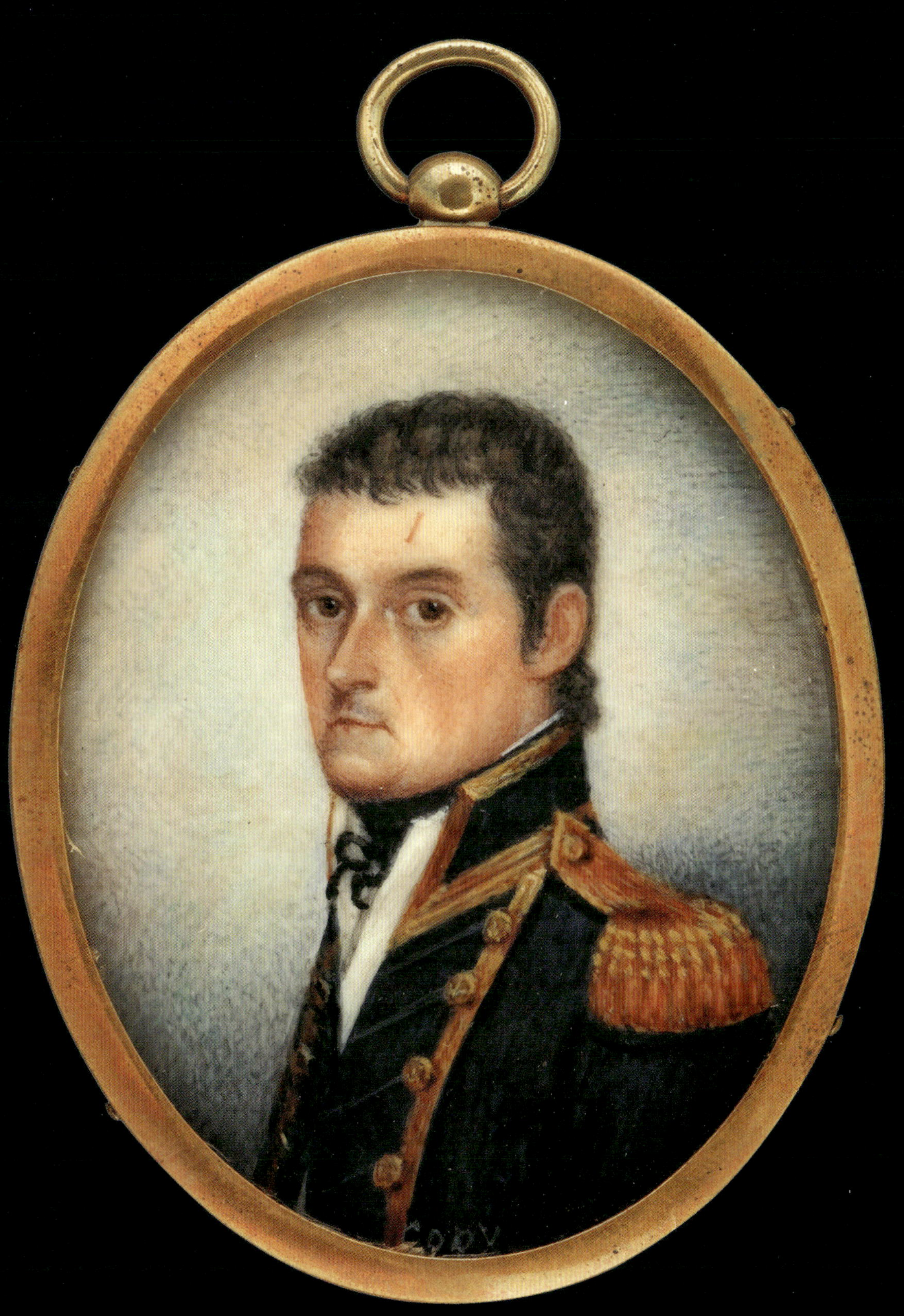

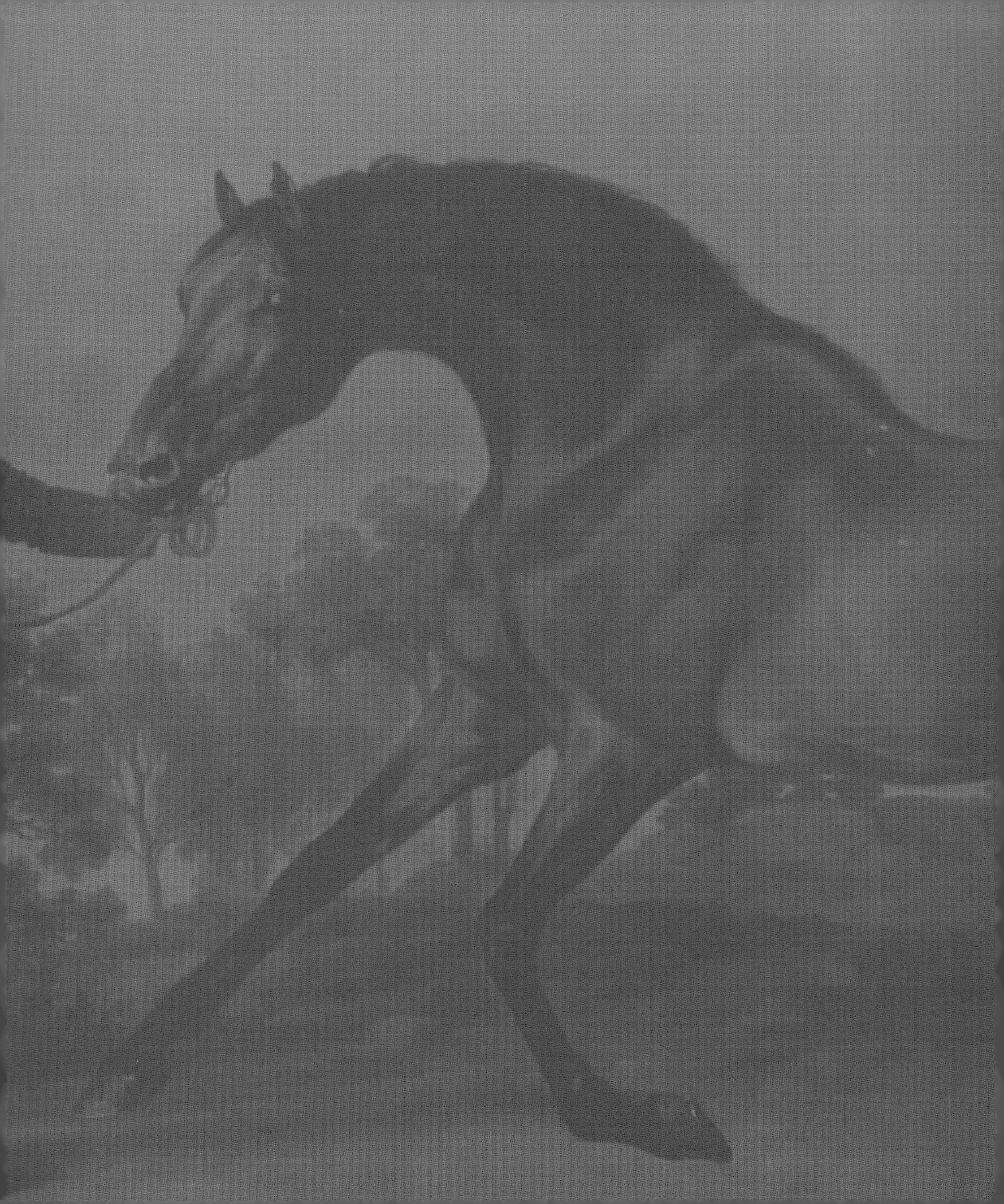

Stubbs and Lincolnshire

ALAN BORG

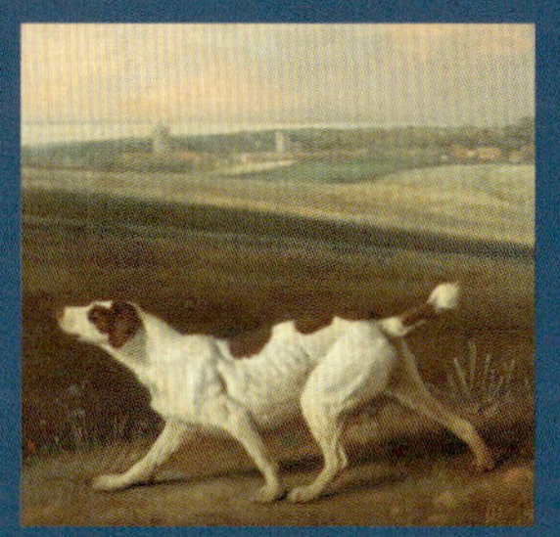

GEORGE STUBBS was born in Liverpool in 1724, the son of a currier and leather seller, but the time he spent in Lincolnshire, both before and after he became famous, was central to his development as an artist. As a boy he worked in his father's shop and at the same time he took up drawing. He was a largely self-taught artist, apart from a brief spell working with the Lancashire painter Hamlet Winstanley. From an early age he had a passion for anatomy and when he moved to York in 1746 he found the recently established Publick Hospital for the Diseased Poor an ideal place to study the living and to dissect the dead. At this time he was primarily a portrait painter, with a growing reputation that was largely based upon his ability to build up a network of clients from the wealthier layers of local society. This ability was later to stand him in good stead both in Lincolnshire and in London. But he was in no sense a national figure at this time.

Few details of Stubbs's early artistic development have survived and what is known derives largely from a memoir written late in his life by a young artist who admired him, Ozias Humphrey. This seems to have been based on conversations that the two men had and represents Stubbs's own views. It is therefore a largely uncritical account, glossing over any unfavourable elements; nonetheless, what it does reveal is generally believed to be accurate. According to Humphrey, it was during a visit to his mother in Liverpool in 1755 that Stubbs 'painted his own Grey mare, which was thought to have succeeded greatly, so that when Mr Parsons, a picture dealer from London saw it, he said that he was sure the author of that picture, if he came to Town, would make his fortune in that line of art'. This is the first record of Stubbs painting a horse, the subject that was to dominate so much of his subsequent career.

He was not yet ready to make the leap to London and instead, as his interest in painting animals grew, he moved from York to Hull in 1752. Here he could develop his network of patrons to include the great families of northern Lincolnshire, for whom fox hunting was an ever-popular pursuit. In 1715 the hounds bred by the Vyner, Tyrwhitt and Pelham families had been combined to form the Brocklesby Hunt, which ranged over thousands of acres stretching from the Humber as far as Scunthorpe and Louth. The Brocklesby rapidly became one of the leading hunts in the country, with its hounds providing the essential bloodline of the foxhound breed in England.

George Stubbs (1724–1806)
***Sir John Nelthorpe, 6th Bt, aged about eleven*, about 1756**
Oil on canvas
Scawby Hall

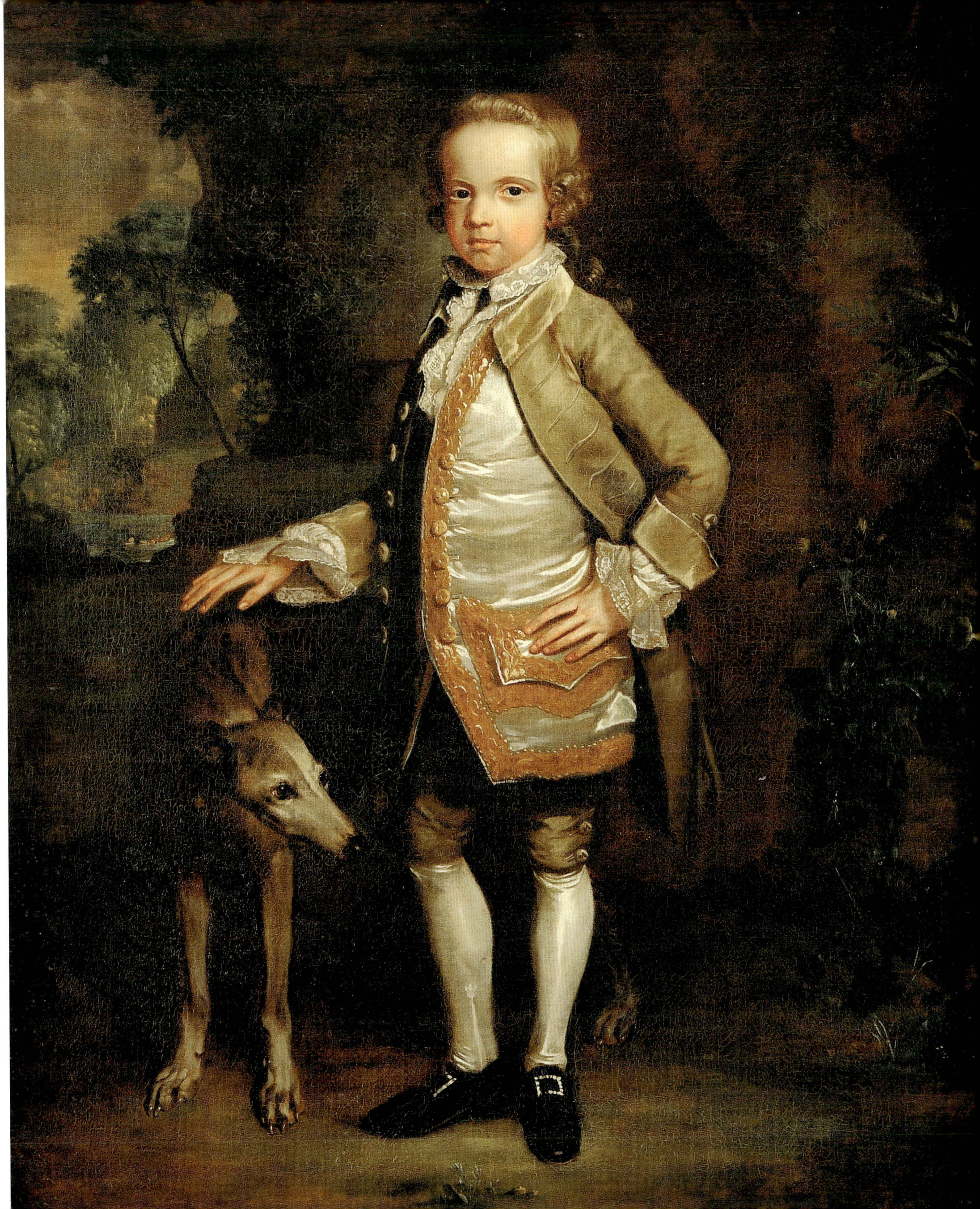

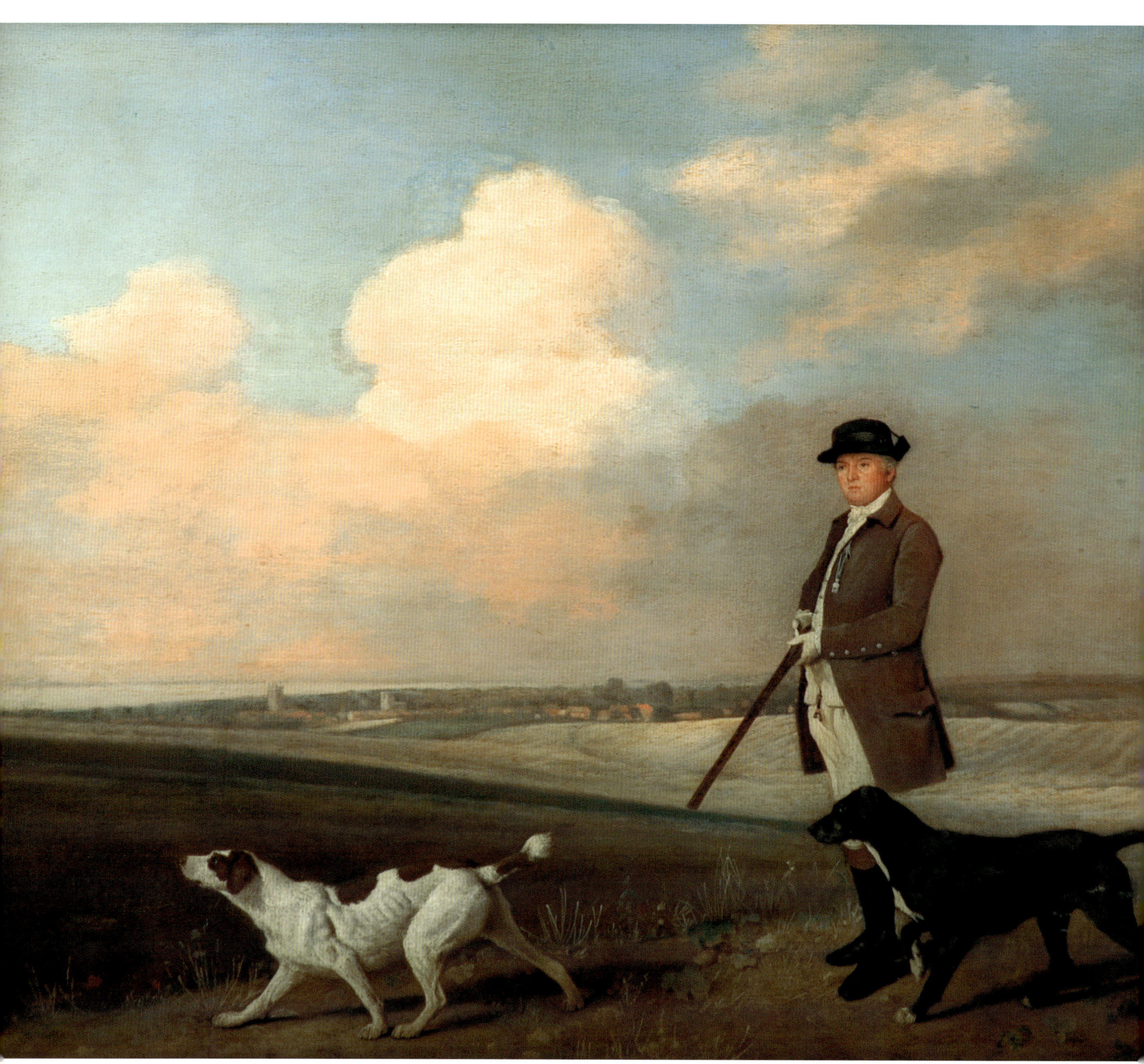

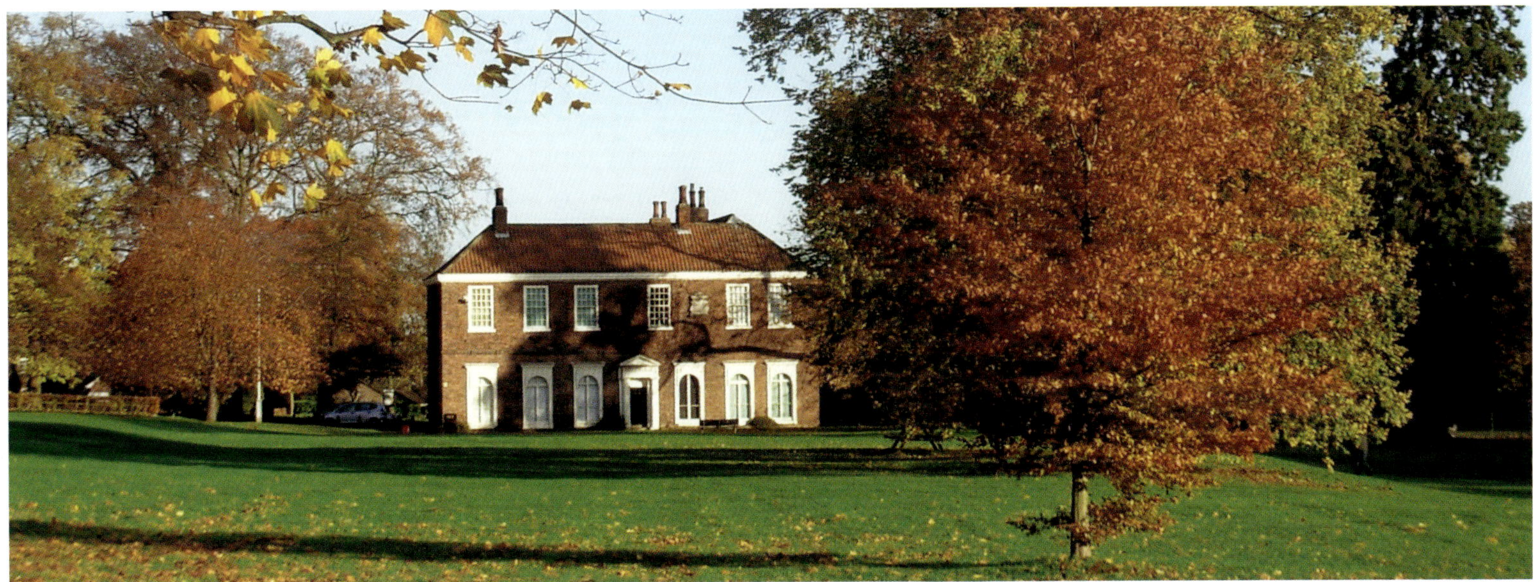

Baysgarth House, Barton-upon-Humber
Photo: North Lincolnshire Tourism Team

OPPOSITE
George Stubbs (1724–1806)
***Sir John Nelthorpe shooting with his dogs over his home ground, Barton Field in Lincolnshire*, 1776**
Oil on panel
Scawby Hall

Although Stubbs probably did make some paintings of horses during his stay in Hull, he remained primarily a portraitist and devoted his time to widening his client base. One family, the Nelthorpes of Barton-on-Humber and Brigg, became close friends and patrons. He also got to know the Constables of Burton Constable, where William Constable had assembled a vast collection of antiquities, many of which he brought from Italy. This may have inspired Stubbs to continue his visual education with a Grand Tour visit to Rome in 1754. There he saw the sights and mixed with various British artists who were living in the city and were inspired by its antiquities. They included Richard Wilson, Gavin Hamilton, William Chambers and Matthew Brettingham, and no doubt Stubbs engaged in many lively discussions with them. At this time it was accepted by almost all who were interested in the arts that the civilisations of Greece and Rome represented the highest achievements of visual culture, matched but not surpassed by the great painters and sculptors of the Renaissance. Stubbs, however, dissented from this view and, as Ozias Humphrey recorded, his 'motive for going thither was to convince himself that nature was and always is superior to art, whether Greek or Roman'. Such an unfashionable view would mean that if Stubbs was to convince both his fellow artists and the wider public, he would have to show that observation of nature was a better way forward for artists than the study of antiquities.

It was this Roman experience that led to Stubbs's next move, to Horkstow in Lincolnshire. It was in some ways a bold and risky decision for an artist with a rising reputation effectively to withdraw from his practice for two years and devote himself to the study of equine anatomy. This was not the only major change in his circumstances, for it was at Horkstow that he first took up with Mary Spencer, described by Humphrey as 'his female relation and friend', who was to remain with him for the rest of his life. His (presumed) wife, by whom he had three children, had died in childbirth in 1755, but it is unclear who exactly Mary Spencer was or how

Jean-Claude Nattes (about 1765–1839)
Horkstow Church, 1796
Drawing
Lincolnshire Libraries

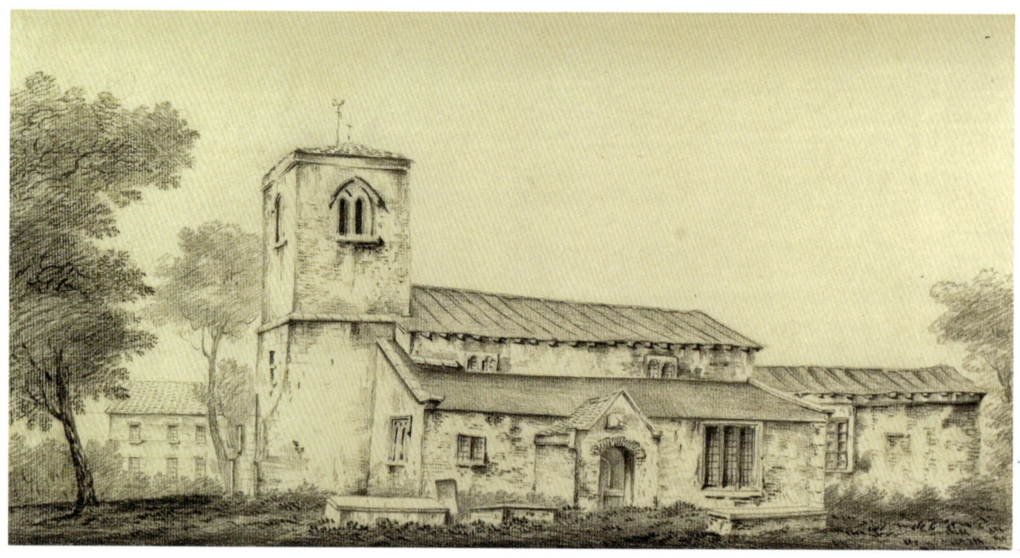

closely she was related to him. What is certain is that she became his common-law wife and bore him a son, Richard, in 1781.

Horkstow is a small and fairly remote hamlet, where Stubbs would have had few friends and which would seldom have been visited by any of his smart acquaintances, yet it proved to be ideal for his purpose. He was not there to paint portraits or to socialise, but to learn all he could about the anatomy of horses. His previous studies in York had shown him the value of the observation of human anatomy; now he determined to apply the same principles to the horse. He probably leased a farmhouse in Horkstow from his friend Elizabeth Nelthorpe and he and Mary remained there for two years. A dissecting room was set up in an adjoining barn, with an iron bar suspended from the ceiling, along with various hooks and a wooden plank on which the horse's hooves could be placed. This allowed Stubbs to arrange his equine carcasses in a variety of positions, including standing, walking, and running.

It was not easy work since horses are large and heavy animals; manhandling the carcasses required great physical strength and Stubbs needed the assistance of Mary Spencer to achieve the postures he wanted. The whole process certainly demanded a strong stomach. Firstly the horse was bled to death and then liquid wax was injected into its blood vessels, so they retained their original form and the animal continued to be pliable. This process had been developed by Leonardo da Vinci in his anatomical studies and was perfected by the Dutch anatomist Jan Swammerdam nearly two hundred years later. Once he was satisfied that the horse was arranged in a lifelike manner, Stubbs would dissect the animal layer by layer, making detailed drawings of each stage of the operation.

Forty-one of these Horkstow drawings are preserved in the Royal Academy of Arts Library, which in itself is something of an irony. Having been ignored by the Academy for several years on the grounds that he was a mere animal painter, Stubbs was elected as a full member in 1776, only to have his election annulled because he

George Stubbs (1724–1806)
Sir Henry Nelthorpe and his second wife, Elizabeth, 1746
Oil on canvas
Scawby Hall

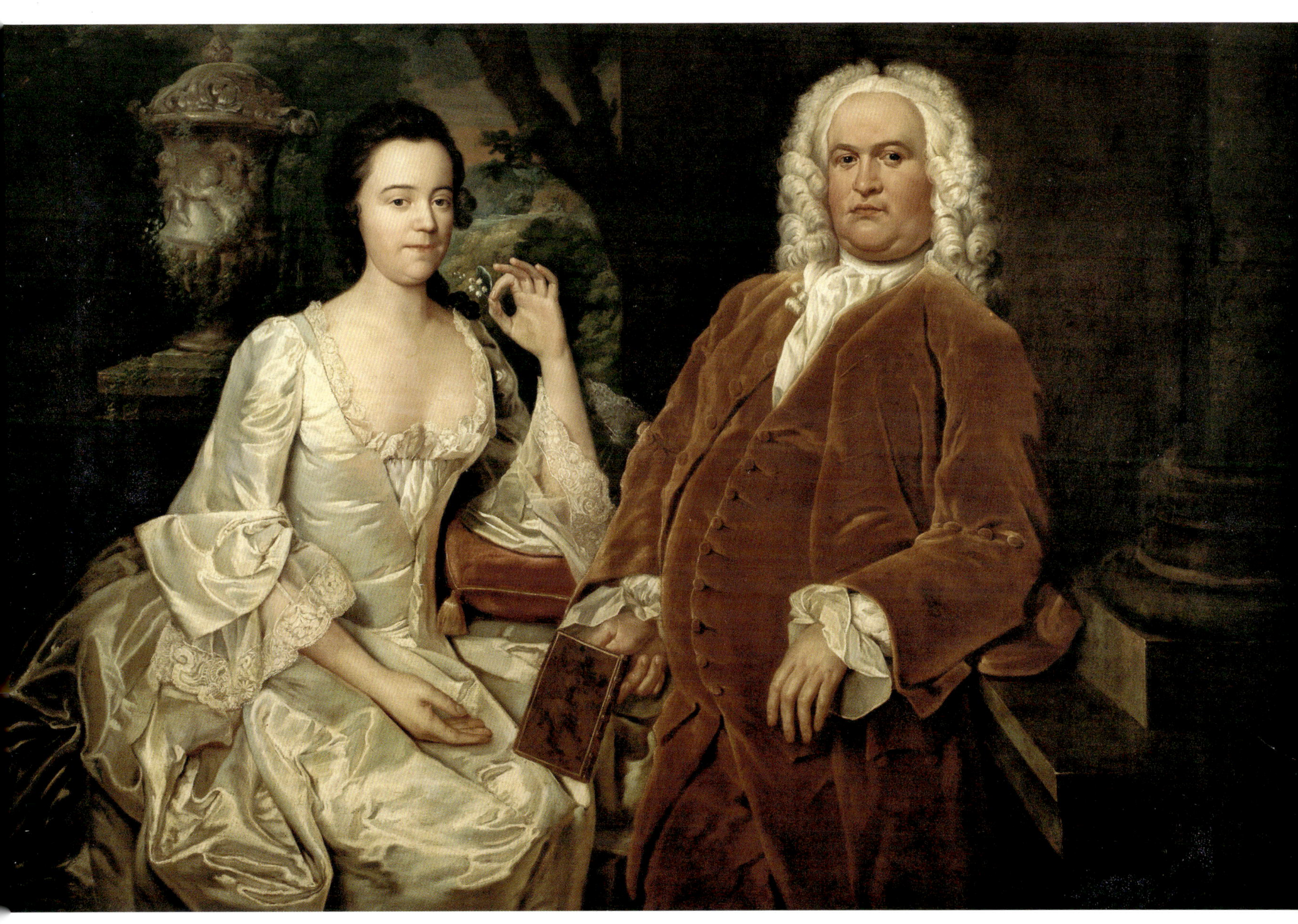

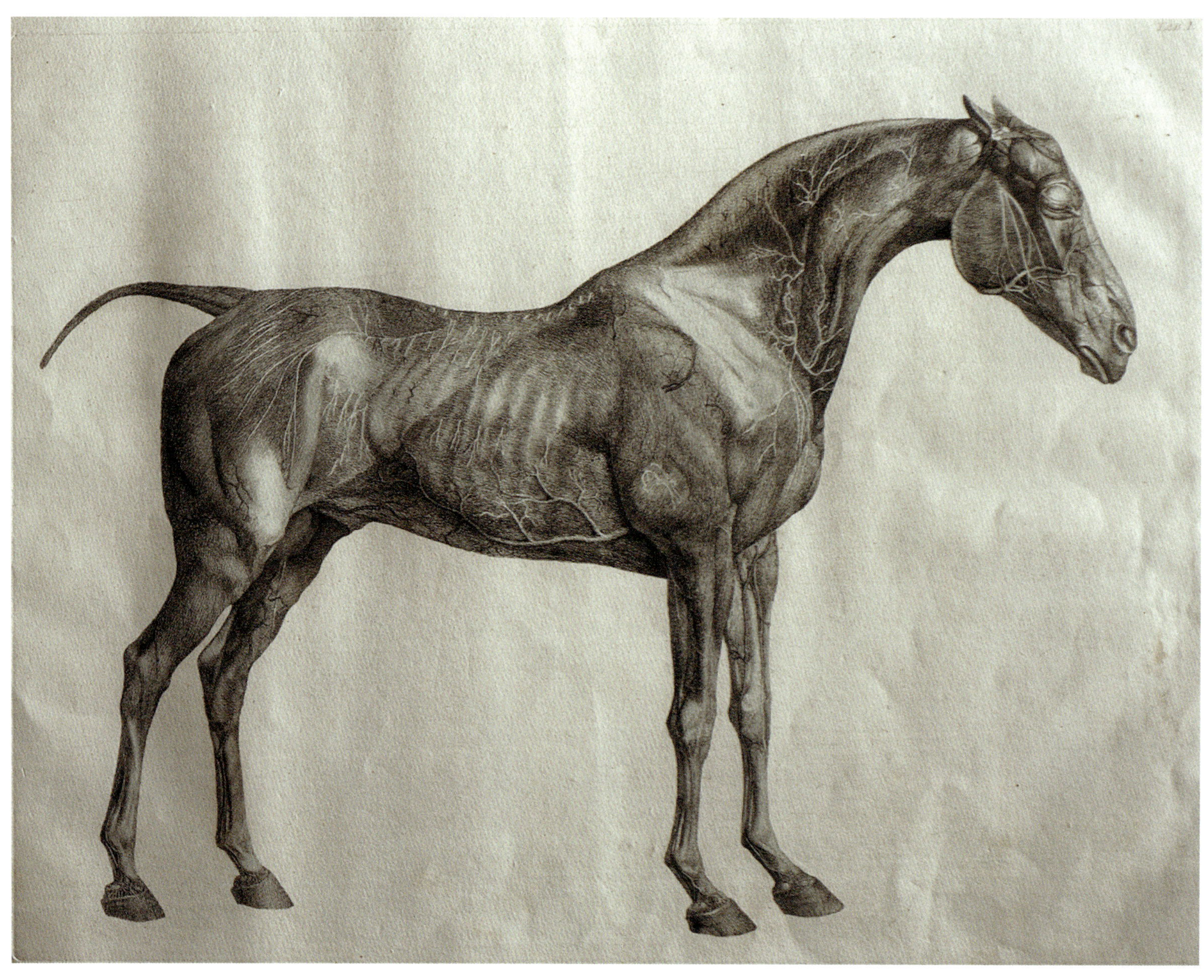

George Stubbs (1724–1806)
Engraving from *The Anatomy of the Horse* (1766)
Scawby Hall

had failed to submit the required diploma piece. However, the Horkstow drawings were acquired by the Victorian artist Edwin Landseer, who bequeathed them to his brother Charles, a long-serving keeper of the Royal Academy Schools.

In 1758 Stubbs moved to London, hoping to find an engraver willing to make the plates for publication of his drawings. Although he seems to have approached all the well-known London engravers, no one was prepared to take on the task. They may well have thought that there was no money to be made from anatomical studies of horses drawn by an unknown artist, since most publications that concerned anatomy were devoted to the human body. He was deeply upset by this rebuff, especially when one famous engraver simply laughed at his drawings, and he determined to take on the job himself. Stubbs was not entirely without

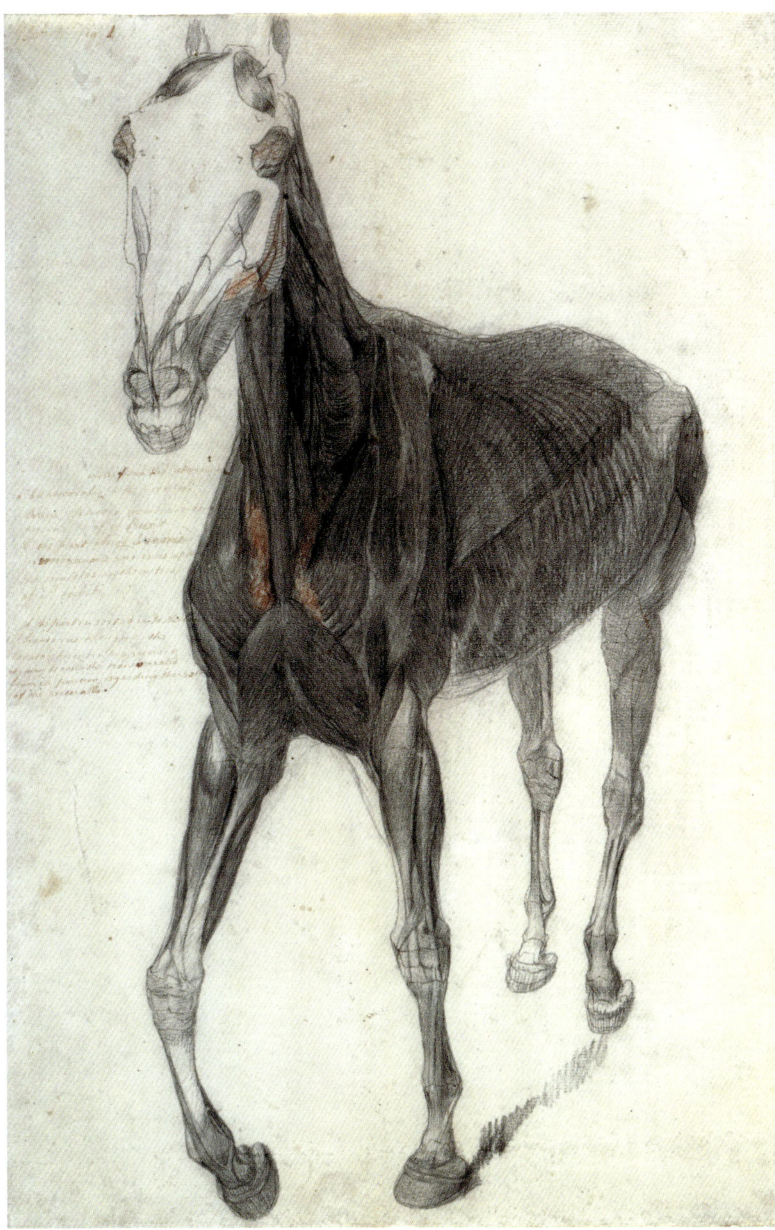

George Stubbs (1724–1806)
Working drawing for 'The Eighth Anatomical Table of the Muscles ... of the Horse', 1756–8
Pencil, chalk and ink
Royal Academy of Arts, 03/5721

experience in this field, since his friend Dr John Burton had asked if he would engrave the eighteen copper plates needed to illustrate his *Complete New System of Midwifery*, published in 1751. He took some persuading, but eventually agreed and set about teaching himself to etch; although he professed to be disappointed with the results, he clearly mastered the art.

In London Stubbs also needed to earn his living, so he could only work on the production of the plates from his horse drawings in his spare time. Progress was painfully slow and the work enormously detailed: it took him six years to make eighteen plates. The book was eventually published in 1766 with its full title *The Anatomy of the Horse including a particular description of the bones, cartilages, muscles, fascias, ligaments, nerves, arteries, veins, and glands; in eighteen tables,*

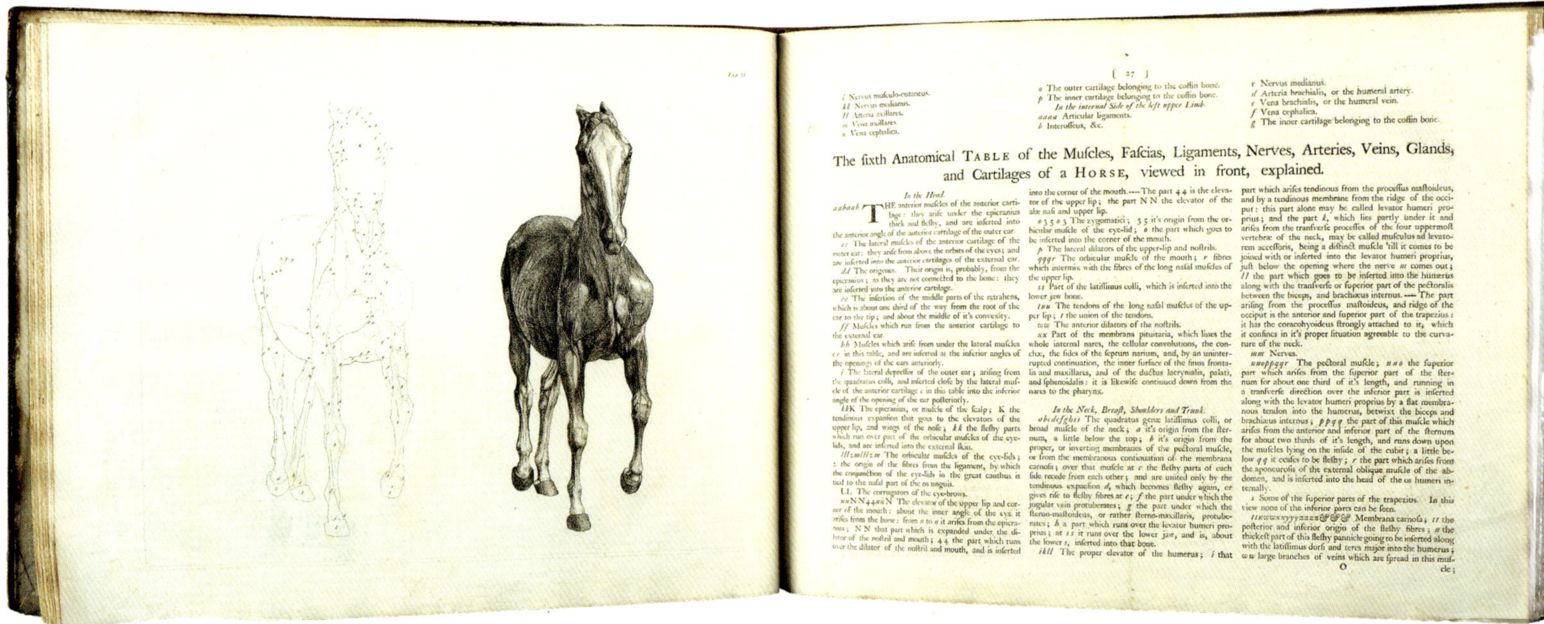

The ſixth Anatomical TABLE of the Muſcles, Faſcias, Ligaments, Nerves, Arteries, Veins, Glands, and Cartilages of a HORSE, viewed in front, explained.

George Stubbs (1724–1806)
The Anatomy of the Horse (1766),
Sixth anatomical table
Scawby Hall

all done from nature. A descriptive text of some 50,000 words accompanied the illustrations. The publication caused a sensation and was immediately hailed as a masterpiece by artists, scientists and, most importantly, by the great aristocrats who pursued their passion for horse racing and fox hunting from their country seats.

Stubbs's reputation was made and he was soon in great demand and earning a fortune. He painted not only in London, but travelled frequently to the great estates of his patrons. In Lincolnshire he went to Brocklesby, where Lord Yarborough acquired several of his works, and also to Grimsthorpe to work for Lord Ancaster. Hunting subjects would normally include figures of the huntsmen with their horses and frequently also with their dogs. It was a natural progression for him to start painting pictures of individual dogs that were specially prized by their masters, and from this he went on to portray a range of other animals. One of the most famous of these portraits was *The Lincolnshire Ox* (1790), belonging to John Gibbon of Long Sutton in Lincolnshire. The ox was a beast of exceptional size, which Gibbon won in a cockfight and then brought to London for exhibition in Hyde Park. Stubbs painted it and his picture was exhibited in the Royal Academy while the ox itself was still in Hyde Park. This was the first instance of what was to become a tradition in Britain of painting enormous farm animals that were much prized by their owners, who would pay handsomely for such pictures. Stubbs charged Gibbon £26 12s 6d for his picture of the ox, a price which put it in the top bracket of the contemporary art market.

Many of Stubbs's works, including *The Lincolnshire Ox*, were made into prints, which both increased their circulation and further boosted the artist's income. He also continued to paint other and more exotic animals, including a zebra from Africa presented to Queen Charlotte. This attracted him because of its obvious relationship with the horse and he painted it not as a commission but out of his

George Stubbs (1724–1806)
***The Lincolnshire Ox, portrayed with John Gibbons and his prize-winning gamecock*, 1790**
Oil on panel
National Museums Liverpool, Walker Art Gallery

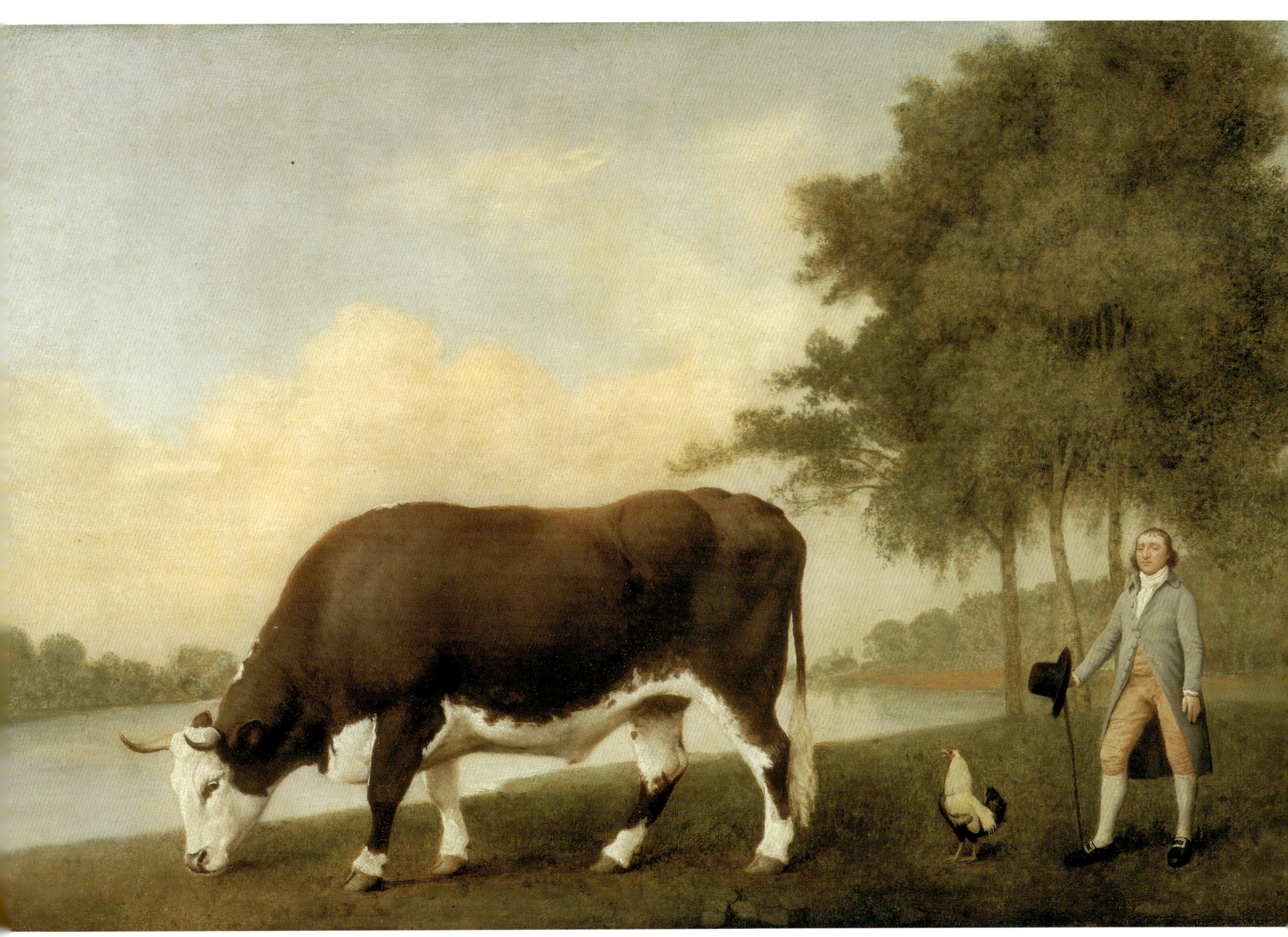

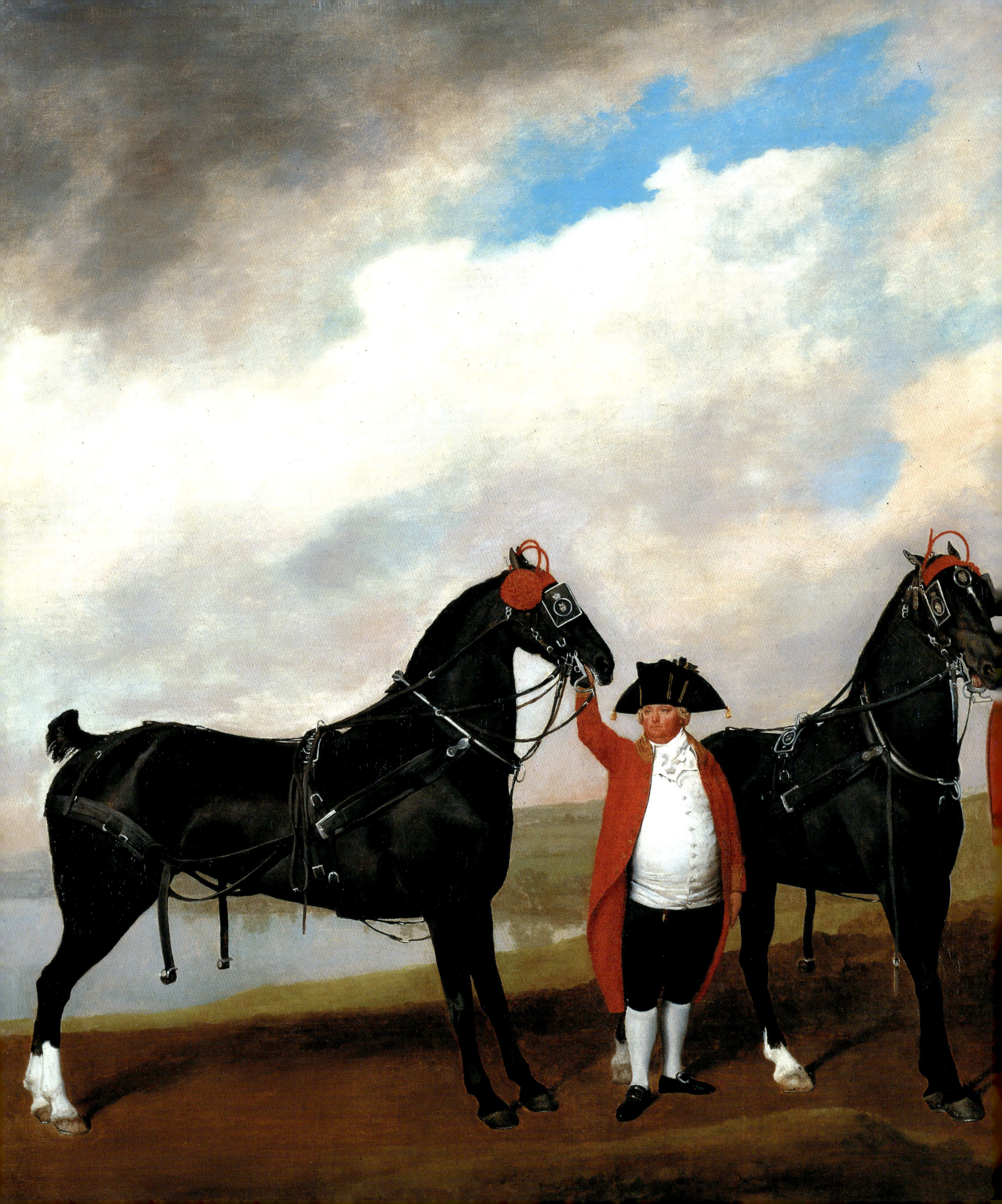

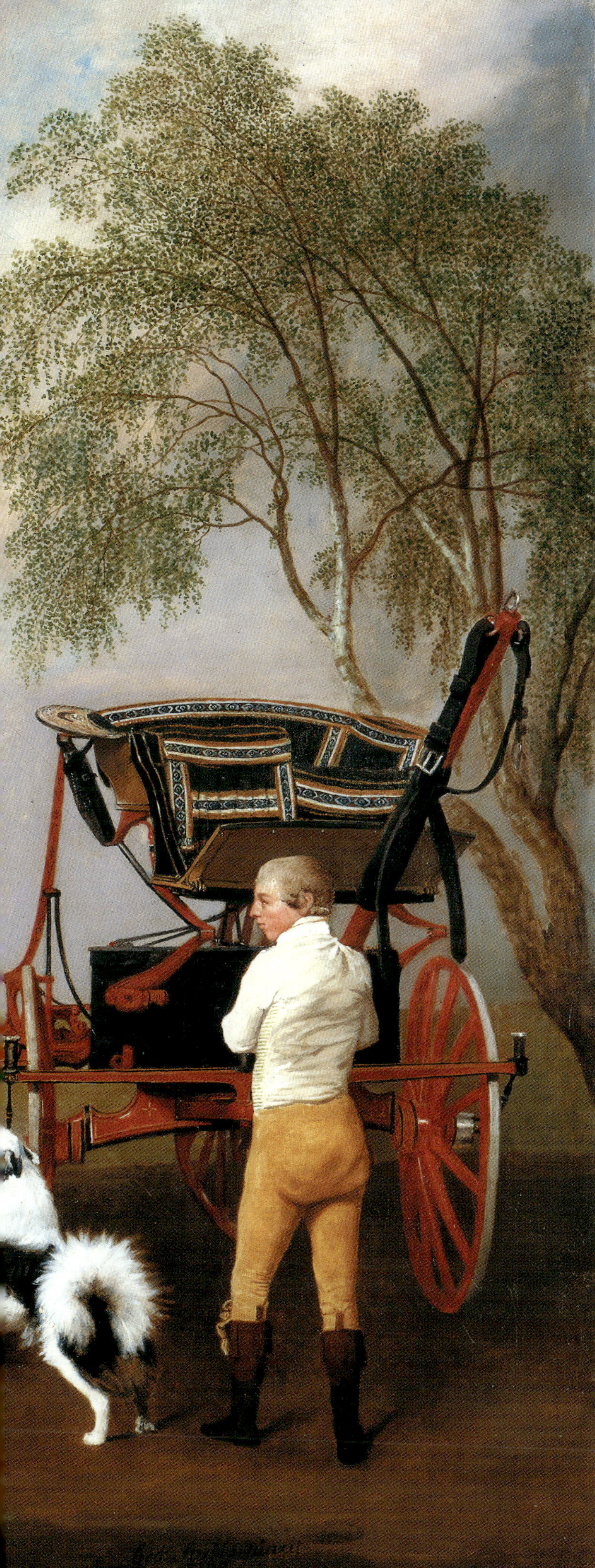

George Stubbs (1724–1806)
***The Prince of Wales's Phaeton*, 1793**
Oil on canvas
The Royal Collection

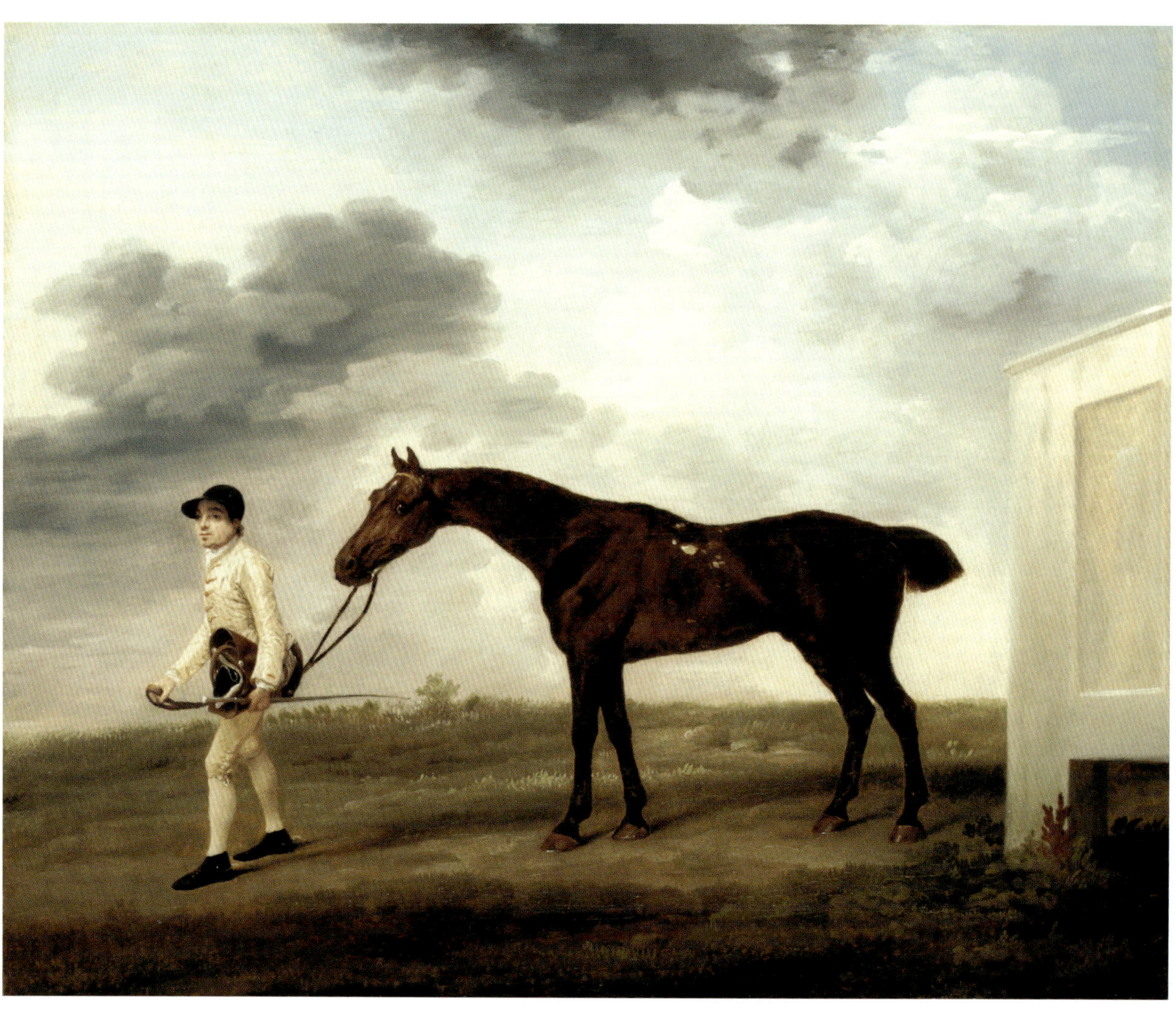

George Stubbs (1724–160/11806)
A bay racehorse belonging to the Duke of Ancaster, led by a jockey, about 1762
Oil on canvas
Grimsthorpe and Drummond Castle

own interest. Other beasts he depicted included a rhinoceros from a circus, tigers at play, and the first Western pictures of a kangaroo (p. 140) and a dingo, which were brought back by Captain Cook from his first expedition on board HMS *Endeavour*.

But it was to the horse that he returned most often. Among the first admirers of *The Anatomy of the Horse* was the 3rd Duke of Richmond, whose country estate was at Goodwood in Sussex. Stubbs made several paintings for him, including *The Duke's Racehorses at Exercise* (1760–1), one of many pictures of horses in training. He visited Newmarket frequently, making pictures that showed particular racehorses with their owners, trainers, stable lads and jockeys. He also went to the Epsom stables of William Wildman to paint the most famous of all racers, Eclipse. He returned to Lincolnshire regularly, to stay with friends and paint their animals. These included the Brocklesby huntsmen Thomas Smith and his son in 1772, out on a morning ride with one of the hounds. Twenty years later, he again painted a pair of Brocklesby hounds for the Revd Thomas Vyner, an avid sportsman and breeder of the famous Lincolnshire dogs.

George Stubbs was now famous and rich, but perhaps the ultimate accolade came when in 1790 he accepted a commission from the Prince of Wales (later

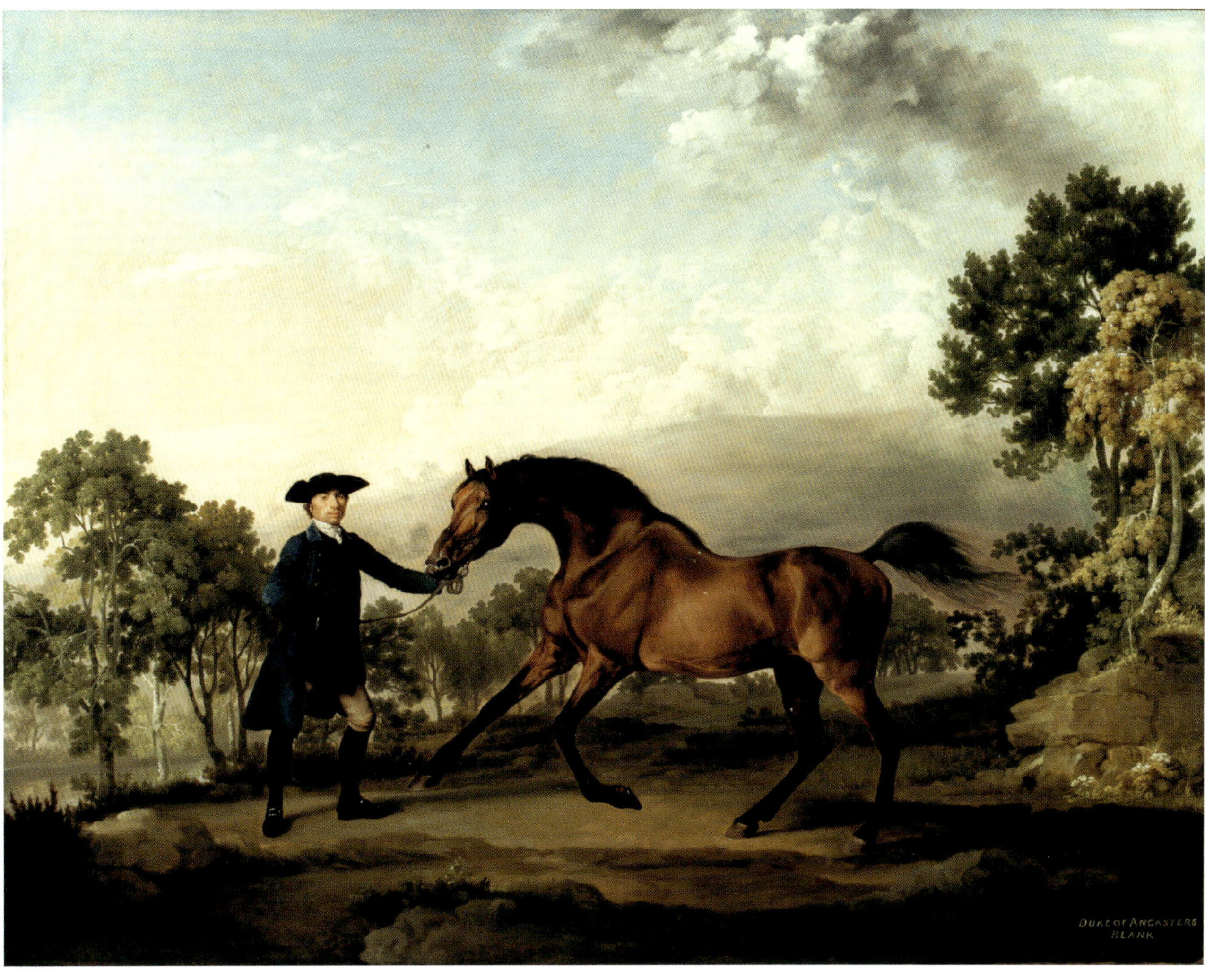

George Stubbs (1724–1806)
***The Duke of Ancaster's bay stallion Blank, held by Old Parnam, his groom*, about 1761**
Oil on canvas
Grimsthorpe and Drummond Castle

King George IV) for a total of fourteen paintings, clearly intended as a series representing the different aspects of the prince's sporting interests. Today there are sixteen paintings by Stubbs in the Royal Collection, thirteen of which are from the original commission. They make up the single largest collection of his late paintings, with horses as usual to the fore.

He continued to paint in his later years and, at the age of seventy, started a new project to produce *A Comparative Anatomical Exposition of the Human Body with that of a Tiger and a Common Fowl*, which was only part published by the time of his death in 1806 at the age of eighty-one. This was an extraordinary, almost philosophical venture that looked forward to Charles Darwin's development of evolutionary theory. Nonetheless, his artistic work quickly fell out of favour after his death and he was largely unappreciated by historians and critics until he was rediscovered in Britain after the Second World War. Today it is recognised that his pictures of horses, while based on the detailed anatomical studies he undertook at Horkstow, transcend mere recording and capture the beauty, strength and poise of these noble beasts. We may perhaps agree with his own opinion that nature always surpasses art, but in terms of painting horses and dogs, Stubbs has no equal.

of men;
thy darkling red
that bubbles fast
of the Past
the dead;

besieged eaves
coming care,
there

breath
rth

th.

I wake, I rise: from end to end
Of all the landskip underneath
I find no place that does not
Some gracious memory of my friend.

No grey old grange, or lonely fold,
Or low morass & whispering reed,
Or simple stile from mead to mead,
Or sheepwalk up the windy wold.

Nor hoary knoll of ash & haw
That hears the latest linnet trill;
Nor quarry trench'd along the hill,
And haunted by the jangling daw;

Nor fountain sparkling from the rock;
Nor pastoral rivulet that swerves
To left & right thro' meadowy curves
That feed the mothers of the

But each

Alfred Tennyson

LEONÉE ORMONDE

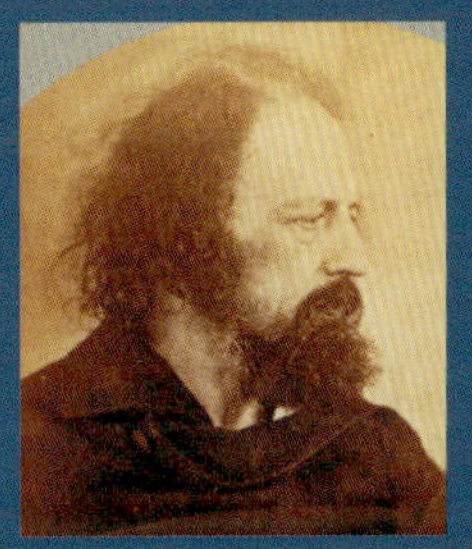

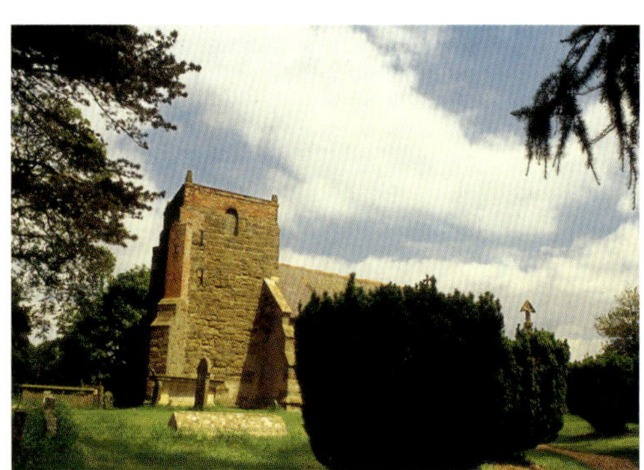

Church of St Margaret, Somersby
Photo: Andrew Tryner. Copyright Lincolnshire County Council

ALFRED TENNYSON was born at Somersby in the Lincolnshire Wolds on 6 December 1809, the third surviving son of George Clayton Tennyson, Rector of Somersby and Bag Enderby. The poet was from Lincolnshire stock on both sides of his family. His paternal grandfather, George Tennyson the elder, was a lawyer based in Market Rasen, who had created a small property empire, while his mother, Elizabeth Fytche, was the daughter of a former vicar of Louth. The poet's uncle Charles, his father's younger brother, built Bayons Manor at Tealby and added d'Eyncourt to his name, in a reference to the Tennysons' distant relationship to the Barons d'Eyncourt.

Apart from an unhappy spell, from 1816 to 1820, at the Grammar School in Louth, the young Alfred was educated by his father at home in Somersby. George Tennyson seems to have been a good teacher, even though his mental state was deteriorating. One of his problems was jealousy of his brother Charles, whom he believed, with some truth, to have been favoured above himself. Faced with a difficult home life, Alfred clearly found it a relief to wander in the countryside. It is said that he only left the county twice before going up to Cambridge in 1828 and he knew his surroundings well.

There can be no doubt of his response to landscape, a response that was to have a powerful effect on his writing. In an early poem, 'Ode to Memory', published in 1830, he writes of the 'The seven elms, the poplars four / That stand beside my father's door'. Later in the poem, he describes the rectory garden:

Or a garden bowered close
With plaited alleys of the trailing rose,
Long alleys falling down to twilight grots,
Or opening upon level plots
Of crownèd lilies, standing near
Purple-spikèd lavender.

Samuel Laurence (1812–84) and Sir Edward Coley Burne-Jones (1833–98)
***Alfred Tennyson, 1st Baron Tennyson (1809–92)*, about 1840**
Oil on canvas
National Portrait Gallery, London

A number of later poems reflect Tennyson's Lincolnshire origins as he recalled the scenes of his childhood. At the bottom of the rectory garden flowed a brook, running into the River Lymn, which, for all the poet's denial, was surely one inspiration for the well-known lines in the poem of that name, published in 1855. 'The Brook' tells the story, largely in the first person, of Lawrence Aylmer's youthful affection for

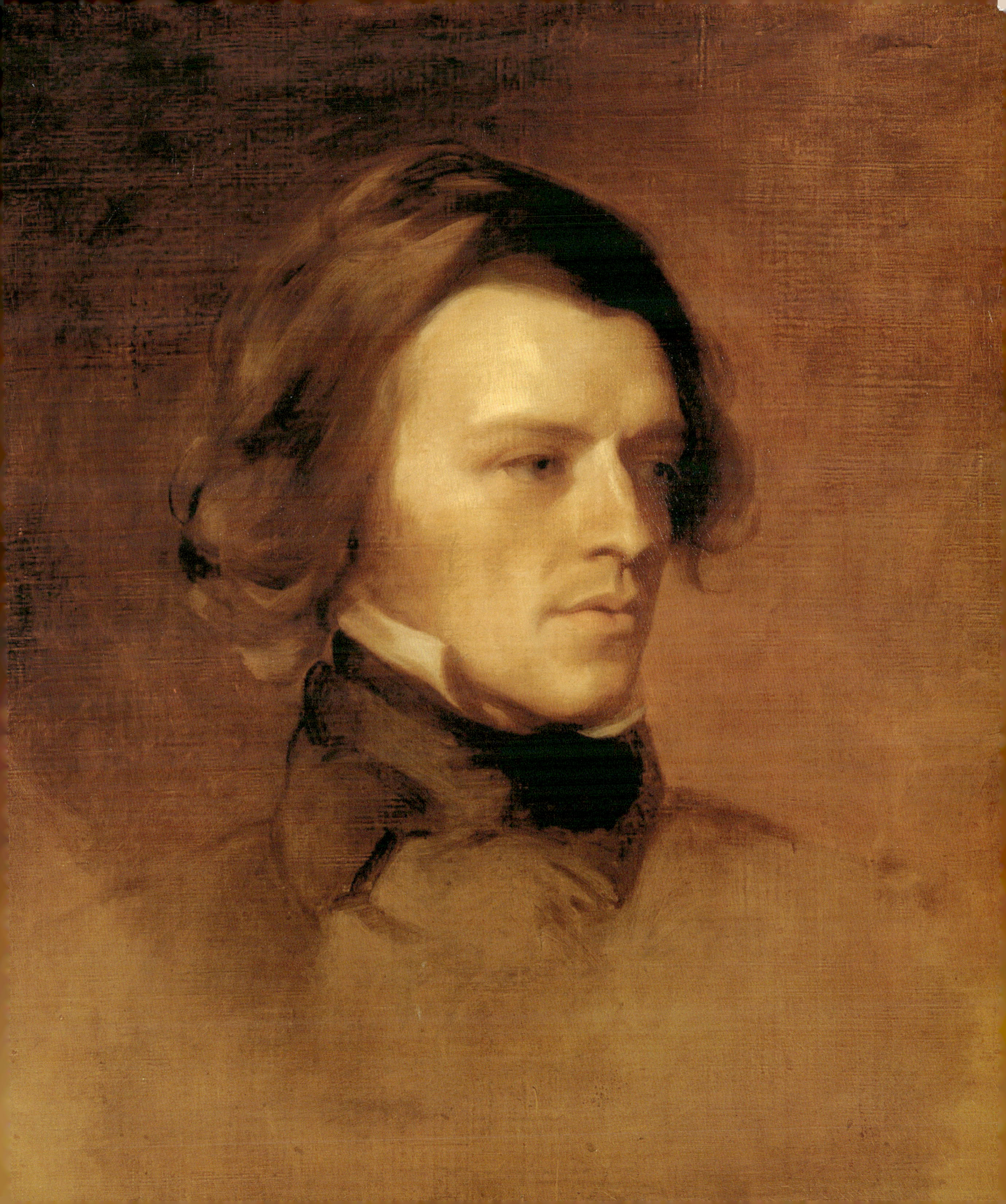

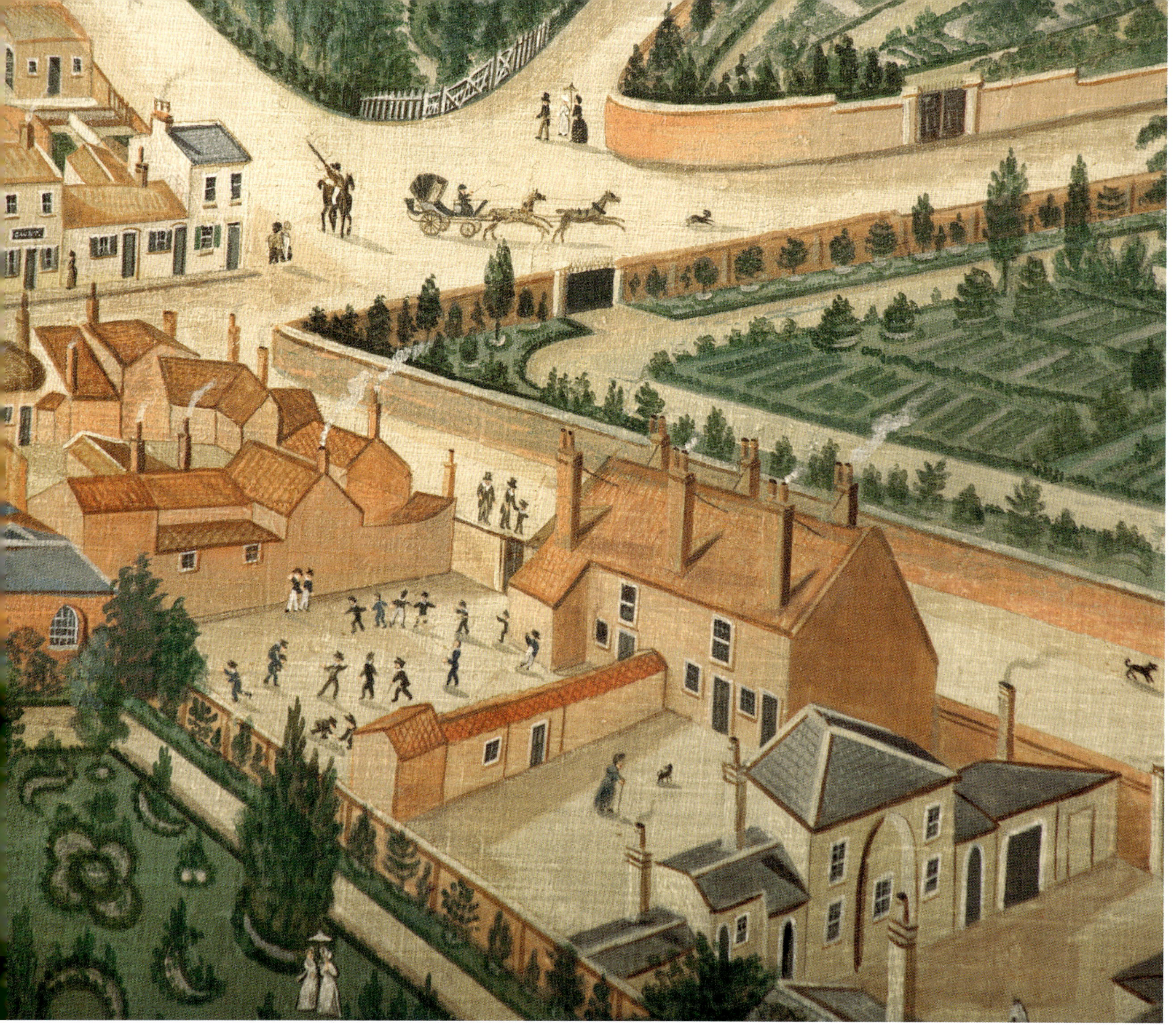

William Brown (1788–1859)
***Louth Panorama*, 1844–7**
Detail showing Louth Grammar School with boys in the playground
Oil on linen
Louth Town Council

Katie Willows, the daughter of a local farmer. He describes how he helped her by distracting her father so that she could talk with her fiancé. Aylmer also recalls his much-loved poet brother, Edmund, who died young in Florence, a clear reference to Tennyson's friend Arthur Hallam, whose death in Vienna at the age of twenty-two had inspired Tennyson's requiem *In Memoriam*, published five years earlier, in 1850. In 'The Brook', the fictional Edmund Aylmer's poem takes the form of the song of the brook itself, running at intervals through the narrative of Tennyson's poem. At one point the brook passes by gardens like that at Somersby Rectory.

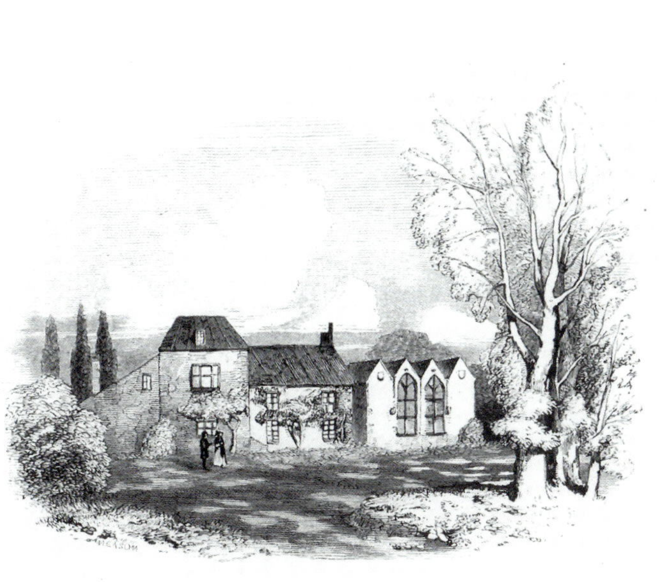

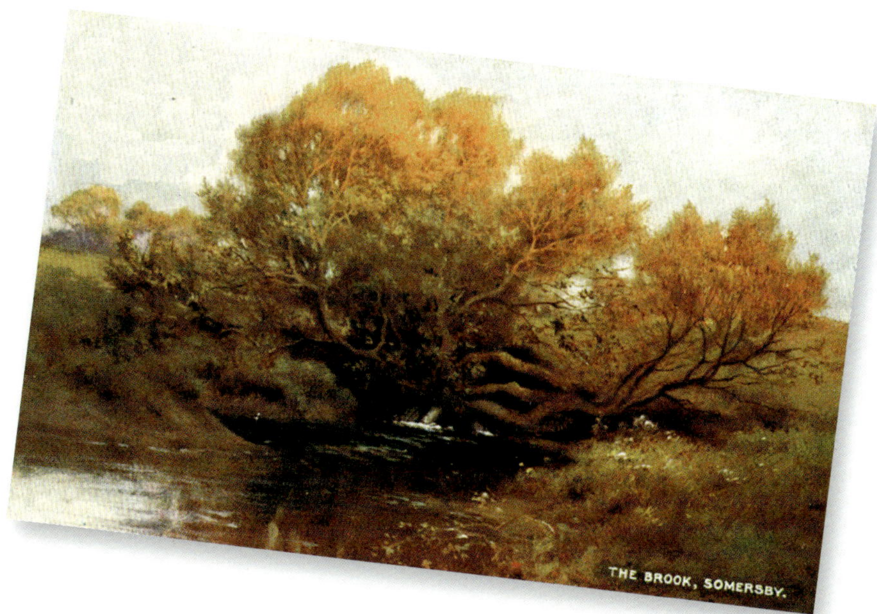

Unknown artist
Somersby Rectory, about 1847
Drawing
Tennyson Research Centre, 5990

Tennyson's 'Brook': 'I make the netted sunbeams dance'
Postcard
Tennyson Research Centre, TRC413

I steal by lawns and grassy plots,
I slide by hazel covers;
I move the sweet forget-me-nots
That grow for happy lovers.

I slip, I slide, I gloom, I glance,
Among my skimming swallows;
I make the netted sunbeam dance
Against my sandy shallows.

Not surprisingly, postcards showing the brook were once on sale, with passages from the poem texting the pictures.

By the time 'The Brook' was written the Tennyson family had long since left Somersby Rectory. They had been able to stay on for a time after the death of George Tennyson in 1831, but had to make way for a new incumbent in 1837. In 'A Farewell', a poem presumed to have been written at the time of their departure for Essex, the brook is invoked as the source of most regret:

Flow down, cold rivulet to the sea,
Thy tribute wave deliver:
No more by thee my steps shall be,
For ever and for ever.

Flow, softly flow, by lawn and lea,
A rivulet then a river:
No where by thee my steps shall be,
For ever and for ever.

The impulse is much the same in *In Memoriam* CI and CII, where Tennyson again describes himself experiencing the rectory for the last time, 'As down the garden-walks I move':

Unwatched, the garden bough shall sway,
The tender blossom flutter down,
Unloved, that beech will gather brown,
This maple burn itself away. (Ricks, II, 423; 421–2)

The Tennysons may be leaving, but the garden will inspire others living in the house:

Till from the garden and the wild
A fresh association blow,
And year by year the landscape grow
Familiar to the stranger's child.

As year by year the labourer tills
His wonted glebe, or lops the glades;
And year by year our memory fades
From all the circle of the hills.

Alfred Tennyson would often walk in the countryside beyond the Somersby garden, sometimes by himself, sometimes with others. Christopher Sturman quotes from a letter written by John Lewis Fytche about the site of the Civil War battlefield of Winceby, three miles from Somersby: 'As a boy I have often walked over the historic field with Alfred Tennyson and my other cousins. It was our favourite walk from Somersby, and the tradition of Slash Lane running down with blood used to startle us.' Sturman argues that this experience influenced Tennyson's early poem 'The Vale of Bones', in which he writes of the earth and flowers stained with blood from Flodden Field: 'How with the red dew o'er thee rained/ Thine emerald turf was darkly stained'.

The immediate neighbourhood of Somersby was not the only source of inspiration for Tennyson's poems on the natural world. In the summer the family

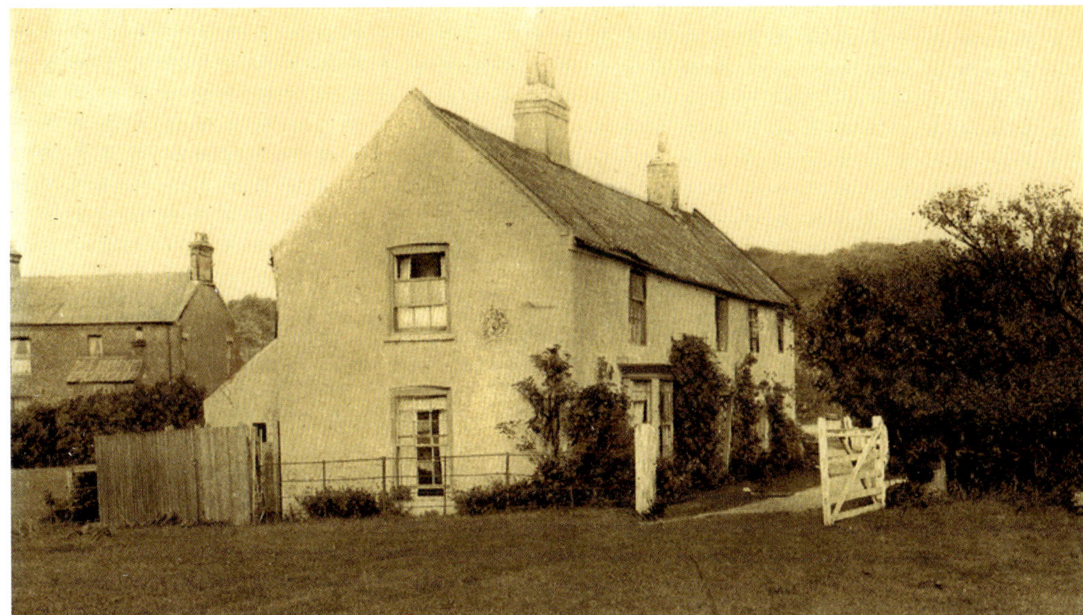

Tennyson's Cottage at Mablethorpe
Postcard
Tennyson Research Centre, TRC423

would travel to the sea coast, staying in cottages in the simple village of Mablethorpe, a very different place from the resort of today. One poem, written when Tennyson was in his middle twenties, although not published until much later, evokes the boy on the beach, bringing alive the classical studies with his father by building his own Grecian fleet like that in *The Iliad* of Homer.

Here often, when a child, I lay reclined,
I took delight in this locality,
Here stood the infant Ilion of the mind,
And here the Grecian ships did seem'd to be.

Comparatively recently, a second verse to this poem was published, from the manuscript:

Yet though perchance no tract of earth have more
Unlikeness to the fair Ionian plain,
I love the place that I have loved before,
I love the rolling cloud, the flying rain,
The brown sea lapsing back with sullen roar
To travel leagues before he comes again,
The misty desert of the houseless shore,
The phantom-circle of the moaning main.

'Ode to Memory', written a few years before, also captures the scene on the North Sea coast, as the young Tennyson imagines himself to be an artist sketching:

Harrington Hall
Photo: Daniel Rollitt

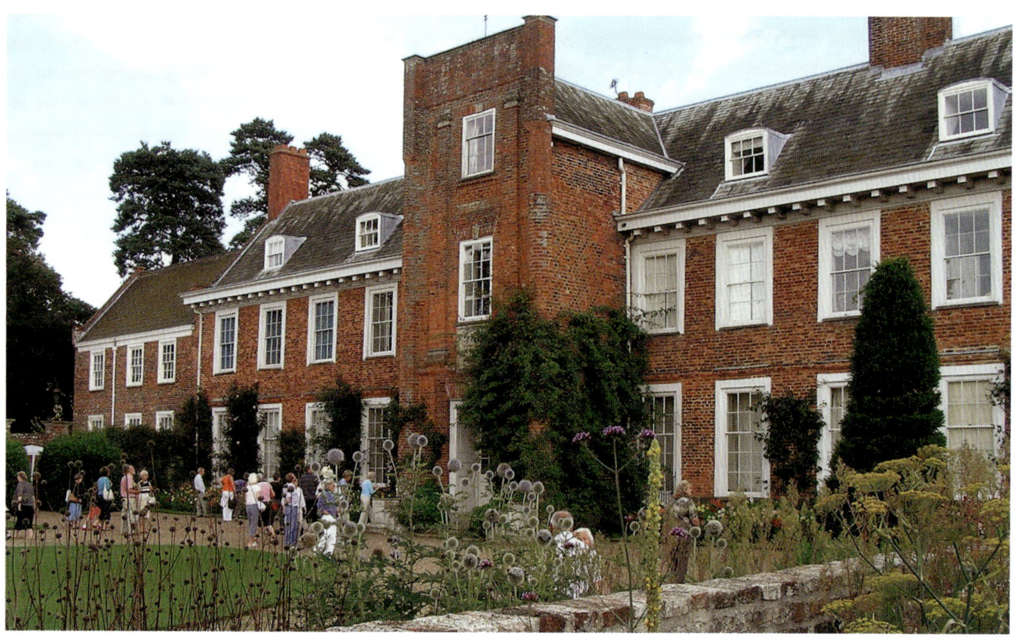

a sand-built ridge
Of heapèd hills that mound the sea,
Overblown with murmurs harsh,
Or even a lowly cottage whence we see
Stretched wide and wild the waste enormous marsh.

Poems by Two Brothers, the first volume to which Alfred Tennyson contributed, was published in Louth by J. and J. Jackson in 1827. In fact the poems were by three brothers: Charles and Alfred wrote the majority, but a few were the work of their elder brother, Frederick. A well-known story tells of Charles and Alfred spending some of the money they had earned on a visit to Mablethorpe, where they 'shared their triumph with the winds and the waves'.

Water was to remain one of the dominant images of Alfred Tennyson's writing, and there can be no doubt that the original inspiration for this came from Lincolnshire, whether from the coast or from playing in the brook in Somersby. He even adapted the last, unpublished, line of 'Here often, when a child, I lay reclined' – 'The phantom circle of the moaning main' – for one of his *Idylls of the King*, *The Passing of Arthur*, published in 1869, where it became 'The phantom circle of a moaning sea'.

While Tennyson's happiest memories of Lincolnshire often evoke landscape, there were also human associations that would leave their mark on his work. The Tennysons had many local acquaintances, among them the family of the Rector of Halton Holegate, Thomas Rawnsley, whose son Drummond and daughter Sophy were close friends of the poet. The younger members of both families were sometimes guests at Harrington Hall, two miles from Somersby. There they met the stepdaughters of the wealthy Arthur Eden, with one of whom, Rosa Baring, a member of the banking family, Alfred Tennyson fell in love. There are a number of

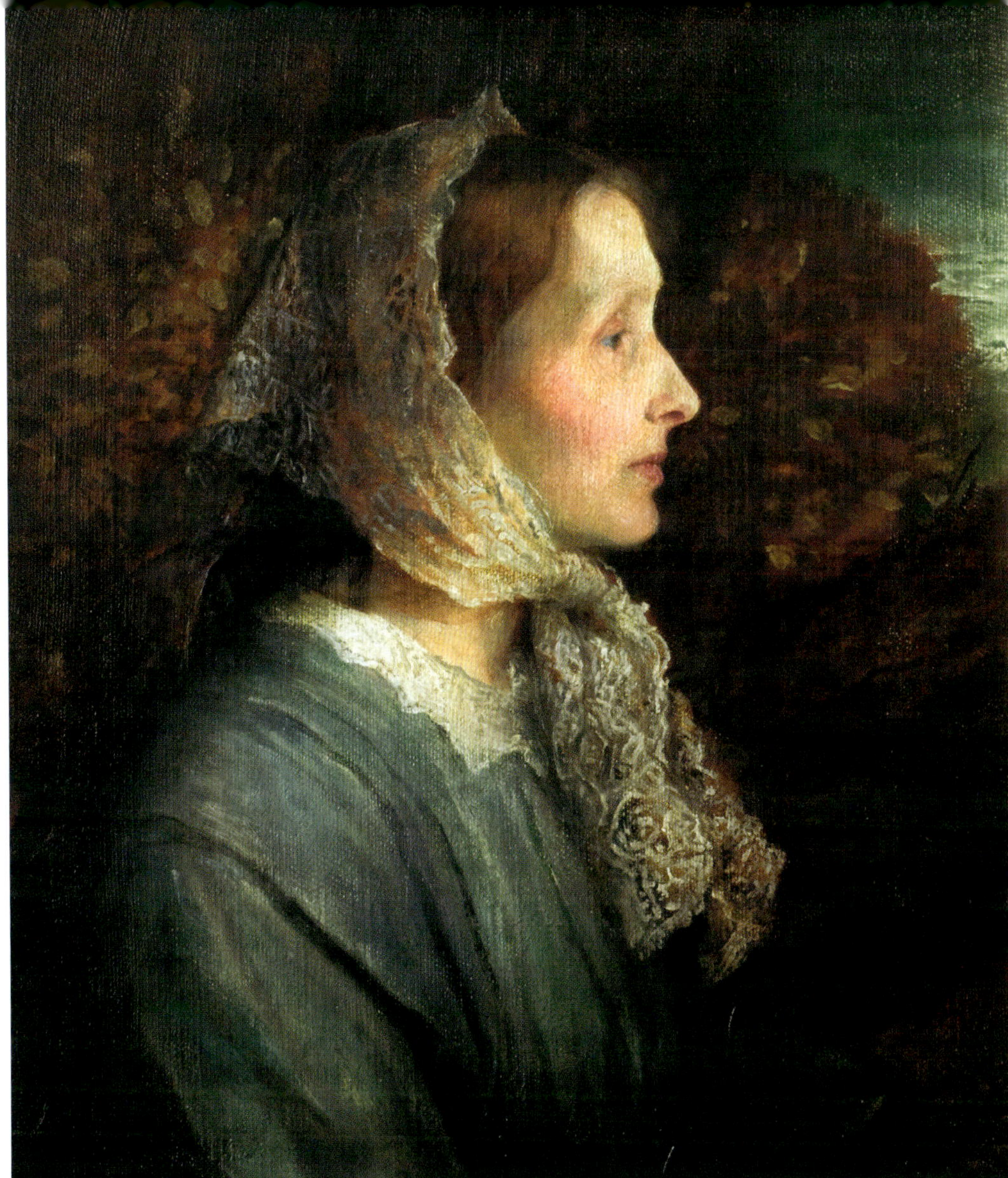

George Frederic Watts (1817–1904)
***Emily Tennyson (1813–96), wife of Alfred Tennyson*, 1862**
Oil on canvas
Tennyson Research Centre

'rose' poems addressed to the young Rosa, who married Robert Shafto in 1838, and she herself claimed to have inspired 'Locksley Hall' where the speaker tells of the woman who gave him up to please her parents, and married another man. However, the most telling effect of this relationship is to be found in 'Maud', published in 1855, long after Tennyson had left the county. 'Maud' tells of the speaker's love for a young woman who is 'above' him in wealth and status. Her brother objects to their relationship and the speaker kills him in a duel and flees abroad. Later he hears that Maud has died and he goes off to fight in the Crimean War.

What might have been another doomed relationship for Tennyson began in 1836, when his brother Charles, who had added the name Turner to his own after inheriting the estate of his uncle, married Louisa Sellwood of Horncastle. Her sister, Emily, attracted his brother Alfred and they became unofficially engaged. The relationship was more difficult after the Tennysons left Somersby in 1837, and the engagement was broken off in 1840. Alfred's comparative poverty and indecision must have been one factor, another may have been Charles Tennyson Turner's

Alfred, Lord Tennyson (1809–92)
'In Memoriam A.H.H.' (1849): original manuscript, known as the 'Butcher's Book'
Tennyson Research Centre

Queen Victoria (1819–1901)
Letter of condolence to Alfred Tennyson on the death of his son, Lionel, in 1885
Tennyson Research Centre

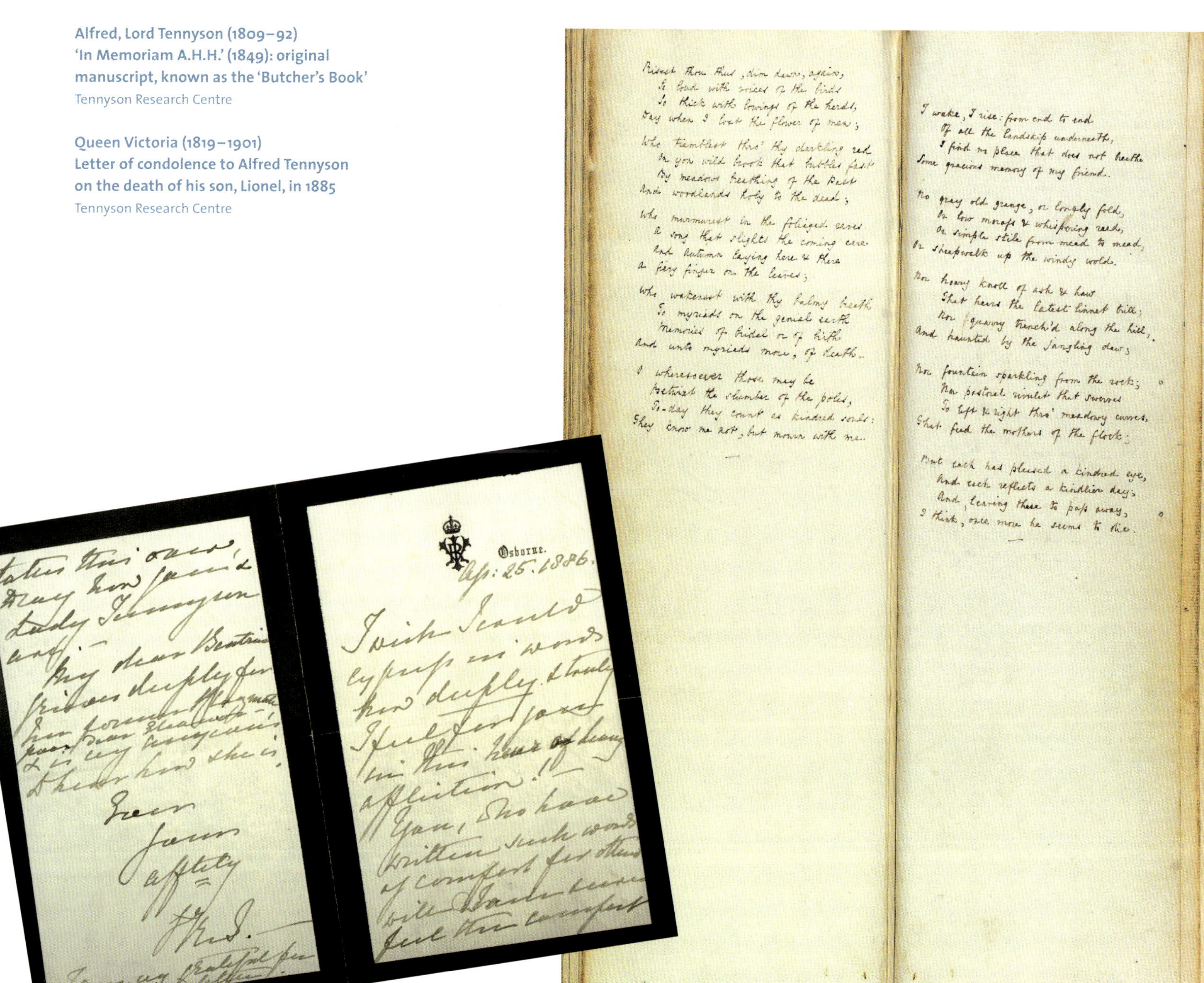

Risest thou thus, dim dawn, again,
So loud with voices of the birds,
So thick with lowings of the herds,
Day when I lost the flower of men;

Who tremblest thro' thy darkling red
On yon wild brook that bubbles fast
By meadows breathing of the past,
And woodlands holy to the dead;

Who murmurest in the foliaged eaves
A song that slights the coming care,
And Autumn laying here & there
A fiery finger on the leaves;

Who wakenest with thy balmy breath
To myriads on the genial earth,
Memories of bridal or of birth,
And unto myriads more, of death.

O wheresoever those may be,
Betwixt the slumber of the poles,
To-day they count as kindred souls:
They know me not, but mourn with me.

I wake, I rise: from end to end
Of all the landskip underneath,
I find no place that does not breathe
Some gracious memory of my friend.

No gray old grange, or lonely fold,
Or low morass & whispering reed,
Or simple stile from mead to mead,
Or sheepwalk up the windy wold.

Nor hoary knoll of ash & haw
That hears the latest linnet trill;
Nor quarry trench'd along the hill,
And haunted by the jangling daws;

Nor fountain sparkling from the rock;
Nor pastoral rivulet that swerves
To left & right thro' meadowy curves,
That feed the mothers of the flock;

But each has pleased a kindred eye,
And each reflects a kindlier day;
And, leaving these to pass away,
I think, once more he seems to die.

Osborne.
Ap: 25. 1886.

I wish I could express in words how deeply & truly I feel for you in this hour of heavy affliction! You, who have written such words of comfort for others will [illegible] feel this comfort

opium addiction, a third Emily's doubts about Alfred's religious beliefs. They did not come together again until the poet's prospects had greatly improved. These were unsettled years, when Tennyson and other members of his family lost a great deal of money through their participation in a mechanical wood carving scheme set up by the proprietor of a nearby Essex lunatic asylum, Matthew Allen. Tennyson's health suffered and he took several cures during the later 1840s. He had, however, some success with the volume of poems published in 1842 and with 'The Princess', his poem on a women's university, which first appeared in 1847 and was later published in several revised editions.

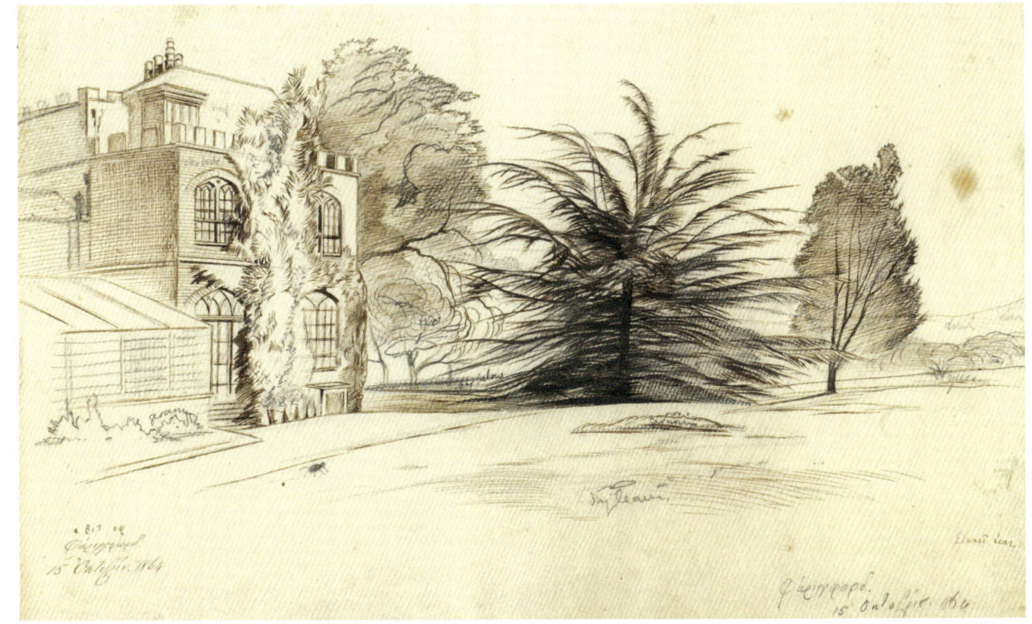

Edward Lear (1812–88)
Farringford, 1864
Drawing
Tennyson Research Centre

Aldworth
Postcard
Tennyson Research Centre

1850 has often been described as Alfred Tennyson's *annus mirabilis*. He had, since Arthur Hallam's death, been working on a series of elegies for his friend. *In Memoriam*, made up of 133 poems, was published in June 1850. His marriage with Emily finally took place in June, the service being conducted by Drummond Rawnsley, Emily's cousin and Tennyson's friend. William Wordsworth had died in April, and the position of Poet Laureate was initially offered to Samuel Rogers, who felt himself to be too old for the post. It was the publication of *In Memoriam*, which Prince Albert much liked, which decided Queen Victoria to offer the Laureateship to Tennyson in November. He proved to be an outstanding Laureate, working for more than forty years to place the Laureateship at the centre of national life and becoming a Baron in 1884. Poems such as 'The Charge of the Light Brigade' and 'Ode on the Death of the Duke of Wellington' won him popular acclaim.

The Tennysons lived for a short time in Twickenham, before moving to Farringford on the Isle of Wight. In his later years, Tennyson became increasingly reclusive, avoiding public attention where possible and even building a bridge across the road so that he could pass from one part of his garden at Farringford to another without being seen. So famous had he become that he had to be helped out of Westminster Abbey through a side door at the close of Charles Dickens's funeral in 1870. He liked, on the other hand, to visit friends in London, and, given an opportunity, he would read 'Maud' aloud on social occasions.

As the Isle of Wight, initially peaceful, became increasingly popular as a resort, Tennyson built a new home in 1868, designed by a young architect, James Knowles, at Aldworth on Blackdown near Haslemere in Surrey. He did not, however, sell Farringford and a good deal of time was still spent there.

Although Tennyson's visits to Lincolnshire were not frequent in these later years, particularly after the death of his brother Charles in 1879, he looked back once

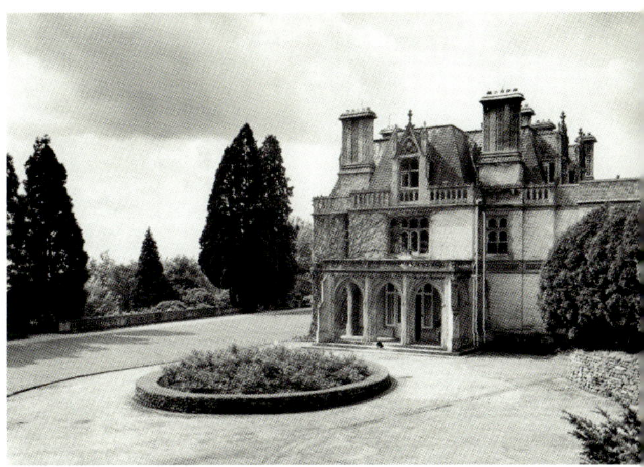

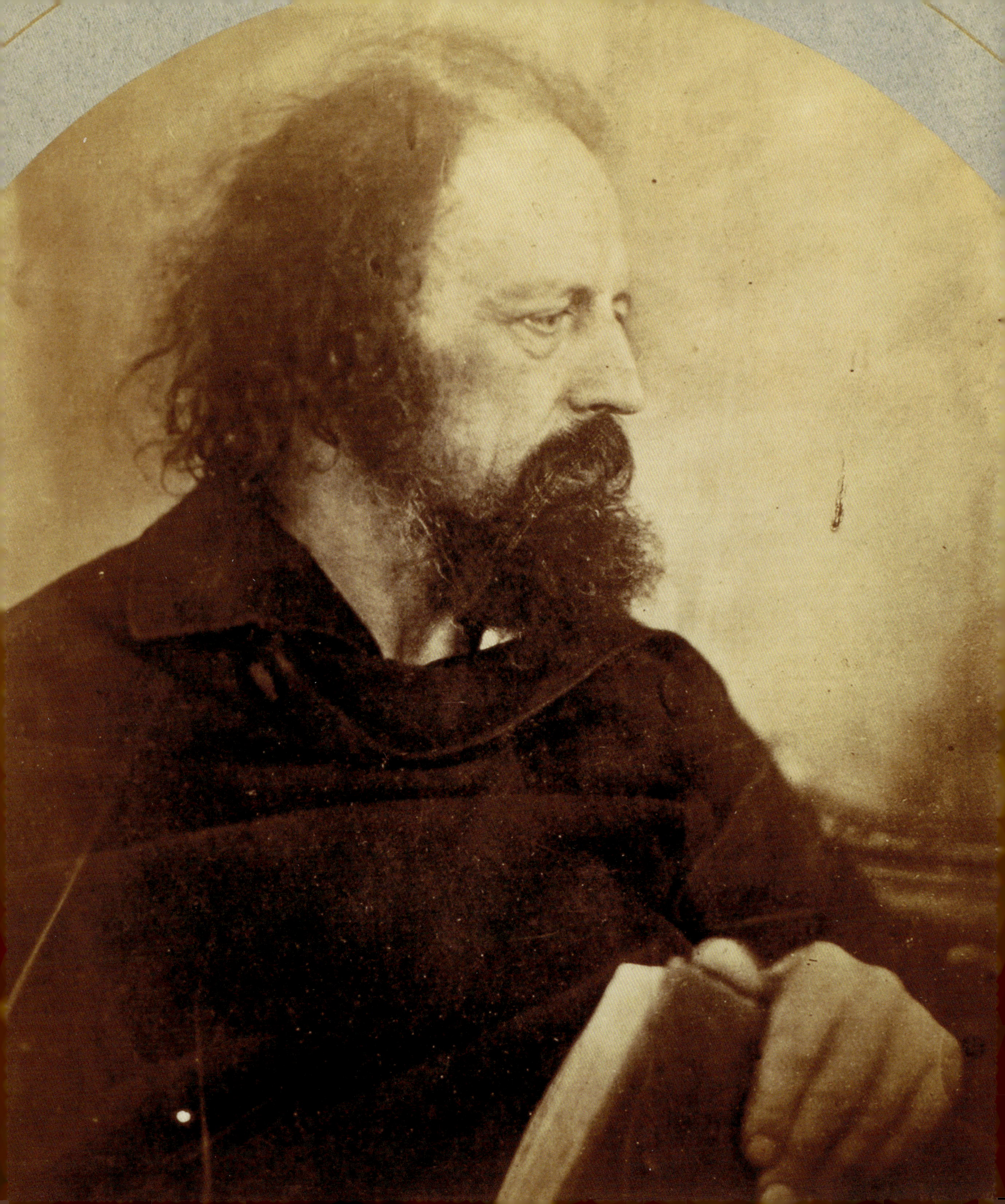

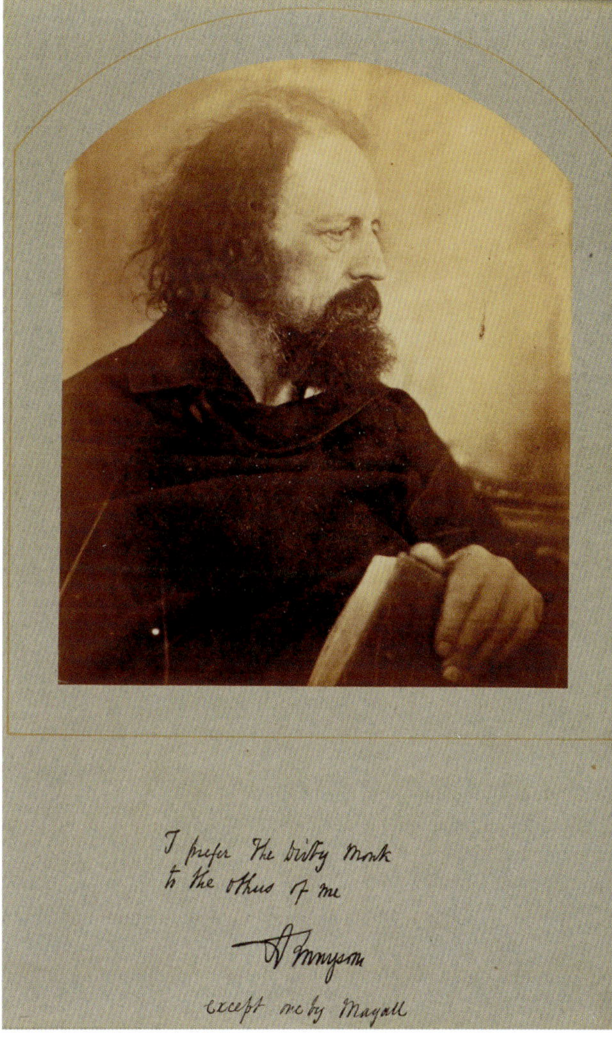

Julia Margaret Cameron (1815–79)
Alfred, Lord Tennyson ('The Dirty Monk'), 1865
Photograph
Tennyson Research Centre

more to his childhood with a remarkable group of dialect poems, written between 1861 and 1890. It is always said that Tennyson himself retained his Lincolnshire accent, but these poems are dramatic monologues in a language that evokes the countrymen and women of the poet's early life. They are people whom he might have known, farmers, in 'Northern Farmer: Old Style' and 'Northern Farmer: New Style', a 'Northern Cobbler', and a 'Village Wife'. As commentators have pointed out, these are not the monologues of the very poor, or of social reformers, but they were a surprising departure for the Poet Laureate.

Tennyson continued to work until the end of his life. One new venture involved writing seven plays, several of which were performed at the Lyceum Theatre. One of the greatest roles of Henry Irving was the lead in Tennyson's third historical drama, *Becket* (1884), but, sadly, this was not performed until after Tennyson's death. The biggest success for Tennyson himself was *The Cup*, which opened at the Lyceum in January 1881. Taking its plot from Plutarch, the play starred Irving and Ellen Terry.

Tennyson's last major undertaking was the writing of *The Idylls of the King*, his twelve-book version of the legend of King Arthur. The epic was many years in the making. 'Morte d'Arthur', a poem written in the aftermath of the death of Arthur Hallam and published in 1842, was the basis for the final Idyll, T*he Passing of Arthur*. The first four *Idylls*, which appeared in 1859, *Enid, Vivien, Elaine* and *Guinevere*, were largely concerned with the female characters from Sir Thomas Malory's *Morte d'Arthur* (about 1470) and Lady Charlotte Guest's translation of the *Mabinogion* (1838–45). Other Idylls appeared over the years and the publication of the final book, *Balin and Balan*, completed the series in 1885. The popular narrative poems inspired, among other works, a series of illustrations by Gustave Doré and of photographs by Julia Margaret Cameron.

If *In Memoriam* and the *Idylls* were admired at home, there can be no doubt that the most (and sometimes the only) popular poem by Tennyson in many European countries was *Enoch Arden*. Published in 1864, it tells the story, suggested to Tennyson by the Pre-Raphaelite sculptor Thomas Woolner, of the wrecked sailor who, after years on a desert island, comes home to find his wife married to his friend.

Tennyson died at Aldworth on 6 October 1892. On his deathbed he asked for his volume of Shakespeare's plays, opened at his favourite lines from *Cymbeline*. His funeral, in Westminster Abbey, was a national event and he is buried in Poets' Corner.

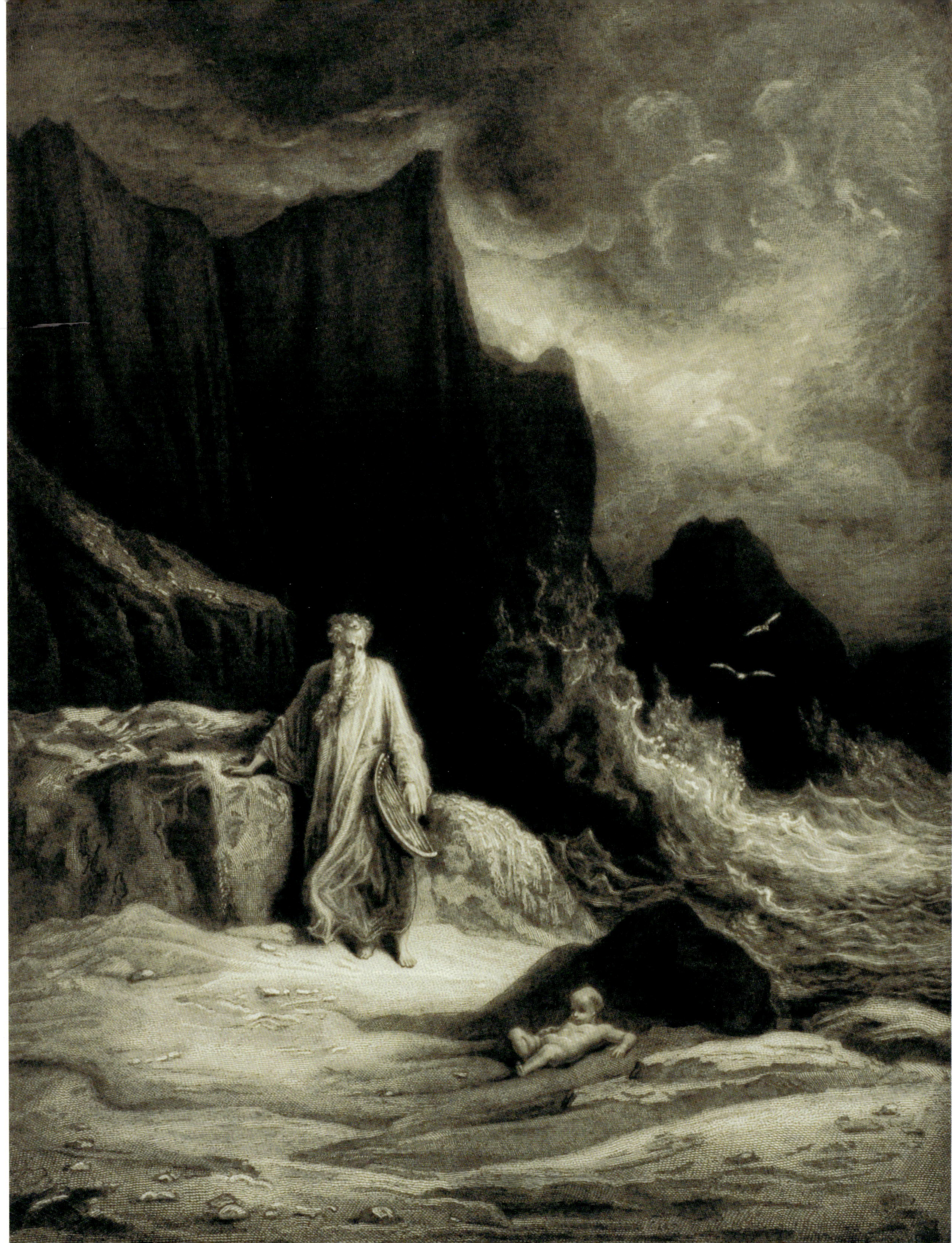

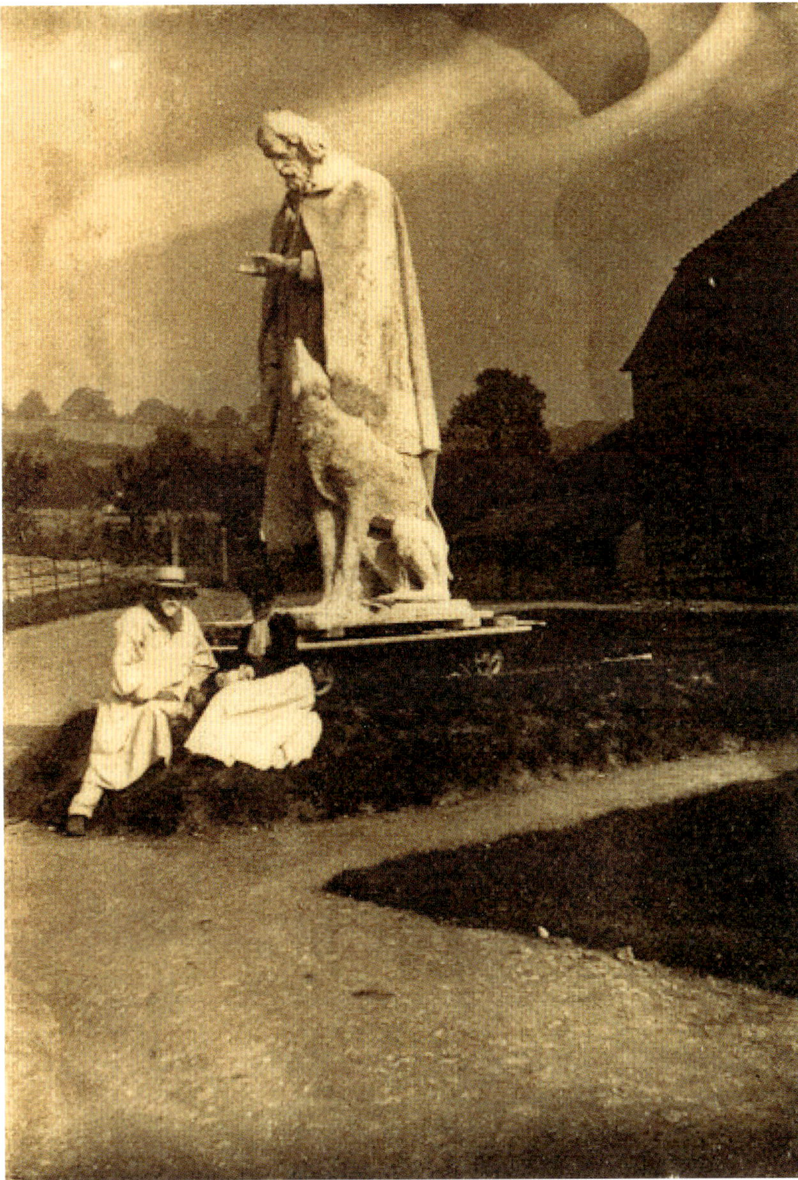

George Frederic Watts (1817–1904)
Statue of Alfred, Lord Tennyson, with his dog Karenina, 1905
Photograph of the gesso grosso model of the statue at Watts's studio, ready for casting
Tennyson Research Centre

OPPOSITE
Gustave Doré (1832–83)
***The Finding of King Arthur*, 1867**
Illustration for Alfred Tennyson, *Idylls of the King*
Tennyson Research Centre

Among the tributes to Tennyson was the statue by his friend George Frederic Watts, which stands beside Lincoln Cathedral. Watts had painted the poet's portrait on six occasions and, when he heard of the planned statue, he offered to work on it for expenses only. In the final bronze (of which the gesso model can be seen at the Watts Gallery in Compton, Surrey) Watts showed Tennyson as he was often to be seen, with a cloak and Spanish-style hat. The wolfhound, Karenina, looks devotedly at her master, who, also meditative, holds a plant in his hand. The relevant poem, 'Flower in the crannied wall', is quoted in a plaque on the base. In fact, Tennyson spent relatively little time in the city of Lincoln, although as a young man he attended balls there. Today, however, the city is the home of the Tennyson Research Centre, with its collections of manuscripts and books – and, indeed, not only of Watts's statue, but also of Tennyson's hat and cloak.

Further reading

Christopher Ricks (ed.), *The Poems of Tennyson*, 3 volumes (Harlow 1987)

Christopher Sturman, *Landscape and Friendship*, ed. Valerie Purton (Stamford 1999)

Hallam Tennyson, *Alfred Lord Tennyson: A Memoir*, 2 volumes (London 1897)

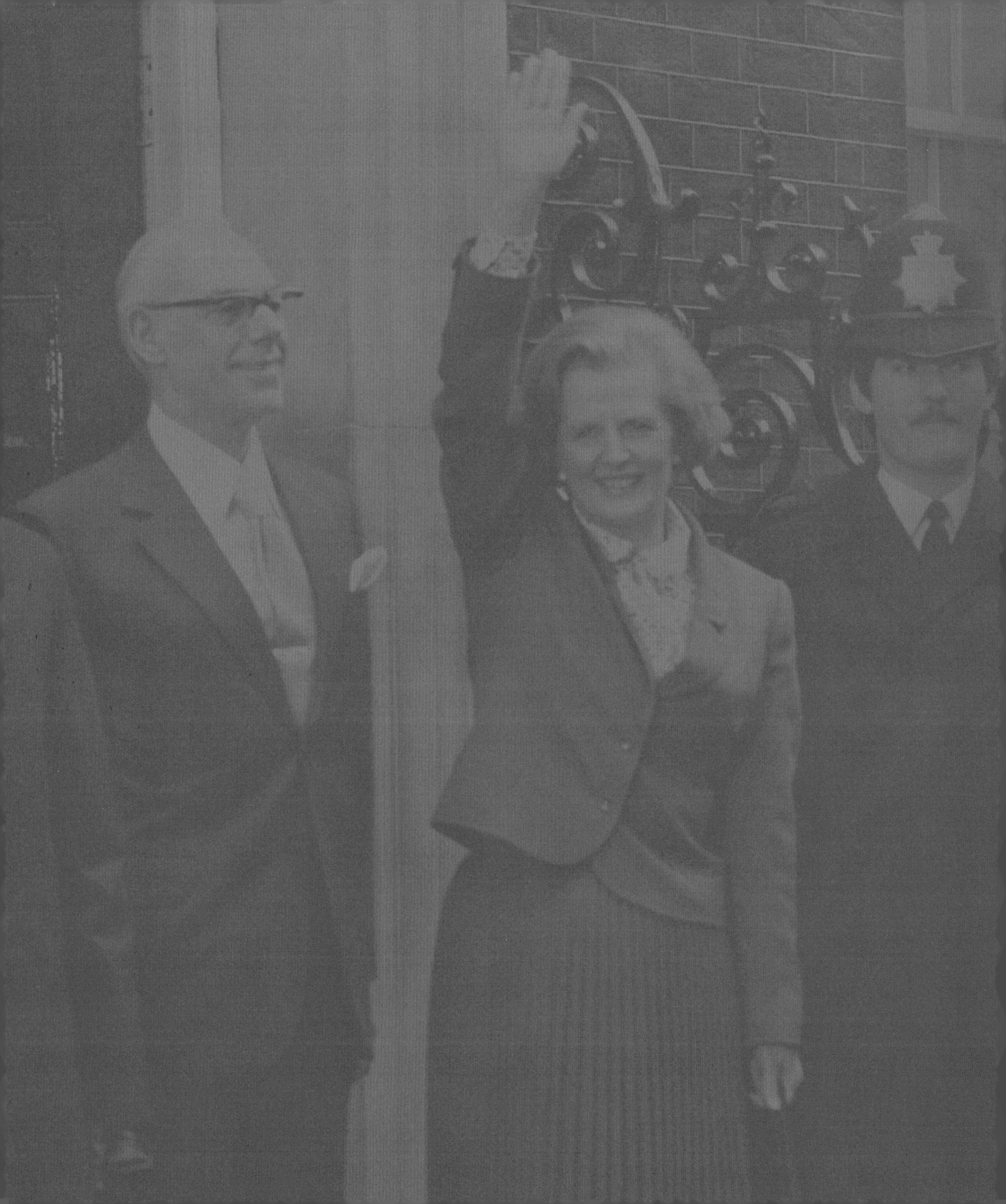

Margaret Thatcher

LORD POWELL OF BAYSWATER

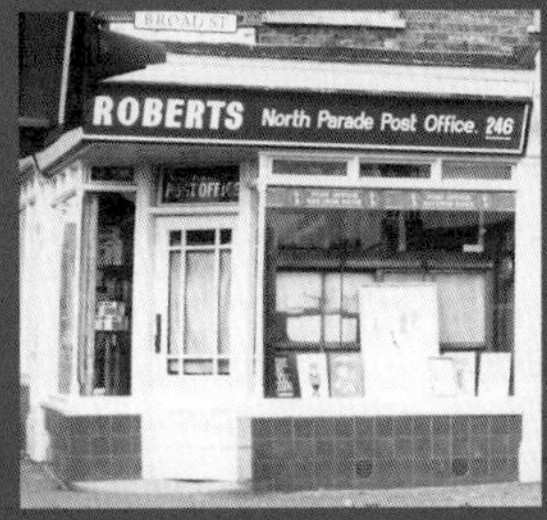

MARGARET THATCHER knew her Lincolnshire. I don't pretend she spent her waking hours, excessively long as they were, thinking about it. Nor as Prime Minister did she have much occasion to visit it. But since I also spent much of my own early life in Lincolnshire in the village of Fulbeck, not far from her birthplace, Grantham, we quite often used to exchange recollections of Lincolnshire people and places during my time as her Private Secretary.

Charles Moore's authoritative biography gives a detailed account of Margaret Roberts's (as she then was) early years in Grantham and how life there shaped her. Indeed, his account is fuller and more revealing than her own in her autobiography, though nothing can match her unforgettable description of how the Roberts family used to spend their Lincolnshire summer holidays: 'We did PT exercises in the public gardens of Skegness … rather than sitting around dreaming'. Yes, Prime Minister!

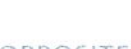
OPPOSITE
Henry Mee (born 1955)
***The Rt Hon. Margaret Thatcher OM, MP, Prime Minister*, 1992**
Oil on canvas
Palace of Westminster Collection

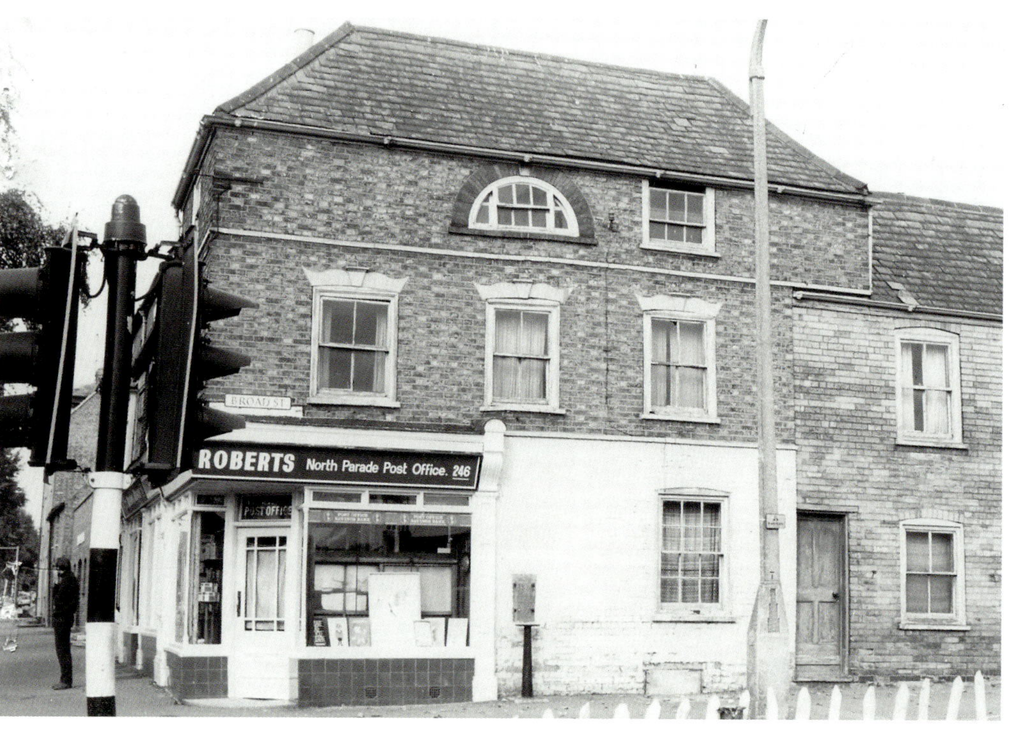

Grantham, North Parade, about 1970
Post Office and grocer's shop on the corner of North Parade and Broad Street: birthplace of Margaret Thatcher
Postcard
Lincolnshire Archives

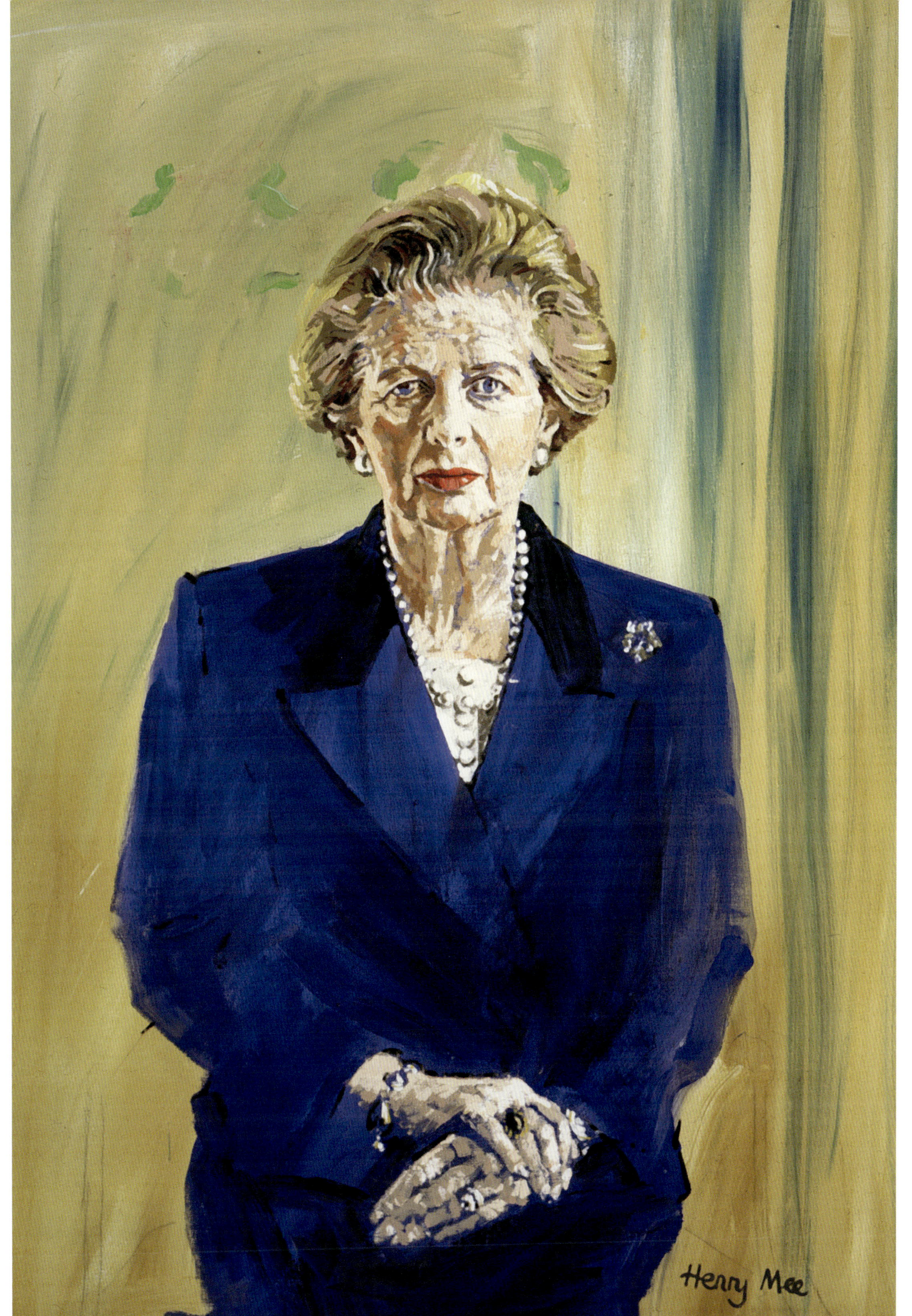
Henry Mee

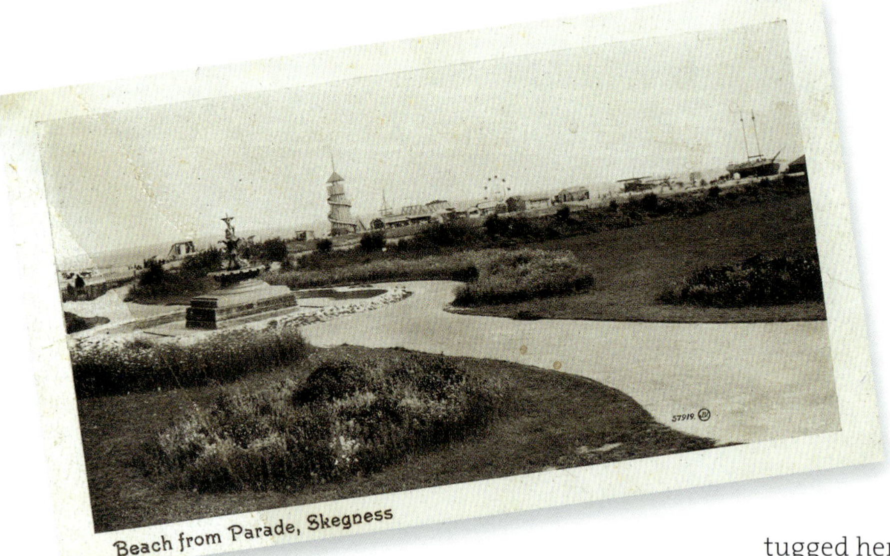

Skegness public gardens
Postcard
Lincolnshire Libraries

Whether she had much nostalgia for her Grantham years is debatable to say the least. But it was there that she developed the roots that later served her well as Conservative Party leader. Not roots that tugged her to stay in Grantham: as an ambitious young woman, Oxford, science and the law offered her a better opportunity to move ahead in life. But roots in the sense of a direct connection to a level of British society where aspirations could only be met by hard work, initiative and enterprise, not by connections and the old school tie. This was to be crucial to her electoral success as Prime Minister decades later. Serving in the shop in Grantham, listening to Council debates and the humdrum aspects of Grantham life gave her a much more direct and personal experience of the aspirations and ambitions of ordinary households than the rarefied lives of the Tory Party elite could ever have. She understood their dislike of slackers and scroungers, their ambition to own their homes, their desire to keep more of their earnings to spend as they wanted rather than at Whitehall's behest, their strong and instinctive patriotism. Friedrich Hayek and Milton Friedman may have provided the intellectual basis for her later

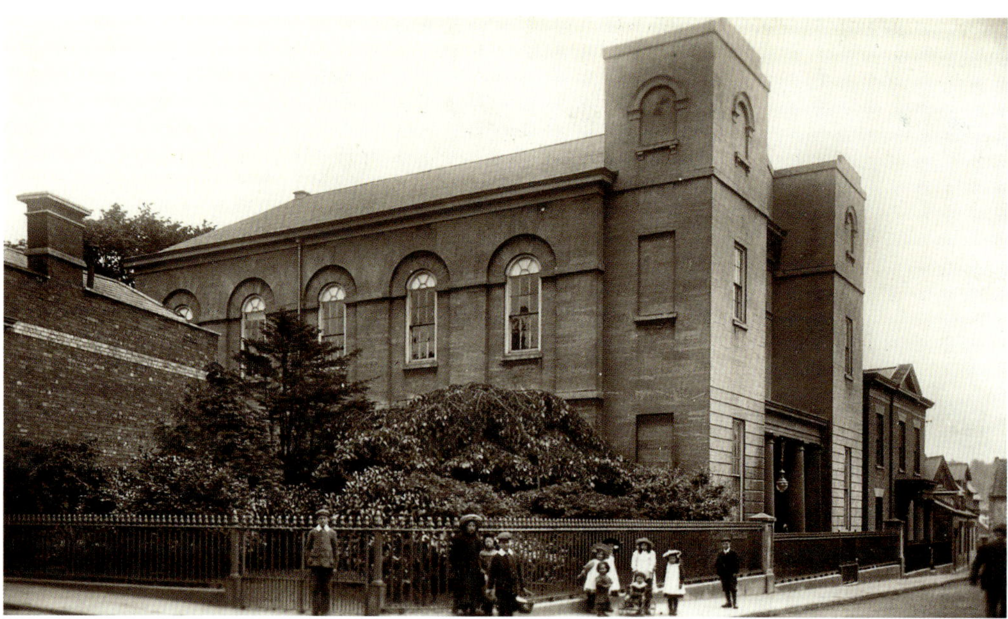

Finkin Street Wesleyan Methodist Chapel, Grantham
Postcard
Lincolnshire Archives

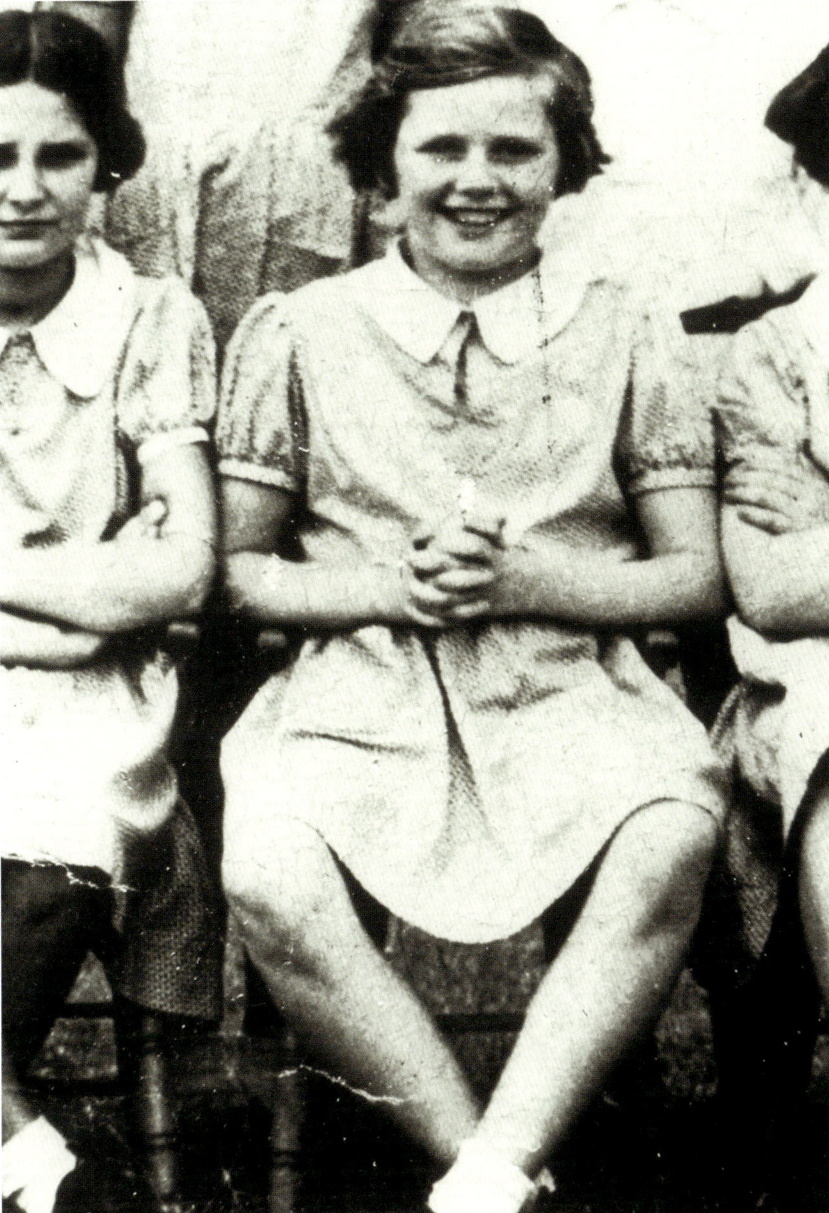

Margaret Roberts as a Grantham schoolgirl, 1930s
Rex

economic policies, but it was her direct experience of 'her' people and their values that shaped what she actually did as Prime Minister. And by winning the support of 'her' people for the Conservative Party she made possible the extraordinary changes in British society which eluded her predecessors, whether Labour or Conservative. I have no doubt that a large slice of her success in politics was due to her Lincolnshire upbringing.

Various connections to Lincolnshire remained with her through her later life and especially in her No. 10 years. She occasionally used Lincolnshire language, in particular the word 'frit' as a jibe directed at weak-kneed political opponents. She knew her Tennyson and was able to quote extensively from his poetry decades after she memorised it at school in Grantham, though he

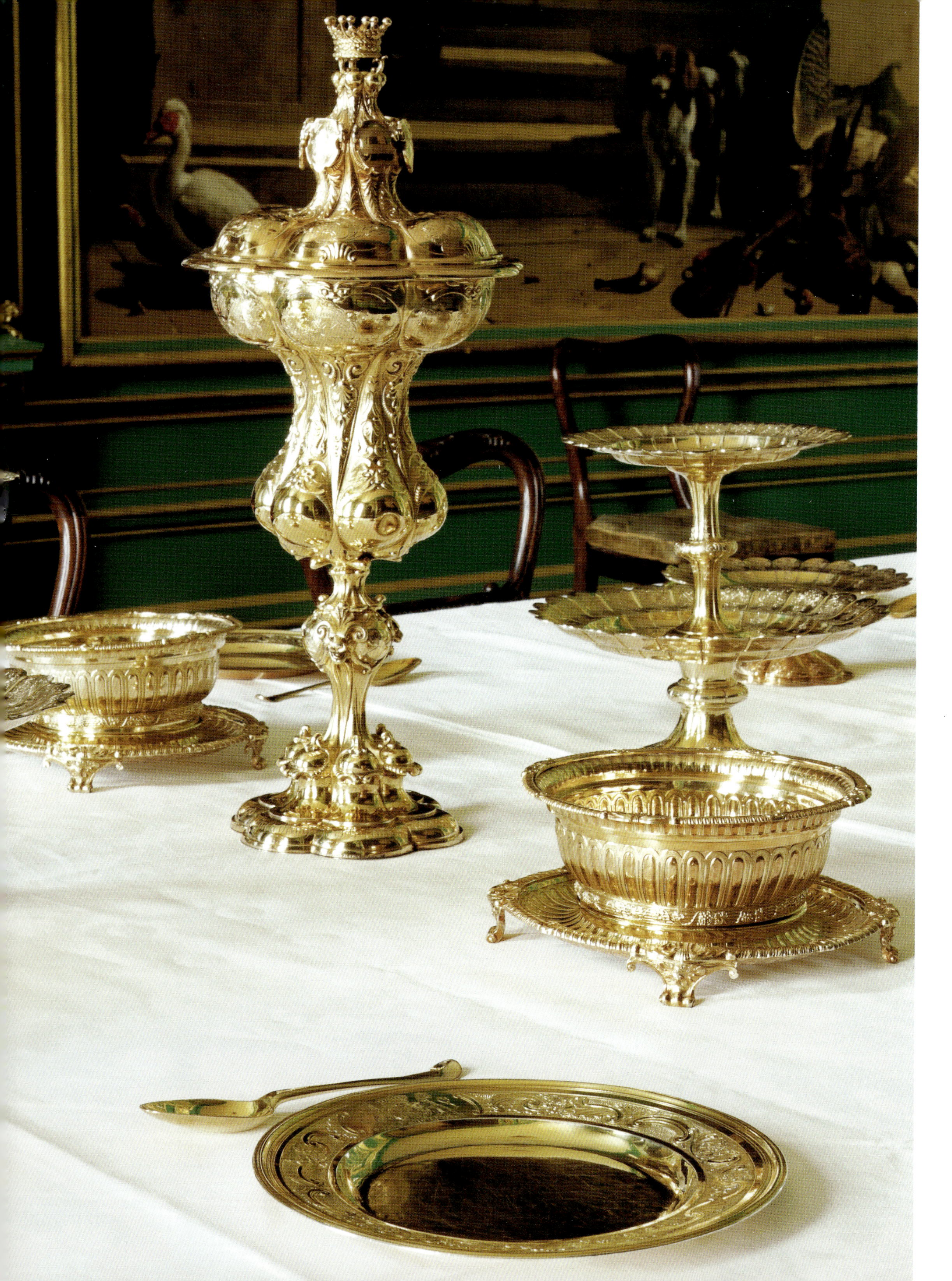

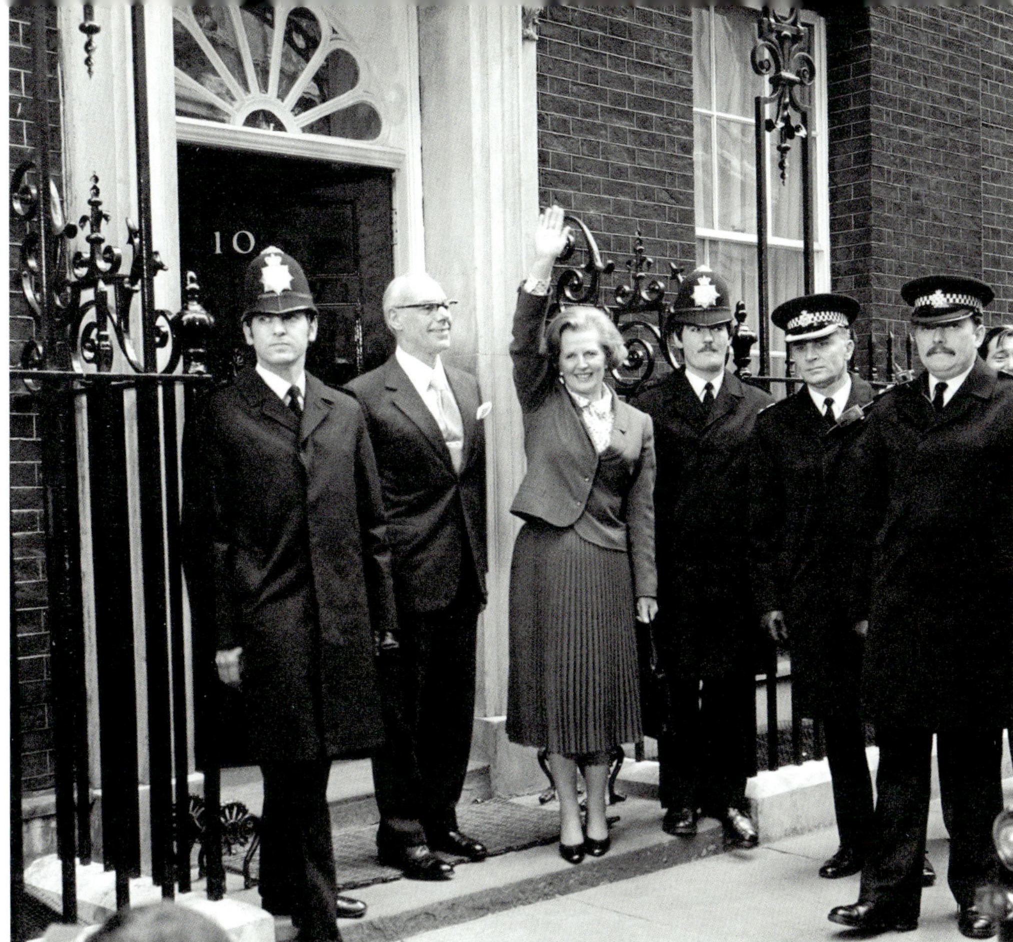

Prime Minister Margaret Thatcher on the steps of 10 Downing Street, May 1979
Press Association

OPPOSITE
The Brownlow Silver at Belton House, loaned to Margaret Thatcher for use at No. 10 Downing Street
National Trust

never quite got the star billing awarded to Rudyard Kipling in her speeches. She borrowed some of the Brownlow family silver from Belton House when she found that No. 10 had none of its own to put on the State Dining Room table for formal occasions. And her coat of arms as Baroness Thatcher of Kesteven has as its 'sinister' supporter Lincolnshire's most famous citizen, Sir Isaac Newton, to recognise her early career as a scientist. She installed Newton's portrait in the main dining room of No. 10 Downing Street soon after she became Prime Minister, along with those of other distinguished British scientists whom she regarded as sadly under-represented among the pictures of monarchs and statesmen. She would have installed more but found that 'distinguished scientists do not devote time to being painted by distinguished artists on canvases of the right size'!

So there was plenty of Lincolnshire in Margaret Thatcher's life. She would have been thrilled by *Lincolnshire's Great Exhibition* 2015 had she lived to witness it, above all because it celebrates eight hundred years of Magna Carta.

Margaret Thatcher shared Lord Denning's view that Magna Carta was one of the greatest constitutional documents of all time. She cited it frequently, alongside the United States Declaration of Independence and the Gettysburg Address, as the foundation for Britain's and America's freedoms. It worked its way into her Bruges speech to illustrate how far back the origins of freedom went in our history in comparison to other European countries. Asked by the Foreign Office in 1989 to give a television interview to celebrate the bicentenary of the

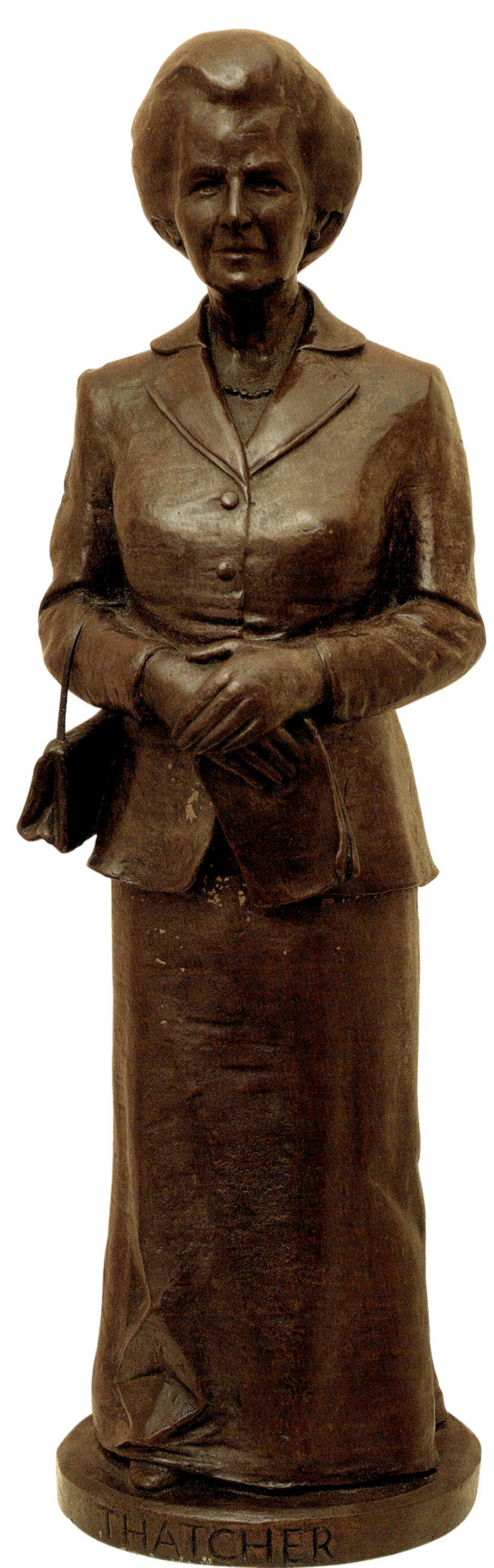

Neil Simmons
***Margaret Thatcher (1925–2013)*, 2002**
Bronze maquette for marble statue commissioned by the House of Commons and now in London's Guildhall
Private collection

French Revolution, she rather spoiled the party by contrasting that bloodstained event with Britain's peaceful evolution stemming from Magna Carta.

Freedom was what Margaret Thatcher was about. It was the foundation of her political beliefs and of her policies as Prime Minister. The clearest statement of those beliefs which I recall was when she defined her vision as 'a man's right to work as he will, to spend what he earns, to own property, to have the state as servant not as master. These are the British inheritance. They are the essence of a free country and on that freedom all our other freedoms depend'. As the *Economist* put it, Mrs Thatcher bet on freedom. In Britain she wanted people to be free of excessive burdens and micro-management imposed by the government. She wanted the economy to flourish based on free markets. And she wanted the people of Eastern Europe and the former Soviet Union to enjoy the freedoms that we had in Britain. Based on those policies and beliefs and her success in implementing them, both Britain itself and Europe enjoyed much more freedom in 1990 than they had at the start of her prime-ministership in 1979.

None of this was achieved without controversy, indeed controversy characterised her political style. For those of us who worked with her in No. 10 Downing Street in those years, it was an exhilarating fasten-your-seatbelts ride. The Soviet Red Army magazine can never have realised what a huge favour it did her by characterising her as the Iron Lady. It was the perfect epithet to characterise her readiness to tilt at every windmill and take on endless battles as she set about the task of changing Britain from the low point we had reached in 1979, when the country seemed condemned to interminable decline. Without the changes she introduced, Britain would have plunged ever deeper into the mire of vertiginously high taxes, trade union control and deteriorating public services. Instead we saw popular capitalism embracing privatisation of the nationalised industries, the trade unions brought under the law, taxes set at a level that provided an incentive rather than penalty and the sale of Council homes to their occupants. It was a social revolution as profound as any that Britain had experienced in its history, and within the very short timespan of a decade.

It was not just in Britain that she made her mark. Many of the policies and reforms to the structure of our economy that she pioneered here were followed, sometimes reluctantly, elsewhere in Europe and more widely too. Indeed,

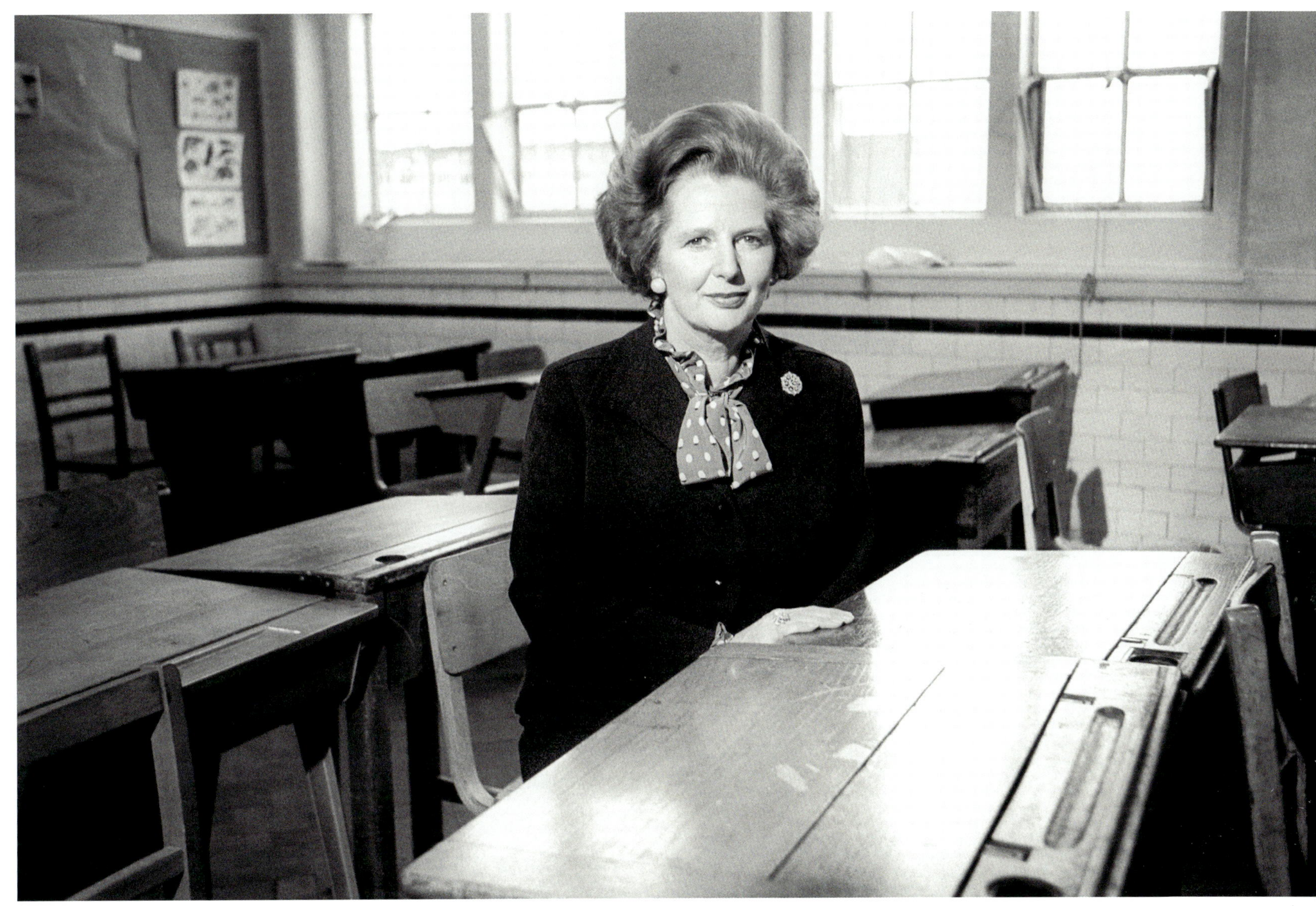

several European countries are under pressure now to do what she did in terms of privatisation and opening up the jobs market. And, together with President Reagan, she had a great part in overturning the doctrines that had caused so much misery earlier in the twentieth century – Communism, dictatorship, the giant state, the crushing of individual choice and initiative – replacing them with free markets, free minds and free people.

One should not over-reach in trying to make connections. But for someone who himself has a modest claim to a Lincolnshire upbringing, the combination of Britain's greatest scientist, one of its greatest poets and our greatest peacetime Prime Minister of the twentieth century certainly makes me proud of my county. We may not be the greatest for football or cricket, but when it comes to contributing to our nation's history and achievements, Lincolnshire has done its bit for Britain, and no-one more than Margaret Thatcher.

Margaret Thatcher visiting her old school, Kesteven and Grantham Girls School, 1982
Press Association

Further reading

Charles Moore, *Margaret Thatcher: The Authorised Biography*, Volume I (London 2013)

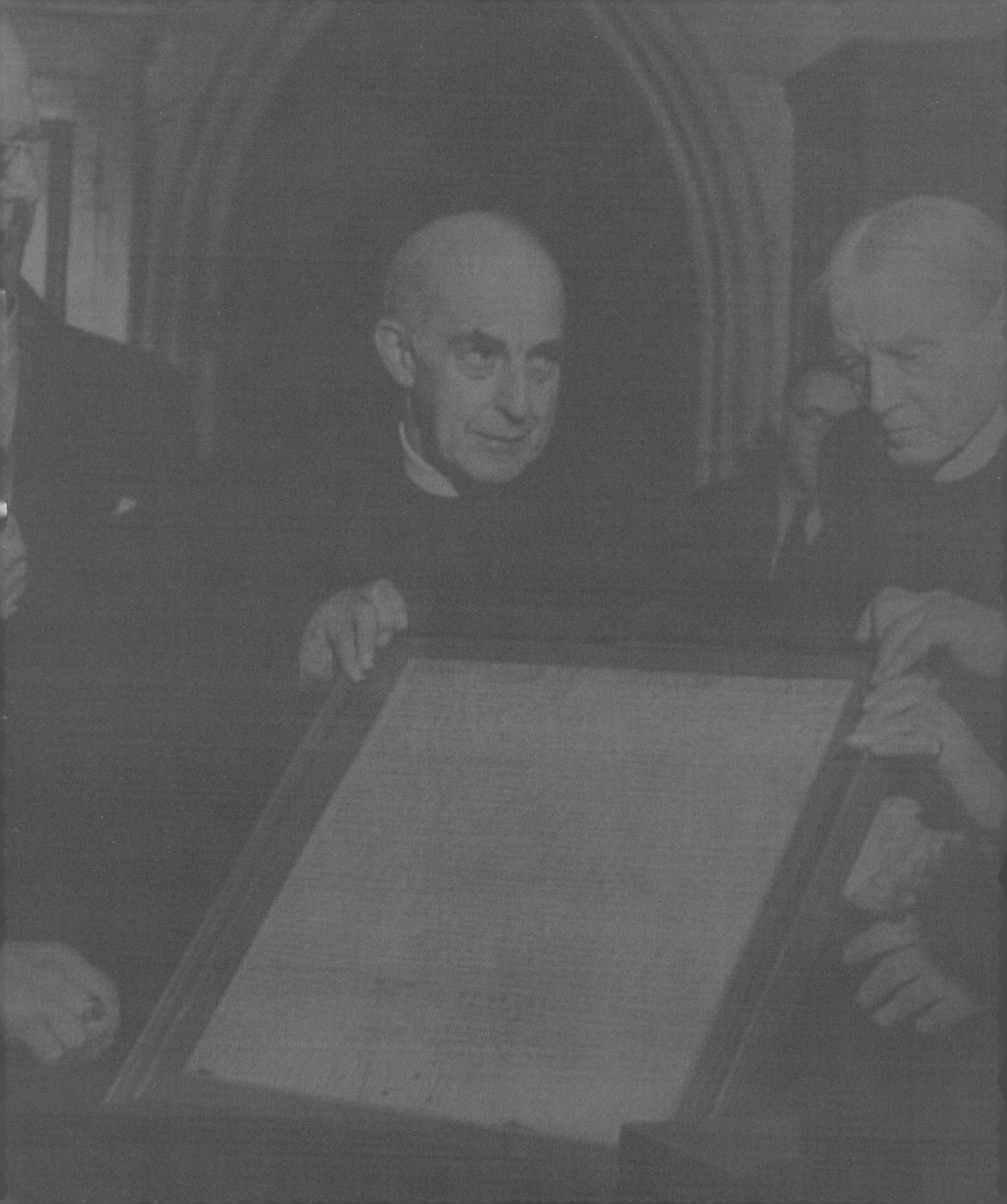

Magna Carta in the USA

PHILIP BUCKLER

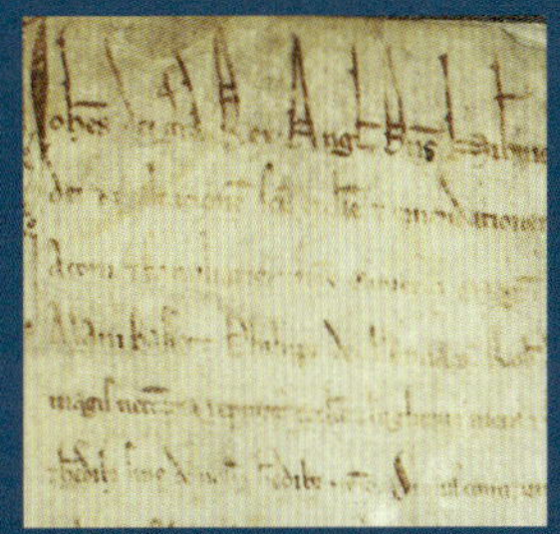

LINCOLN CATHEDRAL's Magna Carta is not only the most settled but also the most travelled of the four remaining 1215 exemplars. It is the most settled in that we know it is in the place to which it was originally sent. On the back of the parchment is written in thirteenth-century court hand 'Lincolnia' – the address for which it was destined. Its home has remained here ever since.

Yet it is also the most travelled of the four copies, and continues to be made available on occasions for exhibition at home and abroad. In 1939 it was sent to New York for the World Fair. When war broke out it was deemed too dangerous to allow it to cross the Atlantic, and so it remained in the United States until the end of the Second World War. At first displayed in the Library of Congress, it was later moved for safe keeping to Fort Knox.

The wartime cabinet papers reveal that in 1941 Churchill had been encouraged by some of his cabinet to gift the Lincoln Magna Carta to the Americans in the hope that they might enter the war sooner. Fortunately it was realised that the government had no power to gift it and the idea quietly disappeared. The Dean and Chapter of Lincoln Cathedral were never even consulted on the matter.

Between 1976 and 1990 Dean Oliver Fiennes took Magna Carta to America again, travelling across many states and enabling large numbers of people to view this seminal document. In 1988 it went to Australia for *Expo 88* and in more recent times it has returned on a number of occasions to the United States. Since 2007 it has been displayed in Virginia, Philadelphia, California and New York. Prior to its anniversary year it was exhibited in two of the 'Charter Towns', St Albans and Bury St Edmunds. Then, most recently, it has once again crossed the Atlantic for displays at the Museum of Fine Arts in Boston, at the Sterling and Francine Clark Art Institute in Williamstown, before returning to the Library of Congress in Washington DC marking the seventy-fifth anniversary of its first appearance there.

The 800th anniversary year sees all four remaining 1215 Magna Carta being brought together for the very first time in February at the British Library in London for three days, and then for one day at the Palace of Westminster.

Lincoln Cathedral's Magna Carta has been viewed by very many people at home and abroad, both young and old alike. It has the power to inspire and to challenge our world today, as it testifies to a belief in the rule of law, the emerging understanding of the rights of groups and individuals, and the concern for justice. Despite its age, it remains a very contemporary document that speaks to issues

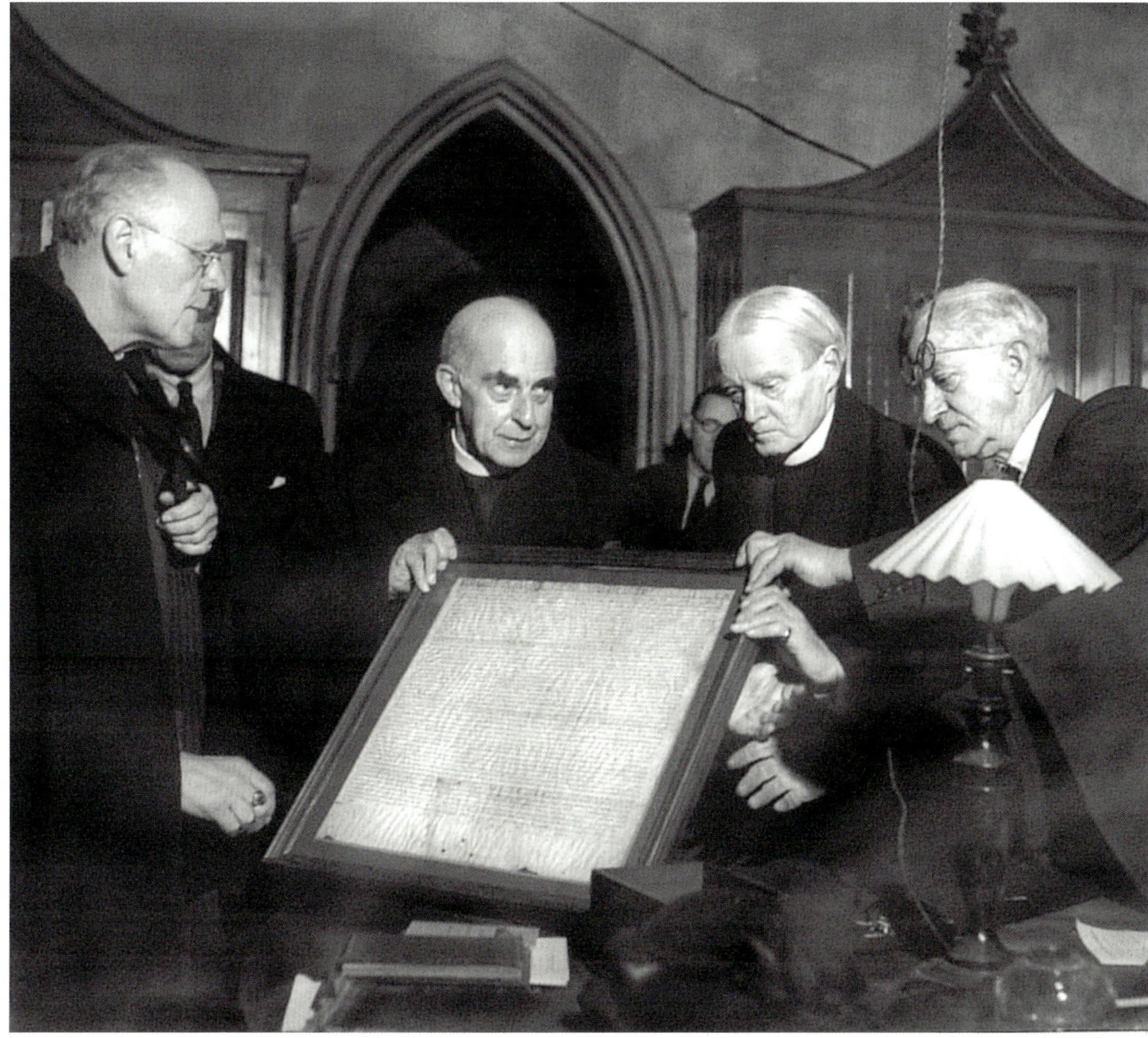

Magna Carta returns from the USA to Lincoln Cathedral in January 1946 and is received by the Bishop, Chancellor, Dean and Clerk of Works
Lincoln Cathedral Library

OVERLEAF
Lincoln Cathedral: the crossing, looking up into the central tower
Photo: James Newton

confronting us in the twenty-first century. In exhibitions around the world it has held centre stage, often surrounded by other documents of international and historical significance, such as the American Declaration of Independence, the US Constitution, the Emancipation Proclamation, and the Universal Declaration of Human Rights. It has been called the 'birth certificate of democracy', the 'grandparent of human rights', and many other such titles. It is entered on Unesco's 'Memory of the World Register' and, together with many other items on that Register, a facsimile of Lincoln's Magna Carta was displayed in Seoul, South Korea, in 2010.

Since 1993 Lincoln Cathedral has loaned its Magna Carta for display in Lincoln Castle. As part of the Castle's exciting refurbishment a new vault has been contracted to house Magna Carta in its 800th anniversary year and beyond. Visitors from across the globe will be able to learn more clearly about this document that has helped to shape the people we are and the world in which we live.

Further reading

Carol and Nicholas Bennett, *Magna Carta: The Lincoln Story* (Lincoln 2014)

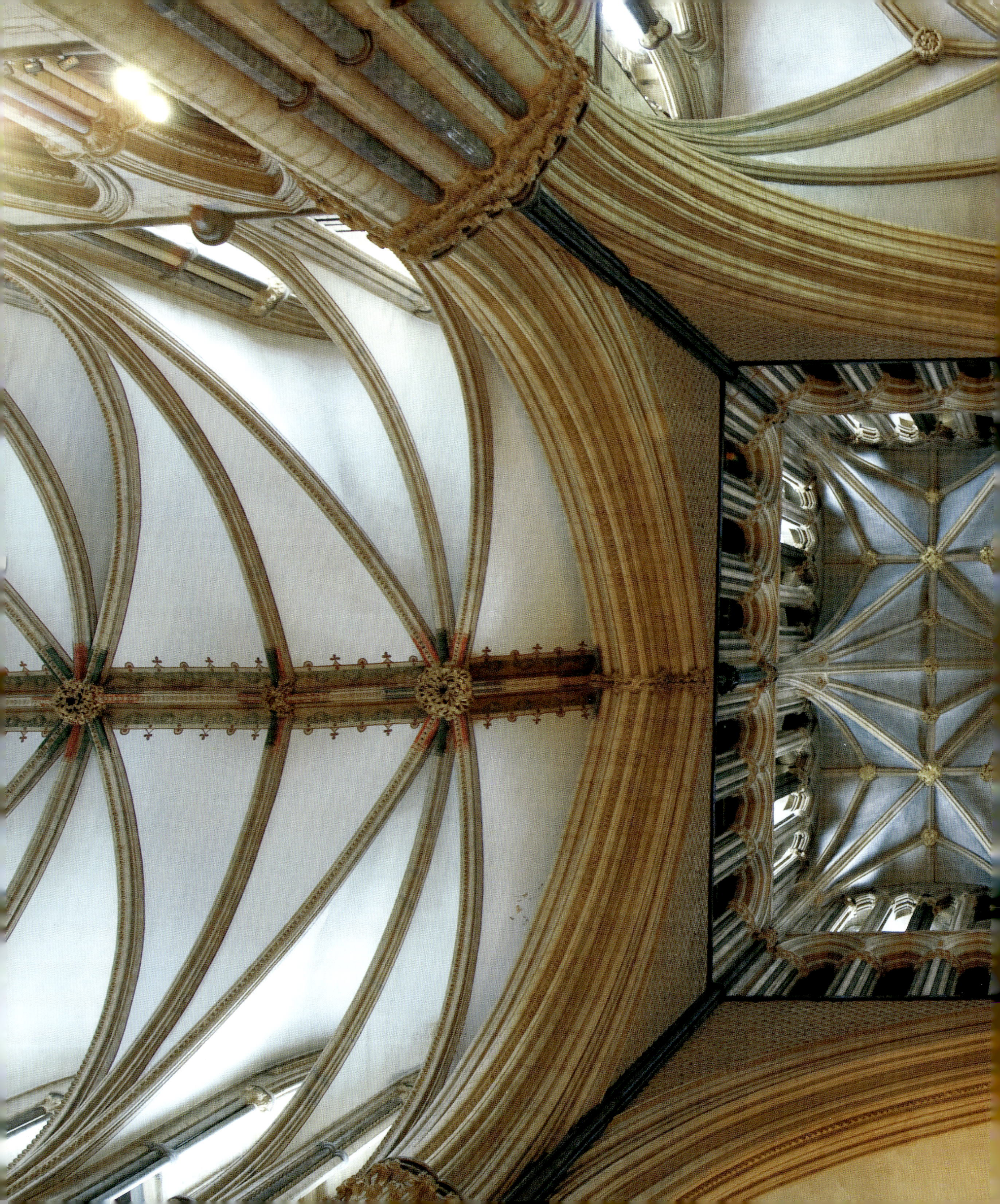

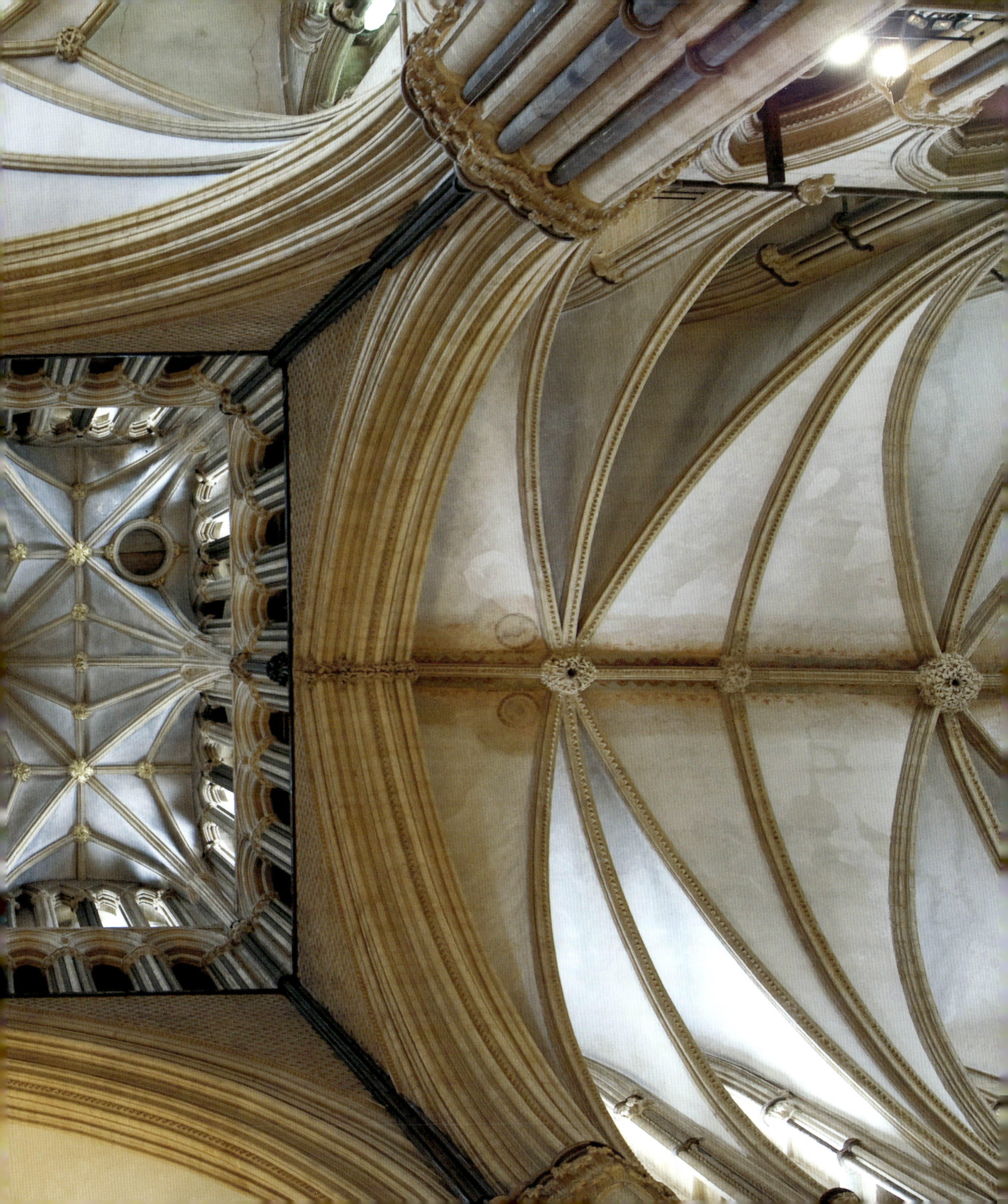

Some highlights of the exhibition

Lincolnshire history, the Church, noble families and notables

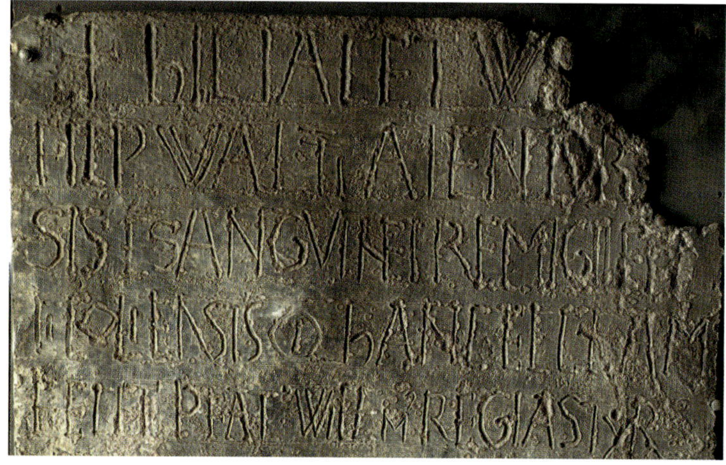

Memorial plaque to William, son of Walter d'Eyncourt, 1090s

Memorial plaque to William, son of Walter d'Eyncourt, 1090s
Lead
Lincoln Cathedral Library

Biblia Sacra Pars I, about 1100
Chapter bible of Lincoln Cathedral, part 1
Lincoln Cathedral Library

Biblia Sacra Pars II, about 1100
Chapter bible of Lincoln Cathedral, part 2
Trinity College Library, Cambridge

Seal matrix, Lincoln Cathedral, about 1150–60
Silver, with nielloed reverse
Dean and Chapter of Lincoln

Episcopal seal of St Hugh of Avalon (Bishop of Lincoln 1186–1200), about 1189–93
Red wax, attached to confirmation for Sempringham Priory
Lincoln Cathedral Library

Archiepiscopal seal of Stephen Langton (Archbishop of Canterbury 1206–28), about 1213–15
The National Archives

Episcopal roll of Hugh of Wells (Bishop of Lincoln 1209–35), about 1214–18
Lincolnshire Archives

Episcopal seal of Hugh of Wells (Bishop of Lincoln 1209–35), 1229
Brown wax, attached to confirmation for Newton Longville Priory
New College, Oxford

Life of Gilbert of Sempringham, early 13th century
British Library

Magna Carta, 1215
Lincolnshire Archives, on loan to Lincolnshire County Council

Magna Carta, 1225
The National Archives

The Charter of the Forest, 1217
Lincolnshire Archives, on loan to Lincolnshire County Council

Nichola de la Haie (died 1230)
Charter granting to Lincoln Cathedral land adjoining the Eastgate in Lincoln, 1224–7
Lincolnshire Archives

The Metrical Life of St Hugh, 13th century
British Library

The Luttrell Psalter, about 1325–40
Illuminated manuscript
British Library

Crowland Abbey
The 'Wrest Park' cartulary, 14th century
Spalding Gentlemen's Society

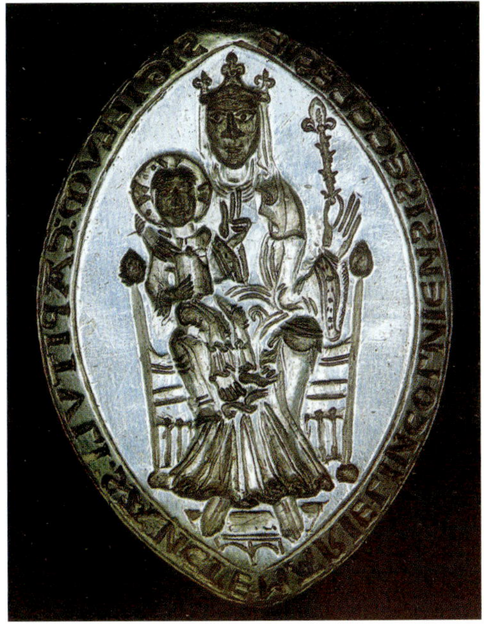

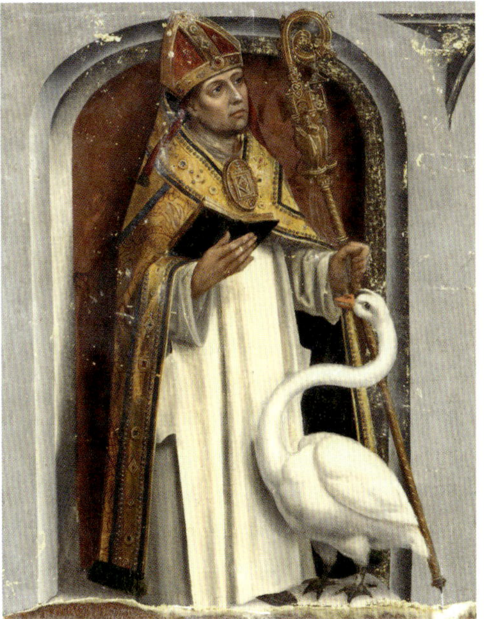

FAR LEFT **Seal matrix, Lincoln Cathedral, about 1150–60**

LEFT **Circle of the Master of the Legend of the Magdalen Martyrdom of St Ursula, with St Hugh and St Bruno (detail showing St Hugh), 1520s**

Pinchbeck Fen Map, mid 15th century
The National Archives

Circle of the Master of the Legend of the Magdalen
Martyrdom of St Ursula, with St Hugh and St Bruno, 1520s
Oil on panel
The Royal Collection

Epworth Mazer, about 1525
Wood with a silver-gilt rim, the central boss engraved with figures of St John the Baptist and St Andrew
British Museum

John de Critz the elder (about 1552–1642)
William Cecil, Lord Burghley, about 1590
Oil on canvas
Hatfield House

John Betts (1570–1616)
Sir Robert Sheffield, Speaker of the House of Commons, 16th century
Oil on panel
Private collection

The Heneage Jewel, about 1595
Locket of enamelled gold, table-cut diamonds, Burmese rubies and rock crystal, enclosing a miniature of Queen Elizabeth I, painted by Nicholas Hilliard (1542–1619) and given by the Queen to Sir Thomas Heneage (about 1532–95).
Victoria and Albert Museum

Nicholas Dixon, John Hoskins, Isaac Oliver and others
Collection of miniatures, including Robert Cecil
The Burghley House Collection

Astrolabe, 1565
Brass
Spalding Gentlemen's Society

Abraham Ortelius (1527–98)
Theatrum Orbis Terrarum (Antwerp 1570)
With annotations by William Cecil, Lord Burghley
The Burghley House Collection

The Walsingham Bowl, about 1580–1600
Ceramic, mounted in silver gilt
The Burghley House Collection

Sir William Dugdale (1605–86)
Book of Monuments, 1640–1
British Library

Circular sideboard dish with initials of James II, 1683
Silver gilt
The Burghley House Collection

Sir Isaac Newton (1642–1727)
Manuscript notebook, 1665–8
Fitzwilliam Museum, Cambridge

William Stukeley (1687–1765)
Manuscript Life of Newton, 1752
Royal Society

Louis François Roubiliac (1702–62)
Sir Isaac Newton, about 1741
Marble
Private collection

Henry Bone (1755–1834), after Sir Thomas Lawrence
George IV, 1820
Enamel, painted
The Burghley House Collection

After George Jones (1786–1869)
Coronation Banquet of George IV, about 1821–2
Oil on panel
Palace of Westminster Collection

Unknown artist
George Boole, 1847
Pencil
National Portrait Gallery, London

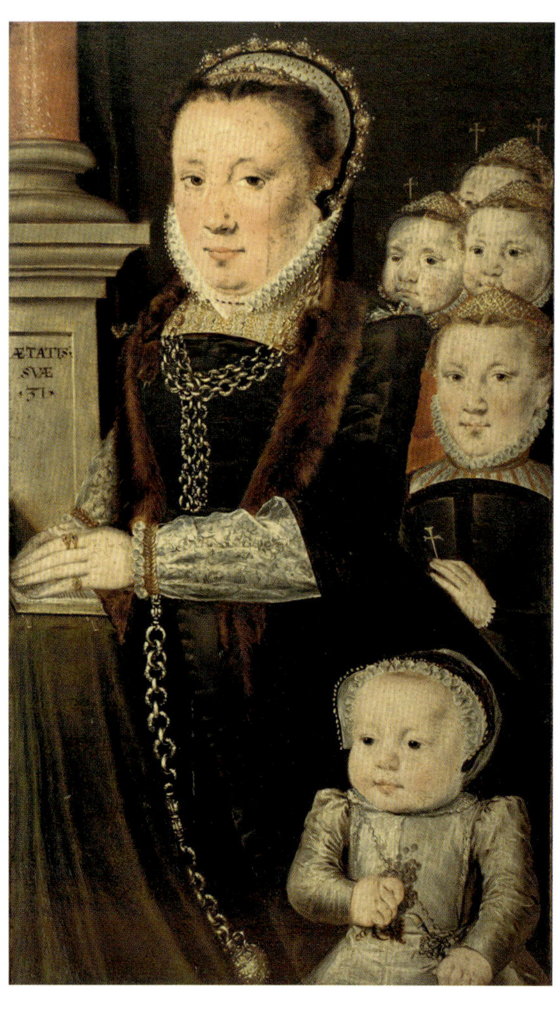

Detail from diptych of *Robert Throckmorton (died 1581) and his wife Elizabeth, née Hussey (died 1554), with five of their children*, about 1550

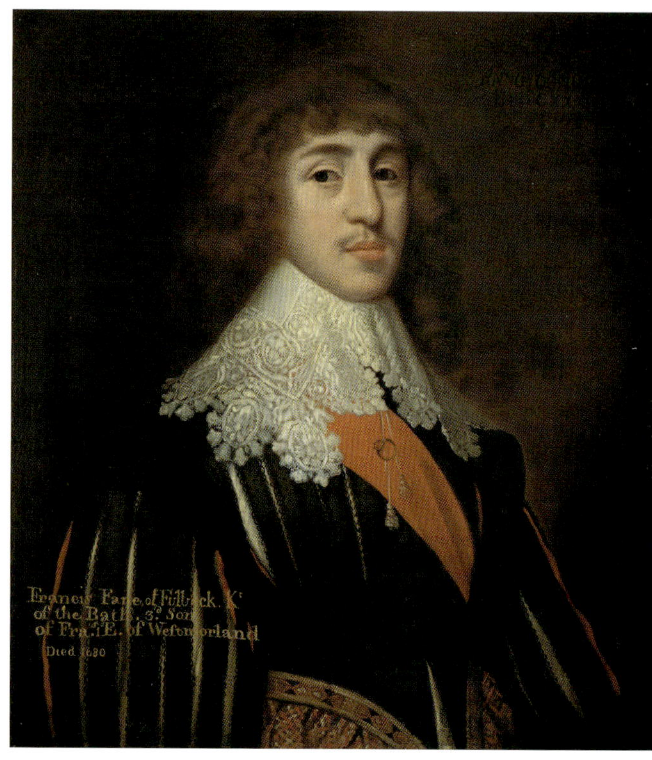

Follower of Cornelis Jonson (1593–1661)
Sir Francis Fane, 1630

William de Fawdrey
Epworth Chalice, 1706
Inscribed 'Epworthia Insula Axholme AD 1706'
Loaned by St Andrew's Parochial Church Council

Nathanial Hone (1718–84)
John Wesley, about 1766
Oil on canvas
National Portrait Gallery, London

Benjamin West (1738–1820)
Sir Joseph Banks, 1771–2
Oil on canvas
Usher Gallery, Lincoln

The King's Champion Saddle, about 1760, probably used at the Coronation of George III, 1760
Leather, covered with red silk velvet, ornamented with silver-gilt lace, braid and fringe
Private collection

Thomas Allen (about 1739–72)
The Disembarkation of Princess Charlotte at Harwich, 1761
Oil on canvas
The Trustees of the Grimsthorpe and Drummond Castle Trust

Matthew Flinders (1774–1814)
Chart showing such parts of Terra Australis and its vicinity, as were discovered or examined by the following vessels: Schooner Francis in 1798, Sloop Norfolk in 1798 and 9, Schooner Cumberland in 1803 and HMS Investigator in 1801, 2 and 3 by M Flinders, Commander, 1804
The National Archives

Helena G. de Courcy Jones (active 1919), after unknown artist
Matthew Flinders, about 1919
Watercolour
National Portrait Gallery, London

Unknown artist
Robert Throckmorton (died 1581) and his wife Elizabeth, née Hussey (died 1554), with five of their children, about 1550
Diptych: oil on two panels
Courtesy of Doddington Hall

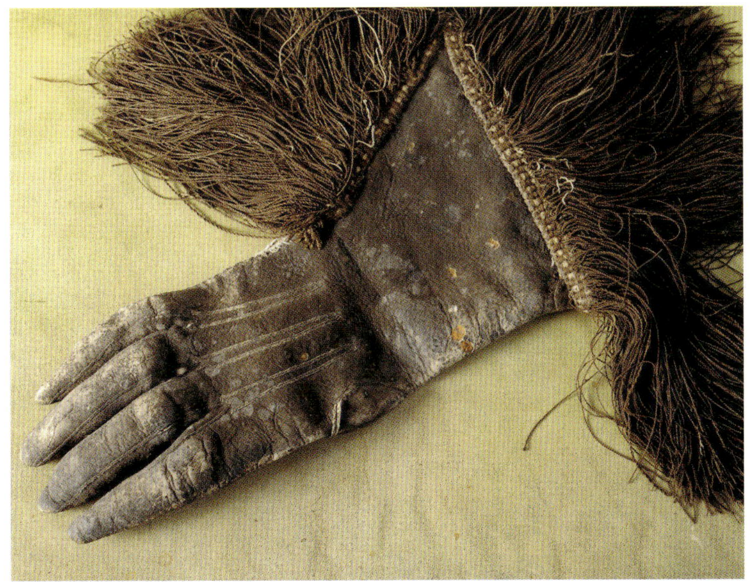

The King's Champion Gauntlet, about 1760

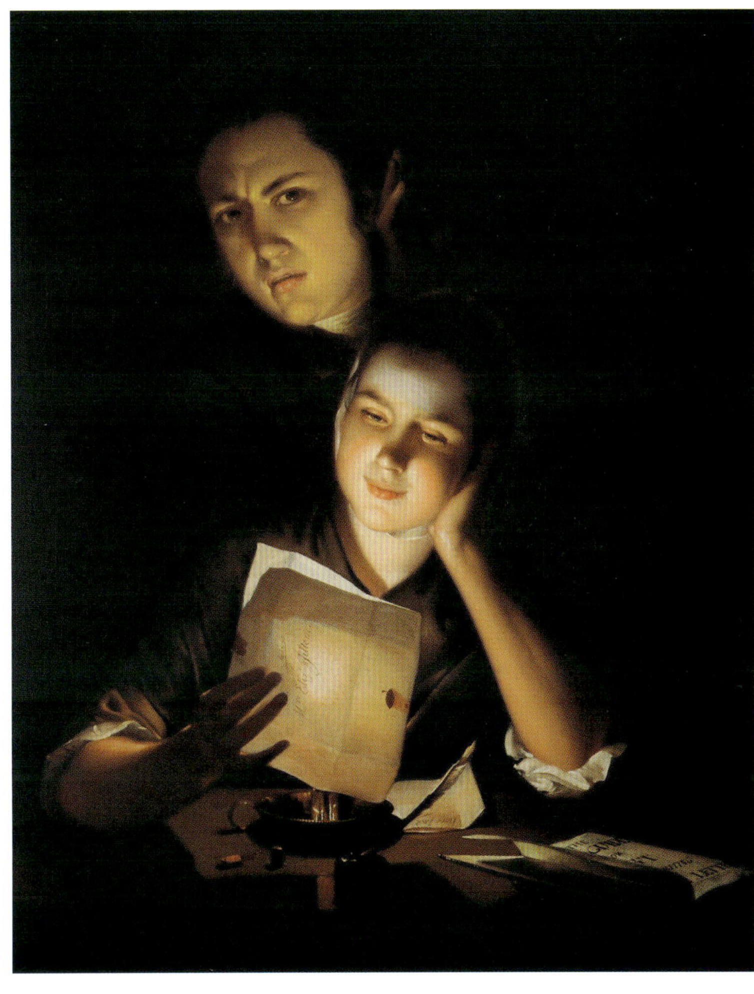

Joseph Wright of Derby (1734–97)
The Letter Writer, 1760–2

John Bridge (1755–1834)
Lincoln Race Cup, 1829
Silver gilt
The Royal Collection

George Frederic Watts (1817–1904)
Emily Tennyson, wife of Alfred Tennyson, 1862
Oil on canvas
Usher Gallery, Lincoln

Samuel Laurence (1812–84) and Sir Edward Coley Burne-Jones (1833–98)
Alfred Tennyson, 1st Baron Tennyson, about 1840
Oil on canvas
National Portrait Gallery, London

Alfred, Lord Tennyson (1809–92)
In Memoriam A.H.H. (1849): original manuscript, known as the 'Butcher's Book', 1850
Tennyson Research Centre

Queen Victoria (1819–1901)
Letter of condolence to Alfred Tennyson on the death of his son, Lionel, 1885
Tennyson Research Centre

Sir Thomas Lawrence (1769–1830)
Lady Georgiana Fane, about 1806
Oil on canvas
Tate, London

Brownlow silver from Belton House
The National Trust

Henry Mee (born 1955)
Margaret Thatcher, 1992
Palace of Westminster Collection

Follower of Cornelis Jonson (1593–1661)
Sir Francis Fane, 1630
Oil on canvas
Mr Julian Fane

Joseph Wright of Derby (1734–97)
The Letter Writer, 1760–2
Oil on canvas
Courtesy of Scawby Hall

The King's Champion Gauntlet, about 1760
Leather and braid
Private collection

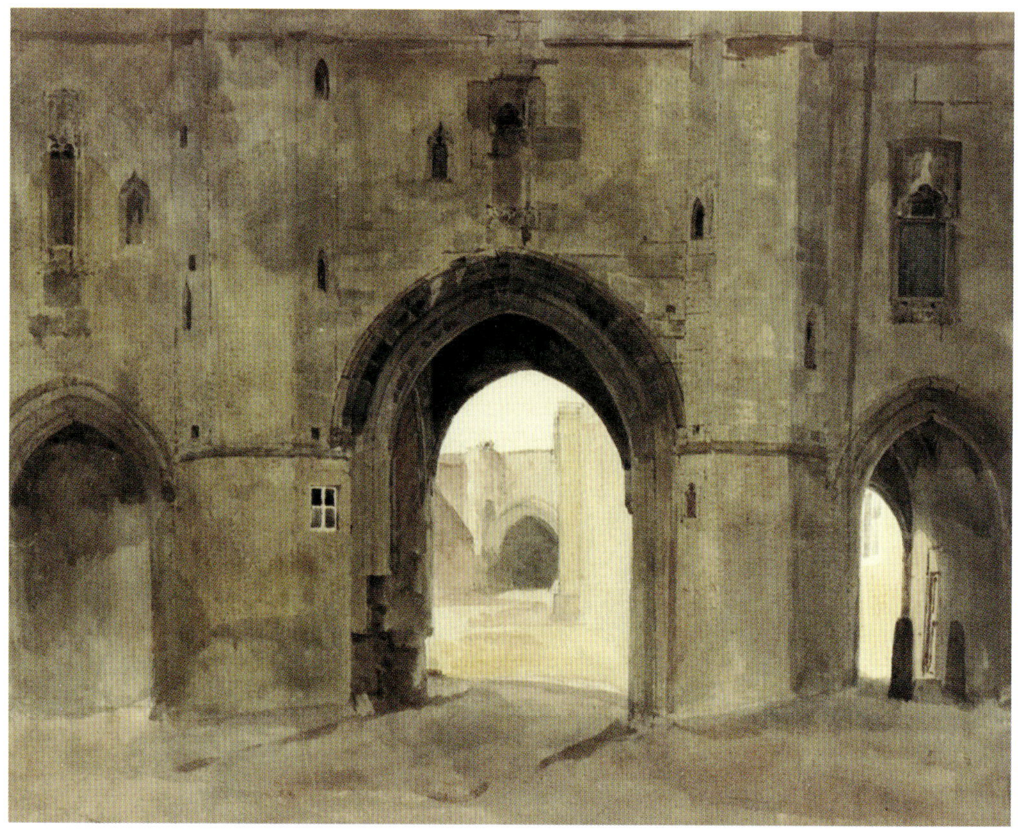

Peter De Wint (1784–1849), *Exchequer Gate, Lincoln*, about 1815

Lincolnshire topography

William Brown (1788–1859)
Louth Panorama, 1844–7
Oil on linen
Louth Town Council

Thomas Wilkinson Wallis (1821–1903)
Wallis carvings, 1848–74
Some of the intricate carvings by this carver, who set up a business in Louth, won medals at the Great Exhibition of 1851, the 1855 Paris Exhibition and the London Great Exhibition in 1862.
Wood
Louth Museum

Thomas Girtin (1775–1802)
View of Lincoln Cathedral, about 1795
Ink on paper and watercolour
Usher Gallery, Lincoln

Joseph Mallord William Turner (1775–1851)
Cathedral Church at Lincoln; the Cathedral towers, seen rising above Exchequer Gate, 1795
Watercolour
British Museum

Joseph Mallord William Turner (1775–1851)
Lincoln Cathedral from the Holmes, Brayford, about 1802–3
Watercolour
Usher Gallery, Lincoln

Joseph Mallord William Turner (1775–1851)
Stamford, about 1828
Watercolour
Usher Gallery, Lincoln

Joseph Mallord William Turner (1775–1851)
St Botolph's Church, Boston, from the River Witham, about 1833–4
Watercolour
Tate, London

Peter De Wint (1784–1849)
Exchequer Gate, Lincoln, about 1815
Watercolour
Usher Gallery, Lincoln

Peter De Wint (1784–1849)
Lincoln from the River at Sunset, about 1830
Oil on canvas
Usher Gallery, Lincoln

Peter De Wint (1784–1849)
Lincoln from the South with Bargate, exhibited at the Royal Academy 1824
Oil on canvas
Usher Gallery, Lincoln

Peter De Wint (1784–1849)
Lincolnshire Landscape (Near Horncastle), about 1813–26
Oil on canvas
Usher Gallery, Lincoln

Peter De Wint (1784–1849)
Torksey Castle (study), about 1835
Watercolour
Usher Gallery, Lincoln

Peter De Wint (1784–1849)
Torksey Castle, 1835
Watercolour
Usher Gallery, Lincoln

John Ferneley (1782–1860)
The Burton Hunt, 1830
Oil on canvas
Usher Gallery, Lincoln

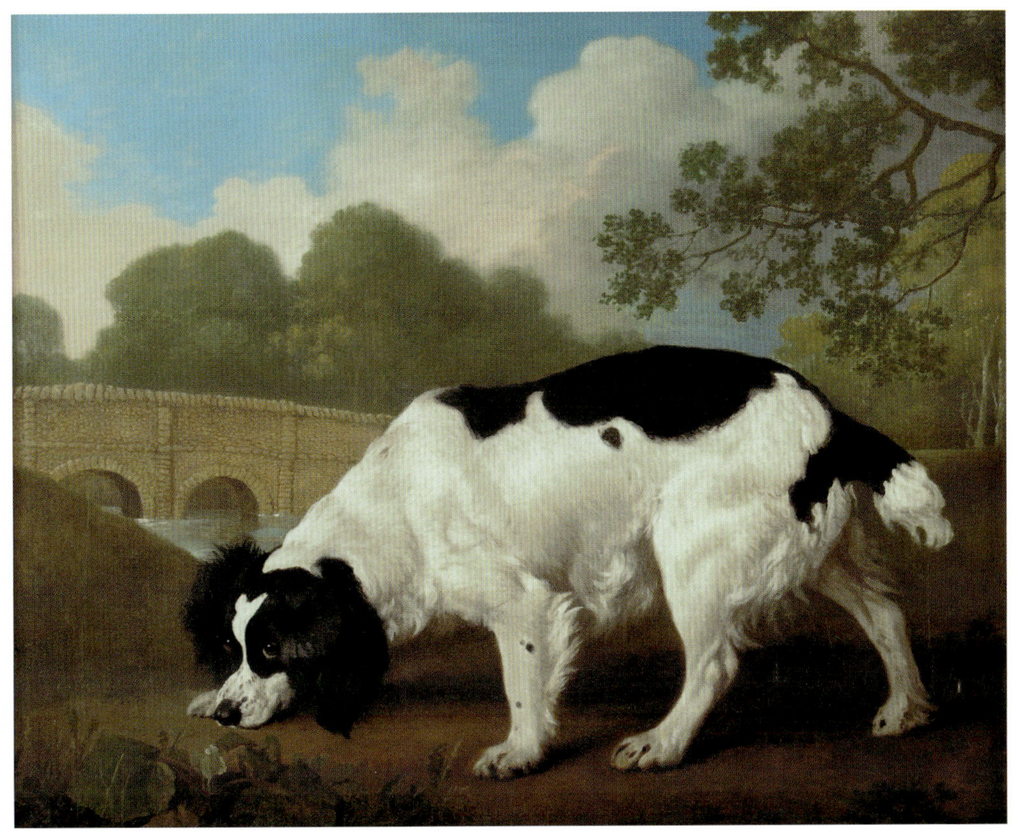

George Stubbs (1724–1806)
Faddle, a black and white spaniel belonging to Sir John Nelthorpe, 1792

George Stubbs

George Stubbs (1724–1806)
Sir John Nelthorpe, 6th Bt, aged about eleven, about 1756
Oil on canvas
Courtesy of Scawby Hall

George Stubbs (1724–1806)
The Duke of Ancaster's bay stallion Blank, about 1761
Oil on canvas
The Trustees of the Grimsthorpe and Drummond Castle Trust

George Stubbs (1724–1806)
A bay racehorse belonging to the Duke of Ancaster, led by a jockey, about 1762
Oil on canvas
The Trustees of the Grimsthorpe and Drummond Castle Trust

George Stubbs (1724–1806)
The Anatomy of the Horse (1766)
Courtesy of Scawby Hall

George Stubbs (1724–1806)
Lion devouring a stag, 1769
Oil on canvas
His Grace, the Duke of Rutland

George Stubbs (1724–1806)
Sir John Nelthorpe shooting with his dogs over his home ground, Barton Field in Lincolnshire, 1776
Oil on panel
Courtesy of Scawby Hall

George Stubbs (1724–1806)
The Reverend Robert Carter Thelwall with his first wife, Charlotte Nelthorpe, and his daughter, 1776
Oil on panel
The Holburne Museum, Bath

George Stubbs (1724–1806)
Thomas Smith, Huntsman to the Brocklesby Hounds, with his father, Thomas Smith, the former Huntsman, with the hound Wonder, 1776
Oil on panel
Private collection

George Stubbs (1724–1806)
An old Shetland pony communing with Driver, a foxhound, with the east front of Brocklesby Hall in the background, 1777
Oil on panel
Private collection

George Stubbs (1724–1806)
George IV when Prince of Wales, 1791
Oil on canvas
The Royal Collection

George Stubbs (1724–1806)
Ringwood, a Brocklesby foxhound, 1792
Oil on panel
Private collection

George Stubbs (1724–1806)
Faddle, a black and white spaniel belonging to Sir John Nelthorpe, 1792
Oil on canvas
Courtesy of Scawby Hall

Authors' biographies

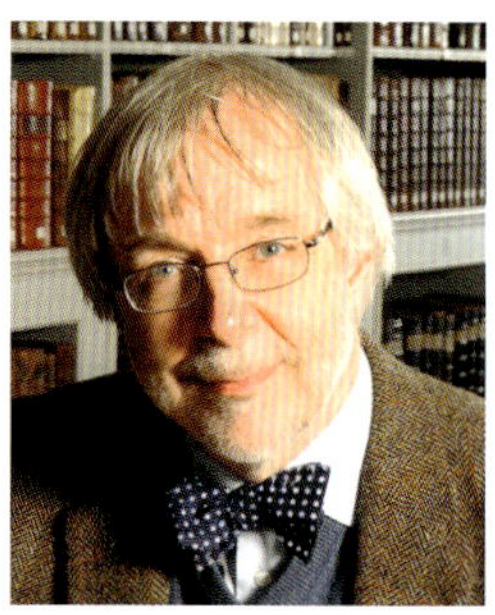

NICHOLAS BENNETT is Visiting Senior Fellow at the University of Lincoln. He spent twenty-three years as custodian of the historic books and manuscripts of Lincoln Cathedral. He has been Honorary General Editor of the Lincoln Record Society since 2002 and has published numerous scholarly editions, including *The Registers of Henry Burghersh 1320–1342* and *Lincolnshire Parish Clergy c.1214–1968* (both in progress).

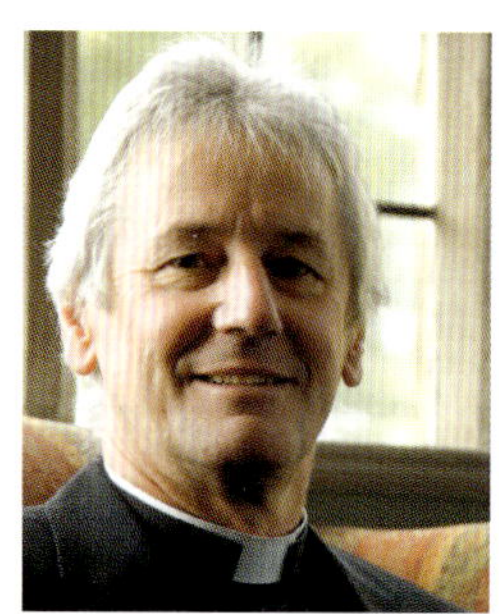

THE VERY REVD PHILIP BUCKLER has been Dean of Lincoln Cathedral since 2007. Prior to this, he was Canon Treasurer of St Paul's Cathedral. He was educated at St Peter's College, Oxford, and trained for the priesthood at Cuddesdon College. He was a contributor to *Lincoln Cathedral: A Journey from Past to Present* (2011).

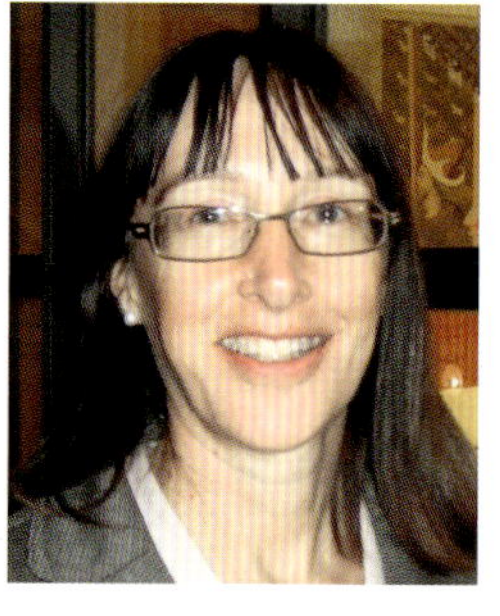

THE LORD CORMACK is chairman of the Historic Lincoln Trust. He is a Visiting Senior Lecturer at the University of Hull and a Senior Associate Member of St Antony's College, Oxford. He has lectured and spoken extensively in this country, as well as the USA, and is a notable advocate of history and heritage. His publications include *Heritage in Danger* (1976), *Wilberforce: The nation's conscience* (1983) and *English Cathedrals* (1984).

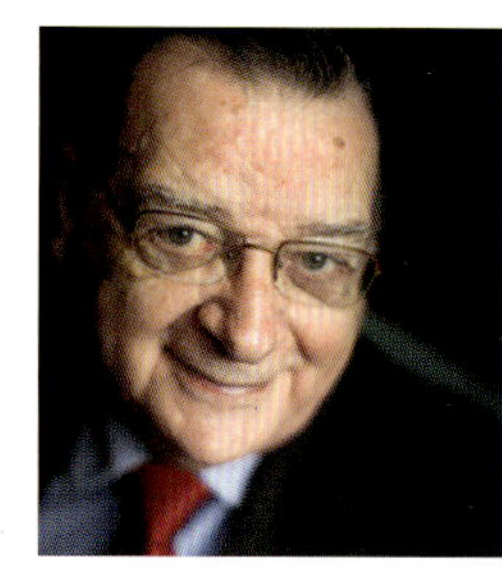

THE LORD GRIFFITHS OF BURRY PORT is an educator, writer, broadcaster and minister. He completed his Ph.D. at the School of African and Oriental Studies, London in 1987. He served as President of the Methodist Conference 1994–5 and since 1996 he has been Superintendent Minister at Wesley's Chapel, London. He was made a Life Peer in 2004.

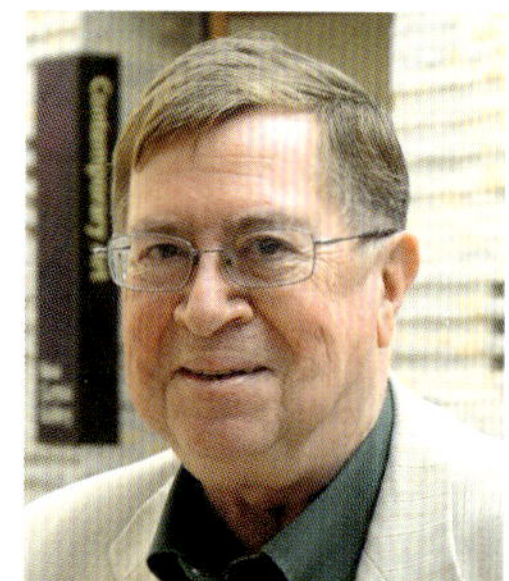

ALAN BORG is one of the Honorary Curators of *Lincolnshire's Great Exhibition*. In 1978 he was appointed the first Keeper of the Sainsbury Centre at the University of East Anglia. Since then he has served as Director of the Imperial War Museum and subsequently as Director of the Victoria and Albert Museum, where he was responsible for remodelling the British collection.

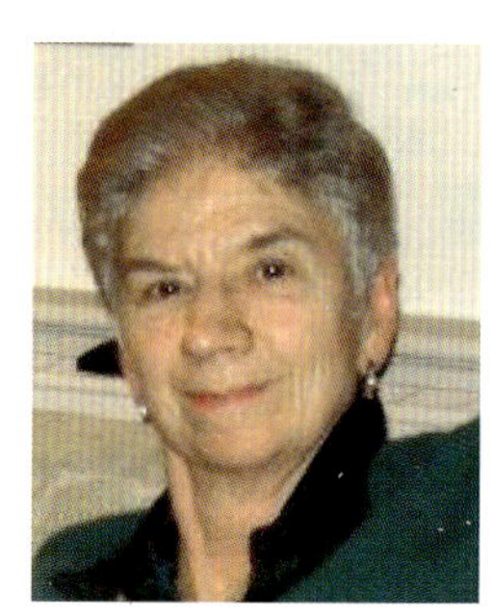

CHRISTINE CARPENTER is Professor of Medieval English History at Cambridge University. Her main research interests are the political and constitutional history of England in the later Middle Ages. She is the author of *Locality and Polity: a Study of Warwickshire Landed Society 1401–1499* (1992). She is currently working on *A New Constitutional History of Late-Medieval England 1215–1509*.

DR KATHLEEN DOYLE is currently the Curator of Illuminated Manuscripts in the department of Medieval and Earlier Manuscripts at the British Library. Her research interests are illuminated manuscripts, Cistercian manuscripts and statutes, and medieval and early modern library history. Dr Doyle's co-authored publications include *Bible Manuscripts: 1400 Years of Scribes and Scripture* (2007).

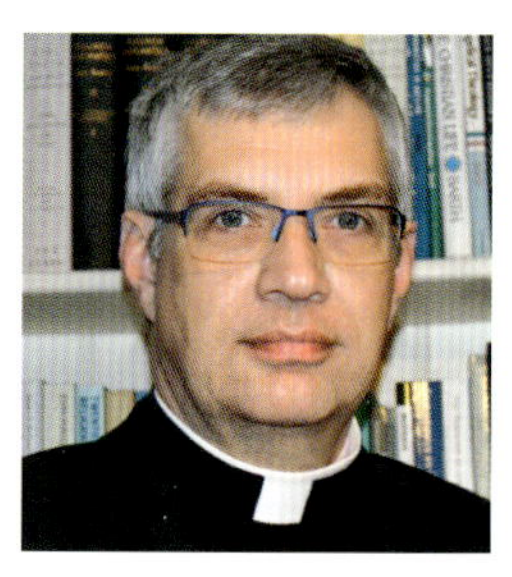

MARK HOCKNULL is Canon Chancellor of Lincoln Cathedral and a Visiting Senior Fellow at the University of Lincoln. He holds doctorates in biochemical engineering (University College London, 1988) and religious studies (University of Lancaster, 2008). His monograph *Pannenberg on Evil, Love and God: the Realisation of Divine Love* was published in 2014.

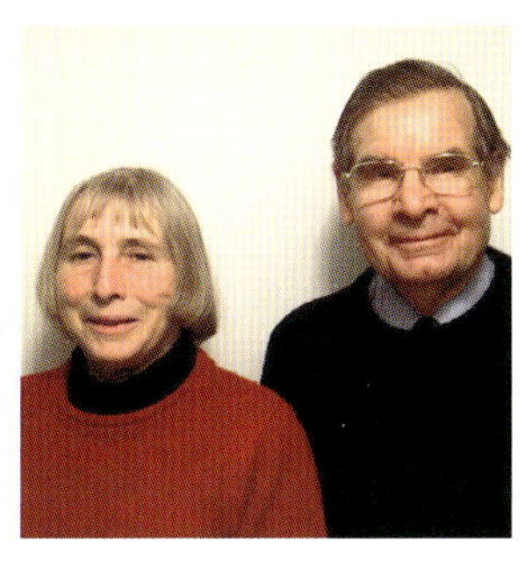

DIANA and **MICHAEL HONEYBONE** have taught history for the Open University and the University of Nottingham, with special emphasis on intellectual activity in the eighteenth century. They have published editions for the Lincoln Record Society, *The Correspondence of the Spalding Gentlemen's Society 1710–1761* (2010) and *The Correspondence of William Stukeley and Maurice Johnson 1714–1754* (2014).

RICHARD OLNEY completed his D.Phil. in 1970 on the subject of Lincolnshire Politics, 1832–85. He worked as an archivist at Lincolnshire Archives Office 1969–75 before his appointment as an Assistant Keeper with the Royal Commission on Historical Manuscripts from 1976 to 2003. His publications include *Rural Society and County Government in Nineteenth Century Lincolnshire* (1979).

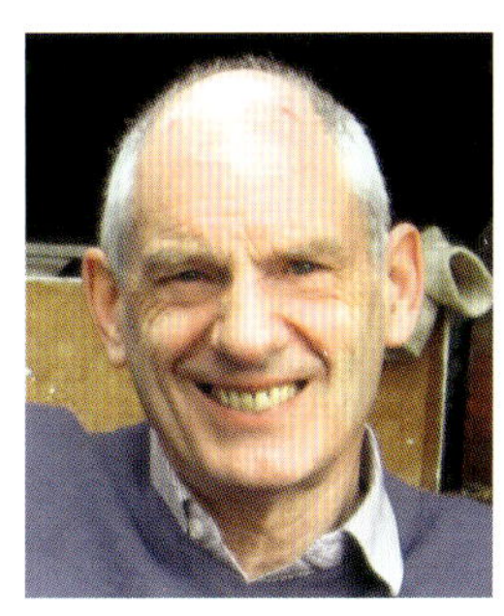

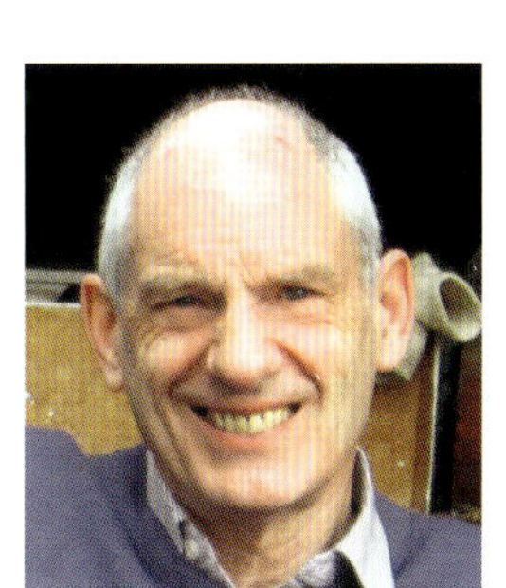

MARY POWELL is Tourism Manager for Lincolnshire County Council. She set up Select Lincolnshire, to promote the county's produce, and subsequently the Lincolnshire Waterways Partnership, which delivered some £18m of regeneration work. In 2005 she became programme manager for Historic Lincoln, majoring on Lincoln Castle Revealed. Telling the 'behind the scenes' stories of these projects is typical of her approach.

PROFESSOR JOHN SIMONS is Deputy Vice-Chancellor at MacQuarie University, Sydney, Australia. He obtained his doctorate from the University of Exeter and has previously worked at a number of universities in the United Kingdom. His publications include *Animal Rights and the Politics of Literary Representation* (2002), *Rossetti's Wombat* (2008) and *Kangaroo* (2013).

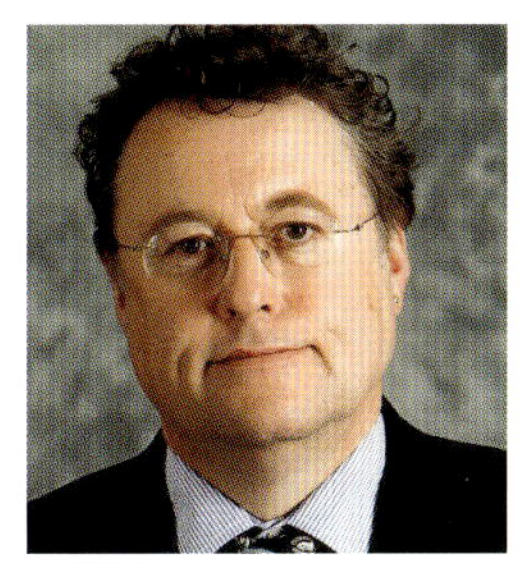

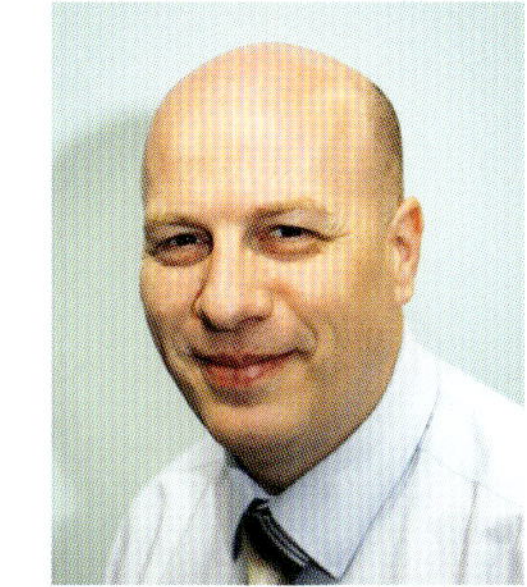

JEFF JAMES is one of the Honorary Curators of *Lincolnshire's Great Exhibition*. He took up the post of Chief Executive and Keeper of The National Archives in July 2014. Prior to this Jeff had worked at The National Archives as Director of Operations and Services for almost six years and subsequently as Deputy Chief Executive at the Chartered Institute for Housing.

LEONÉE ORMOND is Professor Emerita of Victorian Studies at King's College London. She is a specialist in nineteenth-century literature, Alfred Lord Tennyson, J.M. Barrie and George Bernard Shaw. The published works of Professor Ormond include *J.M. Barrie* (1987), *Tennyson: A Literary Life* (1993) and (with others) *Frederic Lord Leighton* (1996).

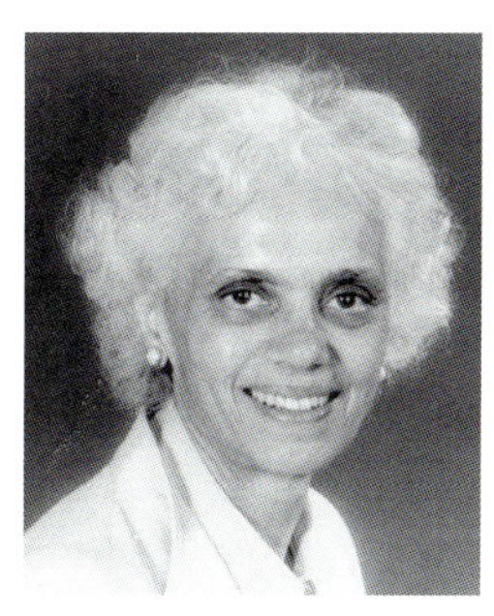

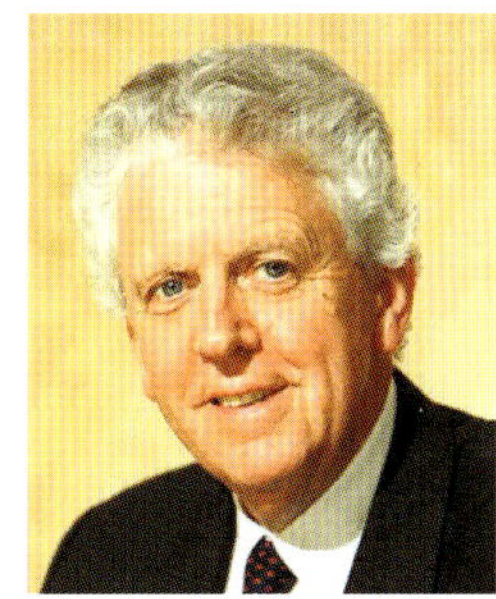

THE LORD POWELL OF BAYSWATER was educated at New College, Oxford. He joined the Foreign Office in 1963 and later became Private Secretary and advisor on foreign affairs and defence primarily to Margaret Thatcher, when she was Prime Minister (1983–91). He has held several directorships and consultancy roles since this time.

OVERLEAF
Thomas Allen (about 1739–72)
***The Disembarkation of Princess Charlotte at Harwich*, 1761**
Oil on canvas
Grimsthorpe Castle

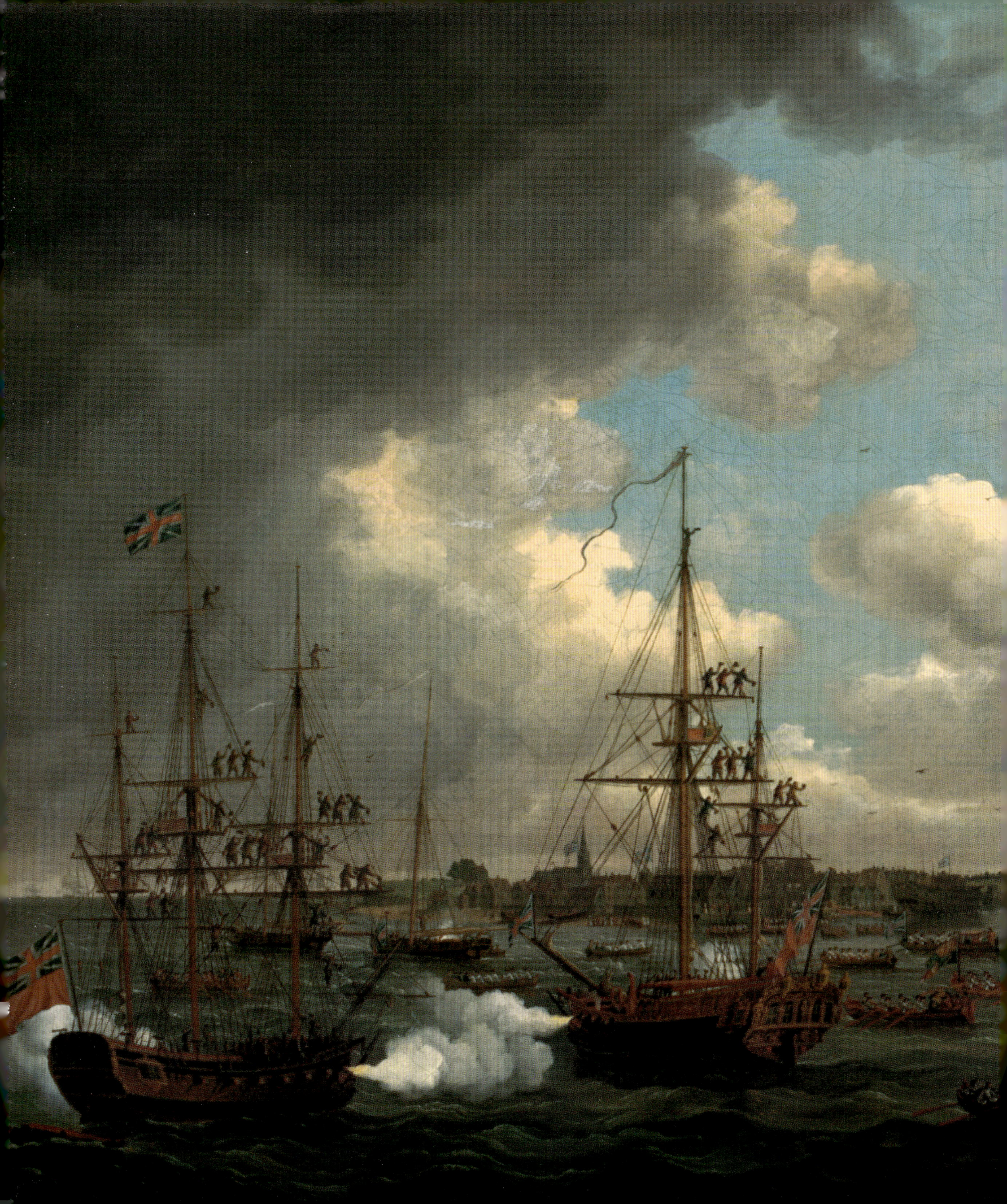

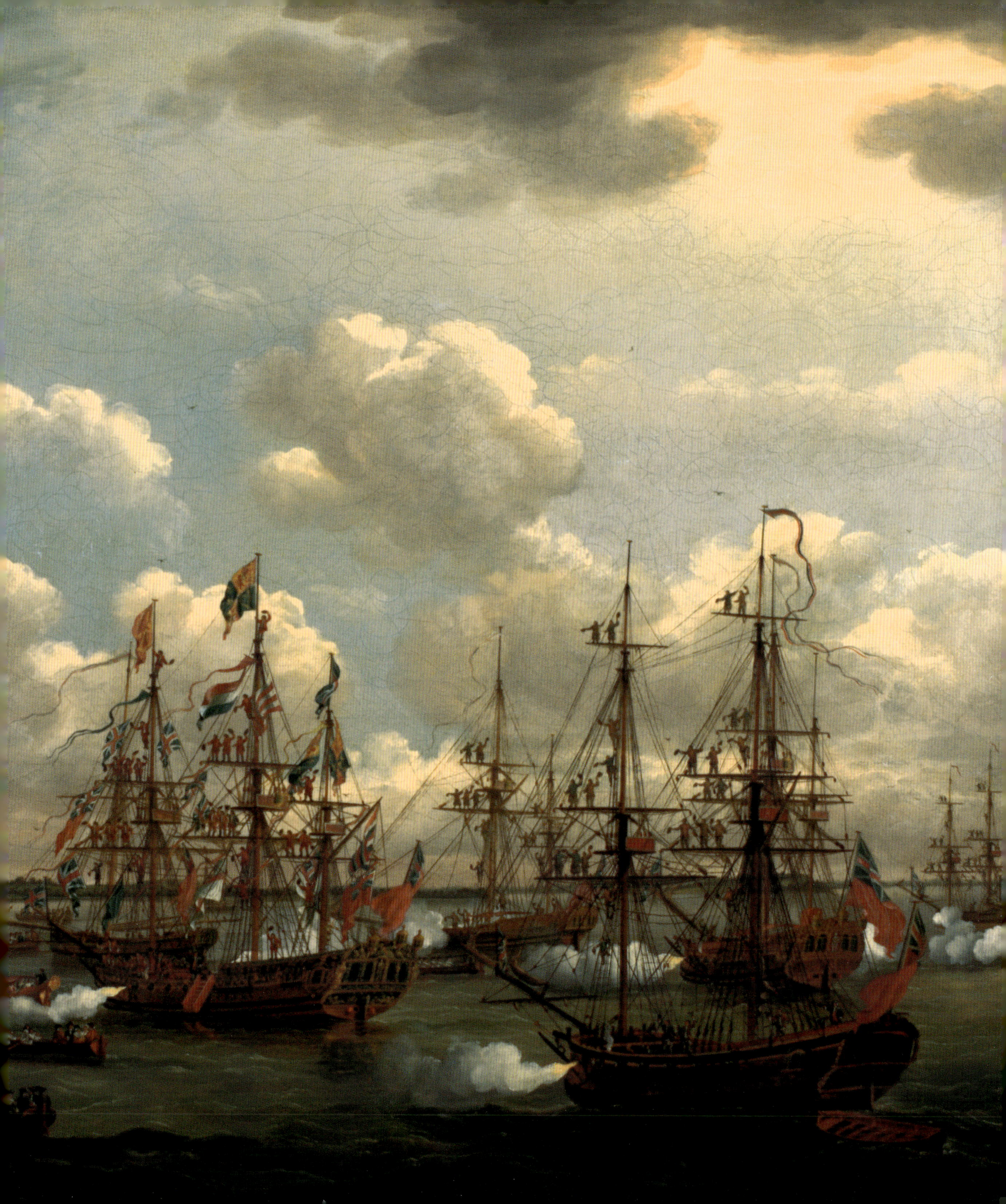

Picture credits

The Art Institute of Chicago, Mr and Mrs Martin A. Ryerson Collection 30, 36 (right)
Photo: Nicholas Bennett 32, 37
© The British Library Board 4, 12–13, 35, 49, 53, 54, 61 (above), 62, 64, 65, 67, 69, 70, 71, 72, 74, 75 (both), 76–7, 78, 83, 94, 132 (both), front cover
The Burghley House Collection 9
The Master and Fellows of Corpus Christi College, Cambridge 58
Mr Julian Fane 196
Fitzwilliam Museum, Cambridge 117
The Trustees of Grimsthorpe and Drummond Castle Trust 160, 161, 202–3
Photo: S. Haimes 113
Lincolnshire Archives 42, 43, 44–5, 48–9, 50–51, 52, 55, 56–7, 59, 61 (below), 115, 179, 180, 182 (below), 189
Lincoln Cathedral 31, 46, 195
Lincoln Cathedral Library 34, 36 (left), 39, 81, 84 (above), 129, 188, 191, 195
Lincolnshire Libraries 22, 92, 152, 182 (above)
Lincolnshire Wildlife Trust 126
Loggan, David (1633/35-92) / Woolsthorpe Manor, Grantham, Lincolnshire, UK / National Trust Photographic Library/John Hammond / Bridgeman Images 114 (below)
Louth Town Council 14–15, 29, 166, 199
The National Archives 16, 17, 33, 40, 136–7, 143
Courtesy of the National Library of Ireland 118
© National Maritime Museum, Greenwich, London 137, 140
Courtesy National Museums Liverpool, Walker Art Gallery 157
© National Portrait Gallery, London 110, 111, 116, 119, 124, 127, 133, 145, 165, back cover
© National Trust Images/Robert Morris 184
Photo: James Newton 18–19, 123, 192–3
Photo: North Lincolnshire Tourism Team 151
© Palace of Westminster Collection WOA 5801 www.parliament.uk/art 7
© Palace of Westminster Collection by kind permission of Henry Mee, WOA 3634 www.parliament.uk/art 181
Press Association 178–9, 185, 187
Private collection 93, 146–7, 186, 196, 197, 199
Private collection. Photo: Mike Fear © The National Trust, Waddesdon Manor 121
Photo: Daniel Rollitt 170
Rex 183
Royal Academy of Arts, London 155
Royal Collection Trust / © Her Majesty Queen Elizabeth II 158–9, 195
© The Royal Society 117
Courtesy of the Marquess of Salisbury, Hatfield House 89
Skegness Town Council/National Railway Museum/Science & Society Picture Library 21, 23
Spalding Gentlemen's Society 100, 101, 102, 103, 104, 105, 106, 107, 108, 109
Tennyson Research Centre 162, 163, 167, 169, 171, 172, 173, 174, 175, 176, 177
Photo: Andrew Tryner, copyright Lincolnshire County Council 8, 14–15, 20, 24, 25, 26–7, 28, 29, 34, 36 (left), 38, 39, 41, 80, 84 (both), 85, 86, 87, 88, 90, 91, 93, 95, 102, 103, 104, 105, 106, 107, 108, 109, 114 (above), 125, 128 (both), 129, 130, 131, 138, 141, 144, 149, 150, 153, 154, 156, 164, 166, 197 (left), 198, 202–3
Usher Gallery, Lincoln 2–3, 98–9, 139, 198
Victoria and Albert Museum, London 1, 97
Copyright Dean and Chapter of Westminster 11, 122, 134–5

The Historic Lincoln Trust

Index

Figures in *italics* indicate illustrations

Acknowledgements

Thanks are due to the many institutions and individuals who have helped to make *Lincolnshire's Great Exhibition* a reality, through the loan of exhibits or in other ways.

The Royal Collection
The British Library
The British Museum
The National Archives
National Maritime Museum, Greenwich
The National Portrait Gallery, London
The National Trust
The Palace of Westminster
Parliamentary Archives
The Royal Academy of Arts
The Royal Society
Tate, London
Victoria and Albert Museum
The Holburne Museum, Bath
Burghley House Collection
Churchill College, Cambridge
The Fitzwilliam Museum, Cambridge
Trinity College, Cambridge
Doddington Hall
Epworth, St Andrew's Parochial Church Council
Mr Julian Fane
The Trustees of the Grimsthorpe and Drummond Castle Trust
Hatfield House
Lambeth Palace Library
Lincoln Cathedral Library
Lincolnshire County Council
Lincolnshire Archives
Lincolnshire Libraries
Tennyson Research Centre, Lincoln
Usher Gallery, Lincoln
The Collection, Lincoln
City of Lincoln Council, Lincoln
Louth Museum
Louth Town Council
Mr and Mrs T.M.S. Nelthorpe
Normanby Estate
New College, Oxford
His Grace the Duke of Rutland
Spalding Gentlemen's Society
Skegness Town Council
Wesley's Chapel, London
The Earl of Yarborough
and private collections, both in Lincolnshire and further afield.

Our principal exhibition sponsor is the David Ross Foundation to which we are most grateful, as we are to our other generous private sponsors and to Lindum Group.